ROADS
A CHRISTIAN
MUST TRAVEL

MERRILL C. TENNEY

ROADS
A CHRISTIAN
MUST
TRAVEL

FRESH INSIGHTS INTO THE PRINCIPLES OF CHRISTIAN EXPERIENCE

Tyndale House
Publishers, Inc.
Wheaton, Illinois

CONTENTS

PREFACE

Anyone who has ever back-packed through unfamiliar country knows the fascination of roads. As they traverse endless plains, or wind through hills where every turn brings some new surprise, or lose themselves in rural cartpaths, they afford constant surprises for the traveler. Sometimes roads are smooth and well-paved, so that progress is swift and easy. Sometimes they are rough and steep, so that one's breath becomes labored and muscles protest vigorously, but in every instance the road has its own promise and its own destination. To reach a desired goal, one must find and pursue the right road to its end.

In this active and bewildering age, we have difficulty in finding the road to our spiritual destination. We become confused, and often despair of ever reaching it. Yet for every one of us, there are roads prepared in a definite direction. God has not left us to muddle our way through life. He has marked the major paths clearly.

Luke, the writer of the third Gospel and Acts, gave a great deal of attention to roads, probably because he had voyaged and marched across the Roman Empire from Antioch in the Middle East to Rome in the west. In his writings, Luke occasionally mentioned the roads that he traveled, and each seems to have some particular significance. They are not presented allegorically, but are a part of an historical narrative.

Nevertheless, these allusions illustrate principles of Christian experience because of their relation to those who traversed them. They are a natural part of Luke's two volumes on the rise and progress of the gospel, and they aptly represent major phases of Christian growth.

Luke's books are not, like *Pilgrim's Progress*, written as allegory. Whatever figurative application may be made of them cannot be attributed to the direct intention of the writer. On the other hand, the spiritual implications of the episodes which he recorded are inherent in the historical text, and may legitimately be included in its interpretation.

On the basis of this principle, the following studies are proffered for consideration in the hope that they may help to "guide our feet in the way of peace."

ONE
THE ROAD
TO BETHLEHEM:
The Road of Faith

Let us now go even unto Bethlehem, and see this thing that is come to pass. Luke 2:15

Seven miles south of the city of Jerusalem lies Bethlehem, a sizable community of about twenty thousand persons which is the center of trade for the surrounding countryside. In Bible times it was much smaller, perhaps not much larger than a village. Even today it is surrounded by open fields where small farmers raise their crops and graze their sheep. Usually nothing very exciting takes place there and before Jesus' time it must have been rather humdrum. On one occasion, however, it became the focus of excited attention, and the road to Bethlehem became the highway for those who sought the realization of a new faith.

Nearly two thousand years ago, the entire land of Palestine was seething with fear and resentment. Augustus Caesar, the ruler of Rome, had decreed that a census of all his realm should be taken and reported to headquarters. The small state of Israel, part of the Roman domain of Syria, was included in the decree, and heads of families were commanded to report to their ancestral homes to register. Rome was unpopular with the Jewish people. Its officials were regarded as interlopers and its brutal legions were an insult to the Jewish state. Why should they bow to Augustus' decree? Taxation

9

was his aim, and they did not wish to fatten the oppressors' treasury with their goods and money. Augustus wanted to recruit men for his legions, and they were averse to supporting the campaigns of their conquerors. Unrest was rife. In some quarters, such as Galilee, revolt was being plotted, but few thought that it had much chance of success. Gloom and despair settled on many as they realized that submission would only confirm their subjection, while open insurrection would be suicidal.

Herod, the puppet king of Judea, had deferred complying with the enactment as long as he dared, but he could postpone action no longer, for he feared the authority of Augustus. Now the census was in process, and crowds of people were streaming into Bethlehem to register. Among them was a carpenter named Joseph who had journeyed back from Nazareth where he had found employment. With him was his affianced wife, Mary, who was in an advanced stage of pregnancy. Probably they would not have made the long trip of seventy-five miles had not the decree of the emperor made it urgent to do so. The journey had been tedious, and the birth of the baby was imminent.

The tired couple looked everywhere for shelter, only to be confronted by an innkeeper who told them that he had no room for them. Perhaps he was not so unkind as might be inferred from the account, because the crowds were great, and they had arrived late. He did offer them shelter in the stable with the animals. To modern men who are accustomed to take the amenities of life for granted, his suggestion seems cruel and degrading. To Mary and Joseph it may have been a blessing in disguise. The shelter which they accepted, probably a cave, would have been warmed by the body heat of the animals, and they would have been hidden from the crowds, with privacy reasonably assured. During that night, in that crude shelter, Jesus was born.

At the same time, as Luke tells us, there were shepherds in the adjoining fields watching their flocks. Just when this took place is uncertain. The traditional date of December 25th is not given in the Gospels. It may have been in the early fall when winter was approaching and the nights were cool, or it may have been in the spring, before Passover, when the animals were being prepared for the sacrifices at the temple in Jerusalem. The time is a minor matter; the fact remains that the shepherds were outside of the town watching their flocks. The stars were bright overhead; the fire which the shepherds had kindled for warmth burned low; the passing hours dragged on uneventfully. Some of the shepherds were chatting, while the rest, wrapped in their long woolen cloaks, were serenely sleeping. For them it was merely one more night's vigil.

Suddenly they became aware of a mysterious glow in the sky that became increasingly brighter. It could not be the dawn, nor the early morning sunlight. Its intensity increased until they found themselves focused in a blinding glare that dispelled the darkness and surrounded them with an unearthly radiance. As they cowered in terror, wondering what would happen, a form emerged from the brilliance and a voice spoke to them, saying, "Be not afraid; for behold, I bring you good tidings of great joy which shall be to all the people: for there is born to you this day in the city of David a Savior, who is Christ the Lord" (Luke 2:10, 11). Then the curtains of the sky seemed to roll back, disclosing rank on rank of heavenly beings, who chanted "Glory to God in the highest, and on earth peace among men in whom he is well pleased" (Luke 2:14).

As abruptly as it came, the vision vanished, leaving the shepherds confused and troubled. How should they interpret this experience? The miraculous light which had briefly broken the darkness really betokened the presence of God, as in the burning bush at Sinai from which God had spoken to Moses. Had the long-expected Messiah really come as a helpless infant wrapped in swaddling clothes? Was this the divine answer to the Roman domination? Could the whole experience be simply an illusion created by the tension or fatigue of the hour?

There would be only one way to resolve the mystery. They needed to take the road to Bethlehem where they would ascertain for themselves whether the utterance of the angel were actually true, or whether they had suffered from a hallucination. They responded positively: "Let us now go even unto Bethlehem, and see this thing that is come to pass, which the Lord hath made known unto us" (Luke 2:15). Without any other corroboration they set out to find the child who would be the answer to their expectation and the Messiah for whose advent they had prayed.

The road to Bethlehem is the road of faith because it begins with *revelation*. All that man can know about God's purpose for the world or about his plans for the human race must come by divine disclosure. The shepherds could have scanned the night skies for years without discovering either. Another shepherd had said as a result of his observations, "The heavens declare the glory of God; and the firmament showeth his handiwork. Day unto day uttereth speech, and night unto night showeth knowledge. There is no speech nor language; their voice is not heard" (Psa. 19:1-3). From nature it is possible to learn of God's glory from the radiance of the sun, of his power from the storm and tides that sweep the ocean, and of his order from the unvarying processes of physical law. Nature, however, does not tell whether that divine glory will illumine the darkness of individual despair, or whether that power will stoop compassionately to our weakness, or whether that order signifies only cold and inexorable fate rather than a plan that provides for human destiny. God's revelation is conveyed by a person who entered human life as a tiny infant, weak and helpless as all infants are. In him "the Word became flesh" (John 1:14), and God's person and intent were perfectly disclosed.

The word that the angel gave to the shepherds was a disclosure of God's purpose. The time had come for the fulfillment of the ancient promise, "Unto us a child is born, unto us a son is given; and the government shall be upon his shoulder: and his name shall be called Wonderful, Counsellor, Mighty God, Everlasting Father, Prince of Peace. Of the increase of his government and of peace there shall be no end, upon the throne of David, and upon his kingdom, to establish it, and to uphold it with justice and with righteousness" (Isa. 9:6, 7).

Admittedly the revelation differed from their expectation. They had not envisioned the coming of the Messiah as the birth of an infant, but they accepted the revelation and acted on it. The road to Bethlehem thus became the road of *resolution*.

12

Faith in God is confidence in the word of God, just as, to a large extent, our dealings with other people are based on our belief in their integrity. All friendship is established on the expectation that one's closest associates will never betray him by treachery or disclose his secrets or abandon him in distress. Commerce depends on faith. A bank lends money because it believes that the borrower has adequate resources and intends to repay the loan according to the stipulated agreement. A merchant exercises faith in a check or in the money that a buyer offers in exchange for his goods. It may be only a piece of paper with some writing on it, but because of his confidence in the writer of the check or in the genuineness of the currency he accepts it without question.

So the shepherds believed the words of the angel and then acted. They did not consider the venture a mere gamble, saying, "Let us see whether these things may have taken place." Rather they said, "Let us . . . see this thing that is come to pass" (Luke 2:15). They regarded it as fact because it had been spoken to them by divine authority and they considered the event as already accomplished. A similar concept is stated in the famous "faith chapter" of Hebrews 11: "He that cometh to God must believe that he is, and that he is a rewarder of them that seek after him" (Heb. 11:6).

Faith is not optimistic passivity that waits complacently for some unexpected event to happen. It is rather the active resolution to depend upon the promise and counsel of God. On the basis of what God has declared, one may step forward with assurance of being led through difficulty however threatening or impossible a situation may appear.

Faith, furthermore, is not a vague assumption that "somehow everything will work out all right." It must be founded on adequate authority. The term translated "thing" in the statement, "Let us go now into Bethlehem and see this thing that has come to pass" really means "word"—particularly a spoken word. It appears in the expression of the angel at the annunciation to Mary: "No word from God shall be void of power" (Luke 1:37). Faith is the exercise of such determined confidence in the promise or command of God that one is ready to expend energy, time, and all resources in putting God's word to the proof. The shepherds were certain that the end of their quest would be neither frustration nor disappointment, but the fulfillment of that which had been predicted, even though they had no idea of what it might entail.

The road to Bethlehem thus became the road to *realization*. The shepherds' resolution to act on God's revelation led to the realization of truth. Obedience to God's command is sooner or later rewarded by the experience of what he has promised. God never makes promises that he will not fulfill, and when they are accepted, they become the realities of life. When the shepherds reached Bethlehem they finally found Mary and Joseph, and the infant lying in a manger. The reality fit and completed the description. Furthermore, the reality gave new significance to the vision. The birth of a baby is not in itself spectacular. Why should this one be introduced by a heavenly vision? The child must have extraordinary significance to be announced by a celestial herald and introduced by an angelic choir. The reality of the infant was a greater revelation yet to come. The ultimate glory of God was not the brilliance of the light that outshone the stars that night, but the light that illumines every man as it comes into the world.

The experience of realization lends new zest to life. The constant fulfillment of God's promises to the believer keeps his daily activity exciting. It is thrilling to take a step of faith and then to see God·work in response as he fits adverse circumstances into his plan and transforms improbabilities and impossibilities into actualities. To the shepherds, whose dull routine had been interrupted by the celestial visitation, the realization in Bethlehem must have been an unforgettable experience. Had they not remembered and cherished it, it might not have been recorded in this Gospel, written probably two generations after the event occurred. Nor did the shepherds realize all that it meant. Its full significance had not yet been completely disclosed, but is still unfolding in the present work of Christ in the world. Its final perfection awaits the day when he will come again.

The road of faith leads forward through an enlarging awareness of the purpose and power of God as he develops the life of the individual believer and at the same time executes his design for the world. Bethlehem is consequently at

14

the end of the road to *redemption*. The road of faith had its goal in the full experience of redemption, for the infant who lay in the manger became the Christ of the cross and the resurrection.

To the astonished shepherds he was revealed as a Savior who is Messiah, or Christ the Lord. These titles would not have been unfamiliar to them. *Savior* was applied to God by the prophet Isaiah, who called him "a just God and a Savior" (Isa. 45:21), and Hosea, speaking for God, said, "Besides me there is no Savior" (Hos. 13:4). *Messiah* means "anointed," a person set apart especially for divine service and invested with peculiar authority. It was applied to kings, priests, and prophets. The term *Lord* denoted sovereignty, the right to rule or to control. All of these titles speak of functions that Jesus was born to discharge. He was destined to be the Savior of his people, for Matthew writes that he was called Jesus, "for it is he that shall save his people from their sins" (Matt. 1:21). As the Messiah, he was declared to be the champion who would ultimately lead his people to freedom. As Lord, he would become the final judge of men and the ruler of their lives.

Obviously this was not instantly apparent to the shepherds. They stood at the threshold of the era that Jesus introduced, and they did not witness all that he accomplished. Nevertheless their united response of resolute faith started them on the road that leads to salvation, not only for the individual, but also for mankind. Simeon, who saw the infant Jesus in the Temple, and who had a fuller perspective on God's revelation than did the shepherds, responded by saying, "Mine eyes have seen thy salvation which thou hast prepared before the face of all peoples; a light for revelation to the Gentiles, and the glory of thy people Israel" (Luke 2:30-32). As the plan of God unfolded, the fullness of that redemption became apparent. By accepting Jesus' person, his disciples were lifted to a new plane of living. By the sacrifice of his death, forgiveness of sin was assured. By his resurrection, eternal life was demonstrated. By his Spirit, new direction and power were granted to them for their daily living.

God's revelation of himself at Bethlehem transcended his previous dealings with man. The person who resolves to act on this revelation will realize a transformation in character, outlook, and destiny. Faith is the first step in walking with God. "He that cometh to God must believe that he is, and that he is a rewarder of them that seek after him" (Heb. 11:6).

It may be that no voice from eternity will wake us from sleep tonight with a new promise, and that no heavenly choir will amaze us with a cantata of salvation, but the written word is before us, and the challenge is the same. From revelation to resolution, from resolution to realization, and from realization to redemption, the road of faith stretches into the future for those who will boldly explore its possibilities. They will see its promises become actualities, and will experience the redemptive power of God that lifts us from sordid depression and frustration into a career of peace and effective living.

TWO
THE ROAD
TO THE WILDERNESS:
The Road of Temptation

And Jesus, full of the Holy Spirit, returned from the Jordan, and was led in the Spirit in the wilderness during forty days, being tempted of the devil. Luke 4:1, 2

Luke begins his account of Jesus' ministry at the river Jordan. There he appeared in public for the first time, requesting baptism at the hands of John the Baptist. To John, as well as to subsequent readers of this story, his action seemed incongruous. Baptism is a sign of penitence and of death because of sin, a symbol that the person baptized is saying farewell to the former mode of life, and that he is entering upon an entirely new existence. Jesus was the Son of God; what need did he have of repentance? The uniform testimony of the New Testament, corroborated by the silence of Jesus' enemies, declares him innocent of all sin. Why should he follow all others in an act which was essentially a confession of wrongdoing? Why must he die to an old life and rise to a new one?

John was bewildered by the request of Jesus, for he seemed to recognize him. He could not reconcile Jesus' person and his desire for baptism: "I have need to be baptized of thee, and comest thou to me?" (Matt. 3:14). The key to the puzzle is Jesus' reply: "Suffer it now: for thus it becometh us to fulfill all righteousness" (Matt. 3:15). Jesus' entrance into the world of flesh and blood did not require him to be a sinner, but it was necessary that he should share the status of humanity. In this first declaration of "the Word made flesh" he took his position among men by saying, "It becometh us to fulfill all righteousness" (Matt. 3:15). Just as sinning men must bow to the judgment of death and experience new life from God, so Jesus must become one with man in his tribulation and triumph. Baptism was the symbolic foreshadowing of his own death and resurrection.

The road to the wilderness began with a public commitment of Jesus to the will of God. If he came "to seek and to save that which was lost" (Luke 19:10) he must go where the lost were. The swimmer who attempts to rescue a drowning man does not need to drown with him, but he must enter the water in order to save him. By this commitment, Jesus pledged himself to the ministry for which he had come into the world.

Jesus' commitment was acknowledged by his visible endowment with the Holy Spirit. Again, it seems that this event was superfluous, for Jesus had been conceived by the Holy Spirit (Luke 1:34, 35). Surely the Son of God did not need a special initiation or anointing by the Spirit. The episode was emblematic of the fact that the Spirit is the seal of God's acceptance of every child of his and the power by which that child makes his way through life according to his Father's will. "As many as are led by the Spirit of God, these are sons of God" (Rom. 8:14).

Following the commendation of John and the manifest presence of the Spirit came the voice of the Father: "Thou art my beloved Son; in thee I am well pleased" (Luke 3:22). To the Hebrews the phenomenon of a voice from heaven was not unknown. There were occasional instances in the Old Testament. God called Moses audibly at the burning bush (Exod. 3:4). He dealt with Elijah on the mountain in the wilderness (1 Kings 19:11–14). Now he had spoken to Jesus in a similar manner. Should Jesus therefore conclude that he was fully equipped for his ministry, and that the enthusiastic introduction by the forerunner, the continuity of purpose and office that the baptism provided, and the divine acknowledgment of him as the Son of God had rendered further training unnecessary?

Just the opposite was true. The exaltation of that moment was followed by a sharp contrast. Jesus found himself, not in the center of popular attention as John had been, but alone in the sandy, barren waste of the Judean desert. Instead of the Spirit's conducting him to a place of ministry among the crowds of Judea or Galilee, Jesus was driven into an empty waste where there were no inhabitants and no food. Instead of the Father's reassuring encouragement he encountered the ominous presence of an adversary who was bent on his destruction. It must have been a devastating shock to Jesus in contrast to the initial joy he experienced at the Jordan.

The road to the wilderness represents the sudden blow that believers experience after the first great ecstasy of salvation. When the new Christian realizes that his sins are forgiven, that he belongs to God's family, and that he has the Spirit to teach and guide him, he may experience a joy that is all too easily dispelled by the first test that comes, especially if that test is not met successfully. The confidence that all problems have been solved and all difficulties removed is rudely shattered by unexpected adversity or by some sudden frustration or failure. There is the tendency to think that God has forsaken one, and that the joy of salvation is a delusion. Discouragement and darkness so envelop the Christian that he can scarcely pray. His faith is tried to the breaking point.

Such trial is what is meant by temptation. It does not necessarily involve solicitation to evil, but rather implies a pressure or testing to see how much a person or thing can bear without breaking under the strain. A prominent automobile manufacturer once advertised his product by a picture of a new model, fresh from the factory, standing in a driveway, with the inscription beneath it, "You will never see this car again." The advertisement explained further that the car would never be sold because it was to be sent to the proving grounds. There, taken fresh from the assembly line, it would be driven at top speed over the hardest, roughest, and most crooked roads that could be devised. It would be subjected to extreme heat and cold and to mechanical abuse of every imaginable kind until it was reduced to a hopeless wreck. The purpose was to ascertain the weaknesses of that particular model in order to correct them before it was released for public sale. That car would become a test case.

Jesus was made a test case. He was to be presented as the perfect example of what humanity should be. Through him God intended to reveal his righteousness and effect the redemption of man from sin. In his person the method of God's salvation would be unfolded. In order to discharge this commission Jesus must be immune to the threats and suggestions of his Satanic enemy.

The same struggle confronts every believer. From the way in which Jesus countered the attack of the devil may be learned the proper tactics for waging this spiritual war. Everyone is exposed to it, for the tempter never forgets us, and often assails us at the most inopportune moments and in the most unexpected ways.

The reality of this enemy is indisputable. Satan is not an imaginary scarecrow nor a mediaeval myth, but an active foe of God who constantly endeavors to divert men from their Creator. His tactics are subtle and his purpose destructive. He is the father of lies and the promoter of disobedience, disorder, and anarchy. Nevertheless, he serves the purpose of testing the integrity and loyalty of God's people. At the beginning of his ministry Jesus confronted Satan to achieve victory for himself, and for us also. In Satan's attack on Jesus can be seen the issues of every skirmish that we may have with him.

The first aspect of temptation is that of *pleasure*, the appeal to appetite. Man is a bundle of appetites; he desires food, sleep, love, and many other necessities of life. Appetite in itself is not a sin. The desire for food is natural, normal, and healthy. Hunger is the internal alarm that informs us when we need refueling. If the appetite is not gratified, the body suffers; weakness, disease, and starvation may follow. Nor is eating merely a necessity; it can also be a pleasure. The taste of savory food can add enjoyment to life, as the existence of novelty restaurants and food stores proves.

Eating, therefore, is no sin, but gluttony is a sin, because it makes the gratification of the appetite an end in itself. The glutton eats more than he needs because he idolizes the food. He thinks only of the next dish or of the next meal, and centers all his life around pleasing his palate. The question, then, is whether appetite is a means to the sustenance of life, or whether life consists in indulging the appetite.

This question faced Jesus as he sat alone for forty days in the desert. The Judean wilderness had no inhabitants from whom he could beg a morsel of bread, and no vegetation that would offer even the coarsest of food. He was desperately and legitimately hungry. Then came the suggestion of the devil, "If thou art the Son of God, command this stone that it become bread" (Luke 4:3).

The kind of bread that Jesus customarily ate was not the rectangular porous loaf that can be purchased in a supermarket. The bread that he knew was more like a flat pancake, often rather dry and coarse. In form and size it resembled the round flat stones of the desert. So the subtle suggestion came: "If you really are who you claim to be, surely God does not want you to starve to death. You have the power to make stones into food; exercise it. After all, the Father has given you work to do, but you will never accomplish it if you die here. Use your power, and live."

Why was the devil's suggestion not acceptable? Would it have been wrong for Jesus to eat? Could he not use his supernatural power to insure his survival?

Jesus came into the world to accomplish the will of his Father. He did nothing apart from the Father's design and consent. Had he exercised this power to satisfy his own desire, apart from the Father's will for him, it would have been sin. Sin does not consist in eating, but in putting personal pleasure or advantage before the express will of God. Sin is placing whim before principle and impulse before purpose. An advertising slogan appeared in a commercial advertisement on television: "Try it, you'll like it." It implied that anything is legitimate if one wants it, that one should try anything to discover whether or not it is pleasant, irrespective of consequences.

Jesus answered the suggestion by quoting from the Law of God as given in Deuteronomy: "Man doth not live by bread only" (Deut. 8:3). He did not say that bread is unnecessary to life, but that it is not the sole need for supporting life. Life does not consist in satiating one's appetite with material things, but in using those things in accordance with God's purpose. Jesus said on another occasion, "My meat (food) is to do the will of him that sent me, and to accomplish his work" (John 4:34). He did not debate the possibility of starvation, nor did he comment on how good a piece of bread would taste, but rather gave his first thought to the relation of his appetite to the purpose of God.

Man does not live by bread alone. To attempt to do so would be only an animal existence. Animals are content if they can find enough to satisfy their physical needs. Man was created for a larger life that is linked not only with the material world but also with the spiritual world. Without the understanding of the Word of God and the appropriation of its provisions for the larger life in God, human existence becomes monotonous, futile, and evil. Had Jesus yielded to this temptation, his dependence on the Father would have been broken, and he would have tacitly declared his intention to place his personal desires above the will of God.

The second aspect of the temptation is the desire for *possession*. Having failed in his first attempt, the devil tried a different approach. He led Jesus to a mountain top and showed him all the kingdoms of the world. In the Judean desert, on the west side of the Jordan just north of the Dead Sea, is the traditional Mount of Temptation. There, supposedly, Jesus stood and surveyed the landscape below him. Far to the east lay the boundary of the Roman Empire, beyond which was the empire of the Parthians, or modern Iran, and its eastern neighbors in India and China, known in those days chiefly by their exports of jewels, spices, and textiles. To the south lay Egypt, the granary of the Mediterranean lands. To the west were Greece and Rome, the political and intellectual centers of the world. To the north were the rich provinces of Asia Minor and the unexplored forests of Europe. It may be that he saw in his vision not only the kingdoms of that moment, but also all those yet to come, for the account says that "he showed them all in a moment of time." As he looked at them and recognized that they were rightfully his, the devil whispered, "I will give you all of them if you will worship me."

Here was a way to avoid the struggle that eventuated in Calvary. It was an opportunity to accomplish his work easily and to claim instant title to the vast realms of human life that otherwise would be won only by sacrifice and suffering. All that was needed was a token gesture of acknowledgment that he had received possession from the one who had usurped these kingdoms.

What a fraud! The usurper was offering to sell the kingdom to the rightful heir. The squatter was impudently informing the owner that he would sell him the title to his own land for the price of submission. It was an insult to Jesus' intelligence and to his authority. If he had accepted the offer, he might have had the kingdoms without opposition, but the devil would have had him. The price would have been too high and the gain only humiliation.

There is no short cut to spiritual victory. Jesus came into the world to establish the kingdom of God. The objective of his mission was to redeem men who were sold under sin, to reconstitute a world that had been ruined by the selfishness and disobedience of its inhabitants. His redemptive work extended to the totality of human life—political, social, and physical as well as spiritual. The book of Revelation predicts the day when "the kingdom of this world is become the kingdom of our Lord, and of his Christ: and he shall reign for ever and ever" (Rev. 11:15). Between the temptation and the triumph lay a long pilgrimage of suffering and struggle, yet there could be no compromise. The victory must be won, not bought. Concession to evil can produce only enslavement, never success.

The reply of Jesus gives the real reason for his refusal of the seemingly easy expedient: "Thou shalt fear Jehovah thy God; and him shalt thou serve" (Deut. 6:13). God demands complete obedience and the recognition of his sole authority over human life. The glittering attractiveness of the immediate temptation has no assurance of permanent advantage if it severs one from the fellowship and power of God. Only the full and final devotion of one's soul to God can ensure that the "kingdoms of this world" will ultimately be his possession.

The devil is an expert advertiser. He knows how to display

his wares in the most attractive setting, and he can dazzle the imagination and beguile the mind with the glamor of his commodities. In themselves they may not be harmful, but if they are not in keeping with God's purpose for life, they can only be injurious to the possessor. The thrill of owning them will soon pass away; the disillusion of disobedience will remain. Jesus chose the hard way to his kingdom.

The third aspect of temptation is *prestige*. On this third occasion the devil took Jesus to the pinnacle of the Temple. When after the Six Day War of 1967 the Israeli people regained control of old Jerusalem, they began a systematic excavation in the area surrounding the Wailing Wall, the ancient retaining wall of the Temple of Jesus' day. The rubble and dust that had accumulated after the destruction of the city in A.D. 70 had buried the land eighteen feet under the level of the present city. When the street of the first century was finally excavated, a piece of marble was discovered that had fallen from the Temple wall. On it was an inscription in Hebrew characters that read, "The place of the blowing of the trumpet." Originally it had marked the topmost pinnacle of the Temple where the priest stood to blow the *shofar* or ram's horn to announce the opening of a feast. Before the destruction of the Temple that place was at the top of the corner, about one hundred and fifty feet above the Kidron valley below. This was probably the place where the devil set Jesus, and said, "If thou art the Son of God, cast thyself down from hence: for it is written, he shall give his angels charge concerning thee, to guard thee: and, on their hands they shall bear thee up, lest haply thou dash thy foot against a stone" (Luke 4:10, 11).

Curiously enough, the devil did not quote the text correctly. The Psalm from which it is taken reads: "He will give his angels charge over thee, to keep thee in all thy ways. They shall bear thee up in their hands, lest thou dash thy foot against a stone. Thou shalt tread upon the lion and the adder: the young lion and the serpent shalt thou trample under foot" (Psa. 91:11-13).

The devil knew the text, but Jesus knew the context. He supplied what was missing. Satan can quote Scripture for his purpose, but when he attempts to use it in order to justify temptation, he always distorts it by omission of something that may be small, but that is significant. The omission of "in all thy ways" overlooked the fact that the promise of protection is only for those who follow the pattern that God has marked out for them. In addition, Satan did not include the verse that promised a victory over himself, who, "as a roaring lion, walketh about, seeking whom he may devour" (1 Pet. 5:8), or over "the old serpent" (Rev. 20:2) who deceives and poisons those who heed him.

The design of the temptation was to test Jesus' desire for prestige. Had he leaped from that height and descended slowly and with dignity one hundred and fifty feet to the floor of the valley below, his reputation would instantly have been established. Everyone who observed him would have said, "This man is supernatural. He possesses incredible power. He can be our Messiah, and we will follow him." The advertising of the grapevine telegraph would have spread throughout all Judea and Galilee, and the multitudes would have flocked to his banner. He would not have been forced to endure a long series of debates or a constant presentation of his powers to gain favor, nor would he have had to take the road of suffering. The marvel of his descent would have accredited his claims, and he would have been acknowledged as a visitor from heaven rather than as the carpenter's son from Nazareth.

Jesus' reply showed that he was not playing for prestige. Again he quoted the Scripture, "Ye shall not tempt Jehovah your God" (Deut. 6:16). The verb in this quotation means to exasperate, to tease, or to provoke beyond any normal limit. The short quotation contains several implications. For one, Jesus was dismissing Satan by calling three temptations sufficient. The devil had already exceeded the bounds permitted to him; God was not a subject for experimentation. Again, he had no right to put God to the test at all. God is to be obeyed, not seduced. Finally, if Jesus were applying this prohibition to Satan's temptation of him, he was claiming deity for himself—a claim which Satan tacitly acknowledged by the wording of his suggestion, "If thou art the Son of God . . ."—a condition like that in verse 3, which assumes the condition to be a fact.

25

Jesus refused the spectacular means of gaining his objective. Had he accepted it, the fickle multitude would soon have forgotten the episode, and would probably have rejected him when his claims on them proved distasteful. The cross was inevitable in any case, but at the end of the devil's road it could only mean stark and irretrievable tragedy: pleasure turned into anguish, possessions stripped away, prestige dissolved in humiliation. At the end of God's road it would mean eternal joy in his presence (Heb. 12:2), the possession of all the kingdoms of this world (Rev. 11:15), and preservation through suffering and death into an inextinguishable life (Heb. 2:9; 7:16).

Finally, the road to the wilderness is the road of *triumph*. "And Jesus returned in the power of the Spirit into Galilee: and a fame went out concerning him through all the region round about" (Luke 4:14). When he emerged from the temptation there was something about him that made his words convincing. His leadership was self-authenticating and the power of the Holy Spirit was manifestly operative in his life. He was tested, proved, and vindicated.

The third chapter of Genesis shows the aspects of temptation initially placed before mankind as the identical three described in the temptation of Jesus. "When the woman saw that the tree was good for food [the *pleasure* of eating], and that it was a delight to the eyes [the power of *possession*], and that the tree was to be desired to make one wise [the *prestige* of wisdom], she took of the fruit thereof, and did eat" (Gen. 3:6). She succumbed to the wily suggestions of the tempter, whereas Jesus did not.

These three elemental temptations confront all men throughout life. In whatever package they are wrapped, the content is always the same: pleasure, power, and prestige. The specific inducements will differ with time, place, and personal susceptibility or temperament; the essence and the alternatives are unvarying. The road to the wilderness is God's means for testing our love for him and our willingness to obey him under all circumstances.

The road to the wilderness is inevitable. God does not make saints by an easy method. One cannot carve a statue without using a knife on wood or a chisel on marble. God employs the temptations of life to chip away the flaws and fragments that are useless in order to bring out of the misshapen block the statue that he intends to create.

Temptation is endurable. Jesus outlasted it. A football game is not always won by the heaviest team or by the one that has superior strategy, but by the one that can stay on the field and hold its own until the opposing side quits or fails by reason of fatigue. Jesus met every onslaught by saying, "It is written. . . ." He adhered to the will of God, and outlasted the devil.

Ultimately, temptation is profitable. Job, who suffered from the attack of Satan, said of God, "He knoweth the way that I take; when he hath tried me, I shall come forth as gold" (Job 23:10). Undoubtedly Job had watched a goldsmith at work, hovering over the crucible in which he was heating the raw ore. As he increased the intensity of the fire, the ore began to melt, and he persisted in blowing on the draft until the seething, tortured mass began to separate. The heavy metal settled in the bottom of the crucible; the lighter slag floated to the top. With a ladle he skimmed off the slag and discarded it, keeping the heat in that terrific furnace until the gold was completely melted and reduced to a glowing liquid. When the gold became so clear that he could see his face mirrored in it, he extinguished the fire. The gold was ready for use.

Sometimes God puts his servants in the crucible. The fire of adversity is hot, and our best intentions evaporate. Temptation presses upon us to escape from pain to pleasure, from weakness to power, from humiliation to prestige. The complexities of life bewilder us and its calamitie. torture us. God is simply trying out the gold to remove the slag. When he can see his face in us, he will put out the fire and finish his work.

To revert to the original figure, all of us must walk the road to the wilderness. It is not, however, a dead-end street. It did not end in the wilderness for Jesus; it will not for us. The road to the wilderness takes us through the ominous desert to a new status where we are better prepared to face the challenges of life and better fitted to do the will of God who has called us to his service.

27

THREE
THE ROAD
TO GALILEE:
The Road of Responsibility

And Jesus returned in the power of the Spirit into Galilee: and a fame went out concerning him through all the region round about. And he taught in their synagogues being glorified of all. Luke 4:14, 15

The account of the road to Galilee in the Gospel of Luke follows immediately after the road to the wilderness. Once the testing was completed and the unswerving loyalty of the Lord Jesus was proved, he was given a commission to discharge. Appointment always follows testing, and all of God's servants from the Lord Jesus himself to the poorest and the most obscure have a work to do that nobody else can perform. Each must take his or her place in God's economy, and must be prepared to give adequate account of his task when it is done.

Jesus' acceptance of his responsibility is given in his own words:

And he came to Nazareth, where he had been brought up; and he entered, as his custom was, into the synagogue on the sabbath day, and stood up to read. And there was delivered unto him the book of the prophet Isaiah. And he opened the book, and found the place where it was written,

The Spirit of the Lord is upon me,
Because he anointed me to preach good tidings to the poor:

He hath sent me to proclaim release to the captives,
And recovering of sight to the blind,
To set at liberty them that are bruised,
To proclaim the acceptable year of the Lord.

And he closed the book, and gave it back to the attendant, and sat down: and the eyes of all in the synagogue were fastened on him. And he began to say unto them, Today hath this scripture been fulfilled in your ears. Luke 4:16–21

As I conversed one day with the president of a large business company, the latter said, "The hardest thing that I have to do is to find men who will take responsibility. I can find many who want a job, and plenty who want a pay check at the end of the week; but where can I find a man who will undertake a task, agree to remain with it until it is finished, and do it thoroughly?" He was dismayed to discover that it was very difficult to find assistants who would discharge their work faithfully and be ready to stand by its results. They were unwilling to risk the onus of failure if it occurred, or to accept willingly the uncertainty of success. As another executive once remarked, "Do not bring me your problems; bring me your solutions."

For the Christian, the road to Galilee is a necessary one. Once having accepted the love and forgiveness of God in Christ, and having passed the initial test of adversity and temptation, he is ready for the second stage of God's dealing with him. Galilee looms before him.

To Jesus, Galilee was the hardest place in which he could begin his work because it was his home territory. Ever since Joseph and Mary had taken up their residence in Nazareth after their return from Egypt, he had lived there. The people knew him only as the son of the village carpenter, and while they knew nothing disparaging about his reputation, they were not prepared to consider him a divine being. His first presentation of himself had to be made to a group of friends, relatives, and neighbors who might regard him as either conceited or demented. Nevertheless, he was obligated to fulfill his commission in spite of possible misunderstanding and opposition.

The primary ministry for anyone who has responsibility is the acceptance of authority. Responsibility involves authority, for any man is responsible to someone for what he does. In any chart that depicts a job description the work of the person involved is always defined by his relation to a superior, who, in turn, is responsible to one above him. The employees of any business must follow the orders of their foreman, who in turn carries out the specifications of the head of his department. He must answer to the manager of the business, who must give account to the trustees or owner for the ultimate profit or loss. If the plans of the owner(s) are to succeed, every person in the company must do his share in perfecting the process of operation.

Following the road to Galilee requires *the acceptance of the authority of the Holy Spirit*. Twice in this passage the power of the Spirit in the life of Jesus is emphasized. When the divine authority is recognized by the disciple, he does not come to God with a plan, saying, "Lord, I want to do something for you, and I have a wonderful plan that I hope to put into action. Please bless it." God expects us to accept his plan and to permit him to work it out in our lives.

One summer the author worked for a contractor who was building homes. Every morning the contractor appeared on the job with a roll of blueprints under his arm. He spread them out on a pile of lumber, and showed the foreman what he wanted done on that day: where the windows and partitions should be placed and what materials were to be used. Suppose that the foreman had called the rest of the carpenters together, and had said, "Listen, men! We're building this house. Let's have a plan of our own. We'll make it the way that seems best to us, and the boss will be pleased when he sees how well we have done it." The boss would have been quite justified in firing all of us because it would not have been his plan.

When we take the responsibility of living the Christian life we must act under the authority that God has established. The Holy Spirit has given the main design in the Scriptures, and the model is Jesus himself, who lived by the Spirit. If the Holy Spirit is in control of us, he will take over our lives and will tell us how we should live it.

31

Seldom, if ever, does God reveal the whole plan of life at once. He does not give us a complete précis of everything that we will do for the next fifty years. If he did, life might become wearisome because nothing new or exciting would ever happen. God always has something fresh and interesting that unfolds as the years pass.

Furthermore, when God plans the way ahead, he makes no mistakes. Often we need to reorganize our own plans because we did not understand the effects of our choices, or because we did not foresee the new circumstances that might arise. To be sure, not all aspects of God's plan may be pleasant or welcome, but the acceptance of his authority always guarantees ultimate satisfaction. The road to Galilee has some rough sections in it and some dangerous turns, but it leads invariably to the right goal.

The authority of the Spirit is not always manifested by some explosive experience. He does not usually speak to us in the thunders and lightnings of Sinai. He spoke to Elijah with "a voice of gentle stillness." When we place our lives at the disposal of the Spirit there may not always be an instant change, but as time progresses, that quiet insistent voice will direct us to new opportunities and new prospects of the path that we are to follow, that no part of our lives will be wasted or futile.

How can the authority of the Spirit become known? The first and best way of discerning it is by the testimony of Scripture. Jesus himself lived by it. Although he was "the Word made flesh," he was operating through the vehicle of human consciousness and through a human body. He lived among us as a man, and was exhibiting to the world what God would do if he were a member of our race. At every turn of his career he was governed by the Scriptures of the Old Testament. His declaration of his calling in this particular instance was taken from the prophet Isaiah (61:1, 2). All of Jesus' actions were ruled by the revealed purpose of God.

Not long after his preaching in Nazareth, Jesus was engaged in a ministry in Capernaum. He exorcised a demon; he healed Peter's mother-in-law of fever; and he conducted a tremendously successful meeting accompanied by many other healings. The crowd begged him to stay with them, but he said: "I must preach the good tidings of the kingdom of God to the other cities also: for therefore was I sent" (Luke 4:43). Two words in his statement afford the clue to the pattern of authority: *must* and *sent*. He was under orders from heaven, and he could not deviate from them to meet popular demand.

These same two words occur in other Gospels in connection with the mission of Jesus. The fourth chapter of John states that on another occasion he "must" go through Samaria by a road which few Jews of his day ever traveled (John 4:4). They tried to avoid Samaritan territory because of their prejudice against the inhabitants. Why should Jesus deliberately take this route? Nobody had persuaded or commanded him to do so. There was one person in Samaria that the Spirit wanted him to meet—the woman at the well. Through her testimony the Samaritan settlement was opened to his ministry. This may have been the precursor of the awakening in Samaria described in Acts, chapter eight. In explaining his action to the disciples he said, "My meat is to do the will of him that sent me, and to accomplish his work" (John 4:34). Throughout his life to the very end, the authority of Scripture directed him. In the last hour on the cross he cried, "I thirst," "that the scripture might be accomplished" (John 19:28). The word of Scripture is the basic criterion for the voice of the Spirit.

There are undoubtedly promptings of the Spirit that are designed for individual conduct. The Bible does not prescribe verbally every detail of personal conduct, and the general principles must be applied by the inner working of the Spirit. To rely on impressions apart from the written word can be dangerous, no matter how sincere one may be. Certainly no one has the right to regulate the lives of others with whom God can deal directly.

This point can be illustrated from life. A young student came one day for counselling and said that she had a personal problem to discuss.

She asked, "Do you know Mr. X?"

"Yes."

"He says that God has told him that I should marry him, and I am not sure that I should."

"Did God say anything to you about it?"

"No."

"Do you have any conviction that you should marry him?"

"None whatever."

"God is a gentleman. When he tells one person something that involves another, he informs the other person also. If God has not told you that you should marry this man, you should not do it. I am not at all certain that the Holy Spirit told him that."

There have been many cases more radical than this one, but the point is that the Lord Jesus Christ, in accepting the authority of Scripture, established the basis for operating under the direction of the Holy Spirit. With the Scripture, the Spirit provides personal guidance to the Christian. Without it, he may fall into fanaticism or delusion. Acceptance of the Spirit's authority is the first step on the road to Galilee.

The second step is *the acceptance of mission*. Certain elements of Jesus' mission are mentioned in the context. The first of these is the place of ministry, Nazareth. Nazareth was his home town. Of all the places where one can serve God, the home town is the most difficult. As Jesus himself said, "No prophet is acceptable in his own country" (Luke 4:24). No man seems exceptional to those who know him well; he is simply ordinary to them. Most of the outstanding figures of history gained their reputations after they left home and lived in other communities. To be able to be a convincing witness among those who know all one's antecedents and limitations, to gain a hearing among those who know as much or more than the speaker, and to exercise authority among one's peers demands unusual character and ability. Often one's past may discredit him, and a long time or a great transformation may be necessary to overcome its persistent memory. That would not have been true of Jesus, but Luke's account shows that his fellow-townsmen would not accept him as the messenger of God. He was, nevertheless, sent to them and he delivered his message. "He came unto his own, and they that were his own received him not" (John 1:11).

There were other places where he preached and was gladly welcomed. Crowds followed him from all the cities of Galilee. The Samaritans urged him to stay with them, and a woman of Tyre sought his intervention for her daughter. In general,

34

however, because Jesus exposed hypocrisy and disregarded conventional attitudes, he made many enemies and was officially rejected by his nation. For him, the road to Galilee was rough and thorny, and beset with perils.

Not only was Jesus sent to a difficult place, but he was sent to four classes of people who were hard to reach. Following the words of Scripture, he declared that he was sent to proclaim the gospel to the *poor*. Poor people are not generally considered to be important, but they are not unimportant in the eyes of God. "Blessed are ye poor," said Jesus, "for yours is the kingdom of God" (Luke 6:20). In that beatitude Jesus was not referring only to those whose pocketbooks were empty, but also to those whose life had been cruelly deprived of the means of subsistence. He did not come to create a church that would be an exclusive religious club for the prosperous. To be sure, they should not be excluded, but it ought to be a fellowship where all can relate to God and to each other irrespective of economic status. Jesus was concerned for the hungry, for the disinherited and for the oppressed. He was sent to those who had been broken on the wheel of life. Poverty refers not solely to finances, but to deprivation of spiritual life and strength, of all the things that God designed for man's benefit.

The second class mentioned here are the *brokenhearted*. In every community there are people who are haunted by regrets, plagued by guilt, and crushed by sorrow. Sometimes the anguish is obvious; more often it is concealed beneath the artificial gaiety of the group or submerged in the incessant routine of daily work. There are few people on the face of the earth who have not suffered heartbreak at one time or another. Some disappointment, some injury, some frustration has left a scar upon their lives that seems ineradicable. Every one carries the memory of some bitter sorrow or of some shattered hope of the past. It may have been assuaged by the passage of time, or it may have left a wound that is irremediable. Whatever the nature of the trouble, Jesus was sent to aid the brokenhearted, and so are his servants. We must walk the road to Galilee with him if we would fulfil our mission. Our hands may be clumsy when our intentions are good. Sometimes when we try to mend the heartstrings of other people we lack the right touch. It takes a peculiar skill, but God can give it; and Jesus certainly had it.

A third group are the *captives* who are imprisoned and forgotten. It includes not only those who are confined in the local jail or state penitentiary, but also those that are imprisoned by their own evildoing. "His own iniquities shall take the wicked, and he shall be holden with the cords of his sin" (Prov. 5:22). Men become the captives of their own evil habits, and of their misdirected desires. Christ offers liberty to captives, first because he frees them from their own guilt and failure, and second because he makes it possible for them to become useful and acceptable members of society. Charles Colson, who for his complicity in the Watergate scandal was finally sentenced to a year in prison that cost him disgrace and disbarment as a lawyer, found in Christ his freedom from spiritual bondage, and has devoted his life to a ministry among prisoners.

The final class mentioned here is the *blind*. This refers to those who are physically blind, but it is peculiarly applicable to those who are blind to truth. In a recent magazine there appeared an article by a former colleague who is now a professor of theology in a Christian institution. He stated that he and another teacher were riding on a plane. The window seat in the row that they occupied was not taken, and his friend moved over to the window to look at the sights, leaving the center seat vacant. At one of the stops a third man entered, and took the vacant seat. They opened a conversation, and the new arrival asked him what he did for a living. He replied that he was a professor of theology, and that his colleague was one also.

"Isn't that funny?" said the third man. "Here I find myself sitting between two professors of theology. You know, I have an employee who is just leaving me to attend a seminary."

"Is that so?"

"Yes, he's a first-class engineer. Something happened to that fellow. I don't know what it was, but he's leaving his job as an engineer and is going to a seminary. He used to live a pretty wild life, but he's changed a lot lately. Maybe it's because he got married."

Obviously matrimony was not the reason. The man had

become a Christian, and had begun to realize that he should not spend his life in engineering when God had something greater for him to do. The road to Galilee lay before him, and he chose to walk in it. The point of the story is, however, that the employer could not understand why any man in his right mind would leave a lucrative position in engineering for the ministry. The former "wild life" of his employee was not so much of an anomaly to him as his new life in Christ. He had no concept of what the new birth meant; he was absolutely blind to spiritual realities.

There are many people who look at a Christian patronizingly and say, "He's got religion." The secular person charges off all spiritual consciousness as a mental aberration. In the Soviet Union believers who practice their faith seriously are sometimes incarcerated in mental hospitals. Jesus was sent to the blind that he might give them light.

These are the people to whom the road to Galilee leads: the poor, the brokenhearted, the prisoners, and the blind. If, however, we are to approach them, what shall our message be? Is this a purely sociological enterprise? There is a necessary sociological aspect. If a person is poor and downtrodden, and needs financial help, we should share with him. If he is brokenhearted, we can lend him a listening ear and offer comforting counsel and sympathy. If he is a prisoner, we may offer our help to unravel the tangled skein of his life and our influence to bring him liberty. If he is blind to truth, we can present to him the Light of the world. All these things may be done on the human level, and are beneficial.

Although the sociological aspect must not be overlooked, however, there must be something more to produce the desired effect. Jesus said, "The Spirit of the Lord is upon me, because he anointed me to preach good tidings . . . He hath sent me . . . to proclaim the acceptable year of the Lord (Luke 4:18, 19). What are the "good tidings"? They are the news that God loves and saves men, that he has a plan for this world that he will execute in spite of all the evil that seems dominant. The road to Galilee leads to the responsibility of proclaiming and living the Word of God.

That responsibility involves knowing the Word of God. One cannot proclaim what he does not know. Any man who assumes the responsibility of the road to Galilee must be familiar with the Scriptures. A doctor can be forgiven if he is not an expert in political science, but if he does not know his pharmacopoeia and his surgery, he can be sued for malpractice. A lawyer need not be required to have skill in repairing a car, but if he does not know enough law to defend his client, he can be disbarred. If a Christian does not know enough of God's Word to deal with men who are without God and hope, he is operating under false pretenses. He lays himself open to the charge of being either incompetent or fraudulent. The Christian on the road to Galilee must take his mission as seriously as Jesus took his.

How far does this road extend? It transcends all national and cultural barriers, and the farther one travels on it, the wider the scope of vision becomes. Dr. A. B. Simpson was the pastor of a large and influential church in New York City. He was diligent and devoted to his work, and his people loved him. Still, he was not content with his ministry, not because it was not well received, nor because there was not enough to keep him busy, but because the church had become ingrown. It paid no attention to the masses of people to whom he wanted to reach out with the gospel. He finally resigned that comfortable pulpit, and began on the back stage of a theater to produce a Bible school and a preaching ministry to the masses of New York. The outgrowth of that ministry has in two generations produced five Christian colleges and Bible schools, a worldwide ministry on more than a score of mission fields, and has sent hundreds of preachers and missionaries who have contributed sacrificially to the proclamation of the message of Christ. His ministry could not be cramped by one small church or by one particular group of people. Whether a man wore a blue collar or a white collar, or no collar at all, whether he spoke perfect English or the jargon of the streets, whether he were a native or an immigrant made no difference. The universal ministry characterizes the road to Galilee.

Finally, the road to Galilee means responsibility for *the consequences* of the mission. For Jesus the end of the road was rejection. That sounds threatening. Does God send his messengers only to be rejected? Not necessarily, but that is a possibility that must be considered. Not everybody welcomes

God's message. At first it may seem that a majority will reject it as they did when Jesus preached in the synagogue at Nazareth. The mob surrounded him, pushed him out of the building, and were taking him to the top of an adjacent hill that they might throw him over its cliff. He had offended their taste and had wounded their egos. He had not restricted himself to the pattern of their thinking. They were not ready to receive his wider vision and his final authority.

When Isaiah was given his commission, he asked how long he should preach. God replied: "Until cities be waste without inhabitant, and houses without man, and the land become utterly waste, . . . and the forsaken places be many in the midst of the land" (Isa. 6:11, 12). It is surprising that Isaiah did not say, "Lord, please excuse me. I do not want a ministry that will be a failure." If rejection is normal, what prospect is there for success?

The ministry of Jesus is an adequate answer. From Nazareth to Calvary he faced rejection by the many, but was received by some. These he taught, and they continued his ministry until today 30 percent of the people in the world are ostensibly Christian. They may not all be genuine believers, but they at least acknowledge him. Isaiah said of him, "He shall see the travail of his soul, and shall be satisfied" (Isa. 53:41). The road to Galilee, walked with him, leads to ultimate success.

Two and one-half centuries ago a Norwegian pastor by the name of Hans Egede became burdened for the inhabitants of Greenland. He thought that some of the people in that forbidding country were descendants of the early Norse explorers. He left his pastorate and sailed for Greenland to find that the only human beings there were Eskimos. Despite the rigors of the climate and the obstinate opposition of the ignorant and thieving people, he learned their language and preached unflinchingly. Finally, in utter discouragement, he preached his farewell sermon from Isaiah 49:4: "I have labored in vain, I have spent my strength for nought and vanity; yet surely the justice due to me is with Jehovah, and my recompense with my God."

He returned to Denmark where he became head of a training school. Three years later a Moravian mission entered

Greenland, and experienced a revival that established a flourishing church in what had seemed to be barren territory. The seed that Egede sowed sprang up and bore fruit under his successors.

Although the road to Galilee may mean rejection, it never ends in failure. For every one it is the path to accomplishment. We are not responsible for producing immediate results from our labors. We are responsible for faithful adherence to the calling of God and for the fulfillment of the task which he assigns. As Jesus took the road of responsibility so must we, knowing that God will lead us to triumph by the same path that he walked.

FOUR
THE ROAD
TO JERICHO:
The Road of Life

A certain man was going down from Jerusalem to Jericho; and he fell among robbers, who both stripped him and beat him, and departed, leaving him half dead. Luke 10:30

The Gospel of Luke is a literary masterpiece. Luke was a skillful writer of short stories. He could have obtained a position as a reporter on a modern newspaper, or he could have written a weekly column. His stories, however, were not wholly original, because he was relating the parables that Jesus told. By the Spirit of God he knew how to state them in language that could be effective. They are brief, expressive, and interesting, and always carry a definite point for the reader.

One of these, recorded in the tenth chapter of Luke's Gospel, deals with a road that Jesus traveled, the road to Jericho. It was a parable, doubtless taken from life, and spoken to meet an actual situation. It reads as follows:

And behold, a certain lawyer stood up and made trial of him, saying, Teacher, what shall I do to inherit eternal life? And he said unto him, What is written in the law? how readest thou? And he answering said, Thou shalt love the Lord thy God with all thy heart, and with all thy soul, and with all thy strength, and with all thy mind; and thy neighbor as thyself. And he said unto him, Thou hast answered right: this do, and thou shalt live. But he, desiring to justify himself, said unto Jesus, And who is my neighbor? Jesus made answer and said, A certain man was going down from Jerusalem to Jericho; and he fell among robbers, who both stripped him and beat him, and departed, leaving him half dead. And by chance a certain priest was going down that way: and when he saw him, he passed by on the other side. And in like manner a Levite also, when he came to the place, and saw him, passed by on the other side. But a certain Samaritan, as he journeyed, came where he was: and when he saw him, he was moved with compassion, and came to him, and bound up his wounds, pouring on them oil and wine; and he set him on his own beast, and brought him to an inn, and took care of him. And on the morrow he took out two shillings, and gave them to the host, and said, Take care of him; and whatsoever thou spendest more, I, when I come back again, will repay thee. Which of these three, thinkest thou, proved neighbor unto him that fell among the robbers? And he said, He that showed mercy on him. And Jesus said unto him, Go, and do thou likewise (Luke 10: 25–37).

The road to Jericho is the road of life on which we all must walk when we undertake a mission for God. Once our responsibility is defined, the practical experience must follow. The narrative was Jesus' illustration to a student of the Law who had asked what he must do to inherit eternal life. A literal translation of that question would be, "Lord, what must I do to inherit the life of the age to come?" He was searching for a life that would be enduring, and, to use the modern jargon, "authentic."

Jesus replied to his question by asking another, "How do you read the Law?" He acknowledged the revelation of the Old Testament as the final authority, and referred the questioner back to the source that he already possessed. The latter responded immediately, "I know all that is required: 'Thou shalt love the Lord thy God with all thy heart, and with all thy soul, and with all thy strength and with all thy mind; and thy neighbor as thyself'" (Luke 10:27). His implication was, "What more do I need? I still am not satisfied, and I want to hear what you have to suggest."

Jesus accepted his answer as correct, but the young lawyer posed a technical question: "Who is my neighbor?" He may have been trying to define the scope of the word *neighbor,* or perhaps he was trying to dodge the issue. He may have felt reluctant to accept as neighbor a peasant who knew nothing about the Law and who did not observe its liturgical precepts with fasting and Temple attendance. Most assuredly a neighbor could not be a heretical Samaritan who lived on the other side of the border of Judea, one of those "foolish people" whom the Jews had despised for generations. The student seemed to think that his neighbor must be someone in his own class with whom he could fraternize pleasantly, and who would cause him no embarrassment. This man had excused himself from the fullness of life and from the enjoyment of God's purpose because he had certain prejudices that debarred him from reaching out to others. Jesus answered his question by telling him the story of the road to Jericho.

The road to Jericho is *the road to pleasure,* for it was the route that the people of Jerusalem used when they wanted a vacation. It had the same relation to Jerusalem that Miami has to Chicago or to New York. When the thermometer plummets to twenty-four degrees below zero and snow fills the roads with drifts, when your wife becomes exasperated because the noisy children are indoors all the time, and when your car develops pneumonia, if indeed you do not have it yourself, you feel like fleeing to Florida. Jerusalem was 2,600 feet above sea level, and Jericho was 1,300 feet below. When Jerusalem was shivering in cold mist and occasional snow, the flowers were blooming, the sky was clear, and the sands of the Dead Sea were beckoning in Jericho. Whether the traveler going to Jericho were indulging in a pleasure trip or not, he would find there a balmy climate, congenial company, and ample chance for relaxation.

The situation was distinctly modern. Jericho represented "the good life" which magazines and brochures advertise today so persistently and so superficially. To them the "good life" is a split-level house with a green lawn, two cars in the garage, two steaks on the outdoor grill, and all the other luxuries and diversions that one can imagine. That is nothing novel; Herod Antipas, the ruler of Judea, had a palace in Jericho and set the social pace for the city. There were inns, amusements, and all the trappings of a wealthy winter resort.

Perhaps the traveler had just taken in a bumper harvest on his estate or had concluded some lucrative business deal, and was going down to Jericho to celebrate.

Again, the road to Jericho was *the road of peril*. This man was literally going *down*. In the twenty miles between Jerusalem and Jericho the road dropped about 4,000 feet, approximately 200 feet per mile, and wound tortuously through country that was utterly rocky, and filled with caves that served as hiding places for the bandits that infested the area. A traveler making his way through the narrow defiles among the hills was often ambushed by robbers who took money, clothes, horses or donkeys, and, not infrequently, his life. The road to Jericho was beset by all kinds of dangers: sandstorms to blind the wayfarer, heat that produced sunstroke, occasional wild animals or snakes, and the wilder men. There were dangers lurking everywhere, and extreme caution was needed if one were to reach his destination unscathed.

The road to Jericho was also *the road of profit*. The influx of tourists and the royal residence which was the winter capital of the kingdom produced tremendous business activity. Jericho was noted for fruits and vegetables that were available in all seasons, and for being a center of trade through which caravans passed from Arabia and Trans-Jordania to the cities west of the river. Perhaps this man was planning some business deal with merchants in Jericho that would net him a splendid profit during the slack period in Jerusalem.

The road to Jericho is also *the road of opportunity*. Life is not solely pleasure, peril, and profit. These all center in man; opportunity is man's outreach to others. Jesus' parable illustrates this vividly by the men who passed that way.

The first of these was the unfortunate victim of the robbers. As his donkey trotted down the steep decline, the traveler may have been anticipating the pleasure of seeing friends in Jericho with whom he could visit at leisure. He may have been dreaming of the social life that the city afforded. Or he may have been counting in advance the shekels that he could accumulate through shrewd business deals with merchants and traders in the city. Suddenly his way was blocked by robbers who appeared from nowhere, both behind and before. They knocked him off his donkey, beat him into unconsciousness, and took all his goods and clothing, leaving him bleeding and insensible by the roadside. There was no house nearby, and nobody was coming down the road. Under the blistering sun his wounds became doubly sore, and his life began to ebb.

Soon a priest appeared. As he came around the bend of the road, he saw the unhappy man covered with blood and dust. Perchance he was dead. If the man were to be rescued, action should be taken immediately. But wait! According to the Law, anyone touching a dead body would be ceremonially defiled, and could not engage in worship nor be accepted in society until he was purified. The priest may have been on a mission to Jericho, and could not risk contamination that would preclude it. Gingerly he picked his way around the man, and passed by on the other side.

Shortly afterward a Levite appeared. Not all Levites were priests; they might be called the sanctified janitors of the Temple. They swept its floors, tended its altar, and guarded its gates. They furnished the choirs for its music. They were the assistants of the priests, and were not subject to quite so many stringent regulations. When the Levite saw the helpless figure lying in the road, he inspected him. Apparently he concluded that there was nothing that he could do. His knowledge of the Temple ritual would have no value for a person in such a condition. He needed a doctor, not a prayerbook; nursing, not instruction in the Temple ceremonies. The Levite was not prepared to cope with the situation, and so passed on his way.

The third man who came that way was a Samaritan. To the Jews, the Samaritans were "that foolish people that dwell in Shechem." Severed from the southern kingdom of Judah by the revolt against Rehoboam, the son of Solomon, the northern kingdom of Israel had long been separated from the life of the Temple. They had developed a worship of their own, and after the exile to Assyria their numbers had been increased by pagan groups whom their conquerors had settled among them. The mongrel religion that developed from that fusion of populations was not pleasing to those Judeans who adhered to the Law of Moses, and in succeeding years the rivalry between the Samaritans and the returning exiles from Babylon deepened the dislike of each group for the other. On at least one occasion Jesus was refused entrance to a Samaritan village, and the woman at the well of Sychar (John 4) expressed surprise that he, a Jew, would even speak to her. The Jews despised the Samaritans even more than they did the Gentiles. The Gentile was ignorant and crude because he did not know the Law; the Samaritan was apostate. In a Gentile world the Gentiles had to be tolerated, but the Samaritans were a perverse sect, and should be exterminated.

In spite of this attitude, which must have been well-known to the Samaritans, he stopped, went over to where the man lay, and inspected him. He might have looked at the helpless figure, and have said, "Another Jew! What do I care about him?" and have returned to his mount and trotted away. On the contrary, observing his critical condition, the Samaritan poured oil and wine over his wounds. The oil had the effect of soothing the pain like an ointment. The wine, because of its alcoholic content, would serve as a disinfectant. Lifting the unconscious man onto his donkey, he took him to the nearest inn.

Today on the road to Jericho there are still visible the remnants of an ancient building which may possibly be that inn. The Samaritan instructed the innkeeper to care well for the man until he returned, and paid two shillings or *denarii* to compensate for expenses. A *denarius* was worth a man's daily wage for unskilled labor. Valued by purchasing power it would cover two days' room and meals in a modern hotel. The Samaritan expected to return by that time, and agreed to pay any additional charges. The "neighbor" of the Samaritan was the person who needed his help.

The road of life had a different significance for each of these persons. To the initial traveler it became the road to disaster. He lost his money, his clothing, his transportation, his vacation or business appointment, and almost his life. To the priest it was the road of potential defilement. He probably congratulated himself that he had narrowly escaped a contact that would have interrupted his planned routine. He scrupulously avoided anything that would endanger his ceremonial purity. To the Levite it was the road of detainment. He could not spare the time from his duties to aid the robbers' victim. To the Samaritan, the road of life meant the possibility of being useful. He accepted the accidental interlude as a part of his day's duty rather than regarding it as a hindrance. He risked defilement, gave freely of his supplies, took the sufferer to a safe place, and provided for his care to the best of his ability. In these three actions are three viewpoints toward life: selfish exclusiveness, preoccupation with business, and generous love. Jesus said that the real neighbor was the helpful Samaritan. Thus the road of life as the avenue of opportunity becomes the road of love.

To pursue this question farther, what is love?

First of all, it is personal interest. In the famous comic strip "Peanuts," one of the little characters said, "I just love humanity; it's people that I can't stand." The incongruity of that remark is comic, but it contains a serious truth. We may be benevolently inclined toward humanity in general, but those who need our ministrations the most are often the most unlovable. One can easily love the person who is pleasant, attractive, friendly, adjustable, and in the circle of our own class. Can we as readily love the narrow, sinister, bitter person who is perverse, abrasive, and possibly degraded and evil? Perhaps one reason for his unloveliness is that nobody ever did love him. Those who have never received love do not know how to accept it, for they are inherently suspicious, nor do they know how to show it, because they do not possess it.

An acquaintance of the author who was a professor of anthropology once described the inhabitants of an island in the South Pacific who had no word in their language for love. They had no concept of such an emotion. How could one translate John 3:16 into their tongue? Certainly it could not be done by an equivalent term; it would have to be translated by life. In that way the Samaritan crossed the bridge to the Jew: he had compassion on him. Compassion is an interesting word. It does not mean merely a kindly feeling or even a sudden rush of pity to the heart, but it implies suffering with the person who is the object of one's neighborly concern. The Samaritan took upon himself the misery of the man who was robbed and beaten. He stood with him in his predicament and supplied what he could not do for himself.

At the great conference on evangelism in Lausanne in 1974 there were 2,000 participants from approximately 150 different nations. Few of them came from countries as affluent as America. While nobody expressed the major need of the Third World in words, the sentiment was clear that they did not desire somebody who would hand down a message to them, but rather someone who would share their circumstances, live in their culture, and exhibit genuine love for them. Such an attitude creates a predisposition to believe the gospel.

Not only did the Samaritan reveal an attitude of compassion, but he did something about the victim's pain at his own cost. He did not stand over the man and make an oration about his sorrow for him. To effect the rescue cost him a walk rather than a ride, possibly a part of his wardrobe, the risk of defilement, the cost of room and board, and exposure to the same fate as the man whom he had salvaged. Perhaps he even shortened his stay in Jericho in order to care for the sufferer. Loving one's neighbor is not cheap sentimentality. The fullness of life depends on fullness of love, and fullness of love comes from giving ourselves completely.

The effectiveness of the Christian's career depends both on what he does and upon the way in which he does it. He may be motivated to reach another man by a complete concern for his needs, or he may be simply using him as a foil to add another good deed to his own credit.

P. W. Philpott, a well-known preacher of a generation ago, was a blacksmith before he was converted. He had lived a very rough life, but after he became a Christian he began to preach. His first pastorate was small, and he provided for his family by working a small farm. Next door to him lived an atheist who loathed preachers, and would have nothing to do with them. He looked upon them as idle parasites who obtained their living by swindling the public. When he vented his spite against them, Philpott offered no comment. One day the atheist remarked to Philpott that he could not find anybody who would plow his garden. The latter promptly volunteered to do it, and refused to take any pay. Some time later the atheist asked him what he did for a living. Philpott replied, "I am a preacher." The atheist almost choked with amazement. "A preacher? And you plowed my garden?" He could not believe that any preacher would know how to plow, much less be willing to assist an atheist. The outcome was that they became fast friends, and the atheist was later converted. If Philpott had gone across his yard, seized him by the lapel of his coat, and said, "Brother, are you saved?" the atheist would have thrown him out of the premises. The road to Jericho puts love to work, but does not minimize the witness.

The road to Jericho was one that Jesus himself walked. The eighteenth and nineteenth chapters of Luke record what he did there. As Jesus entered Jericho he was followed by his disciples and by a curious crowd who wanted to observe what he might do next. A blind beggar sitting by the roadside heard the commotion, and inquired what was happening. Being informed that Jesus of Nazareth was passing by, he cried out loudly, "Jesus, thou Son of David, have mercy on me." Some of the crowd told him not to make a disturbance, but he shouted all the more loudly. Jesus, hearing his frantic appeal, asked what he wanted. Simply and directly he replied, "Lord, that I may receive my sight." Jesus said, "Thy faith hath made thee whole," and the man was cured. Jesus was concerned for the beggar whom the others had tried to brush aside.

As the procession moved down the street to the center of the city another man was looking for Jesus. Zacchaeus, unlike the blind beggar, was wealthy, had a very lucrative position as a tax-collector, and owned a house of his own. Being small of stature, he had been unable to catch a glimpse of Jesus over the shoulders of the crowd that lined the narrow highway. He darted down the street, scaled a sycamore tree, and perched high on an overhanging branch where he could obtain a full view of all that was happening.

It is a psychological fact that men seldom see what is over their heads because they are usually engaged with the immediate foreground. In this instance Jesus did the unusual. As the procession approached the place where Zacchaeus had acquired his gallery seat, Jesus stopped, looked up, and said, "Zacchaeus, come down! I have a luncheon appointment at your house today."

Zacchaeus was so shocked that it is a wonder he did not fall out of the tree. Why had Jesus noticed *him* when he had so many talking to him on the ground? Why should the Prophet of Nazareth invite himself to lunch at the house of a publican and an outcast? What did Jesus want to do with him? Zacchaeus must have been overwhelmed with the mystery. He could not excuse himself on the ground that he had nothing to offer for lunch, for that would have been an unpardonable breach of etiquette, and besides, he was wealthy. His household was undoubtedly well equipped to entertain guests, nor could he refuse so important a personage. To the astonishment and somewhat to the consternation of the crowd, Zacchaeus, the despised publican, slid down from the tree, and went off to lunch with Jesus, leaving the crowd, and possibly the disciples, to their own devices.

The people grumbled, "Doesn't the prophet of Nazareth realize that he is going to lunch with a publican who is a swindler and a thief?" Jesus, however, was impervious to their criticism. He was not seeking popularity; he wanted to reach Zacchaeus. What happened then?

There is no record concerning the nature of the lunch, though on this occasion Zacchaeus would have served the best dishes that his cook could produce. The reaction of Zacchaeus to Jesus' presence is not told explicitly, but one can well imagine that he did not eat much of the meal. There was something about Jesus' person that made Zacchaeus increasingly uncomfortable. Before the Sinless One his dishonest life looked black. Every moment he felt embarrassed and condemned by the contrast of his crookedness with Jesus' righteousness. What about that widow on his street whom he had swindled out of her meager estate? What about the laboring man from whom he seized the savings of a lifetime in excess taxes? What about the family whom he had reduced to abject penury and who stabbed him with accusing glances whenever he met them? As Jesus talked to him those memories came back to haunt him until he could endure them no longer. He rose from his half-eaten meal, looked into the face of Jesus, and said, "Lord, the half of my goods I give to the poor: and if I have wrongfully exacted aught of any man, I restore fourfold" (Luke 19:8). The Greek condition implies not a possibility, but an actuality. It could be translated, ". . . and in those

50

instances where I have cheated, I will make fourfold restoration." Zacchaeus was not asking that his sins be excused, for they were inexcusable. He was repenting and asking to be forgiven that he might begin a new life.

Jesus replied, "Today is salvation come to this house, forasmuch as he also is a son of Abraham." Zacchaeus was not saved because he descended from Abraham, but he became a child of Abraham when he acted on the principle for which Jesus stood and accepted him as his standard of righteousness. As Paul stated it, "They that are of faith, the same are sons of Abraham" (Gal. 3:7).

The road to Jericho became the road to salvation for those who met Jesus there and who made the most of their opportunity. He is our Good Samaritan who, at infinite cost to himself, rescues the helpless, comforts the brokenhearted, gives sight to the blind, and transforms the thief into an honest man. When we walk with him we traverse the road to Jericho. Along its winding trail are the men and women who have been robbed, stripped, and beaten by the sorrows and sins that they have encountered in life. They cry out for help, but how shall we help them? The only answer is given here by the Lord himself: "Thou shalt love the Lord thy God with all thy heart, and with all thy soul, and with all thy strength, and with all thy mind; and thy neighbor as thyself." We can never really love our neighbor unless we first love God, and we can never prove our love to God until we can show love to our neighbor. The two are intertwined and concomitant, and are equally necessary to the Christian's progress on the road to Jericho.

FIVE
THE ROAD
TO CALVARY:
The Road of Sacrifice

And it came to pass, when the days were well-nigh come that he should be received up, he stedfastly set his face to go to Jerusalem. Luke 9:51

These fateful words mark the watershed of Jesus' career. Behind him lay the years of preparation in the village of Nazareth, the baptism at the hands of John the Baptist, the initial manifestation of the Spirit in anointing him as the chosen Messiah of God. He had long passed the testing in the wilderness and had carried on a ministry of teaching, preaching, and healing that had affected hundreds of lives. He had already created a legacy of truth that would change the face of the world. One thing remained: he must validate all that had happened and meet all the problems of the future by the sacrifice of the cross.

The mask of hypocrisy and expediency must be wrenched from the face of evil. The righteousness of God must be manifested not only as a quality of an ideal deity or as a theorem of theology, but as a potent force that could overcome evil. God's identification with man, begun in the incarnation when deity appeared in flesh, must be completed by his assuming the place of the sinner, condemned by his guilt and alienated from God. All of this must be enacted in actual life, not as an artificial drama on a stage, but within the tensions and sufferings that have afflicted the human race since its first disobedience to God. All this is implied in the word *must* which Jesus employed when he said to his uncomprehending disciples, "The Son of man must suffer many things, and be rejected of the elders and chief priests and scribes, and be killed, and the third day be raised up" (Luke 9:22).

The use of this concept is not merely a literary device invented by Luke. All of the Gospels agree that there was a pivotal point in Jesus' life at which time he voluntarily chose the road to Jerusalem. The feeding of the 5,000 had raised the hopes of the multitude and they were ready to make him king. Jesus' ability to organize, and his power to supply material needs convinced them that he had all the potential necessary for restoring their independence as a nation and for ensuring continuing prosperity. Jesus refused this role, for his calling was not limited to political leadership of the nation, but included the salvation of all peoples. He did not simply desire allegiance to a cause or to a political structure, but a new relation to God and to himself. At that time the peripheral following began to shrink, and even the twelve were uncertain, but they stayed with him. As Peter said, "To whom shall we go? Thou hast the words of eternal life" (John 6:68). Yet even Peter misunderstood him, and was rebuked sharply for his lack of spiritual perception. The road to Calvary was an enigma to them.

In Jesus' life there was one overwhelming imperative that compelled him to that route. It was not a brutal threat that made him an unwilling victim, nor was it an inescapable combination of circumstances that hurried him irresistibly to disaster. He knew perfectly well the destiny that awaited him, and he accepted it voluntarily because he could not complete his mission in any other way. Evil could not be exposed and disarmed without a struggle; guilt could not be cancelled without a sacrifice; redemption could not be completed without death. He had come to the point where he must "taste of death for every man" (Heb. 2:9).

Jesus did not expect to walk the road to Calvary alone. When a would-be disciple professed readiness to accompany him wherever he went, but asked permission to return home for his farewell to the family, Jesus said, "No man, having put his hand to the plow, and [continually] looking back, is fit for the kingdom of God" (Luke 9:62).

When any farmer begins his spring plowing, he must set the first furrow straight. He does so by fixing his eyes on some distant object and guiding his tractor straight toward it. He does not look at the earth that he is plowing but at the distant goal. In that way he can make the first furrow straight. When he doubles back he can then use the first furrow as a guide, and so keep his plowing even. If he looks backward he will not guide the plow correctly, and the furrows will be crooked. Jesus wanted to plow a straight furrow to the very end. He had been called to a mission, and he must fulfill its objective. He had a work to perform, a cause to defend, and disciples to teach. Only the straight road to Calvary would take him and the disciples to the rightful end.

The meaning of this road in the mind of Jesus and in the minds of the disciples were two different concepts. For a considerable length of time the disciples had seen Jesus heal the sick, cast out demons, and raise the dead. At the time when he spoke to them of Jerusalem the stupendous marvel of Jesus' feeding of the 5,000 was fresh in the disciples' minds. They entertained no doubt concerning his powers, and were ready to believe that he could easily make himself the ruler of this world; in fact, they were hoping that he would do it.

When he refused to comply with the popular demand for a king, many quit his company. The twelve, despite their misgivings, still clung to him. They had begun to realize that he was more than a potential leader who could procure for them the liberty that they wanted. They not only admired him; they loved him and were concerned for him. They had no intention of deserting him in the crisis, whatever that might be. Simon Peter declared his faith when, upon Jesus' announcement that he would die in Jerusalem, he said, "Be it far from thee, Lord. This shall never be unto thee" (Matt. 16:22). Even though Jesus rebuked Peter for his rash statement, he appreciated the affection of a disciple who did not want any disaster to befall his Master.

Simon's motives were good, but his discernment was poor. At the outset the disciples understood the road to Calvary to be the road of Jesus' ultimate triumph. So, as they marched from Galilee through Samaria to Jerusalem they were expecting some manifestation of Jesus' power that would seat him on the vacant throne of Israel and establish them as official coadjutors and aids.

To Jesus, the road had an opposite meaning. At the end stood a cross, dark and menacing. Crucifixion was probably the most diabolical method of execution ever invented by the mind of man. In it were combined all the elements of torment that one could conceive: the physical pain of wounds, fatigue, thirst, distortion of joints, extremes of heat and cold, nervous tension, and slow strangulation, and the psychological anguish of exposure, contempt, hatred, deprivation of property and friends, hopelessness, and utter futility. In addition, it meant an apparent triumph of his enemies, the failure of his mission, the disillusionment of the disciples whose hopes had been centered on him, and the reversal in fact of all that he had proclaimed in principle. Contrast Jesus' claims with the scene of the cross. He had said, "I am the light of the world," and he died in darkness. He offered the water of life, and one of his last utterances was, "I thirst." He called himself the Good Shepherd, and he fell victim to the teeth of the wolves. He assured Martha that he was the resurrection and the life, and he succumbed to physical pain and mental distress. The cross seems incongruous with the promises and claims of Jesus.

What, then, is its real significance?

It means, first of all, that Jesus gave a full revelation of the will of God and of obedience to that will. God's will is not to destroy men, but to save them. He does not want them to be overwhelmed by the fear of death, but to liberate them from it. He intends to release believers from the guilt and curse of sin by expiating that guilt and by removing that curse. That can be done only in the arena where men live, though it affects powers that are above them. For this reason, Jesus, as God incarnate, did not hold his status as something that must be kept inviolate; but, as Paul says, he humbled himself, becoming obedient to the point of death, and the death of the cross at that! Death itself was humiliation, but death by the cross was unspeakable indignity.

If Jesus is to intervene between ourselves and the just consequences of sin, he must experience our death in order to impart to us his life. He must endure the worst of human agony if he is to impart the deepest of divine comfort to us. He must experience rejection if he is to reclaim those who are alienated from God. The meaning of the road is the revelation of God's love for sinners in the action of Christ, who died for us.

Parallel with the *meaning* of the road to Calvary is the *mystery* of the road. Why was it necessary for Christ to die? It was not because he had sinned, for he was without sin. Four times the writers of the New Testament assert that he was untainted by evil. Peter, one of his closest disciples, said, "He committed no sin" (1 Pet. 2:22). John, another of the inner circle, testified, "In him is no sin" (1 John 3:5). Paul, his greatest theologian, affirmed that "[he] knew no sin" (2 Cor. 5:21), and the writer of Hebrews asserted that he was "tempted like as we are, yet without sin" (Heb. 4:15). He was not guilty of any political offense, for his accusers could find no solid witnesses against him, and his judge said, "I find no crime in him" (John 18:38). Why should such a terrible fate have befallen him?

Why did not God, whom he had served with unvarying devotion, not intervene to rescue him from an undeserved calamity? Had he been a secret hypocrite, outwardly righteous but inwardly selfish, it would be possible to argue that retribution had finally overtaken him; but such was not the situation.

The problem is as old as the human race, for it is essentially the problem of evil. Daniel Defoe, in his famous novel *Robinson Crusoe,* posed this question through Crusoe's man Friday. Crusoe had been explaining the gospel to his savage captive, who listened intently to his description of the good God and the wicked devil. With the straightforward logic that characterizes the untutored mind, Friday asked why God did not kill the devil. Why God has permitted evil to exist through the centuries is not told to us, but one thing is certain: whereas it seems that goodness is often a prey to evil and that wrong seems to eclipse right, God always has the last word. He may seem to lose the move, but he always wins the game. Jesus submitted to death at the hands of his enemies, but by the cross he canceled forever the power of evil. When he died, it could do no more; when he rose, it was vanquished permanently. His righteousness overcame sin; his life rendered death harmless. The road to the cross becomes the road to victory.

The New Testament speaks of the offense, or scandal, of the cross (1 Cor. 1:23; Gal. 5:11). The word means literally the trigger of a trap, the means of capturing or ensnaring an animal. To the Jews, the concept of salvation through the cross was repulsive because they associated it with the execution of a criminal. To the Gentiles, the concept was ridiculous, for if a man could not save himself from such a death, how could he save anybody else? It is an offense to human morality, since it declares that no human righteousness is sufficient to satisfy God's requirements. It is an offense to human pride, because it is the lowest point of humiliation. It is an offense to human desire, because it calls for surrender rather than for gratification. At the cross we abandon our trust in our own merits, and trust only Christ, who has opened the gate to the Paradise of God.

How does one travel the road of sacrifice?

The *method* is made clear by Jesus' teaching concerning it: "If any man would come after me, let him deny himself, and take up his cross daily, and follow me" (Luke 9:23). The first step is the denial of self, which is quite different from self-denial. It consists not simply in the abandonment of something that one cherishes, but rather in the repudiation of his right to cherish it.

A clerk in a business office was so fond of candy that she kept a large box of it on her desk from which she helped herself liberally during business hours. Since she belonged to a liturgical church, her associates wondered what she intended to give up for Lent. When she said that she had decided to give up candy, they were incredulous. To their astonishment, for forty days no box appeared on her desk. Undoubtedly it cost her self-restraint, for she was addicted to sweets. Toward the end of that period, one of them asked her what she would do when Lent ended. She replied, "I shall buy the biggest box of candy that I can find, and eat all of it." The forty days produced self-denial, but not the denial of self.

To deny self means a renunciation of the claims of one's ambitions, appetites, and aims, not because they are necessarily evil, but because life is no longer centered on self but on Christ. Peter denied Jesus not by taking something away from him, but by refusing to recognize Jesus' relation to him. He would not acknowledge him, and said, "I know not the man." To deny self is to refuse to take any longer the road which leads to one's own ease, advancement, or popularity, if these conflict with the straight and narrow road to Calvary. It means to surrender sovereignty over one's own life, and to accept the Lordship of Christ.

To this decision Jesus added, "Let him take up his cross." Taking up the cross is the voluntary assumption of that responsibility which awaits one when he agrees to walk with Christ. As William Clow once said of Jesus, "All his life was lived out upon a cross." It is the sacrifice which alone can make one fit into the will of God. It may not be pleasant, but it means that one accepts the price of a ministry that can be exercised only by the cross. As the cross becomes the supreme manifestation of Jesus' dedication and compassion, so it does for the disciples. Their time is no longer their own; it is spent in his service. Their intellects are no longer theirs; they are directed toward the problems that accompany his cause. Their energy is no longer spent in trivialities, however harmless; it is employed in his errands.

The last command of Jesus complements these two: "... and let him keep on following me." At this point the tense of the verb changes. The first two parts of the command imply an instant and final action; the last implies a process. Of the first two it can be said that the command is fulfilled when the decision is settled and the action is taken. Obedience to the third is a continuing action through life. Following Christ means that every day there is some new turn in the road, some new height to scale, some new expanse to unfold before our wondering vision, some new triumph to achieve.

Among the sometimes strange epitaphs that used to be inscribed on gravestones of the eighteenth century, there was one that became quite conventional:

Reader, stop as you pass by!
As you are now, so once was I.
As I am now, so you will be;
Prepare for death, and follow me.

On one of these stones some wag had scrawled in chalk:

To follow you I'm not content
Until I know which way you went!

Probably this expression voices a universal feeling. If one is to follow another, he wants to be sure of his destination. In the case of Jesus, the end of the road to Calvary was not the cross, because he added, ". . . and to rise on the third day."

It is not difficult for the average man to predict his death. Apart from the coming of the Lord, every one will die. Furthermore, if he is in a situation as perilous as that which confronted Jesus, he can be sure that his life will be short. Jesus was deliberately returning to a city where the governing powers had already set a price on his head, and would not scruple to use illegal means to dispose of him. But what man would dare to predict that he would rise the third day? To make such an assertion would either brand him as a lunatic, or indicate a supernatural character unique in the annals of humanity. Jesus staked the future of their discipleship and of his own credibility on what must have seemed a fantastic impossibility. Furthermore, the import of his words was not understood until after they came to fulfillment. This command called for an immense stretch of faith in him, but it opened a prospect of endless triumph.

Jesus therefore asked them to share his suffering, but he asked the Father that they might share his glory. The former was temporal, the latter would be eternal. As Paul phrased it, "For our light affliction, which is for the moment, worketh for us more and more exceedingly an eternal weight of glory; while we look not at the things which are seen, but at the things which are not seen: for the things which are seen are temporal; but the things which are not seen are eternal" (2 Cor. 4:17, 18). The deepest companionship with Christ is forged not in the moments of ecstasy when a new and marvelous experience fills us with overflowing joy, but is found in those hours of suffering and hardship when we realize that he is making good his word: "I am with you always, even unto the end of the world" (Matt. 28:20).

The disciples lived on the other side of the cross. The account of Luke says that they were with Jesus and on their way to Jerusalem when he said, "Follow me." So they did, and valiantly. We live on this side of the cross with a different perspective. To us it means more than it did to them at that time. When we walk the road to Calvary we can view it from the perspective of the resurrection rather than from the perspective of death. We can realize that he has called us not to death, but to the life that emerges victorious from it. On the other hand, we never appreciate the abundant life which he imparts until we have walked with him who traveled down that road for a sinning world that he might open the gates of heaven to all who believe. When he told the repentant thief on the cross, "Thou shalt be with me in Paradise" (Luke 23:43), he left the gate ajar for all who follow in faith.

The decision to take that road is not easy. George Matheson was a young Scottish candidate for the ministry. In the course of his studies he began to realize that his sight was failing. When he consulted a physician, the latter said, "Mr. Matheson, I regret to inform you that in a short time you will be totally blind. There is nothing that I can do for you."

The young student went away from the doctor's office crushed. He had planned for a career as a pastor and preacher, but what church would want him? Furthermore, he was engaged to be married. Would his fiancée consent to marry a blind man? Realizing that it would be only fair to inform her of his prospects, he told her what the doctor had said. She rejected him completely. With a breaking heart, but with resolute courage, he completed his university and seminary education, and entered the pastorate. With secretarial aid he wrote a number of important and learned works of scholarly, expository, and devotional nature. Twenty years after his personal tragedy, when he had completed half his life of service, he wrote:

> *O Love that wilt not let me go,*
> *I rest my weary soul in Thee.*

I give Thee back the life I owe
That in its ocean depths its flow
May richer, fuller be.

O Cross that liftest up my head
I dare not ask to fly from Thee.
I lay in dust life's glory dead,
And from the ground there blossoms red
Life that shall endless be.

George Matheson had learned how to walk the road to Calvary with Christ. Have you?

SIX
THE ROAD
TO EMMAUS:
The Road to Certainty

*And they drew nigh unto the village, whither they were going: and he
made as though he would go further. And they constrained him,
saying, Abide with us; for it is toward evening, and the day is now far
spent. And he went in to abide with them. And it came to pass, when
he had sat down with them to meat, he took the bread and blessed; and
breaking it he gave to them. And their eyes were opened, and they
knew him; and he vanished out of their sight.* Luke 24:28–31

The events of Jesus' last days in Jerusalem had followed each
other with a dizzy sequence and with distressing results. This
Lord Jesus Christ, who with his disciples had entered the city
riding on a donkey, had been hailed by the people as the one
who was coming in the name of the Lord. Within one week he
had been rejected by the senate of his own people, had been
condemned by their council, and had been remanded by the
Roman governor to a hideous death on a Roman gibbet.
These two disciples whom Luke describes in chapter twenty-
four were on their way to Emmaus that afternoon to escape
from the scenes and the memories that overwhelmed them.
They had seen their world crash around their ears. They had
hoped, they said, that he would redeem Israel. Here was the
One who had fed the multitudes, who had healed the sick,
who by his wisdom had outdone his enemies. He had never
been beaten in an argument. He had provided food for

thousands of people by the miraculous touch of his hands. He had even raised the dead. Their hopes were high that he might take the throne and restore their nation to a position of sovereign independence. In a few bitter hours he had passed from prospective triumph to a tomb, betrayed by a disciple and condemned by the council, crucified by Pilate and buried in Joseph's tomb. He was gone, irrevocably gone! Now they were walking back dazedly to their hometown, reviewing in despair the whole sad occurrence. They were beaten, disillusioned, and thoroughly discouraged. Their hopes had risen to the height of expecting that this man would do for them what they had been awaiting for centuries, and in one short day those hopes had been dashed to the ground.

When people suffer a disillusionment like that they undergo a mental and moral recoil. Can they be sure of anything? Is there anyone whom they can trust? Were all their hopes futile? Must they grind out the remainder of their days remembering this remarkable person who flashed across their horizon like a meteor only to disappear in the gloom of the grave? They were completely disappointed and disheartened. As they walked down the road to Emmaus they were carrying on a dismal conversation concerning their loss, and wondering what life still held in store for them. They had lost their certainty.

Why had they lost their certainty? In the first place, they were intellectually disorganized. Everything that they had thought was true had apparently collapsed. As somebody once said, in the modern hippie vernacular, "Everything that was nailed down is coming loose." Jesus' death was inexplicable in the light of his previous character. He had always been able to answer his enemies when they approached him with a question intended to trap him. When they did so, they found themselves in the trap that they had made for him.

The narrative in the eighth chapter of John illustrates this exactly. Jesus' adversaries brought him a woman whom they accused of being taken in the act of adultery. They reminded him that for such an offense the Law prescribed stoning, and asked for his opinion. Obviously they had no concern for the woman; their chief interest was in creating an inescapable dilemma for him. No matter what answer he gave, it would be

THE ROAD TO EMMAUS

the wrong one. If he declared that they should have mercy, and not stone her, they would insist on the letter of the Law, and accuse him of violating God's plain standard of morality. If he agreed that she should be executed immediately, they would accuse him of cruelty and of inconsistency with his known reputation for kindness.

Jesus stooped down, and with his finger began to write in the dust. One manuscript says, though it may not be correct, that he wrote all the sins of the men who were standing before him. Be that as it may, when he finally straightened up, he said, "He that is without sin among you, let him first cast a stone at her" (John 8:7). That was a legal requirement, for the Law asserted that the eye-witnesses of a crime should be the ones to begin the stoning. In this particular crime, who could be an eye-witness without being implicated? Unwilling to acknowledge their connection with this unsavory situation, the accusers filed out, leaving their intended victim. If Jesus were able to extricate himself from peril by outwitting his enemies, why had he not done it on this last occasion? The disciples could not understand why he had failed to defend himself, when he could so easily have done so.

Furthermore, if Jesus knew in advance that his enemies were plotting his death, why did he not escape while there was opportunity? He had told them plainly that death awaited him in Jerusalem. Even at the last supper, when Judas withdrew to complete the arrangements for his capture, Jesus could have taken the remaining eleven disciples down the road to Jericho, and could have been outside the borders of Herod's territory and of the Jewish authority before Judas could have overtaken him. Why did he not do so?

Beyond all questions of his possible alternatives lay the problem of justice. Jesus had preached that God is just, and righteous, and holy. Why, then, should Jesus, of all persons, be allowed to suffer an unjust fate? What is the rationale behind the cross? The problem of evil had been brought to a climax in the thinking of these two persons on the road to Emmaus, and they could not answer it. Perhaps they reasoned in this fashion: "This man is the holiest and best person that we have ever known. If he had been a criminal, we would have said that he received only what he deserved.

Why should he suffer what he did not deserve? Why would a good God allow a perfect man to undergo such disgrace and suffering?"

The last words at the cross add to this puzzle. The crowd said more than they intended to say: "He saved others; himself he cannot save" (Mark 15:31). Many a word spoken in sarcasm is really the truth. He could not save himself and others at the same time. The underlying purpose of Jesus' life was not apparent to these disciples, and they were completely bewildered by his seemingly irrational action.

Not only were they staggered by the contradictions which they saw in Jesus' death; they suffered emotional shock. Their conversation was not merely an academic debate. They were distressed not because Jesus was a public figure whose death was unaccountable, but because he was their friend. There is a world of difference between noting the name of an acquaintance in the obituary column of the newspaper, and feeling the void left by the loss of a counselor and companion whom one dearly cherishes. All of the disciples were affected. Why did they make so many trips to the tomb that had been declared empty? If he were dead, they could not bring him back. What difference did it make to him or to them if they visited it? The answer is that they were emotionally involved, and were troubled when the body was reported missing. Their whole friendship had been shattered, and when Jesus died in such distressing circumstances they felt it keenly.

Moreover, when Jesus died, his condemnation as a criminal ruined his reputation and theirs also. A man whose father was hanged for murder was asked how his father was killed. He replied: "He was standing on a public platform when it suddenly gave way, and he was killed by the fall." Perfectly true; but why did he not state all the facts? Because if he had, it would have revealed that his father was a felon, and it would have damaged his image. The disciples, who had declared themselves to be friends of Jesus, were already under suspicion as the followers of a dangerous revolutionary and as apostates from the Law. They had hidden in an upper room for fear of the Jewish authorities (John 20:19). The men on the road to Emmaus realized this fact, and were consequently torn between their allegiance to Jesus on the one hand and fear for their reputations and for his on the other. He would now be regarded not simply as a false prophet whose theology was erroneous, but also as a rebel against the Law and possibly as a political plotter against Rome.

Again, they were disturbed by the frustration of their hopes. Jesus had made great promises. He had told some of his disciples that they would be seated on thrones, judging the twelve tribes of Israel. By all appearances that promise had been permanently invalidated. He had been dead for three days, and there could be no question that death was final. All their ambitions had been crushed, and the kingdom, as they had understood it, had vanished into thin air. Life had lapsed back into the dull routine that had been theirs before they met Jesus.

Love was left unrequited. When Peter said to Jesus, "To whom shall we go? Thou hast the words of eternal life" (John 6:68), he was expressing an attitude of love as well as a conviction of Jesus' supreme sufficiency. His death had torn him from them, and though they still loved him, it was like trying to clasp a wraith in one's arms. The unreality of emptiness overwhelmed them, as the bitterness of Thomas' doubt revealed. Instead of redemption, they saw defeat. Instead of revelation, there was only blankness. They stood on the dark side of Calvary, confused and depressed.

That is where people stand when they do not see the certainty that Christ can bring to them on the resurrection side of the cross. How many people there are who are intellectually disorganized, emotionally disturbed, and spiritually depressed because they have not seen the fullness of the purpose of God in the Lord Jesus Christ. They have not walked the road to Emmaus with him.

As these disciples proceeded on their journey they suddenly realized that a third person had joined them. Probably they had been so deeply engaged in their discussion that they were oblivious to everything around them. The man opened the conversation with a question: "What are you talking about? What are these words that you are passing back and forth with each other? They sound strange."

They stopped dead in their tracks and looked at the ground, downcast, and hopeless. Finally one of them replied, "Are you such a stranger in Jerusalem that you do not know these things? Haven't you heard the news lately?"

"What sort of things?" asked the stranger.

"Oh," they said, "the things concerning Jesus, the Nazarene. He was a prophet mighty in deed and in word before God and all the people." Notice the word "was" in their reply. They had closed the books at Joseph's grave. That ended Jesus as far as they were concerned; he had become a part of history, a prophet who spoke marvelous words, but who must be reckoned with the past.

The modern world treats Jesus in much the same way. The *Soviet Encyclopedia* asserts that he never existed, but is only the fictitious emblem of a kind of idealism or superstition that has no relation to reality. Such a statement is ridiculous, for even secular history mentions him and acknowledges his influence. To a great many people he is only a legendary figure who has no significance for the future and not much for the present.

As the travelers brought their brief and mournful explanation to a conclusion, the stranger proceeded to enlighten them. He offered them three things. First, he offered them a divine revelation to meet their intellectual disorganization: "O foolish men, and slow of heart to believe in all that the prophets have spoken! Behooved it not the Christ to suffer these things?" (Luke 24:25, 26). He showed them that the entire occurrence was part of the divine plan. The Messiah was simply fulfilling what he was called to do. His death was not an unfortunate accident but a voluntary sacrifice. To be sure, the rejection of his claims was a national sin, but it was included in the plan of God. The account adds, "Beginning from Moses and from all the prophets, he interpreted to them in all the scriptures the things concerning himself" (Luke 24:27).

What Jesus taught them in that conversation is not recorded; only fleeting hints of its content remain. He must have presented to them the purpose of God beginning in Genesis 3:15, which predicted that the "seed of the woman" would crush the head of the serpent. He probably reviewed the call of Abraham and the emphasis on Abraham's faith which is developed in the presentation of salvation by faith contained in Genesis 16 and Galatians 3. He may have taken the picture of the sacrifice of Isaac, which illustrated the father who was willing to give his son to death, and the son who was willing to die at his father's will. He may have quoted some of the Psalms, such as the twenty-second Psalm which describes graphically a death like crucifixion, which was not a type of execution that the Jews used.

Perhaps he quoted the fifty-third chapter of Isaiah, which is used on several occasions in the New Testament by those who may have heard Jesus make the explanation. As he unfolded the Scriptures he gave them the revelation that could dispel their ignorance and give them a basis for intellectual certainty. God intends that man should have that certainty. He never asks believers to check their brains at the altar. He provides information that may seem irrational to many, but which is really superrational. "Ye err," Jesus once remarked. "Ye know not the scriptures, nor the power of God" (Mark 12:24). The disciples on the Emmaus road were plunged into confusion because they were unaware of what the Scriptures said, and they did not see the power of God to fulfill what he had promised.

The second thing that Jesus offered them was divine companionship. When people are emotionally disturbed, they need somebody to sympathize with them and to help them. As Jesus talked with them, there must have been a growing appreciation of his attitude that comforted and strengthened them so that when they arrived in Emmaus they said: "Come in and spend the night with us. The sun is setting, and you will not be able to travel much farther. You might as well stay with us." They ushered him into their home, and gave him something to eat. They felt in his presence an indefinable strength that supported them. Without realizing his identity, they were aware that here was one who by his presence could fortify them and give them new courage. The silent power of his personality must, at that moment, have met their emotional need.

There are times when one does not need to say very much; he must be a good listener. When discouraged or bereaved people pour out a tale of defeat or of difficulty, such a listener may not utter a single word, but the distressed ones go away with the comment, "You have helped me so much." Why? Simply because they felt the sympathy of a concerned friend. Jesus cheered these despondent disciples who welcomed him into their house at Emmaus.

The spiritual depression was lifted by a divine manifestation. They had not recognized him; to them he was just a casual stranger who seemed to know the Old Testament and who could explain its prophecies. He sat down with them and commenced the meal. How he disclosed himself to them is not stated; the account simply says that he became known to them as he broke bread. Probably on many occasions Jesus had eaten with the disciples. For a few small coins they could buy some bread and a few olives for a lunch as they traveled. When they saw him break bread it may be that there was some mannerism that revealed him. Each one of us has a specific way of performing the ordinary acts of life. The motion of the body in walking, the gestures, or the facial expressions mark each individual.

It may be also that they noticed the scars of the cross on his hands or wrists. Jesus would be the only man they knew who would carry the fresh marks of crucifixion and who would talk as he did. There could be no mistaking him. Despite the improbability that he was still living, he could not be a ghost, for phantoms do not eat. Then, as he vanished from the place where he had been sitting, they realized that they had received a visitation of a person from another realm, and that the person must be Jesus. He had entered into a new dimension of living, and was no longer subject to the limitations of our space-time world. He was the master of matter, of space, and of time; he had risen!

With that realization came a change of vision. No longer did they have to evaluate Jesus merely in terms of his earthly career. They could perceive that their experience was only one aspect of a larger area of life into which he had moved completely. In that experience they were assured of the spiritual reality which had become clouded, if indeed it had not completely vanished, when he died. Their faith had been reconstituted. They promptly closed the house, and walked the seven miles back to Jerusalem. They burst into the place where the other disciples had remained, and announced the tremendous experience that had come to them. Their intellectual doubts were restored to normal, and their spiritual life was enhanced and given new scope by the resurrection of Jesus.

What were the lasting results of this experience? For one thing, conviction took the place of doubt. The episode at Emmaus was unforgettable because it really happened. The long conversation on the afternoon journey, the house in which their guest sat, the bread and the wine; these were not imaginary, nor was his presence. The teaching which left them with burning hearts and the sudden disappearance which shocked their astonished minds could not be dismissed as illusion.

The second effect was this: they became missionaries instead of mourners. They did not return to Jerusalem to establish a memorial society for reminiscing about Jesus; they became the heralds of a new evangel. He was not a great teacher who had left them with a new philosophy of life or with a new system of ethics; he was a living person who was competent to solve their present problems and who would ever be available to them. They may not have comprehended at that time all of the implications of the resurrection, but they acted on what they did know. Life for them had been transformed from grief to joy, from futility to purposefulness, and from despair to hope. They could not mourn in seclusion; they now had a message to deliver.

The final result was that they entered into a new vision instead of remaining in darkness. What would have happened if they had traveled the road to Emmaus without meeting the living Christ? They might have cherished the memory of his person, but there would have been no power to remove their sense of loss and failure. Probably the whole story of Jesus would have died out in one generation except for a few desultory fragments of legend. Instead, the resurrection became a reality to them and to the long succession of believers since their day. Because Jesus lives, our intellectual doubts can be dissipated. Because he lives, our emotional depressions can be lifted. Because he lives, our spiritual darkness can be illumined by his permanent presence. When we walk the Emmaus road with the risen Christ, it becomes the road to certainty.

SEVEN
THE ROAD
TO DAMASCUS:
The Road of Crisis

And it came to pass, that, as I made my journey, and drew nigh unto Damascus, about noon, suddenly there shone from heaven a great light round about me. And I fell unto the ground, and heard a voice saying unto me, Saul, Saul, why persecutest thou me? And I answered, Who art thou, Lord? And he said unto me, I am Jesus of Nazareth, whom thou persecutest. . . . And I said, What shall I do, Lord? Acts 22:6–8, 10

Down the road from Jerusalem to Damascus rode a small cavalcade of stern-faced men led by a young rabbi. They had an important errand in that city. Their intention was to arrest the Jewish believers in Jesus, the prophet of Nazareth, and to bring them in chains to Jerusalem, there to stand trial for apostasy from the Jewish faith. Saul of Tarsus, the leader of the expedition, was particularly zealous to wipe out the last vestiges of the following of the Nazarene prophet, who had drastically criticized the priesthood and the Pharisees for their empty legalism and hypocrisy. He had not observed the Sabbath according to their rules, and had outwitted them in argument. For these offenses they had never forgiven him, and having crucified him, they had begun to vent their fury on his followers.

Saul of Tarsus had been a ringleader in the mob that stoned Stephen, the first Christian martyr, and had become an aggressive head of the persecuting forces. As he and his colleagues approached Damascus, they must have felt that a momentous victory lay within their grasp. If they could check the spread of this pernicious heresy, it would ultimately die quietly and unobtrusively among a host of other forgotten cults.

Suddenly, as they approached the gates of Damascus about noon, a dazzling light shone around them (Acts 26:13). The midday sun in the Middle East is blinding in its intensity, but this light was even more brilliant. While his companions stood amazed at the sudden glare that enveloped them, unable to account for its source, Saul found himself in its focus. An audible voice, not understood by the others, addressed him reproachfully: "Saul, Saul, why persecutest thou me?"

To any Jew, a light of this intensity could mean only one thing—a revelation of God. Whenever the divine presence was manifested to men in the past, it had always been marked by a flash of glory. In the flame of the burning bush, Moses had found God and had heard him speak. When the Law was given on Mount Sinai, "Jehovah descended upon it in fire" (Exod. 19:18; Deut. 5:4), and when Solomon's Temple was dedicated, "the fire came down, and the glory of Jehovah was upon the house" (2 Chron. 7:3). Most puzzling of all was the voice. How could the voice of God accuse Saul of persecuting him, when his whole life was dedicated to the defense of God's Law?

Thinking, perhaps, that some person had spoken to him, he asked, "Who art thou, Lord?" Before making any mental judgment on this strange phenomenon he wanted to be sure who was approaching him in this unusual way. The shock was intensified when the voice from heaven replied, "I am Jesus whom thou persecutest." The unexpected answer filled him with fear. Jesus of Nazareth was to Saul of Tarsus a law-breaker, a charlatan, and an apostate who deserved the humiliating death that had been inflicted upon him. In Saul's judgment, the crucifixion had been God's judgment on a blasphemer who claimed deity. Now this voice spoke from heaven with all the accompaniments of divine revelation. In sorrowful but compassionate tones it accused him of persecuting a risen Lord.

Probably at this moment there flashed through Saul's mind

the last words of the dying Stephen: "I see . . . the Son of man standing on the right hand of God" (Acts 7:56), a phrase which bore striking resemblance to Jesus' own testimony at his trial: "From henceforth shall the Son of man be seated at the right hand of the power of God" (Luke 22:69). There could be only one explanation of this vision. Jesus was what he claimed to be, the Son of Man and the Son of God. Saul thus became the blasphemer for slandering him. The suddenness and the incontrovertibility of this revelation shattered his previous conceptions, and left him prone in the dust of the Damascus road.

It was the pivotal crisis of Saul's life. His entire theology changed in that one moment. From being a blasphemer of Jesus he became a worshiper. The commission of the priests in Jerusalem was forgotten. In the words of his later testimony, these things that had been his spiritual assets he charged off as a total loss that he might gain Christ (Phil. 3:7). From that fateful hour he emerged a different man.

At the beginning of every Christian life there must come a crisis in which Christ is revealed to that person as Savior and Lord. Unless one comes to see himself in the light of God's holiness and unless he realizes that he is incapable of saving himself, there can be no salvation for him. Saul, the persecutor of Christ, became through that crisis Paul, the servant of Christ. He passed from darkness to light, from the power of Satan unto God, to receive forgiveness of his sin and to be set apart to God by faith. The Christian life is not the outcome of receiving new theological information, nor of undergoing ethical reformation, but is the product of a divine transformation effected by the Spirit of God. As Jesus himself said, "Except one be born of water and the Spirit, he cannot enter into the Kingdom of God" (John 3:5).

Not every such crisis is as dramatic or as spectacular as was that of Saul. The sudden reversal in the course of a life already moving at high speed in the wrong direction is cataclysmic, and the contrast between the former pattern of life and the latter is radical. On the other hand, there are believers who, because they have been nurtured in Christian faith and have consequently never strayed far from its doctrines or from the ethical attitudes of life which it inculcates, may not experience so sudden a wrench as did Paul. If one is driving to a destination and suddenly realizes that he is going in the wrong direction, he can either apply the brakes vigorously, skid to an abrupt stop, and make a U-turn in order to retrace his road, or he may slowly and gently curve around the next cloverleaf intersection and make his way back to the route that leads to his original goal. The methods are different, but the result is the same.

The outcome of this crisis becomes manifest in time. The liar becomes truthful, the impure becomes chaste, the hateful becomes forgiving and compassionate, and the selfish becomes sacrificial. With many, the change is a sudden contrast; with others, it is an almost imperceptible shift of interest and of the center of life. How does this crisis manifest itself?

The first evidence is a crisis in thinking. "As [a man] . . . thinketh within himself, so is he." The inner springs of the soul determine the nature of the stream of action. Nor does this refer only to the casual opinions that may be voiced from time to time and that change with kaleidoscopic variety. This aspect of thinking refers to the basic principles by which a man builds his life, and by which he determines his viewpoint and conduct.

Saul of Tarsus began his life by making certain assumptions that were unwarranted. He assumed that the Law of Sinai was God's final revelation. The Law was a revelation from God and could not be lightly set aside at the whim of any man. Paul insisted that the Law was our tutor "to bring us unto Christ" (Gal. 3:24). *Tutor* does not mean the person who instructs the children in the classroom, but rather the old slave who conducted them to the school, keeping them from lingering in the candy shop and protecting them from being run over by the chariots that careened through the busy streets. The objective of the Law was restrictive, in order to control behavior, and directive, to point out the source of revelation in God. The Law as a standard of ethics has never been repealed, but it was not the final revelation of all that God had to say to his people.

Paul, therefore, had to make the living Christ who had arrested him on the Damascus road the center of his thinking. Jesus came to "redeem them that were under the law, that we might receive the adoption of sons" (Gal. 4:5). The Law could prepare men for redemption by revealing the righteousness of God and the sin of man, but it was not the ultimate foundation for building the redeemed life. It was a guide, not a goal.

Another assumption that needed to be changed was that Jesus was an impostor and that his disciples were pernicious heretics. Saul believed that Jesus was a rebel against the Law and a subversive influence in Judaism. Had he not been repudiated by the religious authorities of his nation? Had he not in turn ridiculed their inconsistencies and accused them of hypocrisy? Had he not been condemned by a vote of the Sanhedrin, handed over to the Roman governor, convicted by due process of law, and executed as a rebel? How could any rational person put faith in such a person? According to his viewpoint, he regarded the gospel as a stumbling block to the Jew and as foolishness to the Gentile. Jesus was dismissed as an ignorant blasphemer without adequate investigation of his claims. Paul admitted later that he had acted ignorantly in unbelief (1 Tim. 1:13).

Saul's third false assumption was that he was doing the will of God in persecuting Christians. Undoubtedly he was sincere. He was not trying to gain publicity or to build a name for himself, but honestly believed that by removing those whom he considered to be traducers of the Law he was pleasing God.

While sincerity is an admirable quality, it is not enough to guarantee infallibility. Suppose that you are awakened in the middle of the night with a violent case of influenza. Your fever is high, your head throbs with a painful headache, your eyes run with water, your throat is sore, and you feel utterly miserable. You stagger to the medicine chest, take tablets from a bottle which you assume contains headache pills, and go back to bed. You are perfectly sincere in believing that you took aspirin, but by mistake you swallowed mercury bichloride. Your sincerity will not prevent the undertaker from calling in the morning. In similar fashion, a man may be absolutely sincere in thinking that he is pursuing a straight course to heaven, and find that he is utterly lost because he has not accepted God's way of salvation. A genuine sincerity will be open to God's message, and will not insist on its own self-righteousness.

The crisis in the life of Saul of Tarsus affected not only his assumptions, but also his misgivings. Within his inner consciousness he may have entertained some lingering doubts that were unresolved. For one, he may well have been wondering just how the Law could be related to his own impulses and tendencies. The struggle narrated in the seventh chapter of Romans has been variously interpreted. Some assign it to his post-conversion days, when he became keenly aware of the discrepancy between the righteousness which the Law of God required and the unrighteousness of his own heart.

It cannot be denied that such a conflict exists in the lives of many believers as they attempt to meet the divine standard and realize their own impotence. Yet the conflict is by no means confined to believers. Four hundred years before Christ, Plato, a great pagan philosopher, used the parable of a charioteer who was driving two horses, one that wanted to go to the right, and another that pulled in the opposite direction. He pointed out that such a situation would mean no progress, and probably would bring wreckage. Then he applied it to man's dual nature and impulses, in which the acknowledgement of what is right and the desire to do what is wrong struggle against each other.

It is not impossible that when Paul cried out, "O wretched man that I am! Who shall deliver me from the body of his death?" he remembered his early days when he earnestly determined to live according to the demands of the Law, and probably did maintain the outward righteousness of obedience, but realized that his inner impulse would not conform. Perhaps even as he went down the road to Damascus he was fighting a battle within himself, and persecuted the Christians to compensate for his inward shortcomings. This crisis was resolved when he found that Christ had made provision for salvation of the inner life. He declared that "the law of the Spirit of life in Christ Jesus made me free from the law of sin and death" (Rom. 8:2).

Another crisis of misgiving was memory. The memory of failure or of sin that never could be undone can haunt one like a ghost. Saul had at least one memory from which he could not escape. Shortly before his conversion he had been instrumental in the stoning of Stephen. Stephen had been preaching in the Hellenistic synagogues of Jerusalem, one of which belonged to the Cilicians (Acts 6:9). Saul's home was in Tarsus, a city of Cilicia; and it is entirely possible that the young rabbi was a member of that synagogue and had tried debating with Stephen, only to be defeated in the argument. Losing a debate would have been a humiliating experience for him, especially if his opponent had no rabbinical training. Perhaps his enmity against Stephen was personal as well as theological. When Stephen died under the crushing rocks hurled at him, Saul felt that the case was closed in his own favor.

His conversion must have revived this memory and have made it a bitter recollection. Twenty years later he alluded to it: "And when the blood of Stephen thy witness was shed, I also was standing by, and consenting, and keeping the garments of them that slew him" (Acts 22:20). He could not forget Stephen's words, his face, and his vision. The scene made an indelible impression on him. The forgiveness of God, however, turned its accusing sting into a goad that drove him to Christ, in whom he found forgiveness, and to a career that continued the work that the death of Stephen had abruptly terminated. Saul himself became God's chosen messenger to the Gentiles.

The encounter with the living Christ on the Damascus road produced a crisis in Saul's theology. His entire intellectual life was radically changed. Jesus became for him the center of a new reality. In him the Law took on new meaning, for "Christ is the end of the law unto righteousness to every one that believeth" (Rom. 10:4). No longer was he burdened with the guilt of not having kept the Law perfectly in his heart; he was forgiven and reconciled to God. No longer did he need to struggle with the rebellious nature that made him impotent to keep the Law; he was led by the Spirit of God. Death was no more the dread prospect of descent to the place of mourning and isolation; he looked forward to being with Christ, "for it is very far better" (Phil. 1:23). In Christ he found the basis for a new life which relieved him of the fears and frantic struggle of the past.

The Damascus road led to a crisis in control. As he and his companions set out for Damascus they felt quite self-sufficient. Saul had letters from the chief priest in Jerusalem that would empower him in the Jewish community to arrest and take back for trial those who had become believers in Jesus. Presumably he had a large enough group with him to enforce his action. He was about to complete a mission that would rid Judaism of subversives who were undermining the sacred Law of Moses. All the ecclesiastical authority of the hierarchy at Jerusalem was under his control; he felt that he was master of the situation. When he recognized the lordship of Christ and said, "What shall I do, Lord?" (Acts 22:10), he relinquished command of his own life and mission, and accepted a new control. From that time he was under the sovereignty of the Holy Spirit. He moved from the practice of absolute self-assertion and the assumption of his own righteousness, to that of sitting in darkness waiting for light. In the very city where he had planned to accomplish one of the major triumphs of his career, he found himself helplessly blind, awaiting the pleasure of another who would decide his destiny.

Following the crisis in control was a crisis in activity. He had been a relentless persecutor of Christian believers; now he became their champion and the leader of an evangelistic mission. To the amazement and chagrin of the Jewish synagogue in Damascus he began to preach that Jesus is the Son of God. Although some of the methodology of his rabbinic training remained with him, his theology was no longer based exclusively on the Law, but was rather amplified by the new revelation that came in the person of Christ. In confronting the pagan materialism and mysticism of his age, his approach was centered in Christ, "that in all things he might have the preeminence" (Col. 1:18).

The change of action transformed Saul from a blasphemer into a worshiper. To Saul of Tarsus the name of Jesus was anathema. After this experience he said, ". . . that in the name of Jesus every knee should bow, of things in heaven and things on earth and things under the earth" (Phil. 2:10). He united himself with Christ even in the crucifixion: "I have been crucified with Christ; and it is no longer I that live, but Christ liveth in me: and that life which I now live in the flesh I live in faith, the faith which is in the Son of God, who loved me, and gave himself up for me" (Gal. 2:20).

Still another change in action was his transformation from being a bigoted Jew into being the apostle to the Gentiles. The call of God, in response to the question, "What shall I do, Lord?" (Acts 22:10) opened a new horizon for him, and sent him as a messenger to those people whom he had despised. He realized that the salvation of God was not confined to the chosen race of Israel, but that it was intended to be offered to all nations. He never lost his concern for his own nation, but he came to realize that he was a debtor to Greeks and barbarians, to the wise and to the foolish. He could not confine his ministry to people of one race or of one culture or of one station in society, or of one intellectual and moral level (Rom. 1:14–16). The whole world became his parish.

This is the outcome of traveling the road to Damascus. At the very point where one expects to achieve his greatest success he may suddenly realize that he is on the brink of his greatest failure. Birth, education, morality, or social position are all insufficient to equip him for the problems within himself and for the needs of the world without. Only the crisis of surrender to Christ can fit him to face life adequately. God can forgive the guilt of the past, and transmute its accusing memories into a driving motivation for service. He can manage the inner life so that it will no longer be a hopeless battle between the righteousness of God and the selfish desires of the human heart. He can reshape an egocentric and harsh personality into a gracious messenger of love. He can redirect a career from futility to effective accomplishment. When Paul ended the journey that began on the Damascus road, he said: "I have fought the good fight, I have finished the course, I have kept the faith: henceforth . . ." (2 Tim. 4:7, 8). For those who have never walked the road to this crisis, there is no "henceforth"; for those who follow it to meet the Lord in the way, "there is laid up . . . the crown of righteousness, which the Lord, . . . shall give . . . to all them that have loved his appearing" (2 Tim. 4:8).

EIGHT
THE ROAD
TO GAZA:
The Road of Direction

But an angel of the Lord spake unto Philip, saying, Arise, and go toward the south unto the way that goeth down from Jerusalem unto Gaza: the same is desert. And he arose and went. . . . . Acts 8:26, 27

One of the major lessons of the Christian life is that however good one's intentions may be, he needs direction from God unless his life is to become utterly futile. The best-laid plans of human wisdom cannot take the place of divine guidance. This principle is well exemplified in the story of Philip the evangelist, chronicled in the eighth chapter of Acts.

Philip was one of the earliest choices of the church for a position of responsibility. When the widows in the church were threatened with poverty, he had been appointed one of a committee of seven entrusted with the delicate task of distributing the food and clothing that the poor needed. There had been charges of partiality in this administration, and he, with the others, had been commissioned to remove all traces of suspicion. Apparently he and his colleagues had discharged their duties satisfactorily, so that the problem was removed.

When their work was finished, they took up other occupations, and Philip became a preacher. He went to Samaria, a country despised by the Jews as having no value whatsoever for the kingdom of God. The people of Samaria, however, responded enthusiastically to his preaching concerning Christ, and a revival followed. Many were turning to the Lord in that country that had been neglected and alienated from the Jewish background. God was at work, and the response in Samaria astounded both Philip and the church of Jerusalem.

Despite his success, Philip suddenly suffered a rude shock. The messenger of God said to him, "Leave this place, and go down to the road to Gaza, which is desert." Such a command seemed to be ill-timed, if not indeed foolish. Would it not be necessary for Philip to instruct the converts and to bring them out to a fully dedicated Christian career? Why should God, having blessed his work abundantly, send him down to the desert where there was absolutely nothing to do? The road to Gaza wound down from Jerusalem to the shore of the Mediterranean Sea. It was a twisting path through the hills, where there would be only barren pasture, scrub trees, and, near the sea, empty sand. Why should he waste his time there? The whole idea seemed incomprehensible. Nevertheless, God said, "Go," and when God gave the order, Philip obeyed.

Leaving the prosperous meetings in Samaria, he made his way down the lonely pathway to the sea on the road to Gaza. There were undoubtedly some misgivings in his mind. Perhaps he wondered whether God had really spoken to him, or whether he had only imagined it. Perhaps he was resentful that God was calling him away from the fruitage of his own work. God, however, was on the march. The church in Jerusalem had been crippled by the persecution raised against it. Many of its people had been dispersed into the surrounding territories, and Philip himself had been operating in an alien culture. God had another plan. In obedience to the divine summons, even though it may have seemed irrational, Philip left his station, and went down to the place which seemed empty.

To leave Samaria meant that Philip was taking the road of God's design. Every truly successful life must be planned by God himself. No matter how carefully we outline a pattern for ourselves, however sincere and consecrated we are, we are certain to make a faulty choice if we do not have divine direction. God sees the future as we do not. He knows where the obstacles and the pitfalls are, and he can guard us from stumbling. He has a plan which we have comprehended only imperfectly, and he is waiting for every life to be surrendered to him that he may put it where it is most needed and where God may use it to its fullest capacity. So Philip was lifted out of what seemed to be an ideal situation for him, and was put in a new place.

It is possible to compare this procedure with the experience of Jesus himself. The sixth chapter of John tells how he reached the peak of his popularity at the feeding of the 5,000. At that time he spoke to the greatest multitude on record in the Gospels, probably 10,000 people. At that time they misunderstood what he was trying to impart to them. When he would not allow them to make him king, they turned away from him. Even many of his own disciples deserted him. Since he had not obtained a satisfactory reaction from the Galilean people, his brothers somewhat cynically said to him, "If you really can perform these miracles, go down to Jerusalem and demonstrate them there. In Judea you can obtain a hearing, and make your fortune. Don't stay here in the backwoods of Galilee."

Jesus, however, did not go to Jerusalem until he had the mind of God. He told his brothers that he was not going there, even at the feast time. Later, when God spoke to him and sent him, Jesus went up to Jerusalem quietly and privately. He did not seek publicity nor was he desirous of fame. He went only because the purpose of God had so directed him. Philip therefore had good precedent for what happened to him. Whereas Philip did not initiate his own action, as apparently Jesus did, he realized that he was under the command of God and must await his pleasure.

So it is with us. In life we must learn both to wait and to obey. God's methods often seem inexplicable if not irrational, because occasionally they put us in a situation where we think that we do not belong or where we do not want to be. If God does so act, he has a reason for it. The purpose may not be immediately apparent, but he never wastes his workmen, nor does he send them on futile errands.

Not only is the road to Gaza the road of God's design, but it is also the road of opportunity. Having left Samaria and having reached the main highway, Philip stood there, looking at the vacant landscape and wondering what would happen next. He believed that God had sent him, but for what purpose? As he looked to the north, he saw a cloud of dust approaching. As it drew nearer, he could see a group of travelers coming. There was a chariot, drawn perhaps by two horses, in which a man was riding. He was followed by servants and by pack animals carrying his baggage. Perhaps he was a businessman who had come to Jerusalem for trade, or perhaps he was a proselyte who had visited the Temple and was now returning to his own country.

Scripture tells us that the traveler came from Ethiopia, where he was the treasurer of Queen Candace and an influential functionary of the court. Ethiopia was at that time a powerful kingdom, and its treasurer would have been an outstanding person. He may have been traveling on a diplomatic mission to the Roman headquarters in Caesarea, or he may have been attending a feast in Jerusalem. He presented an opportunity for the gospel that could have tremendous consequences.

As the chariot rolled nearer, Philip could hear him reading. In the Middle East, as in some Eastern countries today, people did not simply scan the written text silently with the eye, but they usually read aloud to pronounce the words clearly and to fix them in their memory. As a psychological device it is quite valid, because one can thus learn simultaneously both by ear and by eye. Philip recognized that he was reading from a passage in the prophecy of Isaiah that dealt with the suffering Servant of God. At that moment the Holy Spirit prompted Philip, saying, "Go near, and join yourself to this chariot." Without hesitation Philip stepped out from the side of the road, and said to the man in the chariot, "Do you understand what you are reading?"

The question may have seemed abrupt and bold, but the man in the chariot did not snub him. He was ready to listen. "No," he said, "I do not understand it. Will you help me? Come up into the chariot and ride with me." Philip accepted the invitation gladly, and joined him in the chariot. Using this contact as fully as possible, Philip "preached unto him Jesus."

Notice what is contained in this guidance. First, the Holy

Spirit did not operate according to the obvious program which would have kept Philip in Samaria to instruct the Samaritan believers. He had a larger field in view, and moved Philip into a point of strategic value. The Ethiopian eunuch could become the agent for reaching another constituency in a land untouched by Jesus' ministry.

The Holy Spirit also works in cooperation with the written Word. Without that Word, impulses that are sometimes attributed to the Holy Spirit may be mistaken. Philip was not introduced to the eunuch's experience to originate the message, but to explain it. He was not guided by his own intuition and desires, but by the Spirit's voice. When the inward impulse and the written Word coincide, the guidance is valid.

Philip realized that the Holy Spirit had prepared the ground for his ministry. The Ethiopian had a definite interest in the Scriptures; he had arrived at the time when Philip had reached the road that he traveled; and the section of Isaiah that puzzled him was the one best suited to explaining the way of salvation. Both the messenger and the audience had been guided to each other, and the subject of teaching had already been selected.

The message of Philip indicates clearly how the Spirit operates when the opportunity is provided. "Philip . . . preached unto him Jesus" (Acts 8:35). When the Ethiopian, in his perplexity, inquired who the subject of this mysterious prophecy might be, whether the writer or some other man, Philip was able to supply the fulfillment of the text in the person of Christ (Isa. 53:7, 8). The work of the Holy Spirit may be illustrated by the light of a projection machine. Without the light no picture can be thrown on the screen; it would remain utterly dark. Yet the light in itself is not significant, but the picture which the light will illumine. The function of the Spirit is to project the picture of Christ on the screen of the human heart. Without the Spirit, there is no light; without Christ, there is no message. Jesus said of the Spirit: "He shall glorify me, for he shall take of mine, and shall declare it unto you."

All too often we try to foresee an opportunity without waiting for God to make the proper arrangements, or we talk about religious technicalities without applying the Word of

God directly to the need of the person with whom we are talking. Only as God's work is done in accordance with his method will it receive his blessing.

The road to Gaza leads to helpful action. Philip's contact with the Ethiopian began with an offer to assist him in his reading. It may be that he was a proselyte to the Jewish faith who had visited Jerusalem for one of the annual feasts and had purchased a scroll of Isaiah in order to find out more about the living God. He had probably read the chapters that spoke of the majesty and power of the one God of heaven and earth (Isa. 40—48) and had noted the allusions to the Servant, initially identified with Israel (41:8ff.; 44:1), and then singled out as a deliverer and messenger to the Gentiles (42:1-4; 49:5-7). The abrupt introduction of the suffering Servant (52:13—53:12) seems to be an alien concept. The eunuch was mystified because he could not understand who the suffering Servant might be. Essentially this is the paradox of the cross, projected in the prophecy, and realized in history centuries later. Philip was able to dispel this man's confusion and to point him to the salvation that Jesus offered him.

Often the Spirit's work is not spectacular, some action that would evoke notice in a newspaper column. It may be that he directs a servant of God to assist someone who is struggling with the truth or who is troubled by what he does not understand. Perhaps he supplies only a quiet word that would straighten out the difficulty. The road to Gaza is the road of helpfulness because the Spirit is working through us to reach other lives and to touch them with new power.

Finally, the road to Gaza is the only road to true success. As the Ethiopian went down the highway, Philip answered his questions, and his heart was warmed. Faith began to grow. There is no record of the exact conversation, but Philip must have presented to him the same truths that Peter preached on the day of Pentecost. When the audience asked Peter what they should do after hearing the message of the gospel, he said: "Repent ye, and be baptized every one of you in the name of Jesus Christ unto the remission of your sins; and ye shall receive the gift of the Holy Spirit" (Acts 2:38).

First, *repent*. The word means to change one's mind, not merely to shift an opinion. It involves a complete reversal of viewpoint and attitude. It is a willingness to reconsider one's relation to God, to repudiate the sin of the past, and to accept the righteousness that only God can bestow on one who has no righteousness of his own.

Second, *believe*. To believe on Christ is more than affirming his historical existence or agreeing that he was a good man and a great teacher. It is recognizing him as the Savior from sin, the Lord of life, and the sufficiency for all needs.

Third, *receive*. The entrance of the Holy Spirit into the life of the believer is not simply a privilege; it is a necessity. The Epistle to the Romans tells us that "if any man hath not the Spirit of Christ, he is none of his" (Rom. 8:9). The Holy Spirit is the seal and hallmark of salvation, who makes the acceptance of eternal life an experiential reality. He provides inner control and guidance.

Philip must have said something like this to the eunuch, for he accepted the conditions and requested baptism, which was a sign of public confession and of entrance into a new life. At a well by the roadside they stopped, and Philip baptized him.

The ministry of the road to Gaza was not a success because of the numbers involved, for there was only one who was brought to Christ on this occasion in contrast to the larger response that Philip had enjoyed in Samaria. The real success was that Philip could see that his obedience had fulfilled the mission on which God had sent him, and that God was satisfied with him. Having done his work, the Spirit removed Philip to another place.

The subsequent history of the Ethiopian eunuch is unknown. Tradition says that he founded the church of Ethiopia, but whether that tradition is accurate or not may be left to the judgment of historians. It is possible that he was not the actual founder of the present church, but in any event, he returned to his country with a new understanding of the Scripture, a new testimony for Christ, and a new readiness to do God's work.

Three questions emerge from this consideration of the road to Gaza. Are we where God wants us? We may be successful in Samaria, but has God opened the way to Gaza, the exceptional and often misunderstood opportunity? If so, have we obeyed? Sometimes God moves people at what seems to be the most inopportune time. Sometimes he demands what we do not wish to give. Sometimes his commands seem irrational. Nevertheless, he has a reason for wanting us on the road to Gaza, and when he speaks, we should respond.

A second question is this: Are we consciously in the plan of God? Do we take for granted that he will bless our labors where we are, or have we discovered where he wants us? God is gracious and longsuffering, and he gives us all he can; but his best blessings are bestowed in the place where he has the opportunity for which he has fitted us.

The third question is: Has God spoken to you lately? The road to Gaza implies not only his control over the total pattern of life, but also over those side excursions we sometimes take at his command. Each day can bring some new adventure and some useful contact. Where does he want us, not tomorrow, but now?

The road to Gaza is the road of direction. There is a promise in the Old Testament that says: ". . . Thine ears shall hear a word behind thee, saying, This is the way, walk ye in it; when ye turn to the right hand, and when ye turn to the left" (Isa. 30:21). We need to take that road if we are to achieve all that God has planned for us.

NINE
THE ROAD
TO JERUSALEM:
The Road to Danger

And now, behold, I go bound in the spirit unto Jerusalem, not know-
ing the things that shall befall me there: save that the Holy Spirit
testifieth unto me in every city, saying that bonds and afflictions abide
me. But I hold not my life of any account as dear unto myself, so that I
may accomplish my course, and the ministry which I received from the
Lord Jesus, to testify the gospel of the grace of God. Acts 20:22–24

A common misconception of the Christian life is that it means
freedom from all temptation, accidents, and failures, and that
the salvation of God assures only peace and prosperity in the
interval between the present moment and a future heaven.
Such a concept is self-delusion, and is contrary to all experience. To walk with God does not guarantee exemption from
all external perils and internal tensions, but rather that these
can be encountered with the confidence that they can be
overcome by God's grace.

As Bunyan pictured the path of God's purpose, it led over
the Hill of Difficulty, through the Slough of Despond, past
the allurements of Vanity Fair, and into the dungeons of
Doubting Castle. The twenty-third Psalm says, "Though I
walk through the valley of the shadow of death . . . thy rod
and thy staff they comfort me." Although the valley of the
shadow of death must inevitably be crossed by all, the sheep
find their safety in the Shepherd. The "rod" which he carried

was the club that he used to beat off the wolves that attacked the sheep. The "staff" was the long crook by which he could pull back into the path the sheep that was straying and about to fall over a precipice or become entangled in thorn bushes. In both instances the danger was unavoidable, but safety consisted not in escaping the danger, but in trusting the strength and watchfulness of the shepherd.

This principle is graphically illustrated by the road to Jerusalem as pictured in the life of Paul. He had completed his European ministry and had collected a generous offering from the Gentile churches to take back to the church in Jerusalem, where the Jewish church was in dire need. In those days he could not take a jet flight from Corinth or Philippi to Jerusalem. Weeks, if not months, would be necessary to make the trip over stormy seas and roads infested with bandits. Even more menacing were the perils of misunderstanding, jealousy, and hatred that might await him at the end of his journey.

Nevertheless, notwithstanding his forebodings and fears, he set out on this trip because he was sure that it was God's purpose for him. The Jerusalem church was needy, and the unity of Gentile and Jew must be preserved. What could be better than to demonstrate the concern that the Gentile churches had for their brethren in Jerusalem? Paul's devotion and courage when confronted with danger are aptly expressed in these words: "I go bound in the spirit unto Jerusalem, not knowing the things that shall befall me there: save that the Holy Spirit testifieth unto me in every city, saying that bonds and afflictions abide me. But I hold not my life of any account as dear unto myself, so that I may accomplish my course, and the ministry which I received from the Lord Jesus, to testify the gospel of the grace of God" (Acts 20:22–24).

There is an old proverb that says, "To be forewarned is to be forearmed." If one can know in advance what his obstacles will be, he can have a better preparation for surmounting them. Jesus himself had to face danger, and he told his disciples that when they followed him they must be prepared for every emergency, and be ready for any sacrifice.

What kinds of dangers confront the Christian on the road to Jerusalem?

The initial danger on the road to Jerusalem was physical. There was first the probability that desperate measures might be taken to kill Paul. A plot against his life was hatched by enemies in Greece, who planned to assassinate him, probably at Corinth, when he embarked for the East. Evading that ambush, he surrounded himself with friends who had been delegated by the church to help him carry the offering to Jerusalem, and then went north through Macedonia to Philippi. From there he sailed across the Aegean Sea to Troas, where he preached. By so doing he avoided his enemies and was able to make one or two further contacts before concluding his journey.

Physical danger is likely to face all messengers of Christ, not only in the remote haunts of savages, but also in the concrete jungles of modern cities and in the fanatical centers of false religions. Believers have risked riots, poisoning, economic discrimination, assassination, treachery of every kind, imprisonment on false charges, incarceration in mental hospitals, slave labor camps, and starvation, all for the sake of their testimony to Christ. It has been said that more martyrs have died in the last fifty years than ever lost their lives under the Roman government in the first three centuries of the Christian era. Probably all of us could name men and women who sacrificed their lives gladly for the ministry of Christ. Even in death God has multiplied the results of their labors, and has made them effective.

When the Italian invasion of Ethiopia occurred in 1935, the infant church among the Wallamo people had just begun to grow. The missionaries were expelled, and the Christians were subjected to oppression and abuse, sometimes resulting in death. Impoverished by the political upheaval, denied the right to worship in public, and deprived of their leaders who were jailed, beaten, enslaved, and sometimes murdered, the church continually increased. When the missionaries returned ten years later they expected to find only broken fragments of the work that they had initiated. To their surprise, they discovered that the church had not only survived, but had multiplied by several hundred percent. It had taken the road to Jerusalem, and had triumphed.

The second danger is that of internal tension. Not all dangers are external and violent. Sometimes the most virulent are those that arise from within the Christian fellowship. Paul must have had a premonition of such tension as he moved toward Jerusalem. He had not gone very far toward his goal when at one of his stops a prophet named Agabus, taking Paul's girdle, bound his hands and feet, saying, "So shall the Jews at Jerusalem bind the man that owneth this girdle, and shall deliver him into the hands of the Gentiles" (Acts 21:10, 11). The prophecy that he made was not new to Paul. In the book of Romans, which was written before he set out on the journey from Macedonia, he asked prayer that he might be delivered from those that were disobedient in Judea, and that his ministry in Jerusalem might be acceptable to the saints (Rom. 15:31). The very fact that he mentioned this indicates that he had some misgivings concerning what his reception might be. He was not sure that the enmity of his opponents might not be greater than the friendship of his supporters. All through this journey he had a feeling of apprehension which undoubtedly increased as he approached his destination. Such a feeling can be very wearing on the nerves. It can upset and disorganize the mind, and consequently affect sleep and digestion. It is much more vexing than the external hardship of a journey. Paul must have felt these tensions keenly. In spite of them, he preserved his confidence in Christ. He asked his readers in Rome to pray for him that he might be sustained on the errand which he had undertaken. He told his friends when they met and tried to dissuade him from continuing his journey that he was ready not only to be bound, but to die for the name of the Lord Jesus (Acts 21:13).

Here is the picture of a man who is courageous, obedient, and ready to do the will of God, but who at the same time feels sharply the perils around him and is quite certain that he will encounter suffering and possible death. The psychological danger rising from such a continuing apprehension can be overcome by the grace of God. Christians should regard themselves not as victims whose careers are to be interrupted, but as persons whose lives are to be invested. God is not obligated to indulge them with comfort and ease, but rather he counts them as those who are dedicated to his purpose of carrying the message to the world. Nowhere can this message be taken without peril. When we receive Christ as Lord, we accept also the devil as an adversary. When we avail ourselves of Christ's omnipotence, we must realize that we shall be plagued with all of the tricks and with all of the menacing evil that a malevolent enemy could raise against us. Internal dangers must be included with the external dangers of this road.

A third aspect of the road to Jerusalem is the danger of misunderstanding. When Paul reached Jerusalem he presented his gift. Curiously enough, nothing is said in the book of Acts about its reception. It must have been a sizable sum of money, but there is not the slightest indication that the church was grateful for it. James, the moderator of the church, does not mention it in his speech to Paul. What James did discuss was a misunderstanding that had arisen. He told Paul that many of the Hellenistic Jews who had come from the province of Asia, possibly including those from Galatia, had looked upon his ministry as diametrically opposed to their ancestral faith. They forgot that as an observer of the Law he was fully qualified to claim all that Judaism could give him, and they pronounced him a traitor. They believed that he had told the Jewish people of Asia and of Galatia that their observance of the Law was unnecessary. That was not true. What Paul said was that Gentiles should not be compelled to observe its ceremonial aspects, but he never said that Jews should not do so. Apparently he was willing to keep its precepts himself, and did so.

In order to convince the critics that Paul had not preached wholesale abandonment of the Law, James proposed that Paul should sponsor two or three men who had taken upon themselves a vow, and that he should go to the Temple with them to assume the responsibility for paying the expense of the vow. This he was quite willing to do, and so up to the Temple they went. When they appeared at the Temple, some of the Asian Jews misconstrued their action. They thought that he had taken a Gentile into the Temple, inasmuch as they had seen a Gentile friend with him in the city a day or two before. To them that would have been a sacrilege punishable by death. On the erroneous assumption that he had done so, they immediately instigated a riot. They mobbed Paul, and would have dragged him out of the Temple and killed him had not the Roman tribune intervened.

The misunderstanding almost cost him his life. His opponents did not stop to analyze the situation in order to ascertain whether or not he really had taken a Gentile into the Temple. He would have known better than that, anyway. They acted on an impulse triggered by hatred.

Misunderstanding is a danger to which any Christian is susceptible. It may be that his words are wrongly interpreted by people who are unacquainted with the background of what he is saying. It may be that his actions have been misinterpreted because motives have been attributed to him which he did not have. Because of such misunderstanding one may suffer heavily and needlessly. Nevertheless, such mistaken judgment must be expected. People who do not know Christ cannot understand his words and cannot understand the motives of those who serve him. All that a Christian can do is to wait patiently until the hostility can be cleared. Fortunately for Paul, he was rescued in time by the Roman guard so that his life was spared, but the misunderstanding was inevitable.

The fourth peril of the road to Jerusalem is the danger of rejection. Not only did the riot endanger Paul's immediate safety, but the attitude that caused it was so violent and so deep-seated that it persisted afterwards. His enemies made at least two subsequent attempts to assassinate him, and at his trial they attacked him with immoderate violence. They were absolutely implacable, and rejected him completely.

To the modern man this may not seem to be a serious crisis. One could say that if Paul's enemies took that attitude, so much the worse for them. They were the losers, not he. On the other hand, he belonged to their company. As he said himself, he was a son of the Law, circumcised the eighth day, of the stock of Israel, of the tribe of Benjamin, as touching the Law, a Pharisee, as concerning zeal, persecuting the church. He had shared their attitude toward the early preachers of the Word. Until his conversion he had been a ringleader in the persecution of Christian believers. Since his conversion his attitude had changed, but he could understand those who opposed him. He suffered a double sorrow: a rejection by his own people, and the realization that they were without Christ.

In the ninth chapter of his letter to the Romans he said that he could wish himself accursed from Christ if only his brethren could be saved. This is the danger that many a Christian incurs by the fact that he *is* a Christian, the rejection that cuts him off from those whom he loves, and that creates a barrier that becomes insurmountable. It thrusts him out into an unsympathetic world unless and until he can find others with whom he can enjoy fellowship.

Some years ago at a Bible conference in Japan, a piece of paper was passed along the platform from one person to another on which were written these words: "There is a young man in this audience tonight who wants to attend a Christian college, and he knows that if he does, his family will cut him off completely. Please pray for him." In that culture he would have been completely disowned by his parents and relatives, and would have been thrust out into the world with nothing to support him. He would be forced to make his own living, and would not be able to pay tuition. He had to make the difficult choice between alienation from his people and a final commitment to Christian service.

These risks are inevitable, but they can be overcome by the power of God. He can sustain us in danger. "The angel of the Lord encampeth round about them that fear him and delivereth them" (Psa. 34:7). That promise is as valid today as when it was first spoken. To be sure, not all are delivered from danger. Sometimes God chooses not to *lose*, but to *invest* his servants. As Tertullian said in the second century, "The blood of the martyrs is the seed of the church." After any sowing comes a harvest, and beyond every hardship there is a reward. Beyond death itself there is a resurrection.

Paul walked the road to Jerusalem, and reached his goal. There he encountered danger, and consequently spent four years in prison; but out of those years came the ripeness of his experience as expressed in the Prison Epistles. God opened to him some vistas of thought that had not appeared in his previous writings. Perhaps without the dangers there would not have been the same heritage that the Christian church has enjoyed during the last nineteen centuries.

Out of the total life, lived constantly in the presence of danger, there came a rich fruitage produced by the harsh experience and discipline of these perils. A sense of the presence of God breathes through all Paul's writing, and the authenticity which marks the man who can say that he has suffered for Christ and has become victorious. Spiritual experience is worth only what it costs; and those who seek its heights of satisfaction find it on the road of danger. To walk that road with God demands undeviating loyalty, constant vigilance, and unwavering trust. Victory comes only from struggle, but in the struggle God assures victory. The road to Jerusalem leads to the suffering that purifies, to the discipline that strengthens, and to the faith that triumphs.

TEN
THE ROAD
TO ROME:
The Road of Service

Now after these things were ended, Paul purposed in the spirit, when he had passed through Macedonia and Achaia, to go to Jerusalem, saying, After I have been there, I must also see Rome. Acts 19:21

Of all the roads that a Christian must travel, the road to Rome is the longest and the hardest, for it continues to the end of life. It is the road of service, which began for Paul within the gates of Damascus when God took command of his career, and which ended at the headsman's block. Along that road were the synagogues where he had preached, the porticoes where he had debated with the philosophers, the prisons in which he had languished, and the churches which he had founded. The road to Rome was the epitome of his life of dedication to God.

The nineteenth chapter of Acts, in which the road is first mentioned, records the point of his career at which he had reached his greatest success. His missionary activity had begun in comparative obscurity. He had preached in Jerusalem, a city located in a remote frontier province of the Roman empire, of which the Romans knew little and which they valued even less. In his travels he had traversed southern Asia Minor, Macedonia, and Greece, planting churches in provincial towns and cities. Little by little his influence widened through his long and varied journeys; constantly he increased in spiritual growth and power. Finally he reached the center of Hellenistic culture in Greece and the Ionian cities, and began to contemplate what the next stage of his work might be.

Ephesus was the scene of a great success. There Paul met the belated believers who had progressed only as far as the baptism of John the Baptist, and introduced them to the fuller life to be experienced in the Holy Spirit. He had preached in the local synagogues, and had made a number of disciples. He had lectured to the philosophers in the school of Tyrannus, and had commanded a respectful hearing. Upon confronting the demonic occultism of the city he had demonstrated the superiority of Jesus over all other spiritual powers. After the riot in the theater which abruptly terminated his visit of three years, he had escaped unharmed, and had raised a generous contribution for the poor church in Jerusalem.

He might have felt that after having carried the gospel to the center of Hellenistic culture in the cities of Greece and of the Ionian coast, he could well have rested complacently on this tremendous achievement. There comes a time in the life of every Christian worker when he seems to reach his highest and final plateau of action. He increases in competence and widens his field of service to the point where he preaches his greatest sermon, wins his last convert, and establishes his strongest church. From that time onward, life may become an anticlimax. Actually that is not the end but a new beginning, for there is always an expanding prospect ahead of him. Even the gates of death do not mark "finis" for a Christian; they are rather the portal to a higher sphere of service.

Such was Paul's experience. The ministry at Ephesus had shown him what God could do in that wealthy pagan city and in the adjoining province. The road to Rome became *the road of imperial vision*.

Paul's decision to go to Rome was not motivated by a desire for sightseeing, but for carrying the gospel to the center of the empire. As Ephesus was the center of Hellenism, so Rome was the center of political life. Paul had a sense of strategy, given him by the Holy Spirit. He approached his mission as a general would undertake a campaign, selecting the important points to be captured, and mapping his progress in advance.

His progress in mission was not the result of chance, but was the outworking of a divine purpose.

When he wrote to the Roman Christians shortly after his departure from Ephesus, he said, "I long to see you, that I may impart unto you some spiritual gift, to the end ye may be established" (Rom. 1:11). The church at Rome was probably begun by migrants who had learned of Christ in other places, and who were slowly crystallizing into one uniform body of believers. The record of Acts states that on the day of Pentecost "sojourners from Rome, both Jews and proselytes," were numbered among the audience of the apostles (Acts 2:10). Paul realized that they needed constructive teaching such as he had given to other churches that he had founded, and he wished to confirm them in their faith.

He must have been thinking of the vast multitude of people in the capital. At that time Rome had a population of about one million people. He saw before him a territory that had not been visited by the message of Christ, and he was not satisfied until he finished his commission to the Gentiles by taking the message to the capital of the empire.

Jesus had a similar vision when he alluded to the people who were like sheep without a shepherd, lonely, fearful, hungry, and disorganized. He had compassion for the multitudes that thronged around him, and he devoted himself to ministering to their needs. Paul shared that vision of Jesus for the world of his day. He was not thinking in terms of the narrow confines of the place where he was living, but he was reaching out to the wider sphere that he might influence.

To state the matter more concisely, Paul was not a politician but a statesman. He was not working for immediate advantage but for future gain. If the gospel were planted in Rome, it would reach the center of the world. In the Roman forum was a golden milestone from which radiated the highways that extended to the Euphrates River on the east, to Germany and Britain on the west, to North Africa on the south. Along those roads marched the heralds who, long after Paul, evangelized pagan tribes, founded theological schools, translated the Scriptures into the vernacular dialects of the day, and brought the illumination of the gospel into the darkness of superstition and cruelty.

Such vision is needed today. With an estimated three billion people now on the earth who have no real knowledge of Christ, and a population that may double in relatively few years, the statesmanship of Paul's vision needs renewal. As with him, so now incalculable results can be effected by a single dedicated life. Such vision has been demonstrated throughout the history of the Christian church. During the twentieth century, a man by the name of R. A. Jaffray left a lucrative family business to go to China. He began the evangelization of South China, where a Bible school was established, a magazine published for Christians, and numerous churches founded. Learning that there was no gospel witness in Viet Nam, he began work in the northern province of Tonkin. In fifty years there were churches in almost every city of that country, a translation of the Scriptures and a hymnbook prepared for the believers, a Bible school begun, and expansion into adjacent countries and among the tribesmen.

Shortly before the Second World War Dr. Jaffray opened a pioneer mission in Indonesia. The work was cut short by the military conflict, and Dr. Jaffray himself died in an internment camp. Today the Indonesian church has passed through a remarkable revival and is flourishing. Dr. Jaffray and others who have accomplished similar outstanding results have been men who could think in terms of what God could do rather than in terms of human limitations and hindrances. Just as the Roman statesmen of the Augustan age envisioned Rome as the dominant power of the world and worked to achieve that sovereignty, so the Christian leaders had the imperial vision of making the gospel a spiritual power. As Paul said to the Romans, "the gospel . . . is the power of God unto salvation to every one that believeth" (Rom. 1:16).

The imperial vision applies not only to missionary policy, but also to the intellectual outlook of believers. The revelation of God in Christ introduces a new reality to history in the incarnation, to ethics in the revolutionary principles of conduct which Jesus taught, and a totally new concept in religious life because it came not as the loftiest example of man's attempt to interpret God, but rather as the compassionate outreach of God toward lost men. Most of the theology of the

New Testament is derived from the epistles of Paul, which corroborate and systematize what is implied in the Gospels and Acts concerning man's relation to God and God's redemption of man. The scope of Christian theology begins with creation and closes with ultimate redemption in the new creation. It is not confined to one period of time, nor to the testimony of one man. "To him [Christ] bear all the prophets witness" is the testimony of the apostle who presented to the church a coherent statement of who Jesus was and of what he did for humanity.

The imperial vision includes also the concept of defense. Paul, in writing to the Philippians, speaks of "the defense of the gospel." Throughout the Christian centuries the message of Christ has been beclouded with superstition, distorted by misinterpretation, and attacked by negation. Although the refutation of unbelief cannot be accomplished solely by the process of logic, misinterpretation and error must be analyzed and exposed. The need calls for dedicated and trained persons who can perceive the trends of error and who can explain truth in lucid and scholarly fashion. It requires the consecration of intellectual ability and learning, so that the Holy Spirit may illumine the servants of God and equip them to combat the fallacies of their age with the truth of God.

The road to Rome is *the road of imperative calling*. Paul did not enter upon it as if he were going on a picnic. He was moved by an inescapable compulsion. When God summoned him, he said, "I will send thee forth far hence unto the Gentiles" (Acts 22:21). A life work among the Gentiles was the last calling that Paul wanted. From his youth in Judaism he had been taught that the Gentiles were unclean heathen who worshiped false gods and were ignorant of the Law of the true God. Why should he be interested in them? The Judaism of his day had become introverted. Although Judaism made proselytes, there was a lack of compassion for men who were locked into the bondage of heathenism and ignorance. On the other hand, Jesus had said of his ministry, "I must go into the other cities also, for therefore came I forth," and "Other sheep have I which are not of this fold; them also I must bring." He recognized that he had been sent to love the unlovely, to teach the unteachable, and to rescue those that were lost. Paul expressed this same sense of obligation by saying, "I am debtor both to Greeks and to Barbarians, both to the wise and to the foolish" (Rom. 1:14).

There is a vast difference between a debt and a contribution. A debt is a compulsory obligation which must be paid; a contribution is a casual gift which is voluntary. Paul considered himself a debtor to the Gentiles because he had the message that they needed. Because of the commission that God had given to him he made the preaching of that message his priority in life, to which all other interests were subordinate. This obligation is expressed more fully in 2 Corinthians 5:14, 18, 20: "For the love of Christ constraineth us because we thus judge, that one died for all, therefore all died: and he died for all, that they that live should no longer live unto themselves, but unto him who for their sakes died and rose again. . . . God . . . gave us the word of reconciliation. . . . We are ambassadors therefore on behalf of Christ. . . ."

The text may be explained in two ways. Either Christ's love for us is the constraining factor, or our love for him. When Paul realized how much Christ loved him, he in turn felt his love for Christ and those whom Christ loved. The other possibility is that since Christ loved all men, those who love him should share his love for others. The two interpretations are different, but they do not clash, for both can be true. Once the love of Christ is experienced it creates a debt to him which can be paid only by fulfilling his call to love others.

The nature of this calling cannot be arbitrarily prescribed for any person. Paul was called to be an apostle; Stephen was originally set apart to serve tables. God himself must determine what the specific activity will be for any individual; all he asks is that life be placed at his disposal. When the first of the imperatives is accepted and a willingness to follow is expressed, he will reveal in his own time what the particular field of labor will be.

The facets of God's calling are always surprising. The obligation of the road to Rome does not mean dull routine and tedious drudgery. Whatever else might be said about the life of Paul, it never lacked excitement. God provides all kinds of unexpected adventures and strange gifts. Sometimes they may seem to be unwelcome, but they invariably bring joy in the end.

There is one more aspect of the road to Rome: it is *the road of implicit faith*. Throughout the disappointments and reversals of his plans, Paul never wavered in his confidence that what God had promised he would perform. He was compelled by the riot to leave Ephesus, and later remarked that the trouble in Asia was so dangerous that he barely escaped with his life (2 Cor. 1:8, 9). He was the target of an assassin's plot in Corinth. The metallurgists' union in Ephesus held a protest meeting, affirming that he was unfair to organized silversmiths because his preaching had destroyed the market for images of the temple. He was falsely accused of desecrating the Temple and was almost killed in the ensuing riot. In Caesarea the Roman governor, being unable to decide whether Paul was guilty of creating a public disturbance, left him in prison for his successor to judge. Paul, knowing that the Roman procurator was ignorant of his case and that he would never receive a fair hearing before a Jewish tribunal, appealed to Caesar in an attempt to bring the issue to a decision. After another defense of his claims before Herod Agrippa II, who was invited to give his expert opinion on the case, he was informed that he could have been released because he was not guilty of any infringement of the law. Since he had appealed to Caesar, however, he must be sent to Rome for trial.

After two years of unnecessary delay, Paul was finally placed in a convoy of prisoners and sent to Rome under military supervision. Apart from the fact that his destination seemed to be within sight, there was little prospect for an opportunity of ministry. He was still a prisoner awaiting a verdict. The final test of faith came during the voyage, when the ship on which they were sailing was overtaken by a violent northeast storm and driven off course. Dismasted and leaking, the craft was in imminent danger of foundering in the high seas. The cargo and fittings had been jettisoned; the passengers had not eaten food for several days and expected death at any moment. After all his disappointments and in spite of the threatening dangers, Paul dared to say to his fellow-passengers, "Be of good cheer." It is a wonder that someone did not throw him overboard! His sheer nerve would have been exasperating. What possible cause for good cheer could one find in that situation?

Paul's faith was founded on the word of God. "There stood by me this night an angel of the God whose I am, whom also I serve, saying, Fear not, Paul; thou must stand before Caesar . . . Wherefore, sirs, be of good cheer: for I believe God, that it shall be even so as it hath been spoken unto me" (Acts 27:23-25). No accident, injustice, or calamity could shake his confidence that God would fulfill his purpose, and that he would be able to complete the ministry for which he had been chosen.

Whatever obstacles may bar the way of the road to Rome, God is able to overcome them. It is the only safe road for the church to travel. To be sure, the ship and its cargo were lost, and the passengers were delayed in their voyage, but not one person perished in the shipwreck. The one man on board who had faith in God held the key for the preservation of all the others, and was the means of rescuing them because he was fulfilling God's purpose.

In the last stage of his journey Paul found himself on the Appian Way. A few miles outside the city the Christian brethren from Rome met him. The account says that when he saw them, "he thanked God, and took courage" (Acts 28:15). For two years, while awaiting an audience with the emperor, he instructed the believers and acted as an evangelist in the city. He had reached his objective by his faith.

Two elements of this faith are outstanding. One is Paul's obedience. In explaining his conversion to Agrippa he had said, "I was not disobedient unto the heavenly vision" (Acts 26:19). He pursued unswervingly the vision of service with which his career as a Christian began. He did not quit under pressure or under difficult circumstances. When God called him to the Gentiles he went as far as he could in responding to God's revealed will. It is impossible to steer a car until it is in motion, and God cannot direct a life that is not progressing in his purpose. It is always too soon to quit following God.

The second element is confidence. Obedience is founded on confidence; one does not obey a person in whom he does not trust, but he shows his trust by his obedience. Paul had learned that he could be sure of the presence and power of God whatever the dangers were that threatened him, and by that trust he triumphed.

The outcome of this faith is expectation. God never leads us down the path of service only to arrive nowhere. He has a goal to achieve, and a new revelation to disclose. Whatever the thrills and pleasures of the journey here, there will be much more beyond the prospects that are presently visible.

A group of men engaged in a hunting expedition among the Himalaya mountains of India were snowbound by a sudden storm. In order to occupy the hours while they were confined to the lodge, each narrated the most exciting experience of his life. Finally they turned to a man who had remained silent, eager to hear what he would tell. "The most thrilling experience of my life," he said, "will occur in the first five minutes after my death."

A Christian has an even better prospect. For him the supreme experience will be when the Lord comes. Then the strange turnings of the road will be explained; then the hardships will be forgotten; then the pattern and purpose of God's dealings with him will be consummated when he sees what his mission has accomplished.

Before every one of us stretches the road to Rome. The weary track may seem endless, its terminus lost somewhere on the distant horizon. Some have traveled it for a long time; some have taken only the first few hesitant steps. God will not supply us with a road map, with all points marked and all distances measured. He may say only, "Take the next step." One can never take the last step until he has taken the first, and many more between them. What shall the procedure be?

First of all, take the first step by accepting the challenge which will become the major motivation of life. Remember that, once having begun, God will not change his call, for "the gifts and the calling of God are not repented of" (Rom. 11:29). Whatever one's occupation may be, it will be fruitful provided that it is the calling of God.

Last of all, trust in God, and move onward. Whether one experiences immediate acclaim and success or repeated interruptions and protracted disappointments, God is the only sure guide for life. Follow him to the destination which he has prepared, and you will enjoy the blessings on the road to your Rome.

"Caldwell's writing is rich, hypnotic, and allegorical. He creates a magical story where place is as important as plot. Caldwell's Naples both delights and assaults the senses."
—*San Francisco Chronicle*

"Joseph Caldwell hits a perfect high C with *The Uncle from Rome*, an elegant, entertaining tale of an American tenor seeking personal and musical salvation in Naples. Under its shimmering surface lie starker, tragic truths, rendered with subtlety and metaphysical grace. A book that, however many readers it finds, can never find all it deserves."
—Richard Hall, author of *Fidelities*

"*The Uncle from Rome* always feels like an opera—it is grand in scope and framed by betrayal of one sort or another. And each character has a full half hour or so in which to sing his or her aria. They all perform brilliantly, and you believe every note author Joseph Caldwell has given them to sing."
—*Lambda Book Report*

"A literary opera that is both buffo and Grand Guignol, this odyssey into the unknown of our souls is richly inventive, highly compelling, and as darkly comic as our own absurdist times. A latter-day *Death in Venice*, this Neapolitan adventure is both moving and hilarious, the story of passion and its expression in a numbed and numbing world."
—Michael Lassell, author of *Decade Dance*

"Shrewd and splendid...the finale is nothing short of extraordinary."
—*Publishers Weekly*

"Through ornate emotion and operatic excess, Caldwell tells, paradoxically, a pointed, elemental tale of the human heart and shows how we are scalded and strengthened by our losses. *The Uncle from Rome* is an astonishing, unpredictable novel, as rich and densely layered as torte." —Bernard Cooper, author of *Maps to Anywhere*

"Bravo, *Uncle!*" —*The New York Times*

"A comic novel that, despite a real penultimate tragedy, resolves itself—with a final snort of laughter—in a triumphant, serious happy ending. Moreover, it's really wonderful all the way through—phrase for phrase, as good as any American comic novel, a peer of the best of Henry James and J.F. Powers."
—*Booklist*

"*The Uncle from Rome* has the intricate play of the lightness and darkness of the Mezzogiorno itself as well as the comedy, tragedy, and absurdity of Naples, a city as singular as Mr. Caldwell's gifts."
—Barbara Grizzuti Harrison, author of *Italian Days*

"A surprising amalgam of the tragic and the comic, the bizarre and the everyday; a novel, in short, like Naples, with all the virtues of grand, grand opera...splendidly entertaining."
—*The Village Voice*

"*The Uncle from Rome* is a fiery novel that singes the reader on almost every page. Set against the backdrop of Naples and with the music of Puccini as an underscore, this story of love and death is itself grand opera delivered at perfect pitch. I swallowed it down in a single radiant gulp."   —Richard Selzer, author of *Down from Troy*

"This sometimes shockingly funny comedy of sex and grief careens with ease between the heightened emotions of the opera stage and the more layered and subtle ones of real life. Caldwell reveals the complicated ways we all deal with sex, love, and pain...*The Uncle from Rome* is surprisingly original; a provocative look at how AIDS affects our innermost lives and thoughts that manages to entertain as well as move us."   —Michael Bronski, *The Guide*

"A delightful book—witty, original, knowledgeable about men and music, and the arcane life of Naples."
—Shirley Hazzard, author of *The Bay of Noon*

PENGUIN BOOKS

THE UNCLE FROM ROME

Born in Milwaukee, Wisconsin, Joseph Caldwell is the author of the novels *In Such Dark Places*, *The Deer at the River*, and *Under the Dog Star*. He was awarded the Rome Prize by the American Academy of Arts and Letters for his work in fiction and twice received the John Golden Fellowship in playwriting at Yale. He lives in New York City.

JOSEPH
CALDWELL

The *Uncle*
from
Rome

PENGUIN BOOKS

PENGUIN BOOKS
Published by the Penguin Group
Viking Penguin, a division of Penguin Books USA Inc., 375 Hudson Street,
New York, New York 10014, U.S.A.
Penguin Books Ltd, 27 Wrights Lane, London W8 5TZ, England
Penguin Books Australia Ltd, Ringwood, Victoria, Australia
Penguin Books Canada Ltd, 10 Alcorn Avenue, Suite 300, Toronto, Ontario,
Canada M4V 3B2
Penguin Books (N.Z.) Ltd, 182–190 Wairau Road, Auckland 10, New Zealand

Penguin Books Ltd, Registered Offices: Harmondsworth, Middlesex, England

First published in the United States of America by Viking Penguin, a division of
Penguin Books USA Inc., 1992
Published in Penguin Books 1993

1 3 5 7 9 10 8 6 4 2
Copyright © Joseph Caldwell, 1992
All rights reserved

Grateful acknowledgment is made for permission to reprint excerpts from William
Plomer's libretto for "Curlew River" by Benjamin Britten. © 1965 by
Faber Music Ltd. London.
Reprinted with permission.

Publisher's Note:
This is a work of fiction. Names, characters, places, and incidents either are the
product of the author's imagination or are used fictitiously, and any resemblance to
actual persons, living or dead, events, or locales is entirely coincidental.

THE LIBRARY OF CONGRESS HAS CATALOGUED THE HARDCOVER AS FOLLOWS:
Caldwell, Joseph.
The uncle from Rome: a novel / by Joseph Caldwell
P. cm.
ISBN 0-670-84058-0 (hc.)
ISBN 0 14 01.5707 7 (pbk.)
PS3553.A396U48 1992
813'.54–dc20 91–16587

Printed in the United States of America
Set in Bembo
Designed by Francesca Belanger

Naples, the paradise of Italy,
as that is of earth . . .

John Fletcher,
The Double Marriage

. . .

V'a Napoli!

Italian epithet,
the equivalent of
"Go to hell!"

Acknowledgments

The author wishes to thank the American Institute and Academy of Arts and Letters for the Rome Prize, which introduced him to Italy and to Naples, the city in which this novel takes place. He is also grateful to the Ludwig Vogelstein Foundation for financing a return to Naples at a time crucial to the writing of this book, and to the Cockayne Fund, which also gave its valued assistance.

For Yaddo, the MacDowell Colony, and the Virginia Center for the Creative Arts, he feels a continuing gratitude for their sustained and sustaining help, and to the singer Michael Chiusano he gives special thanks for sharing his knowledge about the joys and melancholies of that profession. He also expresses a particular gratitude to Federico Stampa—himself *un figlio di Napoli*—who corrected or confirmed the author's amazed and affectionate sense of the sovereign people of Naples.

The Uncle from Rome

I

Michael Ruane—Indianapolis born, Indianapolis bred —had planned to climb Vesuvio that morning and look down into the volcanic crater, but he was persuaded instead to go to a wedding in the basilica of Santa Chiara and present himself as the "uncle from Rome." Persuaded is perhaps too weak a word. Actually, he was there by the near-royal dictate of Aganice Calefati, the soprano in whose *Tosca* he would sing a minor role the week after next at Naples's Teatro San Carlo.

La Calefati had had no less than the stage director of the production phone Michael early the morning before and "beg" —a soprano's word for command—beg him to see her at the opera house in an hour. She would be having a costume fitting, and he'd find her in the costumer's atelier. Michael had other things he wanted to do, but he was a *comprimario*—a singer of secondary, even tertiary, roles in opera—and it wouldn't hurt to have a lead soprano, and one of Calefati's presumed ascendancy, in his debt.

Calefati, after asking his honest opinion about her costume and accepting somewhat skeptically his nods of approval, got down to business. Would he please, for her sake, and as a favor to her—which would excite no end of gratitude—go to a wedding as the family's "uncle from Rome"? It was, she explained, an old Neapolitan custom, not that much in favor anymore, but what it came down to was this: To impress one's friends and neighbors, one would ask—even pay—a distinguished-looking person, a man, to attend an important family function and be pointed out in tones of reverence and respect as the "uncle from Rome." That the family had connections to the capital and possibly to the Vatican would ensure a status obtainable in no other way. The family itself would pretend to shrug off the uncle's presence as nothing of note, but the guests would immediately intensify their participation in the event, convinced of attributes in themselves newly revealed, since they'd been invited along with the uncle from Rome. They would consider themselves wittier, taller, more profound; some would become outright giddy from the sudden ascent up the social ladder. Others would become insufferable snobs for the duration of the gathering.

The idea intrigued Michael. He was, after all, an actor as much as he was a singer, and he invariably reveled in any role that came his way. And to play an Italian, a Roman, *and* an uncle was an opportunity he couldn't expect to have tossed his way every week of the year. Then, too, he was especially eager these days to grab at identities other than his own. Being an uncle from Rome—like playing the other roles, the operatic characters he'd come to Naples to play—could be a welcome invitation to identity that might relieve the sense of absence and vacancy that pervaded his own psyche at the moment. He was more than usually receptive to possession; gladly would he assume another's attitudes, needs, and prerogatives, even if it was only for a few hours. Since he didn't particularly appreciate Michael Ruane these days, he might find at least temporary refuge from his confusion by cloaking himself in the robes of someone defined by circumstances other than those that had so recently altered his life, someone he could create and control within his imagination.

What gave him pause, however, was that in this instance

he'd be dealing not with ordinary mortals but with Neapolitans, and to be honest, Neapolitans scared him. They were too unpredictable, too inscrutable. Several times during his student days in Rome he'd come to Naples for the usual release from responsibility and commandment, a needed exploration of the possible. More often than not, he'd return, a sated weariness murmuring along his bones. But there had been several experiences, none of which he was prepared to divulge to La Calefati, that had given him a certain unease as regards the Neapolitan disposition. Yet how could he tell the pleading, implacable soprano, herself *una figlia di Napoli*—a daughter of Naples—that he found Neapolitans too contradictory to allow for ordinary human transaction and exchange? To Michael, her fellow citizens could be completely open and friendly, but at the same time more closed and private than any people he'd ever known—accepting and welcoming, but ultimately tribal and exclusionary. They were a gentle people, but fierce as well, the one characteristic equal in intensity to the other. That they were cunning is well known, but they were also generous and genuinely caring. Joyful they could be, more joyful than most, but the melancholy, the sorrow, was always there, and for all their prayerful piety, they were completely and irremediably fatalistic. Even their sensual and sensuous lures were desperate yet, at the same time, indifferent. And all these contradictions, all these opposites, were kept in precarious balance by an energy not famous for its stability. Sudden shifts, inexplicable tilts of the scale, were forever possible, and the results could, to say the least, be unsettling.

The source of these native traits, of course, was geographical. There, spread out before all of Naples, serene and nourishing, was the bay, calm and peaceful, the waters themselves easy and yielding. And there on its eastern flank was a volcano. What else but contradiction in the extreme could be expected of a people born within sight and sound of such primal and opposing forces? Here were older gods, and the Neapolitans perhaps were still made in their dual image, possessing a larger humanity that ranged beyond the usual restricting covenants and intimate redemptions.

That Michael should involve himself so closely with these people was daunting enough, but to claim a right to their respect, to pretend a social superiority, to *lie* to them, would be just plain stupid.

He wanted to tell Aganice—she'd asked him to call her that in anticipation of his acquiescence—that he was not a coward, but neither was he a fool (although there was sufficient evidence accumulated over his thirty-seven years to suggest that he was both), but he settled instead for listing his disqualifications for the part. One by one, Aganice knocked them down.

Michael said he wasn't Italian, to begin with. No, Aganice replied, but he was black Irish; he could pass without difficulty. And besides, she added, he'd lived and studied in Rome; his Italian was accurate and impeccable. Very *romano,* almost *toscano.* To that she swore, and Michael had to admit it was true. But he then protested that people would ask him questions about the family, questions he wouldn't be able to answer. No, Aganice told him, they wouldn't have that much of a chance to ask anything. All Michael had to do was attend the church service. Then, because he was from Rome, it could be assumed that he would have to hurry back.

The groom, Peppino, Calefati explained, was the son of a woman with whom she'd studied piano as a child, Assunta Spacagna. The bride was Rosalia Attanese, and that was as much as Aganice could tell him about her. But why Signora Spacagna wanted to revive the old custom, she had no idea. It might have something to do with there being no father. He was dead, killed eight years ago in the 1980 earthquake. He had gone to Laviano, a village in the mountains, to search for a cousin thought to be trapped in the rubble. During the search, a wall of stones fell on him. Michael would be his long-lost baby brother, given at birth to a charity—which in turn had sent him to yet another charity, in Rome—because the family had no food. The story was too common to be questioned. If anyone should require further details, Michael had only to say they were too painful to be recalled. Michael stated flatly that black Irish or no black Irish, Roman Italian or Tuscan Italian, he'd never be convincing. No one would believe him in a million years.

It was here that La Calefati got him.

"I have seen you in rehearsals. You are such a superb actor. I have sung in opera houses throughout Europe, in South America, even, and nowhere—*nowhere*—have I seen such acting. Your Spoletta, especially in Act Two, sends chills, I will not tell you where. The way you've conceived the part, the way you act it, with that complete conviction, I am almost more repulsed by you than by Scarpia."

Michael had no choice but to accept this as true. He was, he knew, becoming an exceptional *comprimario*. He'd worked hard at it, and he had ambitions. He was a singing actor, an acting singer, in the great tradition, and whatever doubts and exasperations he may have concerning his life, his career, for the moment, wasn't one of them. He was a valued New York City Opera *comprimario*—and rumors had reached him that spies from the Met had seen his Basilio in *Figaro* and his Goro in *Butterfly*. No doubt he'd hear from them soon and be invited to make the short stroll across the Lincoln Center Plaza from the State Theater to the Met, a journey he had rehearsed in his mind with unflagging fidelity.

Michael's final objection to Calefati's proposal was—and even he had to admit it was rather weak—that he didn't really look the part. He was a bit too young, of only medium height, with no authoritative gray in his hair, and if one looked closely, there were freckles on his nose. He was not, in effect, distinguished-looking enough.

La Calefati took care of that. "Ah, Michele," she said, "how can you say those things? I look at you and I begin to see another Toscanini. Taller, of course. Younger than in most pictures that come down to us these days. Be honest. You are a very handsome man. And if I didn't have so many distractions, I might show a little more interest myself." With that, she chucked him under the chin, puckered her lips, and made a kissing sound.

Michael could hardly voice the real reasons for his reluctance—his fears and his susceptibilities—and so he agreed to do all that she asked, but only as a favor to her, and please, no money. She took his head in both hands, kissed both cheeks, then, to complete her condescension, gave the left one a light slap. But when, as he was leaving, she said, "*Grazie, caro Michele,*" it was obvious that she really meant it.

When Michael got to Santa Chiara, the wedding party was no-where to be seen, and nothing was as he'd expected it to be. Since this was in Naples, and in a basilica, no less, he'd prepared himself for an extravagant exaggeration of the Italian weddings he'd seen at Our Lady of Pompeii in Indianapolis when he was a boy. There would be three to six bridesmaids, with the groom attended by the equivalent of, if not a brigade, at least a hockey team. The bridesmaids would wear enough tulle to scrim an entire *Ring* cycle, and the groom's crew would be costumed in cutaways with striped pants, yet manage to look confident no matter how foolish they might feel.

A soprano would sing "*Ave Maria*" at the Offertory and "*Panis Angelicus*" at Communion. The church would be filled, with an overflow in the choir loft. The littlest children, *i bambini,* would test to see how far they could go in disobedience and sacrilege, chasing each other into forbidden side altars, playing hide-and-seek behind statues and candle racks. Gossip would occupy the wives, indulgence the husbands, who didn't exactly like to be seen at what was, after all, a women's affair. The young people, *la gioventù,* friends and cousins of the bride and groom, would be, by turns, grave and silly, more nervous in their way than the couple themselves.

Flowers and candles and perfume would compete as to which would be responsible for the imminent asphyxiation of everyone present. The colors of the women's dresses would suggest a garden that one would never want to tame—chaotic, tipsy on its own nectars, indifferent to its own gaudy excess. Everything would be both bright and warmly glowing, excited and content, expectant and resigned. Then the organ would sound out, descending, rising in majesty, announcing the first step of the first timorous bridesmaid as she would begin the long, inexorable approach to the altar.

Michael had walked halfway down a side aisle of Santa Chiara, past the columned arches that opened onto the small side chapels, then stopped. He'd obviously come at the wrong time. Right in front of him was a small congregation of elderly and, it seemed, underfed women, scattered among a dozen pews that faced a chapel on his right. They were droning in Italian the *Sanctus* of the Mass being celebrated by a gnome of a priest, who, without waiting for them to finish, had gone on to the words of the Consecration.

Ahead of him, far down at the end of the nave, he could see the first five or six pews randomly occupied by worshipers bundled up against the chill that had obviously been given sanctuary in the church—as if the winter cold, now that it was March, was a threatened species and Santa Chiara herself had made its preservation her very own cause. There were two sprays of white flowers near the main altar. Gardenias? He couldn't tell. Candles had been lit, but no more than for the least celebratory Mass of a common Sunday. The only indication that something unusual might possibly take place was the red plush kneeler placed in front of the altar and the two spindly gilded chairs placed a few feet behind. Also, as he'd entered, he'd seen two workmen unrolling a red carpet that would have to go all the way from the main portal to the steps of the altar. The rug, he was certain, could never make it. The basilica was almost a city block long. Surely it would run out a little past halfway. But no, its final curl now lapped the sanctuary step, and the two workmen, to put an immediate stop to such familiar behavior, were busy tamping it down onto the aisle stones.

Michael wondered if he should wait at the side chapel until after the Consecration of the Mass now in progress or if he should just skirt the worshipers and continue on to the front pew, where, he'd been instructed, he'd find a spare but handsome woman with gray-streaked black hair, wearing a fur coat with a white flower at the neck. He was to go to her, open his arms, say, "Assunta! *Cara!*" embrace her, kiss her on both cheeks, then allow her to pin a white flower similar to her own on his lapel, indicating that as the uncle from Rome he was an important part of the celebration.

Michael decided to move down the aisle and get the first part of his act over with, but before he could make his way around the pews facing the chapel, a bell rang as if to warn him to go no farther. He reverently bowed his head as the host was raised, then the chalice. The priest, his slightly lopsided head coming to no more than a foot above the altar table, invited the assembled to proclaim "*il mistero della fede,*" the mystery of faith. Not sure which of the several possible prayers had been prescribed for this particular day, Michael waited for someone else to say the first word. The priest began.

"*Annunziamo . . .*" was enough. The others joined in. "*. . . la tua morte, Signore, proclamiamo la tua risurrezione, nell' attesa della tua venuta.*" When we tell of your death, Lord, we proclaim your resurrection, in expectation of your coming.

The reference to death and resurrection made Michael wonder if now might be the time to say a prayer for his friend, his once-upon-a-time lover, Damian, now three months dead. Michael thought he should at least try.

His first thought was a familiar one: Damian is dead, and I feel no sorrow, no loss; I have no pity, no tears. One of the women, better fed than the others, with a face like a brown moon, turned and glared at him as if she'd heard his admission and had been scandalized. She got up and, without genuflection, headed for the back of the church. Michael took her departure as something of a rebuke and did what he could to prove himself a minimally decent human being.

Down on one knee he went. He begged that Damian be given eternal rest, eternal love, eternal joy. Then he waited, his head bowed, his knee still poking against the stone beneath it. But his patience was prompted not by piety or even by the wish for some assurance that his petition had been heard. He was waiting to see what feelings his prayer might awaken not in the Almighty but in himself. He wanted to see what this nearness to Damian might do, what response he might have at this joining of the two of them—himself and Damian—in the intimate presence of the author of love, a spiritual coupling before the divine witness.

Nothing happened except that his knee began to hurt. He considered lowering the other knee to relieve the pressure, but he didn't want to move, as if some shift in posture might put him at a remove from the sensations that could, at this moment, be headed his way, not exactly a thunderbolt but at least a tightening in his chest, a gasp of breath, a twitch in his cheek, the coming of grief.

As others in bereavement ask for comfort and release, he had prayed instead for sorrow and for desolation. He begged to be allowed to feel again the aching loss of his friend, the loss he'd felt for four years, from the time of their separation. He asked that at least the sorrow he'd known then be returned to him now. Absurd as it seemed, he was suffering from the loss of loss. It was as if he'd never loved his friend, had never during all those four years desperately wanted him back.

Kneeling on the aisle stones, Michael thought he might pray just one time more, but he knew it would be useless. Perhaps, like wisdom and fortitude, sorrow and grief were gifts of the Holy Spirit and not to be had just for the asking. Like the assurances of faith, the desolations of loss could be given or withheld according to the divine will. If emptiness was to be his burden, he must accept it and not complain.

A distant organ made a somewhat feeble foray into the reaches of the great Gothic church. The wedding had begun, and Michael had yet to present himself to his *cognata*, his sister-in-law, Signora Assunta Spacagna (born, Aganice had told him, Gallifuoco), and prepare himself for the uncertainties that lay ahead.

He turned to see the first bridesmaid place her slippered foot on the red carpet. Instead he saw what must be the bride herself, since she was striding forward on the arm of a man who seemed a little old to be her father. Where were the bridesmaids? He looked again toward the altar, expecting to see the waiting groom, his best man, and a respectable complement of ushers. To one side of the step leading up into the sanctuary stood a pale and fair-haired boy, or, to be more exact, a young man. He was wearing a double-breasted black jacket, its only button down near his waist, giving it a low-slung appearance and making it look outsized, as if he had yet to grow into it. A very small black bow tie seemed to be clipped not to his shirt collar but to his Adam's apple. There was a white flower in his lapel, and he stood looking straight ahead at a stone on the far wall.

Michael had seen him before, in the portico, talking to three small boys, one of whom had held a soccer ball. The boys, as far as Michael could make out from the dialect, had been asking him questions about the wedding, and he had been asking them questions about soccer. Michael had made it a point not to look too long at the young man; it would be distracting when he should be concentrating on other matters. But he did remember feeling sorry for the groom, who couldn't possibly equal, much less surpass, the beauty of this presumed usher or best man. The bride would, at the sight of him, repent her decision or at least realize at a very crucial moment that she was settling for decidedly inferior goods. It wasn't just the soft fair hair and the soft fair skin, nor was it his soft brown eyes or soft fair lips; it was the quiet way he had been talking to the younger boys. There had been a tender patience in his voice, and on his face an eager sweetness. Michael had quickly paid the tribute that is beauty's due, an amalgam of awe, envy, exhilaration, and lust—with a strong dash of covetousness thrown in—and continued on into the basilica.

But this was not one of the ushers. This was the groom. He was Peppino Spacagna, Michael's presumptive nephew. And there were no ushers, any more than there were any bridesmaids. This was not what he'd expected.

Rosalia Attanese, the bride, was now almost halfway to the altar, the ceremony was about to begin, and the "uncle from Rome" had not yet made his appearance. But Michael waited another moment so he could look more closely at the bride. He was hoping she'd be very beautiful, dark and luminous, with, perhaps, a proud modesty. She would wear the near-sorrowful smile of the conqueror, reflective and anticipatory. Yet she would glow with consent; she would advance with stately grace to the man she was destined to raise from the dust with all her cherishing and all her sly intelligence. If Michael was to play a supporting role, he at least hoped for the main characters to be worthy of the artistry he was prepared to bring to his *comprimario* part. The groom was acceptable indeed, but the event in general, with the drab congregation, the dusty, mustard-colored walls, the ancient sarcophagi as the only offered decoration, required an equally superb bride, an added assertion of the glories of the flesh to bring into perspective the supreme austerity of the surrounding stones.

Now Michael could see her, one arm looped into that of her father—or grandfather. Her bearing was stately yet easy. She was indeed beautiful, more beautiful than even he had required. She was indeed dark and luminous, with, no doubt about it, a proud modesty. Everything his imagination had demanded had been granted, and more besides. There was an impishness, suggested probably by the nose, which nature had turned up slightly just before it could become too long. And a sympathy, obvious from the way she was adjusting her pace to that of the elderly man at her side. It was as if she were leading him, helping him to a place where he might find, if not rejuvenation, at least rest and quiet. She was making no apologies for his infirmity. She was doing honorable service, and it was giving her a great and mischievous joy.

Only when Michael began his own swift stride toward the front pew did he recognize what the organist was playing. Surely it had been chosen at random, without thought, without knowledge. Maybe it had been there on the music stand, left behind by some master of the organ who'd forgotten to pack it up and take it with him. But then, it could be right after all. It could be absolutely right. It was Handel, which made it somewhat appropriate, and it was from an oratorio, another point in its favor. But the oratorio was *Judas Maccabeus*—a celebration of release from oppression—and the music was the great choral march "See the Conquering Hero Comes."

Before Michael had taken six more steps, he thought the music completely appropriate. It was being played for him, for Michael Ruane, to give him courage, to buttress his faltering determination, to summon up a dignity, a conviction, suitable to his role. For the moment, he must transcend the *comprimario;* he must be Rhadames, he must be Chenier, he must be Rodolfo and, come to think of it, Judas Maccabeus as well.

He presented himself to the woman in the front pew. In fulfillment of what La Calefati had said, she was wearing the fur coat, the white flower. "Assunta! *Cara!*" he cried in a stage whisper intended for everyone unto the tenth pew behind them. He embraced her, kissed her on both cheeks, then held her slightly away from himself, the better to drink in the sight of her, watering to full flower a kinship that had lain too long in the dust.

The woman looked at him, startled. Michael felt the first twinge of horror; it tweaked the right edge of his upper lip and was preparing to give instruction to his eyelids, whether they should widen in aghast awareness or close, never to open again. He'd made a mistake. This was not Assunta Spacagna, not the mother of the groom, not the long-ago piano teacher of the about-to-be-acclaimed *diva,* Aganice Calefati.

And he was not the uncle from Rome. He was a known madman given to assaulting important personages at sacred functions. This was probably not the first time he'd done it; he'd been known to strike before, at funerals, at ground-breakings, at the blessing of the fleet. In Rome, the prison was Regina Coeli, Queen of Heaven. To what saint of Naples would he be thrown in sacrifice for this latest transgression? Michael then remembered the massive hilltop fortress dominating the city, Castel Sant'Elmo. He would be sacrificed before nightfall to the greater honor and glory of Sant'Elmo.

Just as Michael began to rehearse in his mind the part of Florestan in *Fidelio,* just as he was beginning to see himself emerge out of the dungeon dark, the woman began reaching toward him, either to wring his neck or to pluck out his eyes, or some other response appropriate to his criminal gesture.

"*Caro! Zio!* All the way from Rome! *Bravo! Grazie, Zio, grazie.*" She, too, took care that her words reach at least a dozen pews back. The outstretched arms gathered him into the cool animal fur; his cheeks were to be kissed, not clawed. Then it was she who held him at a slight distance, not just to radiate gratitude but to acquaint herself as quickly as possible with this fraud she'd just embraced.

The organ, satisfied that the conquering hero had arrived, ceased its exhortations as both Assunta and Michael turned to watch the groom step out toward his bride. Michael saw mostly the back of Peppino's head, the light-brown hair reaching gently to his white collar, the drape of the jacket still loose even as it stretched along the wide shoulders underneath.

Peppino was kissing Rosalia's father on both cheeks, then accepting Rosalia's hand, offered by her father. He bent down, but before he touched his lips to the flesh of his bride, Michael was being introduced to the people in the pew behind him.

"*Lo zio,*" Signora Spacagna was saying with an almost defiant satisfaction. "*Lo zio, da Roma.*" The uncle, from Rome.

"*Piacere, piacere, piacere,*" Michael said. A pleasure, a pleasure, a pleasure. He took in his own hand first one, then another, and then another hand of the people in the second pew, squeezing, in his nervousness, a little too hard, making one woman gasp and quickly pull away. Meanwhile, the ascent of the bride and groom to the altar was all but ignored, so important was it that he be introduced. There were quick bows of the head, repeated pressures of the hand, stares he hoped were of awe and not of scorn.

Now Rosalia's father had come into the front pew, next to Michael, forcing him closer to Signora Spacagna. Still not having looked at her son or his bride, the Signora was insistent on introducing Michael to Rosalia's father, who turned out to be not her father but her *padrone,* her employer in the linen shop where she worked. When the Signora faltered and began to mumble, the man said, "My name is Scarano," his voice much less feeble than his step coming down the aisle. "And yours, Signore?"

Only with effort did Michael not turn to the Signora and ask her his name. In his anticipation of the part he was to play, in his anxiety over failure, he'd neglected to find out what his name was. He made sure he was opening his mouth very slowly, to give the mother of the groom time to speak his name and complete a proper introduction. But from behind him there was only silence, and his mouth was completely open by now. "Michele," Michael said, expecting a jab in the ribs to indicate error. No jab came, only the moment when he was supposed to give his last name. He couldn't say "Ruane," his own name, without giving the whole show away. Then, with a suavity that recalled him to his role, Michael spoke the obvious. "Spacagna," he said. "Michele Spacagna." He bowed to Signor Scarano, not out of respect for his person but in congratulation to himself for his powers of recovery, his newfound genius for swift-wittedness.

So readily did Signora Spacagna subscribe to this identity that she leaned slightly backward and introduced Michael to the first two pews on the main aisle. "Michele Spacagna, the uncle, from Rome. Don Michele, from Rome, the uncle." By the time he had become "Don Michele, from Rome," Michael felt sufficiently secure in his imposture to pinch the cheek of the five-year-old girl to whom he was being introduced. The girl accepted the honor by slapping his hand, then turning her attention to the bride and groom, now standing firmly between their gilt chairs and their plush kneeler.

Two middle-aged men had come into the sanctuary, each one stationed in front of what looked like a handsomely crafted and beautifully finished wooden cube. The witnesses, Michael assumed, but obviously peripheral to the event. They looked professional, hired. Was that, too, a Neapolitan custom? Before he could worry about it, the nuptial Mass began.

During the *Kyrie,* two late arrivals, a woman in a silver-fox stole and a teenage girl in a leather miniskirt and knee-high boots, came and kissed the Signora. "*Tesoro,*" the woman purred. Treasure. Michael was then introduced, kissed ritually by the woman and ignored by the girl. While the letter of Saint Paul to the Ephesians was being read—bidding wives to be subject to their husbands as to the Lord—a man in gray cotton shirt and pants

—something of a custodial uniform, Michael guessed—his face extraordinarily cheerful and his voice gravelly and low, thrust his arm past both Michael and Signor Scarano and scratched at the arm of Signora Spacagna. "You must introduce me," the man said. When the Signora realized, perhaps, that she was not merely having a nervous reaction to the peculiarities of the epistle, she looked toward the man, who then nodded his head up and down a few times. The Signora herself nodded in return, as if to indicate her approval, if not pleasure, at the way the man was moving his head.

"You must introduce me," he repeated.

"Oh, yes, of course. Don Michele. The uncle. From Rome."

"I know, I know," the man said. He and Michael shook hands, the man continuing to nod his head, prompting Michael to do the same in return. The man then retreated and the Signora confessed in a not particularly hushed voice that she had no idea who that was.

The gospel, the wedding feast at Cana, had been read, and now the homily began. The priest, instead of mounting the pulpit, placed himself directly in front of the kneeler and addressed his words primarily to the bride and groom but with the assembled well within earshot. He was speaking of San Giuseppe—Saint Joseph—whose feast would come the following week. He spoke of the saint's blessings on marriage and on the family, of his fidelity to his wife and to his child.

"Fra Callisto," Signora Spacagna whispered to Michael. "A cousin of mine. That's why we're in the basilica. He insisted." The prim satisfaction with which the Signora spoke the words "he insisted" told Michael that the priest had done nothing of the kind. Underneath her words Michael thought he heard the Signora's timid request, then her insulting demand, and, finally, her impassioned plea that the marriage take place in Santa Chiara. He thought he saw Fra Callisto's benign doubt, then his angered refusal, then his pitying acquiescence. It pleased Michael to know that, as Don Michele Spacagna, he had Franciscan connections.

The priest continued, and the little girl who'd slapped Michael's hand walked around in front of them, came into their pew, and hugged herself against the Signora's fur coat as if frightened by the words being spoken by the kindly friar.

Michael was patting the top of the girl's head when he saw the Signora stiffen, then gasp, then relax her body as if preparing for some action not yet decided upon. Her eyelids lowered, and her head moved back, but very slowly. There was an intake of breath but no exhalation that Michael could hear. He looked toward the altar.

In what seemed to be yet another difference between an Italian wedding in Naples and an Italian wedding in Indianapolis, a youth with crow-black hair and the taut face of a young hawk had come into the sanctuary and positioned himself next to the bride, at her left. He was talking to her, not very loud, even as Fra Callisto was delivering his homily. The young man suggested a troubled tempter, quietly telling the bride not to heed the good priest's words. Rosalia didn't move. Erect in her gilded chair, her head tilted slightly upward, she seemed to be studying the details of a stone sarcophagus above the altar.

Peppino shifted backward, took his hands from his lap, and put one hand on each knee, giving support to his upper torso. The two witnesses, sitting upright on their wooden cubes, seemed to see nothing either in or out of the ordinary.

"Gaetano, go sit down," Fra Callisto said, the words spoken in the same tone of voice and volume as those of his homily, an integral but not too important part of the message he was giving to the bride and groom. Continuing, he expanded on the Holy Family's acceptance of what God had sent them and was beginning to tell about the abundant grace God gives to the family to help it accept its acceptance.

In the middle of a phrase concerning God's gifts to those married within Church sanction, Fra Callisto interjected the words "Gaetano, stop," then continued as if that, too, were one of God's blessings.

The young man had moved even closer to Rosalia, still at her side, his head bowed a little toward her left ear. An angle of black hair fell forward, shading rather than covering his eyes and forehead. Rosalia continued her study of the sarcophagus, neither more nor less intent than before. Peppino's only move was to claw a little deeper into his kneecaps.

"Tell Peppino to get up so I can sit down," Michael heard the young man say.

"Gaetano! Come here!" The Signora's voice was both a whisper and a shout.

With no change in posture or tone, the young man, Gaetano, continued to talk to Rosalia. "Peppino will do it if you tell him to. Just say, 'Peppino, go sit with Mamma so Gaetano can sit down and listen with me to what Don Callisto is saying.' "

Sit next to Mamma? This, then, must be Peppino's brother. And he was insisting he take Peppino's place.

Signora Spacagna was on her feet, pushing past the child, past Michael, past Signor Scarano, who whimpered in pain as she shoved against his chest. Her fur coat smelled like lilac shampoo.

As both Fra Callisto and Gaetano continued, neither trying to drown out the other, the Signora advanced toward the altar. Only now did Michael notice that she walked with a cane, but the walk was so determined, so firm, that Michael decided immediately that the cane was more an emblem of authority than a support, a sort of secular crozier that, like its canonical counterpart, held a history of power, an irrefutable right to command and to sway.

Fra Callisto, unperturbed, continued to concentrate on the young couple, certain perhaps that the mild distraction to his right was about to be removed. Only Peppino gave any acknowledgment of this new presence in the arena; he glanced sideways to watch the cane as it passed behind Rosalia's chair, then he faced front again but didn't bother to raise his head to its former position. The witnesses relaxed into a slump; they would resume their erect positions once the fuss was over.

Out of respect for the Signora, Fra Callisto halted his homily so the congregation could witness with full attention the imminent and easy defeat of the doomed intruder. The Signora did not hurry. With each step she hit the tip of her cane on the floor as if warning the stones themselves not to try any funny business.

Gaetano moved his head closer to Rosalia's ear and went on talking, but now in a voice so low no one else could hear. The Signora reached his side. She, too, bent down, and it wasn't clear at first whether she was talking to Gaetano or to Rosalia. Peppino raised his head, arching it backward as if trying to get rid of a crick in his neck, then held the position, his neck seemingly locked halfway in its attempt at relief. His mouth was open, perhaps in awe at something he saw in the stained-glass window high above the main altar.

Signor Scarano snorted, stood up, yanked the flower from his lapel, threw it down onto the pew, got out into the aisle, genuflected, crossed himself, and started out of the church with a step decidedly more sure than the one with which he'd entered it.

"You don't listen to your mother?" the Signora was saying. "And in church? I told you not to be here if you couldn't behave yourself." The Signora took a step back, the better to aim her words directly at her son, who continued to speak only to Rosalia, quietly, whispering to her like a lover.

"Come with me and with your uncle, or else leave the church," the Signora said.

That would be Michael. He was the uncle. Aganice had promised a simple drama, a decent role, and an easy triumph. There'd been no mention of possible plot complications. For the first time in his life, Michael would have preferred that his part not be expanded.

"Do you hear me?" the Signora was saying. "You'd better hear me. Because if you don't . . . !" She stopped, hesitant to say aloud the terrible thing she had in mind. "I'll call down your father if you don't! He'll see that you do what you're told. Is that what you want me to do? Call your father, out of his grave?" She raised the cane, now a conjuring rod that could strike open the tombs of the dead and call them forth. "I'll do it!" The cane, it seemed more likely, was about to come down on Gaetano's back, which is probably why he shifted a little out of its reach, allowing himself to face for the first time the imperturbable Rosalia. This silenced him, but only for the moment. He then said her name—"Rosalia"—as if surprised by her beauty. He said it again, this time a long exhalation of wonder and yearning. "Rosalia . . ." Peppino unlocked his neck and looked away from them, toward the sacristy.

"Uncle! Help me! Come, come. Come!" Signora Spacagna was looking directly at Michael, and her plea was genuine and heartfelt.

Now stage directions were being added to the drama, and soon, he was sure, there'd be a need for dialogue, with no script available. His entire Italian vocabulary would flee from his brain; grammatical constructions and idioms would desert him, the irregular verbs leading the way. If words were required, he'd have to speak English. His imposture would be revealed; he would disgrace both himself and the needful Signora. And what the young man, Gaetano, might do to him was mercifully beyond his imagining.

"Don Michele! Come!" the Signora called.

"She wants you," the little girl whispered.

Knocking against the front of the pew, then stumbling over the kneeler at his feet, Michael managed to get himself into the aisle. Whether he would retreat or advance, he wouldn't be sure until the final moment. Wishing he, too, had a cane, he found himself starting toward the sanctuary, resolving that he would not trip over the step and he would not tread on the bride's veil. Beyond that, he could think of nothing.

"Gaetano! This is your uncle. From Rome. Gaetano? Do you hear me? This is your uncle, your father's brother I told you might be here. Don Michele. He's come from Rome. You'll listen to him. To your uncle."

Michael continued in the direction of the voice, helpless against it. He was in the sanctuary now; he had negotiated the single step in fine fashion. Perhaps things would go well after all. He passed the witness on the right and reached the edge of Rosalia's veil. With stately deliberateness he sidestepped it and advanced toward the Signora and Gaetano.

He saw that the young man was older than his brother, that his eyes were dark, closer to black than brown, and that his eyebrows met above the bridge of his lean and lengthy nose.

"Speak to him, Don Michele," the Signora commanded.

"Gaetano," Michael said, "I am your uncle, Don Michele. You will hear what I have to say." He was amazed and impressed by the authority in his voice, to say nothing of the perfection of his accent. Surely some saint, some angel, some god kindly disposed to the fraudulent—and resident only in Naples—had come to his aid. If Gaetano would keep from laughing, Michael might get away with what he was doing. So far, Gaetano responded not at all. "You will either come with your mother and with me and bear solemn witness to this marriage of your brother to Rosalia Attanese, or you will leave this house of God in peace." He almost added, in English, "and no more shenanigans," but the spirit possessing him exerted its protective powers just in time. "Have I been heard?" Michael asked.

Gaetano continued to stare at Rosalia. Then he turned slowly and looked at Michael. He's going to spit at me, Michael thought.

But he saw the young man's face. It appeared so helplessly bewildered that Michael was ashamed. The dark eyes were anguished; the lips, slightly parted, seemed about to ask a question, but without knowing what the question might be. The angle of black hair shot out straight above his forehead, trying to shield his face, to protect it in this unguarded state.

Michael felt obliged to continue, if for no other reason than to cover his shame. "Please, Gaetano," he heard himself plead. "Come with me, with your uncle Michele." Never had Michael heard himself so humbled. He meant what he was saying. "Can you do that? Come with me, with your uncle? With Don Michele?"

Gaetano drew himself up, then slowly shook his head from side to side, not in refusal but in sorrow and in pain. Michael expected the young man to moan, to keen, but instead, as if dismissing the words as hopeless even as he spoke them, he said, "Oh, Uncle, Uncle! Help me. Please. Don't let this happen to me. Don't let this happen to my brother. Or to my *fidanzata,* Rosalia. Help us. Tell them I am supposed to marry Rosalia. She is engaged to *me*. Peppino mustn't marry her. She mustn't marry Peppino. You can help us. Take Peppino with you into the pew. Let *him* bear solemn witness. It will be terrible if he doesn't. Please. Don Michele. Uncle. Help me."

Tears had come into his voice. Michael stepped toward him, but before he could make another move, a curdled scream bumbled and rolled through the sanctuary. It was Rosalia, and for a moment it seemed as though Michael's advance toward Gaetano had given rise to the screech that was still finding its way into the great beams above the nave. Then he saw what had happened. Peppino had fainted dead away and was lying in a heap, with his handsome head cushioned on the kneeler.

"Rosalia!" Gaetano reached toward her, but his mother's cane, coming down swiftly like a drawn sword, stopped his hand.

"No!" she said. Then, with equal vehemence, she turned to her other son, who lay unmoving. "Peppino, get up. Rosalia, fix your veil. Fra Callisto, continue."

Gaetano turned to Michael. "Uncle . . . Uncle . . . ," he

whispered, then rushed from the sanctuary and headed up the main aisle.

"Don Michele, go after him. Keep him out."

Michael began to protest, to proclaim his inadequacy, to petition for release from the role of uncle, but the Signora continued. "He must not come back. See to it."

And because he was too confused to find the words of refusal, he obeyed. As he strode between the two witnesses, they quickly righted themselves, brought to attention by the passage of so important a person.

Far in the back of the church, in front of the fragment of an ancient fresco showing the faces of some anguished saints, Gaetano had dropped to his knees. His head was bowed. Michael stopped about fifteen feet away, then started toward him again. At the sound of his step, Gaetano jumped up and dashed out the center portal.

In the great doorway, Michael gave a backward glance, as if hoping for further instruction. He saw that Peppino had been restored to consciousness and was seated on his gilded chair. Rosalia's head was tilted upward as before, and Fra Callisto, from the distance, seemed to be continuing his homily to the young and blissful couple, oblivious that any interruption had taken place.

The only change of scene was provided by Signora Spacagna. Just to the side and slightly behind the groom and bride she stood, her cane gripped firmly in her fist, a sentinel and a guard over the marriage of her younger son, Peppino Spacagna, to the dark and radiant Rosalia Attanese.

2

Michael came out of the church just in time to see Gaetano round the corner near the bell tower. He followed, not rushing, not even certain he wanted to continue his participation. He certainly had no intention of pursuing the young man through the narrow cobblestoned *vicoletti,* streets no more than two strides wide, which he'd heard referred to as the *"budella di Napoli,"* the entrails of Naples. All he had to do was make sure Gaetano didn't reenter the church. That had been Signora Spacagna's final order, and beyond that he'd need further direction.

When Michael turned the corner, he saw Gaetano enter a door set into a high stone wall. It could lead to another entry to the basilica, and Gaetano might be headed for it. Michael speeded his step along the broad paved area that ran alongside the church. He was only half aware that on a small raised plot of ground to his left, a group of boys, aged about ten and eleven, were kicking and battering their way through a game of soccer. Then the ball bounced in front of him, and a cry of *"Capo! Capo!"* caught his attention. "Chief! Chief!" was what they were saying, but it wasn't flattery at all. It was a kind of robust respect that had, implicit within it, the expectation that the ball would be returned—noblesse oblige—without their having to come and get it.

Michael very expertly slowed the ball with his toe and tipped it up just enough so he could give it the perfectly aimed kick that landed it in the exact middle of the playing area. Not for nothing had he lived in Italy during his student years. If his ambition to be a great and glorified leading tenor had been thwarted, he had at least a skilled and talented toe, trained on Italian soil.

The shouted *"Grazie!"* from the boys, who—the ultimate praise—showed absolutely no amazement at Michael's prowess, was quickly buried in the shouts and calls as the bumping and kicking resumed with no noticeable appreciation that they had been the beneficiaries of a skill Michael had long forgotten he possessed.

When Michael reached the door, he questioned again whether or not he should continue the role in which La Calefati had cast him. Suppose Gaetano *did* go back into the church. What could Michael do? Repeat the scene already played? No one, to his knowledge, had shouted *"Bis! Bis!"* And Michael was definitely not one of those singers who'd apparently had ear implants that allowed them to hear cries for an encore when no such call had been made. Then, too, anticlimax should be avoided at all costs. And what if the scene turned physical, even violent? Was he expected to overwhelm Gaetano with his superior strength? To wrestle him to the stone flags of the sanctuary? Gaetano, though hardly massive, was taller than Michael by half a head and seemed, especially in his tense and fevered state, to possess a strength and energy Michael couldn't hope to match.

Besides—and far more important—Michael was too busy, too involved elsewhere, for this distraction to be extended or intensified much further. Within two hours he had to be at a meeting to arrange for rehearsal space. His first purpose for being in Naples was not to sing the *comprimario* part of Spoletta at San

Carlo but to stage, sing in, and present to the people of Naples, in an Italian translation made by Michael himself, a production of Benjamin Britten's "Parable for Church Performance," *Curlew River*.

The project was, at the moment, even more precarious than his native anxiety had previously projected. The chapel already contracted for by the Santo Spirito Foundation—the estate, actually, of his Roman mentor, the great teacher of his student days, Ugo d'Alessio—was completely unsuitable. It was the Cappella Sansevero, a seventeenth-century funerary chapel, something of a mausoleum for the noble family descended from Duca Giovan Francesco Paolo de' Sangro, and right smack in the middle of what would be the playing area was *Il Cristo Velato, The Veiled Christ*. A work in marble, eight to ten feet long and at least four feet wide, it depicted exactly what it said it depicted, the marble body of the dead Christ shrouded by a thin veil, carved also in marble, through which one could see the features of the bearded face, the gash in the wounded side, the nail marks in the hands and feet. At its side lay the crown of thorns and the extracted nails, all in marble.

It was a ghostly presentation, more eerie, more unsettling than a completely exposed corpus could ever be. It suggested that the veil might stir at any moment, that the dead body could, as one looked on, begin the first few tremors shuddering through the bone-white flesh, that it would rise, still veiled, still not revealed as the resurrected God but seen only as a bewildered shade, a looming specter brushing against its whispering shroud.

Michael's dismay when he first saw the sculpture became complete after he realized that it could not be moved even if the necessary powers would allow it. It was secured to the stone floor with bolts that, in heresy, defied the rising on the third day. When he voiced his objection, Signor Crescenzo, the foundation's representative, mentioned the obvious: The chapel was small and the "Parable," after all, was something of a chamber opera, needing only seven musicians, four male soloists, a boy soprano, and a small chorus of monks. Also, the chapel was dedicated to the Virgin Mary of the Pietà, popularly known as *La Pietatella,* and the parable itself concerned a mother driven mad by the death of her son. Then, too, sarcophagi and memento mori lined the walls, and *Curlew River* dealt not only with loss and grief but with a promise of the resurrection. The spirit of the dead child appears to his maddened mother and restores her to sanity with the words "The dead shall rise again and in that blessed day we shall meet in Heaven."

In all these aspects, Signor Crescenzo claimed, Sansevero was most appropriate, and the foundation had, in its own way, displayed an informed sensitivity in its selection. Michael admitted all this was fine, but one fact remained: With the marble effigy hogging all the space, there was no room—he repeated the words: "no room"—for the performers. Signor Crescenzo assured him that the appointed designer, supported by artisans of Neapolitan skill, would *create* room. There was no need to worry. However, if Michael should continue his protest, it might be taken as a sign of bad faith toward the foundation and close to an insult to the Neapolitan genius for circumventing natural law, including that pertaining to space. It would have to be Sansevero or nothing.

Michael had considered withdrawing completely but couldn't quite bring himself to do it, to pick up his marbles and skulk back home. The project was to be something of a memorial to d'Alessio. Michael, as his pupil, had done a translation of the opera into Italian, with the youthfully exuberant notion that it could be performed by himself and some of his friends, with d'Alessio as the Madwoman. D'Alessio, even at that time, was long retired from performing after a career as one of the world's leading (if the word was not contradictory) *comprimari*. His Emperor in *Turandot* was legendary, and his Simpleton in *Godunov,* his demented bleatings that end the epic opera, were said to have competed in pathos with the death scene of Czar Boris himself.

D'Alessio was touched by his student's efforts, but before a production could be arranged, his arthritis made it all impossible, and that seemed to have been the end of *Curlew River*'s Italian career.

Then, less than a year before, the foundation had contacted Michael. Funds had been specified in d'Alessio's will for a performance of *Curlew River* in Michael's translation, with the further specification that Michael direct and sing the Madwoman himself. And the production was to be not in Rome but in Naples, the only city in the world, d'Alessio claimed, that really knew and appreciated music. Michael, without thinking, accepted. It would be an homage he was more than eager to pay. And he didn't exactly object to the idea of playing a lead part for a change.

Then, after Damian died, Michael had wondered whether it was coincidence, fate, or simple irony that he should be scheduled to do this opera about grief and mourning. It did pass through his mind that he'd been given a source for sorrow that he might use as the Madwoman, but considering his own "loss of loss," it wouldn't have worked. He would play a monk playing a madwoman, and his grief would be the actor's grief, the artist's grief, imagined and therefore as real as any grief that was ever known or felt.

When he opened the door set into the wall, Michael saw beyond it a paved space that looked like an enclosed parking lot but without the requisite cars. Gaetano was nowhere in sight. But there, to Michael's right, was another door.

He opened it and found himself in a small shop where religious books and pamphlets were sold. Gaetano wasn't there, and Michael considered asking if he'd passed through, but he didn't want to waste any more time. Straight ahead was another doorway. As Michael pushed it open, he half expected to find himself facing the congregation gathered for the wedding. Instead, he was in a large and spacious cloister, the size of an Indiana acre. The sudden quiet made him stop short, not so much to look around for Gaetano as to allow himself, his inner and outer being, to acclimate, to equalize itself to the absolute stillness. If he'd rushed ahead, surely he would have been attacked with some spiritual equivalent of the bends. Peace was here, an almost palpable presence that not even Michael's pursuit of Gaetano could disrupt.

Nor, Michael also realized when he'd looked around some more, could the cloister's peace be canceled by the partial disarray he saw around him. Half of the area had been closed off with chicken wire. It was *in restauro*—in restoration—though Michael often thought when he saw the phrase, one of the more ubiquitous in Italy, that it really meant "taking a rest." In the part not caged with wire, there was a deep trench along the church side, with the makings of a terra-cotta water conduit stacked nearby. The trellises that supported the grapevines were rusted, and, this being March, the vines themselves were still a hoary interweaving of frayed ropes, the ancient bark peeling away in tatters as if it had been burned by a black sun.

The gardens, set off in squares, had been dug up and a crudely lettered sign stabbed into the loosened ground: ATTENZIONE. TERRENO TRATTO CON VELENO. Attention—or, more likely: Beware. Earth treated with poison. A few clumps of shrubbery, weary from the winter, gave some indication of the garden this was intended to be, and here and there an orange tree, a little spindly, with early spring oranges the size of apricots, suggested most strongly of all a failed Eden where no temptation had ever taken place.

Yet in spite of the disarray and the drab sky overhead, sunlight was somewhere present. Another glance cleared up the mystery. The wide stone-paved walkways between the elevated plots of turned earth were walled to a height of about three feet with shining tiles, like pieces of mosaic really, forming scenes that celebrated the bounty of the earth: flowers and fruit, men, women, animals, set in scapes of field, mountain, and sea. The people fished, they played at *bocce,* they rode donkeys, they looked out of windows and out of doors. The colors were varying shades of gold and blue, as if the tiles were fallen bits of sun and sky collected by some faithful hand and placed here, comfortably, confidently, near the center of a city as driven as Naples, a needed antidote to the poisoned earth.

Michael had almost forgotten he was there to search for Gaetano, but then a small group of students came down the center walkway, notebooks and sketchbooks clasped with curled fingers at their sides. They turned into the arcade where he was standing. A brown-sweatered teenage boy purposely bumped into a girl wearing a sweatshirt on which was printed, in English, Rugby Team of Ohio, Members Only. A girl with thick glasses, speaking in Neapolitan dialect, which Michael could barely comprehend, was instructing a boy with even thicker glasses in the specifics of something archaeological. A lone teenager was scribbling in his notebook even as he walked past Michael, knocking him with his elbow, all unaware.

Michael waded through the rest of the class as it straggled toward him, about seven more students in all, until he came to the walkway that bisected the cloister. He started down the path that ran perpendicular to the arcade, heading straight for the chicken wire, certain by now that he'd lost Gaetano for good. There was probably another doorway, which Michael hadn't seen. Gaetano was at this very moment probably in the church, tormenting Peppino, Rosalia, his mother, Fra Callisto, and, most of all, himself.

Then Michael saw him, Gaetano, sitting on a tiled bench halfway toward the far wall of the cloister. He seemed to be tracing with his eyes the route the grapevines were traveling from one overhead trellis to the next. Slowly his upturned head moved to his right, then, looking higher, he moved it back to his left.

The angle of black hair, exempted from gravitational pull, slanted upward like the visor of a baseball cap. Gaetano, it seemed, would always view the world through shaded eyes. His elbows were resting on the top of the low wall behind him, and he looked like a man completely at ease. Maybe the worst was over.

Michael considered leaving him as he was. The quiet of the cloister had seemingly stilled even Gaetano's troubled heart, and perhaps Michael should consider this the end of his adventure. The cloister had done his work for him; Gaetano's torment had left him. The young man obviously had no intention of going back into the church; he was hardly the man to bother anyone. Michael started to turn toward the arcade that led back to the entrance.

"Why do you live in Rome? It's such a filthy place."

So completely was the stillness broken by this soft-spoken question that Michael couldn't tell at first who might have said the words or where they came from. They could have come from a stone or from a tree, or from Santa Chiara herself, speaking gently from beyond the sky. When he looked down the walkway at Gaetano, the young man was turned toward him, his elbows still resting on the wall that backed the bench, the expression on his face not one of challenge or disgust but one of genuine perplexity. Implicit in the tone and inflection of the slightly accented Italian—Gaetano had no doubt been taught modern Italian in school, a second language to his native dialect—implicit was the notion that he, Michael, was too good for Rome and that if one could only understand his reasons for living there, one would have solved a seemingly insoluble puzzle and come perhaps to a valuable wisdom.

How should Michael answer? He didn't know why he lived in Rome, since he didn't live there. He couldn't give his reason from the old days, that he was studying voice. He was a little too old to be a student still. Perhaps it was time to reveal his true identity, to wish Gaetano well and go on his way. It might even cheer the young man to know that he'd participated in a *commedia,* that the scene in church, for all its obvious drama, was really part of a game. Gaetano might even smile; he might enjoy having been fooled. He would offer Michael congratulations on his abilities and thank him for getting him out of the church before he'd made an even greater fool of himself.

"I was so ashamed to hear you came from Rome. You— my uncle I never met before. I was so ashamed, I was glad I had to leave the church."

So completely startled was Michael by the very idea of what Gaetano had said that he answered without thinking: "What's wrong with Rome?"—a leading question if ever there was one.

"It's dirty. In the streets, under the bridges, in the piazzas, there's garbage everywhere. And the Romans, they don't wash, they don't even have bathtubs or showers. And then, with their dirty hands, they steal. How many times have you been robbed? They're thieves, all of them. Cutthroats. And the whole city is run by drug dealers. Cocaine is sold in the confessionals at the Vatican. But you know that. And the stink, how can you stand it? They don't even have the sea to clean the air. They have a river that's a sewer, and the dead fish make the stink even worse. How can you live there? Aren't you afraid? Aren't you ashamed?"

Gaetano, of course, had just accused Rome of all the faults of which a Roman, his equal in ignorance, accuses Naples. Michael thought of throwing it all right back at Gaetano: He lived in Rome because Naples was filthy and all Neapolitans thieves. He was, after all, something of a Roman. He'd lived there and been happy as a student. He had his allegiances. But then, he also had his affinity, however wary, for Naples. And both cities, Naples and Rome, were certainly less dirty and less smelly than New York, the one city that claimed his loyalty more than any other, including Indianapolis. So he decided neither to attack nor to defend.

"But Rome," Michael said, "is where I've lived almost all my life."

Immediately—even as the words were being spoken—he realized that were this an opera, he would now launch into the famous first-act aria *"Roma, Sempre Mia Città,"* known among the knowing as "The *Sempre Mia.*" It would celebrate not the monuments and the grandeurs but the simple sights and daily doings. It would tell of first love, young struggles, old yearnings, and lost happiness. Then, in climax, the aria would rise to a paean of praise: Rome, the eternal city, because love is eternal. Rome will never die because the love found there will never die. Let conquerors and calamities come, the triumph will be forever his, the tenor's. And Rome's. And love's.

A high C, maybe two. Applause and shouts that flake the paint from the walls. Tears. A humble bow, the tenor almost too moved by both aria and audience to continue the scene. But he does. Brave tenor. Commendable tenor. Tenor immortal and—yes—eternal.

But in its stead Michael settled for a slightly apologetic telling of the backup story concocted by La Calefati. Some facts, he told Gaetano, were unknown even to his mother, some were too painful to be recalled or repeated. But—and here Michael managed to work in a little melancholy, a little fatalism that proved he was Neapolitan born—he accepted Rome as his own, and Gaetano must not scorn him for his misfortune.

When he finished, Michael became aware that he had—it was unavoidable under the circumstances—performed a passable aria after all, and from Gaetano's response, he knew it was not without effect. The young man said nothing, his silence indicating that his disdain had been revoked and no more accusations would be made.

This bewildered Michael. Why was Gaetano so accepting of his lies? Why hadn't he challenged him, found him out, forced him to tell the truth? Why, in fact, did he believe Michael was his uncle? Gullibility was not known to be a Neapolitan trait, yet here was Gaetano, calmed, even chastened by the sentimental melodrama Michael had just spoken. He searched the young man's face for some hint of doubt, the beginnings of a skepticism that would end with accusation, scorn, and who could guess what else. But Gaetano was merely thoughtful, even meditative, as if still taking to himself all that Michael had said, making it his own, a part of his genetic memory.

Surely now would be the time to leave, to let the drama end, and quietly. Michael allowed himself one more look at his nephew, at the eyes, fierce even in repose, and the splayed shock of sprung black hair that seemed the eruption from a brain uncomprehending and unheeding. Gaetano was contemplating the tiles across the walkway, as if looking for some detail he couldn't find, resigned already to the failure of his search.

Before Michael could make a clean break toward the arcade, Gaetano raised his head to point with his chin at the tiled scene he'd been studying. "When we were kids," he said, "Peppino and I used to say that would be us when we grew up."

Michael looked over and saw a blue sky that modulated to a pale yellow, two men under a tree, a wide and quiet valley between two peaceful cliffs. Each cliff was topped by an ancient and comfortable house, and in the distance, two small towns, each on its own blue hill, seemed about to meet on the lower slopes. One man was sitting on the ground, the other standing, supported by a stick that served as a crutch. Their backs to the viewer, they were looking toward the higher of the two hill towns, the man with the crutch pointing off in the opposite direction, into some unseen valley in the distance.

"You and Peppino? One of them has a crutch."

"I know," Gaetano said. "Sometimes I was the wounded one, sometimes it was Peppino."

"Wounded?"

"We're coming home from the war. We've just beaten the Saracens. Or the Amalfitani. We've walked a long way, and now we see Naples and we're pointing to it. We know, from all the trees, that we're almost home."

"The trees? The orange groves, the olive trees, outside the city?"

"Oh, no. The trees of Naples. We know it's Naples because of all the trees."

Naples, in Michael's mind, was one stone-paved street after another. "Trees," he said. "In Naples?"

"Yes. You know. The trees along Corso Umberto. The trees in Via Duomo."

"Oh. *Those* trees. It's *those* trees you can see." Now Michael could recall the trees lining those particular avenues, their leaves showing all the exhaustion they must feel from having had to hang there all winter, the Neapolitan sun too stubborn to retreat and allow them a graceful autumnal fall to the ground.

"And San Martino—we can see the trees of San Martino and the trees of Capodimonte. Everywhere we see the trees. The trees here in the cloister. The trees of Piazza Cavour, Via Caracciolo, the Villa Comunale, and the Palazzo Real. From the trees, we know we're almost home."

Why the simple sight of Vesuvio didn't tell them where they were, Michael would never know. Let it be, then, as Gaetano had just said. It was the trees, the precious exhausted trees, that proclaimed the nearness of Naples. So be it, Michael thought. Naples, the City of Trees.

But before Michael could voice his acceptance, he heard Gaetano say, "Now I have to kill Peppino."

Michael parted his lips to say some words not yet decided upon, but Gaetano had leapt up and gone to the bench opposite. He knelt one leg on the tiled seat and, with his right hand, scooped up a fistful of the poisoned dirt and shoved it into his mouth.

"Gaetano!"

Gaetano worked his jaw, chewing up and down. Michael, now at his side, began to hit him on the back, not to save his life but to punish him for scaring his uncle. Gaetano bent forward, opened his mouth, and let the dirt flop out onto the walkway.

After spitting three times, he clawed his tongue with his fingers, then spit again, twice.

Michael straightened him up, turned him toward himself, and said, "Open your mouth! Let me see!" Gaetano opened his mouth. Crumbs of earth flecked his tongue and his teeth. "We have to get you some water to rinse you out."

Gaetano closed his mouth and swallowed. "The ground, it tastes like last week's fish oil." He shuddered through his whole body, spit again, then swallowed.

Michael looked around. There was a fountain down the walkway, the sound of water splashing into water. He took Gaetano by the arm, but he pulled himself free.

"Rosalia is mine. She is engaged to me. It's me she has to marry. Me!" With the side of his fist, he beat his chest, then he reached out both hands, the thumbs and first fingers touching, shaking them loosely from the wrist as if he had touched something hot and was trying to cool himself off. "She is mine. Can't anyone understand? And Peppino, who is he?" With that, Gaetano bent his legs at the knees, making himself seem bowlegged. He opened his hands wide, fingers spread, and brought them down to his thighs. Then, thrusting his pelvis forward, he framed his crotch with his hands and said, "Who is he? Eh? Who is he?" Up the hands came again, again the touching thumbs and fingers, again the loose shaking from the wrists. "He took her because she is mine." Bringing both hands together, he touched one palm against the other in a position of prayer and, pointing them toward Michael, moved them up and down. "Rosalia knows this is wrong. Why did she do this to me?"

He swung around and dug his hands into the dirt. As he was raising yet another fistful to his opened mouth, Michael knocked against his arm, sending the dirt down onto the bench in front of them. Gaetano swung back toward Michael, but not to return the blow. He put his forehead on Michael's shoulder. "Don Michele, you are Spacagna. What am I going to do?"

Over Gaetano's shoulder, Michael could see a man seated where the two pathways crossed. He was reading the morning paper, *Il Mattino*. Though close enough for Michael to see a photograph of two soccer players on the front page, the man didn't seem to notice Gaetano's display. He simply turned the page and looked even more casually at what he was reading.

Michael placed his hand on Gaetano's back. Slowly the young man drew away, then reached up and put his hands on Michael's cheeks. "Peppino raped her," he said softly. "That's why she has to marry him and not me." He took his hands away and put them in the prayer position again. He looked directly at Michael. "He raped her," he said, his head straining forward a little so he wouldn't have to say the words too loudly.

Gaetano's eyes were wet now and shining. The lashes were tangled, some stuck together, others pointing in varying directions. It would take a comb to force them back to where they belonged.

"You need to rinse with some water," Michael said. "Your mouth. Before you swallow any more of the poison." He'd deal with the poison now. What Gaetano had said about killing his brother, about rape, were surely Neapolitan exaggerations, the threat and accusation of a rejected suitor. He'd deal with all that later or possibly never. Perhaps he'd just ignore, forget, what Gaetano had just said, a courtesy to a man not responsible for what he was saying.

They went to the fountain, a huge basin spouting an arc of water two feet into the air, filling the pool at its base. "Take some into your mouth, rinse around, then spit it out. Like mouthwash. Keep doing it."

Gaetano bent over and repeatedly scooped water into his mouth, rinsed it, then spit the water onto the walkway, careful not to pollute the pool. Finally, he gargled deep in his throat, then spat that out and wiped his mouth with the palm of his hand.

"I don't know when I will kill him or how I will kill him, but I know I'll have to do it, and before too long."

"You're not going to kill him," Michael said. He was tempted to put a firm uncle's hand on Gaetano's shoulder, but considered the gesture too trivial. Instead he bent down and scooped up some water for himself. As he felt the water pass his lips and flood his mouth, he sensed that a bond was being forged between himself and Gaetano, that the shared drink from the fountain's flow might unite them in some silent way. An unspoken pledge could be made. All Michael had to do was swallow the water, and the bond, the pledge, would become indissoluble. Perhaps he would become, in truth, Gaetano's uncle. Perhaps the water would change into blood, and they would be joined by a common lineage that could never be denied.

Michael spit the water out. "The poison from the ground —it's in the water too," he gasped.

"You think so?"

"Couldn't you taste it? Isn't that how the dirt tasted?"

"No. Not at all. Taste the dirt. You'll see. They don't taste the same at all." Gaetano dipped into the pool and put his fingers on his tongue, then licked his lips, frowning thoughtfully as if he were testing soup for the proper flavoring. After he'd done this a second time, he said, "It tastes the same as it's always tasted, all my life."

Michael wanted to believe that his own mouth wasn't coated with poison, but he couldn't quite convince himself. He wrinkled his face and kept scraping his tongue against his teeth. Gaetano laughed. "The water's very good," he said. "Watch."

He stooped, put his face into the pool, and began lapping the water like a dog. Then he stood up, still laughing, the water dripping from his chin down onto his jacket and shirt. "You want to see me do it again?"

He began to stoop, but when Michael said, "No, I believe you," Gaetano settled for another quick dip of the fingers and another thoughtful taste.

"Then go ahead," he said. "You were thirsty."

"No, it's all right. I'm not really that thirsty."

"Yes, you are. Drink. Then you'll know it's not poisoned."

Michael scooped up a handful of water, letting as much drip through his fingers as possible without it being noticed, then clapped the palm of his hand over his mouth and made a few swallowing sounds in his throat. It still tasted like poison.

Gaetano watched, waiting until after he'd swallowed, then said in the quiet voice Michael had heard before, "After Peppino raped Rosalia and he told Mamma what he'd done, it was Mamma who made them get married. First she asked me if I had ever been with Rosalia, and when I said no, never, not really, that's when she said Rosalia must marry Peppino. If I were to marry Rosalia, Peppino, whenever we were together with her —Peppino, Rosalia, and me—he would sit there and Rosalia would sit there and I would sit there, and all three of us would know that Peppino knew what it was like to be with my wife. Mamma said I would get over my feelings for Rosalia, but Peppino's knowing what it's like to be with her, that would never change. So I must agree to their getting married."

"But you didn't agree."

"Oh, I did. But first I jumped out the window. Just to make my mother scream. She did. She screamed." This fact, it seemed, was the most mournful of all.

"You weren't hurt?"

Gaetano shrugged. "We're on the second floor. But I almost ruined myself when I hit the clothesline. That hurt for a while, but it's gone now."

"Well, maybe your mother's right. Maybe you'll get over it after a while. You probably don't think so, but you will."

Gaetano shook his head. "I will never get over it. Because how will I forget that I killed my brother?"

"You won't kill him. You probably want to—"

"No. I don't want to. But I have to. He knows that. He's waiting for me to do it. It makes him nervous."

"But if you don't really want to do it—"

"He raped my *fidanzata*. Now he's married to her. To Rosalia. Rosalia . . . !" He put his open hands against his stomach. "Oh, *Zio*. It does something to my stomach. Something is alive in there. It keeps tickling me until it hurts, but it won't stop. I want to shit it out, but I know it will still be there. I want it to move into my cock, so it can turn all hard and stop the tickling, and I could use my hand and shoot it all out. But I do shoot. I shoot and I shoot, three times, four times, one right after the other, and it's still there, in my stomach. When I get home now, I'll shoot right away. I have to. Two times, three times. Four times. I can't stop. I eat. I work. But before I finish eating, I have to get up from the table and go shoot. At work, I have to go shoot, in the toilet. Once, when I was under a car, in the garage, working, I stopped and made myself shoot up onto the axle. No matter what I'm doing, I try to get rid of it. But it's there. Here." He punched his stomach three times, grunting each time his fist hit. Then he sucked in his breath. "*I* will rape Rosalia! This thing in my stomach, I'll pass it into her. She'll be pregnant. And it'll be my kid that's born. And someday when Peppino thinks I've come to kill him, I'll tell him what I did. I raped his wife and got her pregnant. And then see what he does." He shook his head. "He won't do anything. And poor Rosalia. How could I do that to her. She's my *fidanzata*. I love her. I would protect her with my life."

Gaetano slumped down onto a bench and jammed his fists into his pockets. Michael looked down at him. Gaetano made some snorting sounds through his nose as if, quite literally, he was letting off steam. Michael sat down next to him, leaning forward a little, his hands folded between his knees. He watched the water plop down into the basin, uneven spurts like an uncertain rain, as if some distracted cloud couldn't quite control its own release.

He wanted to help. He wanted to offer comfort and ad-

monition. He wanted to be sympathetic. Slowly, he started to
sit up straight so he could reach a hand over and put it on Gaetano's shoulder. But if he did, would he be accepting a contin-
uation of himself in the role of uncle?

Now Michael was sitting up straight. He reached his hand
over and put it on Gaetano's shoulder. He'd accepted the part.
This touch was his contract, as good as his bond.

"Yes," Gaetano said.

Michael didn't look at him. He waited, then said, "Yes? Yes,
what?"

Gaetano stood up. Michael let his hand suspend itself in the
air a moment, then slowly drew it back to his side. He, too,
stood up. Gaetano was looking again along the grapevines overhead, this time not to trace their ancient twistings through the
rusted trellis, it seemed, but to marvel at their simple existence,
their presence just a few feet above him. "I'm going to kill my
brother," he said, his voice hushed as if he'd been given a revelation that had left him awed and sorrowful. He turned and
started down the walkway toward the path that led to the arcade.

Michael followed, but not too fast. When Gaetano stopped
just before the turn toward the arcade and looked at the tiled
scene of himself and Peppino coming home from the wars, Michael had no choice but to catch up. He looked at the scene: the
hills, the houses, the two men, the wounded brother pointing
toward the unseen distant trees of Naples.

"Today," Michael asked, "which one is you?"

"I don't know," Gaetano said. "Without Peppino here for
us to fight about it, I can't tell."

They looked for another moment. "Don't kill your
brother," Michael said. "He's my nephew."

Gaetano lifted his arm and placed it along Michael's shoulder. Together, not talking, they reached the arcade and turned
toward the entry. On the gray wall beneath the faded frescoes
was a small framed notice, and Michael, as if he wanted to read

what it said, stopped and turned toward Gaetano. "Did you hear what I just said?"

Gaetano didn't answer. Instead he read the notice fixed to the wall. Michael leaned forward to see what it said:

SE PENSATE DI PASSARE ALLA STORIA SCRIVENDO IL VOSTRO NOME SU QUESTO MURO VI SBAGLIATE, SARÀ CANCELLATO AL PIÙ PRESTO. If you think you will pass into history by writing your name on this wall, you are mistaken. It will be erased more quickly than quick.

While Michael was reading, Gaetano went over to one of the signs warning of the poisoned earth and found a stone. Holding it firmly in his hand, he scratched "Peppino" into the wall, then held out the stone to Michael.

"Go ahead. Write a name. Yours. Why not? Don't worry. It'll be erased."

Michael accepted the stone. Gaetano kissed him on each cheek, respectfully, almost solemnly, smiled a rather wan smile, then turned, walked toward the exit, and was gone. As Michael looked down at the stone in his hand, a brown-robed friar came into the cloister. Michael had thought to scratch the name Gaetano into the wall, next to that of his brother, but he dropped the stone into his pocket instead and started toward the exit. The friar, as they passed each other, cast a sideways glance at Michael, but neither spoke or nodded. Just as Michael was going through the door, out of the cloister, he heard the friar's voice. "Peppino! Peppino! Shame on you, Peppino! Shame! Shame!"

And before the door had closed behind him, Michael felt and accepted the shame. He was, presumably, part of the family.

3

The rehearsal hall was like the interior of a giant cube, the ceiling as high as the walls were long. Used usually for ballet classes, it seemed to have gone to something of an extreme in its anticipation of the dancers' leaps and elevations. The room wasn't freezing, but it was cold enough for Michael to keep wiggling his fingers as he talked, rubbing them into his palms, making fist after fist, then splaying the fingers outward as if preparing for a piano recital instead of an opera rehearsal. What made the room seem even colder, almost glacial, was a mirror, about ten feet high, reaching from wall to wall. This made for an additional difficulty. The men he'd been given by the foundation for his production of *Curlew River* kept looking not at him but at the mirror behind him. This in turn caused them to constantly adjust themselves, moving strands of hair from one side of the forehead to the other, checking profiles, scratching the tip of a nose, rubbing a chin, rearranging their crotches. One of the baritones kept drawing himself up, then slouching, to see which was the more flattering posture. A bass kept puckering his lips as if, could he have his way, he would reach them across the room and give himself a great big kiss.

Michael could change the seating, a collection of kitchen chairs and what looked like an army cot covered with an Italian flag so old it still had the coat of arms of the deposed monarchy on the field of white, but he didn't want them to know he was aware of, much less bothered by, their rampant narcissism.

And he could hardly blame them for looking at themselves. They were extremely interesting, collectively as well as individually. All the conquerors, colonizers, traders, and travelers from the north, the south, the east, and the west seemed to have left behind some small deposit in the genetic pool of Naples, and its flowering at its most various faced him now. True, there were more black- and brown-haired singers than blond, and there were no towheads in the room, but still, there was a redhead—a bass—and the man cast in the part of the Abbot was black, a second-generation Neapolitan from Ethiopia. Expecting the short, dark Neapolitan of Greek origin—Naples took its name from the Greek *Neapolis,* New City—the kind that provided Indianapolis with its Italian stereotype, Michael had been surprised and a little disappointed on each visit to find that Naples provided not much in the way of human presentation that wasn't readily available in New York or any other fair-sized American city. If he wanted to see the "real" Neapolitan, he'd perhaps have to go to Cumae or to Athens—or to Our Lady of Pompeii in Indianapolis.

"Let's go once more through 'Birds of the Fenland'—first the pilgrims, then the Ferryman and the Traveller, then everyone including the Abbot. Begin."

Michael nodded to Signor Zongola, at the harmonium; he gave the musical lead-in, and they all began to sing. Michael could hardly believe his ears. This is what he had come to Naples to hear. As if they'd been rehearsing for weeks instead of not more than an hour, the voices blended, separated, made their harmonies and their entries almost, if not quite, on cue.

Michael detected only one problem. A tenor, one of the pilgrims, had a voice so pure, so effortless, that he tended to rise up above the others, to sound too much like a soloist. Several times, Michael had indicated *meno voce,* and the young man would, after a quick self-critical grimace, all but fall silent, clearly both pleased and embarrassed by his singularity. Michael would then motion him to bring the voice up a bit, and the young man would oblige. For a time anyway. Then the old enthrallment would assert itself again, and there he'd be, floating up and above everyone, the perennial lark ascending. Now, however, he seemed to have settled in perfectly. He was one pilgrim among seven, crossing the Curlew River.

> Ferryman, she begs of you
> to let her come aboard.

In Michael's translation:

> *Traghettatore, ti prega*
> *Lasciarla imbarcar.*

Michael was elated. He began to believe that his enterprise, his homage to d'Alessio, might actually be a success. That morning, Crescenzo had shown him the set design, and even though it clearly assumed space that didn't exist in Cappella Sansevero, Michael would just proceed on the same assumption. His one hope was that Neapolitan indifference to reality drew upon a wisdom unavailable to the rest of mankind and that, in the end, the special blessings given to Neapolitan optimism would be extended to include the skeptical Irish-American who had presumed to challenge Neapolitan certainties. Naples, apparently, had been dispensed from the laws of logic and physics and engineering, and who was Michael to contradict divine favor? He was prepared to give the opera all he had—and more, if it could be found.

There was, however, the continuing and not unwelcome distraction of his role as uncle. He'd done what he'd said he wouldn't: He'd taken on Neapolitan complexities, including rape, marriage, and possible fratricide—and in a somewhat intimate way. The complexities, of course, made the role all the more attractive, at the same time offering full warning that he was ill prepared for these particular intensities and ill advised to encourage himself in any deepening participation. Which made them all the more intriguing, all the more inviting. Every reason he gave himself to suggest his withdrawal only confirmed him that much more completely in his commitment.

Here was a part he could hardly refuse. High drama touching the several fates of that most self-dramatizing breed, the Neapolitan. That tragedy, *true* tragedy, might be the outcome was considered, and Michael warned himself to be more genuinely apprehensive, but it did little good. He wanted the drama, he wanted the role, he wanted this rare chance to insinuate himself into Neapolitan life—which, by definition, would be life at its most tribal and its most intense. And if tragedy was to be the result, it pleased him, it flattered him, it inflated him, to find himself, if not at the center, at least at the near periphery of so important and so devastating an event.

Fortunately or unfortunately, the drama seemed to be in intermission for the moment. Michael had phoned the Signora to warn her of Gaetano's plans for his brother, but no one ever answered. Then Calefati told him Assunta had gone to see her sister in Caserta and would return the following week, the same day Peppino and Rosalia would be coming back from their brief honeymoon in Sorrento.

Eager to proceed, even without the main characters, Michael had phoned Fra Callisto, the priestly cousin who'd presided at the wedding. The priest, of course, would know who he really was, but Michael could still inform him of the family difficulties and beg his advice, hoping the two of them could become co-conspirators in search of a solution to the problems at hand.

On Tuesday he'd meet with the good friar—who'd been too busy to talk at any length on the phone—but their meeting, at the ungodly hour of eight-thirty in the morning, would probably get the drama moving again. Of course, the priest would be busy then too, so busy, in fact, that the only appointment he could give Michael was during his assigned duty in the confession. No other time was available. Absolutely none. But Michael could come then, present himself as just another penitent, and the two of them could talk. The priest promised to give him as much attention as he could, as much as he'd give any other sinner, and Michael agreed. He hoped that by ten o'clock on Tuesday he could tell La Calefati, at that day's rehearsal of *Tosca*, that he was doing very nicely indeed in the part she'd given him.

His report to the soprano about the wedding itself had gone rather well. He'd minimized Gaetano's intrusion, as a silliness more than a threat, and said nothing at all about either Peppino's precarious hold on life or the role Fra Callisto would assume on Tuesday. Aganice was so grateful that in the rehearsal for the second act, she suggested a bit of business involving Michael's character, the henchman Spoletta, that would heighten his presence in the scene. In a production of *Tosca* she'd sung in some German town or other, Scarpia, the villain, hearing that the escaped prisoner, Angelotti, hadn't been found, had picked Spoletta right up off the floor, and as he sang the words *"Ah, cane! Ah, traditore!"*—Ah, dog! Ah, traitor!—he'd flung him five feet across the room. This would land Spoletta on his stomach, and he could scream his *"Gesù!"* from there, then crawl, trembling and hurt, during his *"C'era il pittore . . ."* In other words, Michael's reward was to be picked up and thrown down. He liked it. And so did the Scarpia. Michael was being more than satisfactorily compensated for his Santa Chiara performance.

There had been one problem, however, and a lot of rehearsal time was spent solving it. The director, a staff member assigned to stage faithfully a *Tosca* previously set by a more celebrated regisseur, said it couldn't be done.

"But I can do it," said Enzo Darida, the Scarpia. "Watch." With that, he raised Michael up by the front of his sweater and flung him five feet away. Michael obligingly landed on his stomach. Before the director, Attila Rigutti, could object, Michael immediately went into his *"Ei sa dove"*—He knows where—giving his four lines all they were worth, from terror and rage to the triumphant *"ch'io lo trassi in arresto!"*—that I arrested him! The opera, for that moment, would be his. It was a minor *"Vissi d'arte,"* and he was prepared to weep if that would guarantee its inclusion.

"But then what will Tosca do for her '*Vissi d'arte*'?" Rigutti asked. "Scarpia lurches at her, she stumbles, falls, and sings the aria on her stomach. We can't do both on the stomach. And '*Vissi d'arte*' is, I think you'll all agree, a more important moment."

"But I do not do '*Vissi d'arte*' on my stomach," Calefati said.

"You do. In your desperation to escape, you stumble, you fall, and you sing on your stomach."

"I do not do '*Vissi d'arte*' on my stomach. I do *nothing* on my stomach."

"But it is the way it must be done."

"No!" Calefati pulled herself in, drew herself up, and said, "I will show you how *I* do '*Vissi d'arte*.' I, and no one else." She turned to Darida. "Scarpia reaches for me. And yes, I do stumble. Darida, reach for me."

Darida, who apparently saw Scarpia as something of the athletic type, made a lunge for her, forcing her to rear back, turn away, and, finally, stumble. Calefati stretched out a hand to steady herself, then quickly drew herself back, keeping her arm outstretched.

"There is a crucifix there," she said. "The one I put on his corpse after I stab him. But now I see it for the first time. It is the sight of the crucifix that gives me the motive for my prayer, for '*Vissi d'arte*,' not a bumping on my stomach. My back is to the house. I begin." She began singing phrases of the aria. "Here I kneel." She sang more phrases. "Then, to give my prayer even more emphasis, I rise." Slowly rising from her knees, she continued the phrasing. "Then, humbled by my prayer, I turn myself away from the crucifix, unworthy but pleading all the more. Now I am facing front. I finish, my eyes downcast, submissive to heaven's decree. And there you have my '*Vissi d'arte.*' "

"*Brava!*" Darida began to applaud. Both Michael and Nunzio Cappozolli, who would be singing Scarpia's other henchman, Sciarrone, joined in.

"But I am here," Rigutti said, "for the specific purpose of telling you that '*Vissi d'arte*' is from the stomach. And at San Carlo, if you keep your back to the house too long, someone will shout and tell you to turn around so he can see you sing. Then the shushing will start, then more shouting and *more* shushing. The whole aria will be lost."

"But, Rigutti," Calefati was pleading, "how many times has '*Vissi d'arte*' made sense to you in the opera? Why does Tosca pick that moment to pray? This beast here is about to do beastly things to her. She sings the aria because she is the *diva* and it's time for her second-act show-stopper. On her stomach is all right, but it's been done. I saw it in Rome, I saw it in Paris, I saw it in Liguria, for God's sake. Let's try something new."

"But, *tesoro,*" Rigutti said—and the battle was joined. First Calefati smiled and touched Rigutti's ear, then she used a straightforward, commonsense approach, and from there to a piteous pleading, then on to a towering rage, then to a frighteningly cold denunciation that would end, Michael was sure, with Aganice Calefati taking Attila Rigutti in her hands and breaking him in two over her right knee. The pieces would then be tossed aside, and she would do "*Vissi d'arte*" the way she'd always known she would do it.

Rigutti himself was no slouch in the A-to-Z emotional gamut department. He was, in turn, condescending, authoritative, flustered, insulted, and, finally, suppliant—telling Calefati what would happen to him when the famous regisseur saw that his instructions had not been faithfully enforced. The implication was that he would be caned within an inch of his life, and he begged that this not be allowed to happen, for his sake, for his wife's sake, and for the sake of his seven children.

Darida broke the impasse by saying, "We'll try it, and if it doesn't work we'll go back to the stomach." Then, without giving Rigutti a chance to enter yet another plea, he started his declamation "*Ella verrà, per amor del suo Mario*"—She will come, for love of her Mario—and continued to Sciarrone's, then Spoletta's entrance. Very much in the spirit of things, Darida lifted Michael up and threw him down. Michael began his "aria," all four lines of it, trembling and giddy, not so much out of fear of Scarpia as in dread that his moment might be taken from him.

By the end of rehearsal, Calefati had sung her "*Vissi d'arte*" to the crucifix, and Michael, just so they could get it right, had been thrown to the floor five times. Spoletta was becoming one of his favorite roles.

· · ·

"Te lucis ante terminum,
rerum creator, poscimus,
ut solita clementia
sis praesul et custodiam."

Michael, with his complement of monks, joined in the rehearsal of the recessional to be sung after *Curlew River.* "In hope, in peace, ends our mystery," the Abbot had intoned. The Madwoman from the Black Mountains had been restored to sanity by the vision of her dead son, and now the monks who had performed the parable would make their way from the church, singing their evening hymn.

Michael wondered how many of them knew what the Latin meant. He assumed they understood the Italian into which he'd translated the opera itself, but not quite as a formality, he asked, "Does anyone have any questions?"

No one stirred.

"Is the opera fairly clear to all of you? The words, they have meaning for you, don't they?"

Still, no movement. They didn't even turn to see if someone else might have a question or a comment. The only encouraging sign was that they were looking at him, not at the mirror.

Michael then asked what he'd been extremely reluctant to ask. "What do you think of this work—I mean for here, for Naples?"

Again he got no response, but at least there seemed to be a minimal stir. He repeated the question. This, unfortunately, put an end to the stir but still got him no response.

Not without cause was Michael worried about what answer they might give. *Curlew River* was hardly Neapolitan fare. Its source was closer to plainchant then to *bel canto* or street songs, and he feared the listeners would find it too distant from their traditions to appreciate what they were hearing. Audiences could even become belligerent. There could be a fiasco, an out-and-out scandal.

Then, too, there was his own part, the Madwoman. The opera, a program note would explain, is presumably being sung by a group of monks in their chapel. All the parts are sung by men, including that of the Madwoman. What will the response be to that? Audiences everywhere had accepted women in male roles—Cherubino, Octavian, Orfeo—but try as he might, Michael couldn't think of a single work that asked a male to sing a female role.

Signor Crescenzo had dismissed the entire concern. "Have you never heard of the great *castrati* of centuries past? Naples more than anyplace has a history of a man singing a woman's role."

"You mean they'll consider me a *castrato?*" The idea made Michael extremely uncomfortable. And it didn't help that Signor Crescenzo paused before his next dismissal.

"No," he said. "I don't think so. Your voice isn't the right timbre. It's all wrong. No, no *castrato*. No."

"Then what will they think?"

"What they always think."

"And what," Michael asked, "is that?"

"No one ever knows. Not in Naples, one doesn't."

After he'd unburdened himself of this cheery insight, Crescenzo added, "Of course, the tradition itself continues."

"You mean they're still castrating . . . !"

"No, no, no, no, no. The tradition, I said, not the practice. And even the tradition has become only a remnant of what once was one of the specialties of Naples. I mean the famous transvestites, who still ply their wares in certain parts of the city. It's not an unhonored profession, and it's sometimes passed on from father to son, like any other craft. I don't suggest that the audience will think of you as a male prostitute. But I do suggest that your presentation, the part of a woman, is not completely outside an accepted Neapolitan experience."

This calmed Michael somewhat, but then, of course, the good Signor Crescenzo had repeated his earlier thought. "Still, in Naples, what they're going to think, what they're going to do, one never knows." He brought his hands together, then separated them, as if to surrender the whole subject, to release it, like so many fluttering doves, into the uncharted air.

To try for some notion of what lay ahead, Michael asked his singers, "What did you think when you first looked at the libretto, when you were learning your parts?" Certainly the cast wouldn't be shy about that, about the parts they themselves were to play. But Michael was wrong. They continued to regard him with all due respect, but beyond that they would not go. "Were you sorry for the Madwoman? Were you moved when you heard the Ferryman's story about how the child had asked to be buried near the chapel where the shadow of one of his countrymen might fall across his grave? Did you accept the appearance of the child's spirit, up out of the grave?"

It was this last question that finally got someone to speak. It was the enthusiastic tenor, Piero Esposito, if Michael remembered his name correctly. "Oh, yes," he said. "How could anyone not accept that?" The tone of his voice hinted that what Michael had said approached absurdity. "Of course everyone believes people rise up from their graves."

Michael nodded his gratitude, but when, pressing his luck, he directed some of the other previously unanswered questions to the young man, he got nothing but shrugs. Soon everyone was shrugging and watching himself shrug in the mirror opposite.

Michael dismissed them with thanks and encouragement. He set the time for the next rehearsal. They got up and left, speaking little to each other, much less to him. Because there were no women in the cast, there seemed to be no reason for delayed departures and long-drawn-out farewells. The flirtations and pursuits that gave the dispersals at San Carlo a party atmosphere were completely absent here. At San Carlo they'd go downstairs to the bar to talk, to drink, to pursue. Here they crowded out the door like schoolboys dismissed from a Latin class.

Outside the rehearsal room, there was the revving of more than several motor scooters, each rider seeming to need the reassurance of at least five or six full-throttle snarls before trusting the bike completely. When the scooters drove off—more or less together—the sound suggested *The Texas Chainsaw Massacre*.

Michael dismantled the "ferryboat," the chairs he'd placed in rows to indicate where the pilgrims would sit when crossing the river. As he was replacing a heavy ladder-back—green, with enough paint chipped away to show a coat of yellow and, beneath that, some flecks of blue—he caught himself in the mirror across the room. He saw the way he was placing the chair, how he shoved it a few inches this way, then that, so it wouldn't stick out from the others, so it wouldn't touch the wall.

From then on, lining up the chairs became not a chore but a performance. He watched himself pick up a chair, take it to the wall, and place it next to the previous one. He watched himself pull and shove until the chair was exactly where he wanted it. He saw as well a reasonably strong and agile man, dark, with thick and moderately sloppy hair, a nose perhaps a bit too long, a chin that stuck out slightly farther than he might have wished, appropriating to itself a prominence he preferred would have been given to the lips.

The last chair was where it belonged, but instead of turning out the lights, locking the doors, and leaving, Michael sat down and looked again into the mirror across the room. He, too, moved a strand of hair from one side of his forehead to the other. He, too, rearranged his crotch, then tried the slouch and the no-slouch. He was, he realized, lonely. In defiance, he aimed his puckered lips at the mirrored mouth beyond the far wall.

Reflected there, opposite him, was the enthusiastic tenor, Piero Esposito, standing in the doorway to his left. He was looking, not at his own reflection, but at Michael's. Michael simply sat there.

"I left my music," Piero said. He walked over to the harmonium, and there, on top, was his copy of the score. This brought him into Michael's line of vision, so that he could see both the image of the young man and the young man himself.

He was taller than Michael had thought he would be, almost six feet, and he moved with the possessive ease of one who casually lays claim to whatever room he may be in. He was wearing an unzipped dark-blue jacket made of what seemed to be sailcloth, a little short in the sleeves, so that bits of his denim shirt stuck out at the wrists. The jacket had a hood, which lay across his shoulders, the tip pointing down his spine, making it seem that he had monastic inclinations, if only from mid-hip up. His pants, unpressed and loose-fitting, were dark-gray flannel, and his shoes, scuffed brown, were large and wide, suggesting comfort and an unself-conscious stride.

After he'd picked up his music, he closed the lid of the harmonium, a task Signor Zongola had obviously failed to perform, then ran his right hand along the top of the instrument as if calming it. He stuffed the score into his jacket pocket and gave it a light tap, as if it had somehow misbehaved.

Michael noticed that he was wearing what looked like a college ring; he must remember on the night of performance to tell everyone to remove rings, watches, bracelets, whatever might be unseemly vanities among a group of monks intent on parable.

Then he thought of using the ring now as a conversation ploy, but before he could say anything, Piero, looking at Michael's image across the room, spoke. "Forgive me," he said, "but are you an American?"

"Yes. American." The question surprised Michael. He thought everyone in the cast knew where he'd come from and why he was here in Naples. He'd assumed that the story of his mentor was familiar to them all, that Signor Crescenzo had filled in the background of the production, telling them why it was being done and by whom. Now he realized he should probably have given a short talk before rehearsal. He'd do it next time.

"You're not from Rome?"

"No. I'm from New York."

"Yes, I know. That's what Signor Crescenzo told us. But I thought maybe you were from Rome instead."

Michael nudged a chair away from the wall so he could realign it. "No. New York." Having moved one chair, he discovered that the one next to it was even more offensively misaligned. He moved that chair too, one millimeter this way, two millimeters that way, never quite achieving the ideal position.

The young man had come to his side. Michael moved the chair one more time. "In church," Piero said, "I was told you were from Rome. I just wasn't sure."

Michael stopped playing with the chairs. He looked at the young man. Piero was smiling, a kind of pleased smile, mildly sly. A lock of brown hair was flattened against his forehead, falling just below his right eyebrow. The eyes themselves were brown and narrow, giving the impression that he viewed what he saw with an amused skepticism.

"Oh, that," Michael said. "I only did that as a favor for a friend."

"No, it's all right. I understand. One must get by as best he can."

"Get by?"

"You take whatever jobs you can get. I understand."

"Oh, no. It wasn't a job. I mean, I wasn't paid. I was—"

"No, it's all right. I told you. I understand."

"But you don't understand, not if you believe—"

"Gaetano thinks you're really his uncle."

"Well, it won't be for much longer."

"But you should do it for as long as you can. Signora Spacagna can afford it. She gets a pension no one knows about, since her husband was killed in the earthquake."

"But I'm not getting paid. I didn't do it for money."

"Signor Ruane, please, why do you feel it's shameful to be paid? You should be proud to be able to earn some money."

"But I told you. I'm not being paid."

The young man lengthened his smile, narrowed his eyes, and held out his hand. "You don't have to worry. I'll keep your secret from Gaetano, that you're not from Rome."

When Michael reached out his hand, he felt he was becoming complicitous to yet another lie. He *wasn't* being paid, but apparently nothing would convince the young man otherwise. Resigned, Michael shook his hand, a firm shake on both sides. Before letting go, Piero said, "Gaetano is very respectful of you. He'll do whatever you say. But please don't worry—I won't even let him know that I know you."

Michael was tempted to tell him that he should feel free to say whatever he wanted to say. Except he didn't like the idea of

Gaetano being told he'd been paid, that he'd done what he'd done for money: the concern he'd shown, even felt, in the cloister, the sympathy. And even less did he want Piero Esposito to think him a liar. Michael decided to shrug, to give him permission to do whatever he wanted—especially since the smile, the narrow eyes, told him that here was someone who would, under any circumstances, do and think precisely what pleased him most.

"No, no," the young man said. "You're still worrying, and you mustn't. I like secrets. And I'm very good at keeping them. I've never told anyone about Signora Spacagna's pension. So there you are."

He looked directly into Michael's eyes, cocked his head to the left, straightened it, then went to the door. Without looking back, he said, "Gaetano and I, we sang for the Pope together. That's how we're friends."

"I didn't know Gaetano sang."

"He doesn't. But the Pope wasn't listening anyway. It was a long time ago. Four years. Four and a half. We've been friends ever since. That's why he invited me to his wedding. Except it didn't turn out the way he told me it would. It wasn't his wedding after all."

"There seem to be . . . complications."

"Yes. It was the best wedding I've ever been to. You were very good. Even *I* believed you. Sometimes I still think you're from Rome, not from New York."

"No. I'm from New York." Michael spoke the words in English to help substantiate his claim.

Piero laughed. "That is exactly what a man from Rome would say." He, too, spoke in English, but with a heavy accent.

"You speak English."

"On occasion. It is not my preferred language."

"But it sounds very good." Piero nodded, accepting the compliment, while his smile said he doubted its sincerity. "But believe me," Michael continued, "I'm from New York."

"Why should I doubt it?" This, too, he said in English, then went quickly out the door. Michael stared in its direction. And as if he'd expected it, the door opened almost immediately. The young man didn't come back into the room but connected with Michael's image in the mirror. Reverting to his preferred Italian, he said, "I hope you won't forbid Gaetano to kill Peppino. It would make him feel very bad to disobey you."

The door closed again, but Michael kept looking at it, uncertain whether or not it had been closed for good. When he heard the sound of a motor scooter under the windows, he felt reasonably sure the young man had indeed gone. As Michael turned out the lights, he listened to the sound of the motor fading in the distance down Via Santa Teresa degli Scalzi, not the snarl of the chain saw, but the light and busy buzz of the mosquito. Then even that sound moved off, and everything was quiet.

4

Four people were waiting to go to confession: a young woman in a three-quarter-length fur coat with a red-and-gray silk scarf tied at her neck; a bald man who seemed, in spite of the cold, to be sweating; the moon-faced woman he recognized from the day of the wedding; and a teenage boy wearing a sweatshirt that had the words Bull's Eye emblazoned across the front. It hadn't occurred to Michael that there might be a line and that he'd have to wait his turn before he could unburden himself. He genuflected and started to enter the pew but was stopped by a voice that was obviously upbraiding him for something he was doing wrong. He turned to the right. A woman who appeared to be a cleaning lady—gray hair in a pug, dirty brown skirt slightly askew, thick woolen sweater, unbuttoned, showing a gray rayon blouse the color of scrub water—was leaning on top of the half door to the confessional. The confessional itself was like the setting for a triptych: three arched frames of dark polished wood, the priest in the center, one penitent at each side—though, as indicated by the gray-haired woman, a more direct approach was available, the confessor confronted directly at his very doorstep, the penitent sharing the central panel instead of relegating himself to the lesser station a side panel might imply. The woman seemed to be giving Fra

Callisto not a listing of her sins but a sizable chunk of her mind,
all cast in the accusatory mode. The friar was receptive if not
quite as remorseful as the woman seemed to demand. What was
suggested to Michael was a patient neighbor sitting behind the
closed bottom half of a doorway to one of Naples's *bassi*—the
dark, cavelike rooms that open right onto the narrow streets—
listening to a harangue from the local scold.

Relieved that he'd committed no breach of protocol, Michael
continued into the pew and knelt down, a matter of form, the
prompting of an old habit. He considered again that he might
try saying a prayer for Damian, but he immediately felt the
familiar reluctance. He wondered now if the reluctance might
not come from Damian himself. Maybe Damian didn't want
Michael to pray for him. Maybe he'd even be annoyed. Michael
had the idea that in response to his prayers, Damian would say
to God, "Oh, *him* again."

Michael heard a voice and looked up. The moon-faced
woman, behind him, was saying something to him in dialect.
And the teenage boy and the woman in the fur coat had gone.
The woman kept jerking her head toward the confessional. She
finally raised her two hands in frustrated supplication and bent
herself toward him. In a whisper reminiscent of the whirlwind,
she told him that he should go ahead of her into the confessional,
that she didn't want him trying to hear what she would have
to say. She knew that was why he'd come into the pew—not to
line up for confession but to overhear her sins. She seemed to
be demanding that he prove he was there for some purpose more
legitimate than the enjoyment of the revelations intended for the
priest alone. Michael thought it best not to protest. He moved
out into the aisle.

From which angle should he approach Fra Callisto, full face
over the half door, or at his right or left ear on the other side of
the crosshatched grille? Remembering that he was the uncle from
Rome and therefore a figure of some importance, he quickly
strode toward the half door.

Fra Callisto's head was leaning against his propped hand; he seemed already wearied by what he'd have to hear. But then his head straightened. He moved his face slightly forward, and his expression was one of eager yet tender welcome. His eyes were shaded with sorrow, as if he were dispensing not just forgiveness but the remorse that was its indispensable component. He seemed to be both priest and penitent, and Michael couldn't help wondering if Fra Callisto didn't complete the sacramental act by performing the penance as well.

Before there was any chance for Michael to say anything, however, Fra Callisto erased all sorrow, all forgiveness, all eager welcome from his face and returned his head to its propped position. He had recognized Michael. Implicit in his posture was the message that he didn't want to hear what Michael had to say.

Reflexively, Michael began with the words "Forgive me, Father—" then quickly managed to switch his thinking so that he could continue with words closer to his purpose: "but I heard a few things from Gaetano the day of the wedding that I think you should know about."

The friar waited a moment, then said, "And you think I haven't heard them myself?"

"You probably have. But I wanted to make sure. And I was even hoping you might be able to do something about it."

Fra Callisto breathed a heaving sigh, as if shifting off to one side the heavy stone under which he had buried this entire subject. "Perhaps you'd better tell me first what you came to tell me."

"Gaetano says he's going to kill his brother Peppino."

The friar paused a moment, then said, "Yes. And what else?" as if he were waiting patiently to hear the sinner's next transgression.

"He claims that Peppino . . . well, that Peppino . . ."

"That Peppino raped Rosalia."

"Yes. At least that's what Gaetano said."

"And what else did he say?"

Michael was, to say the least, flustered. He'd come into the confessional with words like "murder" and "rape," and the priest seemed to have heard it all before, to the point of indifference. The stiffened incredulity Michael had expected to arouse, the troubled concern he'd feared to awaken, showed no sign of imminent arrival. If anything, Fra Callisto's weariness seemed to have spread into the arm propping up his head. He lifted its burden and let the hand fall limply to his lap. His head he let hang down so that Michael could see the tonsure cut into his thick gray hair. It was just past the bristle stage and looked like a cultivated field set among tempestuous outcroppings of bush and brier.

"He said Peppino's and Rosalia's marriage was at the insistence of . . ."

"Of your sister-in-law. Of Assunta. Is that right?"

"Yes. That—that's right."

Michael was surprised; he'd assumed that the Signora had told Fra Callisto of his deception. Here, in the one place on earth where the truth had to be told, Michael must now set the record straight. "Father," he began.

But before he could continue, Fra Callisto raised his head and looked at him. His scorn, his contempt, were obvious. He knows the truth after all and will now confront me with his disapproval. He will castigate me for the fraud, then dismiss me with the prescribed "Go and sin no more."

"Signor Spacagna," the priest said, his voice barely able to contain itself within the confines appropriate to the confessional. "Consider this. Consider that Gaetano has said nothing that was true beyond his own imagining. Consider that his attraction to Rosalia was engendered by the prospect of his brother's marriage. Consider that he is a most inventive young man, one of deep feeling, of genuine feeling, even, but with nothing to substantiate his claims against his brother, against Rosalia, or against your sister-in-law, Assunta."

"Is that what you believe?"

"Why shouldn't I? It was all explained to me by Assunta herself."

"And what if Gaetano acts on what he's imagined?"

"Kills Peppino?"

"Yes."

"Then he has killed Peppino."

"But that's why I'm here. To see what can be done to stop him."

"And what do you propose?"

Michael was stunned to realize he had no answer to the obvious question.

"Tell him not to?" the priest continued. "Is that what you came here to do? To ask me to go to Gaetano and say, 'Gaetano, don't kill Peppino'? And then turn away, assured that my words had uprooted the murder in his heart, that my mere asking would have dissolved his passion and swept away all his darkest determinations? Is that what you came here to do?"

"You sound as though you accept that Gaetano is really going to kill his brother."

"What can be done to stop him? Prayer, perhaps. But does anything else come readily to mind?"

"But it can't happen!"

Fra Callisto heaved another sigh, this one indicating that the stone had been replaced, the subject buried again. "Signor Spacagna—"

"I am not—"

"You are from Rome." The priest's voice interrupted and rode over Michael's words, trampling them beneath his own. "Go back to Rome. Stay in Rome. This is Naples. Forever you people come from Rome and interfere. Forever you intrude. You have no place here, and there is nothing here for you to do, nothing that is worthwhile. Leave us to ourselves. We are Neapolitans. And Rome has nothing to do with us—or we with Rome. Go back. Don't interfere. There's nothing you can do."

The dismissal was too abusive for Michael to let pass. "Then you'll do nothing. And an innocent young man and an innocent young woman—"

"Signore! Who is guilty and who is innocent? What is true and what is false? You don't know. And you'll never know. Of course, you have your own version. Rome always has its own version. But do not inflict it on us. At birth you were sent to Rome, and that's where you belong. You are a Roman. Go back. Naples has no need of you. Not now, not ever."

With that, he turned away and slammed open the sliding panel to his left, indicating in no uncertain terms that he was finished with the one penitent—Michael—and ready for the next. Michael, who hadn't bothered to kneel for the encounter, turned and started toward the pews. The moon-faced woman was making her approach to the confessional, slowly, head bowed, as if straining for a shyness, a reticence, that had not the least chance of survival once she started to confess.

Michael went into one of the pews. He was tempted to raise his arms and shake his fists at the distant beams under the church roof, but he knew it would do no good. He slumped down, hoping that that would at least be a partial display of his frustration and his anger. Peppino's death would be a just punishment, a proper judgment on Fra Callisto. He could hardly wait for it. Given the chance, he'd hand Gaetano the knife, the gun, the poison, needed to do the deed. He'd even hold Peppino's hands behind his back so Gaetano could all the more easily strangle him. Or was it to Fra Callisto that Michael wished all this to happen? Or even to Gaetano, for having stirred up the fuss in the first place?

Michael straightened himself, his spine against the back of the pew. He wanted to lower his head into his hands, but he forced himself to look directly at the altar. Cold stone was all he saw, the carved tomb elevated behind the great crucifix, an offer to one and all. Death was raised triumphant here.

And then he realized he was wrong. He became aware for the first time of the quiet simplicity of the basilica. There was warmth in the soft yellow of the great stones that made its walls. There was a gentle modesty to the narrow stained-glass windows that lined the clerestory of the nave. The pillars and pilasters were plain, claiming no more strength than was necessary to hold in place the rounded arches leading to the side chapels. The statues, like the tombs, were dignified ungilded stone. The Gothic window high above the main altar was mostly blue, to assure the constant presence of the sky, and its scene was limited to the Father's quiet meditation on the stable of Bethlehem.

It was not death that triumphed here; it was repose. And the offered dead in their graves of austere and crafted stone were a celebration of rest, of the sweet end of things, of acceptance and of peace. Michael was in precincts dedicated to Santa Chiara, Saint Clare, the friend and follower of Francis, the saint of Assisi. Now the simplicity made sense; now the reigning quiet was explained. And the tranquillity of the cloister—that, too, he understood. A meeting place for the things of heaven and the things of earth, where neither warred against the other, an attempt, perhaps, to see what Eden had been like.

Michael would leave the church restored. He got up and walked the center aisle toward the main altar, a gesture of thanksgiving. Just before he made the step up into the sanctuary, he saw a woman—a girl, it seemed—busy rubbing her finger over a small area of stone on the side wall of the chapel to his left. She took a handkerchief out of her purse, put it over her finger, wet it with her tongue, then scrubbed against the stone.

For just a moment, he thought it could be Rosalia, but it wasn't. Rosalia had long dark flowing hair; this woman's hair was brown and barely touched the collar of her coat. Also, the woman here was taller, less robust. Rosalia wasn't exactly delicate, but there had been about her a refinement of feature that he couldn't imagine on the face of the girl he glimpsed in profile now. Still, Rosalia or not Rosalia, Michael was fascinated by what she was doing. Had she been given as a penance the job of scrubbing the walls of the great basilica with no more than the tip of a finger and a white handkerchief?

Michael made his way over to the tomb on the side of the sanctuary. The girl's back was to him, but he could tell from her movements that she was diligent and determined in her task. She stepped back to examine the effects of her labor. One look at the shoulders told Michael that she considered her efforts hopeless. He took special note of the spot on the wall that had demanded her attentions. He would wait until the girl was gone, then go and satisfy his curiosity about what on earth she'd been doing.

To occupy himself in the meantime, Michael looked at the carved effigies slumbering on the lid of the sarcophagus on the wall above him. The stone was chipped, the features of the faces eroded, the carved clothing no longer luxuriously folded and creased but smoothed now to the simple homespun garments available to any peasant. Time had not confined its labors to the bodies within.

"Don Michele?" The voice behind him was bright with uncertainty and pitched at what seemed a little higher than its usual tone. Michael had only to turn halfway around. There was Rosalia, not ten feet away. Her hair, within the last few minutes, had lengthened and darkened. The skimpy coat she was wearing wasn't so skimpy after all; it merely accommodated the slender and healthy body underneath. Close by, the features of her face had withdrawn to the delicacy he had noticed at the wedding. She was smiling, and her eyes were opened to a fullness he hadn't seen before, as if they, too, were now unveiled and ready to present themselves without their bridal protection. She seemed happy to see him.

"Rosalia? What a wonderful surprise." Michael, to defend himself from the accusation of a lie, quickly insisted to himself that the sight of the girl had indeed filled him with wonder.

There was pleasant wonder and unpleasant wonder, welcome wonder and unwelcome wonder. Unsettling wonder was what he was filled with right now, but wonder nevertheless. "You've been to Sorrento," he said.

"Yes. We got back last night."

"Was it beautiful? Sorrento?"

"Everyone says it is."

"But you didn't think so?"

Rosalia glanced down to her left. Without looking up again, she said, "I have to go to work now. I can't be late. I just wanted to say hello. Signor Scarano, my boss, agreed to come to the wedding if I wouldn't take too many days away. He even agreed to walk down the aisle with me. He's very kind, Signor Scarano. But I mustn't take advantage, or he'll fire me. I have three hours free between this morning and this afternoon. From twelve o'clock to three. May I meet you? I would so much love to get to know you. Since you came all the way from Rome. I want to thank you."

"Well, I—"

"But no, I can't see you after all," she said quickly, wanting the fault to be hers, not his, that they would be unable to meet. "What am I thinking? I have to do the shopping for tonight, or we won't have anything to eat. I would have gone this morning, but—well—I wanted to come here. It's not my church. San Giuseppe dei Ruffi is where I go. But now, now that I am Spacagna and not Attanese anymore, I should come here to pray. Don't you agree?"

Even if Michael didn't agree, she was so desperate for his assent that he had to give it. "Oh, yes, I agree. I agree."

"But I have to go to work now. And then I have to shop." She tried without success to smile again, as if she had to apologize to Michael for having to shop and go to her job. When she gave up on the attempted smile, her lips seemed to tremble slightly as they relaxed themselves into something less rigid, yet less hopeful. She turned first her head away, then her body, and started toward the step that led down from the sanctuary. Without stopping, she said, "You didn't go back to Rome. I thought you'd go right back."

"I . . . I have some business here in Naples. Then I'll go back."

Rosalia nodded, then stopped and looked back at him. "Can you come to see me? Later? After my shopping? At my—at our apartment? I would like you to see where Peppino and I live. So when you come again to Naples . . ." Realizing the hopelessness of her invitation, she let her voice trail off. Her head was bowed; she seemed ashamed of suggesting something so impossible.

And it was impossible. He had a rehearsal at San Carlo and a luncheon meeting with Signor Crescenzo and a scheduled session with the lighting man, who had never been inside Capella Sansevero but had promised that he would have no difficulty in giving Michael whatever he might need, the same promise given by the set designer, who had designed a set that couldn't possibly fit into the chapel confines. "I don't really think I—"

Rosalia nodded again. She understood, and she accepted.

"Unless tomorrow is all right," Michael said. "I can come then, if it's all right with you. How far is it, say, from here?" He hadn't intended to say it, but he had.

"Oh, not far! Not far at all! Via Giganti. A few minutes away. And you'll come? And I can thank you for coming all the way from Rome for my wedding. I'll cook for you. Something for you to eat. You're my family now. And I am your family." Her smile was effortless, and there was more gratitude shining in her eyes than Michael ever wanted to see again in his entire life.

"No, no. I'll just stop by. A short visit. So I'll know when I come another time."

Rosalia, chattering away, gave him directions. He should approach from Via del Duomo, a few streets up from the cathedral, and turn at San Giuseppe dei Ruffi, her church. He would see four arches reaching over the street, over Via Anticaglia. After the third arch, he must turn left, because that would be Via Giganti, her street. She gave him the number; it would be just before the shrine of Maria Santissima delle Grazie. If he saw the shrine, he'd gone too far. He should turn back. But to see the shrine, she warned, he would have to look up. It was high in the wall. But he probably wouldn't see it, because he would easily find the number.

She grabbed both his hands, squeezed them, then kissed both his cheeks and squeezed the hands again, only this time not quite so hard. She lowered her eyes, let go of his hands, and the smile faded; her lips twitched a little, as if there was more that she wanted to say. The best she could manage was a breathy *"Ciao, Zio,"* before she rushed down the side aisle.

When she was out the door, Michael went to the chapel where she'd been scrubbing. Three saints, carved in the same rough stone he'd seen elsewhere in the church, presided over a small altar. Michael had little interest until he noticed that the one nearest Rosalia's wall had, very neatly sunk into his head, a meat cleaver. He glanced at the other two. The saint in the middle held a book and a ciborium—a Church Father, he assumed—but the one on the other side had a sword thrust into his chest. Part of the sword was broken off, an accident of time, but the blade plunged into the heart remained. Michael tried to see if he could figure out who they were, then remembered he wasn't there to decipher iconography.

The stone that had given Rosalia such frantic employment just a few moments before was beneath yet another tomb, set high in the wall. He expected at first that the carved and lengthy inscription would provide his first clue, but before he could read it, he found clues that interested him more. Written or printed on the gray stones, mostly in pen, in letters no larger than one might use to make notes in a notebook, were phrases like *"Fa*

che Laura sia felice in tutto sopratutto con Ciro." Let Laura be most
happy most of all with Ciro. *"Fa me essere promosso."* Let me get
promoted. (The words of petition were spun like a fine web over
the stones.) *"Fa che non sia bocciato."* Don't let me flunk. *"Fa
trovare un posto a mio fratello Gianni e a Nicola il mio ragazzo te ne
prego."* Find a job for my brother Gianni and also Nicola, my
boyfriend, I beg you. There was, even in church, the inevitable
"Ti amo se tu leggerai questo messagio. Io ti amo. Telefonami . . ."
The rest was scratched out, the stone itself pitted in the attempt.
Roughly translated, it said: I love you if you will read this message. I love you. Telephone me . . . The declaration of love had
been allowed to remain, but the means of possible consummation, the telephone number, had been dug out and spilled as dust.

Michael looked to see which might apply to Rosalia. *"Fammi
andare a una festa domani"*—a request that the petitioner go to a
party the next day. *"Fa che stiamo in buona salute: Armando, Lella,
Viviana, Valeria per sempre."* Let us stay in good health: Armando,
Lella, Viviana, Valeria forever.

Just a little higher and to the right, Michael found what he
was looking for. The words were especially visible against the
newly wetted stone. It was these words that Rosalia had been
trying to scrub away with her handkerchief. *"Fammi mettere con
Gaetano felice sempre. Fa che sua madre acconsenta."* Let me be happy
forever with Gaetano. Make it so his mother consents.

The handwriting on the wall clearly contradicted what Fra
Callisto had said. The priest's assumptions had indeed come from
a prompting by Assunta. How else could she have persuaded
him to preside over the marriage except by anticipating—and
denying—whatever objections her son Gaetano might raise. Peppino, then, may very well have raped Rosalia, and Gaetano, true
to his word, might well kill his brother. And what this would
do to the injured Rosalia he couldn't begin to imagine. Michael
looked over at the saint nearest him. Indifferent even to the cleaver
planted in his skull, the stone martyr had nothing to say.

5

The young man leaned back in the chair and stretched his legs out alongside the table to show Michael the boots he was wearing. The leather was tooled in an intricate design of curls and sprays that showed black against brown. He pulled the leg of his pants to mid-calf, so Michael could appreciate the scalloped boot top bordered with interlacing loops cut into the thick brown hide. "If you want to buy them, I might be able to sell them. If you're interested."

The voice was not insinuating, but the indifference of the tone seemed more blatant than the most direct invitation could possibly have been. And the hiking of the pants leg was surely the equivalent of a flirt lifting the hem of her skirt to reveal a well-turned ankle. The young man was lanky, his long face topped by a huge puff of unruly brown hair that stuck out under the high-domed duck-billed cap sported by so many Americans, who apparently want their heads to look like oversized gumdrops.

His manner was slow, almost languorous, his eyes doing all the work. Heel on the floor, he waved his right foot back and forth a few times like a sluggish metronome, then slid down a little more in the chair so his body could stretch itself out in an almost unbroken line with his legs.

The restaurant was filled but not crowded, the decibel level rising and falling with the irregularity of a rough but unthreatening sea. Just off Piazza Garibaldi, it had become Michael's favorite restaurant in all Naples. He'd been sitting there, waiting for his pasta, trying to think about *Curlew River,* about the part of the Madwoman, but he hadn't been too successful. Thoughts of Rosalia had kept intruding. Michael felt sorry for her, trapped as she seemed to be between forces originating in the primal rivalry of the brothers Spacagna. In Santa Chiara that morning, she had been so needful, so forlorn, yet so determined to be cheerful, that he couldn't resist wanting to see her, if that was what she wanted, to help her in some way, no matter how paltry and inadequate it might be.

Her attempt to erase the words she'd scratched onto the stones of the basilica had touched him by its futility. Her effort to revoke a simple act of faith and hope and love—"Let me be happy forever with Gaetano. Make it so his mother consents" —seemed such a lonely thing to do. Her acceptance of the saints' decision not to take up her cause, the quick smile she summoned to assure Michael that she was resigned to heavenly indifference, her sad forgiveness of those who had dismissed her simple plea —all this pressed upon him, but lightly, as if it were too gentle in itself to weigh heavily on the thoughts he had of her.

But thoughts of Rosalia, of her loneliness, had brought to the surface a sense of his own solitary life, especially here in Naples. Soon he was meditating on his solitude, his need for companionship—and more besides. He became newly aware of how loneliness heightens rather than dulls the senses. Sight, smell, touch, all seemed pitched a few tones higher, their sensors drawn more tightly across the resonator of the emptied heart, the better to pick up the least vibration, the easier to alert the searching flesh that possible satisfactions had entered the area, that one must remain poised, aware, and ready. Nature, it seemed, had evolved an apparatus that would aid the lonely in their detection of the antidote and cure for what ailed them but, in the process, had, with the cruelty and irony once ascribed to the gods, increased the capacity for torment in the very act of providing the means for its release.

Michael knew from experience that his loneliness, especially since his separation from Damian, had given him a heightened existence, that his yearning had intensified, clarified, even made brilliant, what would otherwise have been an experience too common to notice. But grateful as he was for this intensification of his life—and he *was* grateful—he was also, at times, exhausted. Often he begged for a slackening, a relief, however temporary, from the drawn senses upon which this scent, that touch, this sight, would thrum again and again the one word only: "alone, alone, alone."

Michael had seen the lanky young man eating with a woman who seemed to be doing all the talking, leaving him free to eat without interruption, slowly, with great concentration. Michael could not remember paying any attention either to him or to the young woman. Then, as he'd been gulping his red wine, before the waiter had brought him his pasta, the young man had come up to him and said, "You're the singer, at San Carlo."

After Michael, surprised and pleased, had admitted that he was, the young man reminded him that it had been he—his name, he said, was d'Arezzo, Antonio d'Arezzo—who had delivered one of Michael's suitcases, the one that had been lost in Rome en route to Naples. He worked for the airline. The suitcase had had to be brought to the opera house, because there'd be no one in the apartment. Guido, the *portiere* who guarded the San Carlo stage door—*l'ingresso degli artisti*—had sent for Michael, and the suitcase had been handed to him directly. Michael, too occupied with the rehearsal, had given his deliverer only passing attention but had tipped him lavishly and been rewarded with a slow nod of the head and a slow turn away from the stage door.

Michael had acknowledged remembering him and had

thanked him again for retrieving his suitcase from that vast limbo of lost luggage called Leonardo da Vinci Airport; Signor d'Arezzo had then asked if he might join him for just a moment, a question that seemed to derive more from a mild curiosity as to what the answer might be than from an actual request for permission to sit down. Michael had nodded, his nod quicker than the one he'd been given in return for his ten-thousand-lire tip. The young man sat, asked a few questions about the opera, about Michael's part, and seemed, in his own thoughtful way, to be interested in the answers.

It was during Michael's rather ardent panegyric dedicated to the voice and talents of Aganice Calefati that Signor d'Arezzo chose to stretch his legs out and show the boots in all their glory, as if this increased visibility of his frame indicated an increased receptivity to what Michael was saying.

"She will be the next Tebaldi," Michael had said. Pretending not to have noticed the outstretched legs, he continued with an even more ardent tribute to Tebaldi, whom he'd heard only on recordings. Halfway through his praise for her *Butterfly*, Signor d'Arezzo interrupted by saying, "They're pretty good boots, don't you think?"

True, Michael had been looking at the boots, and his concentration on the artistry of the great Tebaldi had been growing weaker and weaker by the moment. He decided it was time to give Tebaldi a rest. "Yes," he'd said, leaning forward a little, not to give himself a more unobstructed view but to indicate a casual acceptance of the interruption.

Signor d'Arezzo then gave Michael a history of the boots, the city of origin, the fame of their maker, the singularity of their tooling, their sturdiness, reliability, comfort—as if he were speaking of a horse rather than of some nailed, stitched, and decorated chunks of dead hide. To conclude his sales pitch, he'd said, "If you want to buy them, I might be able to sell them. If you're interested."

"Well," Michael said, "I . . . I really hadn't thought of it."

"Really? From the way you were looking at them, I had the idea you might want them for yourself."

"Oh. Was I looking at them?"

"Intently." He paused. "Very intently."

"Oh. I wasn't aware."

"But I can't blame you. You have to admit you won't find anything like them anywhere. I can promise you that."

"Yes. I'm sure."

The young man was looking not at the boots but at Michael, and with an appraising eye. "I'd prefer," he said, "that you make an offer rather than me name a price. Consider, however, that I've gone to the trouble of breaking them in. By now they're very comfortable." He paused, then added, "They won't give you any trouble at all."

To release himself from the young man's stare, Michael looked again at the boots. Damian had had a pair of boots, brown, square-toed, scuffed to a light gray. At first he'd never worn them. They stood in the back of the closet, upright, two stiff stumps, like prosthetic devices left behind at a sacred shrine after one of the devout had miraculously grown back his lower legs, feet, and toes.

Then, after Michael and Damian had been together for a little more than a year, Damian began to wear the boots. In retrospect, Michael saw this as the first signal that their time together was coming to an end, as if Damian donned the boots when he went off in search of someone other than Michael. Michael had no proof of this beyond his own imagining, but he soon considered it an irrefutable truth.

And what the memory summoned now was not the old yearning for his lost friend but the jealousy, the hopelessness, the anger and fear of their final days. The bitter and not funny thought crossed his mind: Damian had died with his boots on.

"Of course I don't have anything with me to wear in their

place," Signor d'Arezzo was saying, "so if you decide you want to buy them, we'll have to go to my apartment, but it isn't that far. I'd have to take Anna home first, my girlfriend, but I'd come back and we could go then, just the two of us."

Michael wanted the boots. Very much he wanted them. Still, there was his earlier vow of reticence when it came to Neapolitans, a vow already compromised by his sometime assumption of the name Spacagna. He also thought of the danger he might be putting himself into, but that only increased his interest—the uncertainty, the joining of fear with desire. Risk had often provided an intensification, even when none was needed.

But now the word itself—risk—entered his mind like a disturbing rather than a reinforcing element, rather like the wicked godmother at the feast, proffering not the promise of a blessing but the prophecy of a curse. And his bitter phrase returned to him: Damian had died with his boots on. He could hear the epidemic intone its variation of death's ancient Arcadian truth: "*Et in Napoli ego.*" Even in Naples am I.

Early in the onslaught of AIDS, Michael had had himself tested for antibodies to the virus and come up negative. He was determined to keep it that way, but there had been lapses. These would be followed by terror, regret, remorse, and anxiety, until finally he'd go and have himself tested again. It was rather like going to confession in the old days, complete with contrition and a resolve not to repeat the offense. And like confession, he'd had to make more than one trip and always for the same infraction.

So far he'd escaped the doom he'd been courting, but he knew that luck came in very limited quantities and the time had come and gone when he could expect to be exempt forever from the statistical certainty that he was next. For Naples he must make a special resolve. He knew that the seductions of the Neapolitan setting and the Neapolitans themselves could persuade him, as they'd persuaded countless generations before, to throw caution to the winds and dare to do those deeds whose sanction never seemed to reach beyond the Vesuvian plain. Not without reason is Naples said to be a city sacred to the ancient *sirena* Parthenope. As legend has it, she had thrown herself into the sea when her song failed to attract the wily, "many-minded" Odysseus. The peaceful waters through which her drowned body found its way to the shore formed now the Bay of Naples, its slopes her burial place, the city itself her monument and shrine. Drowned she may be, and buried, but still the siren songs are heard, whispering, echoing through the cobbled streets, along the stony shore, among the silent trees, and anyone with less cunning than many-minded Odysseus would be well advised to travel by another route.

"You're very kind," Michael said. "They're beautiful. Extraordinary. Excellently made, anyone can see that. But they're really not for me. Still, I thank you. It was very kind. Truly. Truly kind. And I thank you. Kind. Really kind."

He was repeating himself; he'd said what he had to say, and now all he had to do was shut up. But he didn't, because now the young man had drawn his legs toward himself and was sitting up almost straight in the chair, looking again at Michael, but this time with a steady, unwavering gaze.

"Too bad they're not my size," Michael continued. "And not my style—which I suppose is more a commentary about me than about the boots. But you've been very kind. Very . . . thoughtful."

Now he'd shut up at last. The waiter had put in front of him the pasta he'd ordered, *penne all'arrabbiata*. It steamed up into his face, and he could catch the smell of the dark sauce, the peppers and the tomatoes. Paying no attention to the young man, the waiter poured more wine into Michael's glass, then moved to a table at the other side of the room.

"You're sure, Signore? Think about it a moment. Look at them and then decide." Signor d'Arezzo lengthened himself again, stretching his legs, the boots, out in front of him. His hands he slipped into his pockets, looking all the while directly at Michael.

After the required pause to prove that he'd been reconsidering his refusal, Michael said, "Thank you. But no. Very kind. Very kind. Many thanks. Many thanks."

Slowly the young man stood up, his bones moving with supple ease inside his flesh. He brushed the side of his right leg to make sure his pants were straight, then put his hand on the table. The fingers were long and sturdy, the hand itself huge, the cords mapping the back more like sinews than veins. But the touch on the tablecloth was light, almost tender.

Michael watched as the hand withdrew itself. "You should have bought the boots," Signor d'Arezzo said. "Because they *are* very beautiful. Extraordinary. Like none other. I promise you." By now the hand was gone completely. "Good night, Signore. And I wish you well at the opera."

He went back to his table, slowly, and sat down. The woman, Anna, seemed to take up the conversation where she'd left off, with, as far as Michael could make out, no reference to her friend's absence. The young man put both his hands on the table, one on either side of his salad. Michael watched only a moment, tracing the raised veins, sensing the deft touch of the fingertips on the spotless cloth.

He leaned over his plate and again inhaled the steam, the dark sauce. Quickly he took a good gulp of the red wine, swallowed, then lifted a forkful of pasta to his mouth. It was hot and spicy, enough so to have been made, as its name indicated, by an angry woman, an *arrabbiata*. He ate another forkful, then another, the spice-coated *penne* slipping into his mouth with indecent ease. He chewed, swallowed, took another gulp of wine, then drank more *acqua minerale*.

He still wanted the boots, wanted to motion Signor d'Arezzo back to his table. He would ask that negotiations be reopened with the assurance the boots had found their destined owner after all. He'd eat one more forkful of *penne,* then signal boldly, shamelessly, for the young man to come back.

"Vasco! Vasco!" The words, mean and threatening, seemed to be directed toward Michael. He lowered his fork to his plate. "Vasco! *Vieni qui!*"

An older woman, wearing glasses the shape of cat's eyes, her hair the color and consistency of stiff bleached straw, was looking at Michael. A cigarette hung from the left side of her mouth; the lips themselves were drained and dried, like two withered sections of a peeled orange stuck together. She was wearing loop earrings that dangled like handles on an ancient vase, and at her throat was a silk neckerchief held together by a large brooch that looked as if it had entered life as a belt buckle. Uncertain as to what might enhance her beauty most, she had obviously opted for everything available.

"Vasco! Vasco!" The sound was somewhere between a snarl and a bark, which, as it turned out, was more than apt. A dog, mostly German shepherd, came out from under Michael's table and looked at the woman, who had apparently learned to speak to her pet in its native tongue. Michael hadn't known the dog was there.

The woman, satisfied that she'd been understood if not obeyed, said something to the waiter, and they both laughed. Her laughter was pleasant—intelligent, as if it came not from her throat or her nose but from her brain, the humor rippling through and among the soft gray coils, finding in the curls and crevices a whole series of unsuspected delights. Vasco retreated back under Michael's table and lay across his feet. The woman, indifferent to this recidivism, sat at the table right next to his. Again she said something to the waiter, and again they laughed.

Now Michael could never invite the young man back. Not just that the German shepherd had appropriated part of young d'Arezzo's space, but the proximity of the woman seemed to preclude a renewal of the bargaining process. D'Arezzo would not only have to circumvent Vasco; he'd have to stretch his legs out in front of the woman's table. Michael didn't think she'd appreciate that. Or—and the possibility couldn't be ignored— *she* might wind up buying the boots.

The waiter took his *penne* away and served Michael the fish and the spinach he'd ordered for his *secondo*. The dog was warming Michael's feet, its breathing a slow measured pressure against his legs.

And then his dinner was over. Without his having noticed, Signor d'Arezzo and his friend Anna had left. But now Michael had finished the wine and the half bottle of *minerale*. The fish had been both firm and tender, though Michael suspected he still had a scale attached, like a misplaced contact lens, to the roof of his mouth. It was time to go home.

Where Via Libertà met Corso Garibaldi, a bonfire had been lit against the chilled March night, and Michael could see a smaller one farther down the Corso near Piazza Principe Umberto. He walked at a pretty good clip, head down to show that he was in search of nothing but the spot on the pavement where his next step would land. By now Piazza Garibaldi itself was filled with the orange buses that had come here for the night after what must have been a trying day. In the dim light of the streetlamps, they slumbered on. Through the aisles between the buses Michael could see on the far side of the piazza the North African blacks lined along Via Indipendenza, their frail tables set out, spread, he knew, with sunglasses, watches, and golden chains. By what seemed a prearrangement, they always replaced after dark the white Neapolitans who during the day sold cigarettes, toys, shoulder bags, household utensils, and postcards, as if, being the most recent complication to the local scheme of things, they had to start with the night shift.

Just as Michael was walking opposite the statue of the great Garibaldi himself, he saw a woman approaching him. She'd come out from behind the statue and was headed his way with an assurance that suggested she and he had an appointment and she was eager not to be more than a minute late.

"*Bello*," she said in a low voice, deeper than Michael had expected. "It's too cold for you to be out alone like—" Before the sentence could be finished and certainly before Michael could say his "*No, grazie*," the woman had turned away and started, even faster, back toward the base of the statue. Then, like a phantom, she disappeared behind it.

She had spoken even her few words without the least trace of dialect, in an accent reserved for professional exchange. Michael continued on, the bonfire of Piazza Principe Umberto his beacon. It took him more than a few steps to realize that he'd been confronted not by an ordinary prostitute but by a true Neapolitan transvestite. But it took him less than another step to become aware that it had been the young and enthusiastic tenor, Piero Esposito, whose singing he'd had to restrain, then encourage, the one who'd returned to the rehearsal room to retrieve his forgotten score.

Michael considered going back and searching for him. He had it in mind to reassure him that he, Michael, had no objections to his profession and was even intrigued. He might even go so far as to say he was respectful of it. With that, Michael realized a faint hint of hysteria had entered into his thinking and he would do better to continue his homeward course.

His eyes intent on the bonfire ahead, Michael made his way toward Vicolo Venezia, his steps slightly slowed by regret and by memories he had no power to refuse.

6

What Rosalia had suggested as a possibility became a fact. Michael had gone too far down Via Giganti. There, above his head, built into the wall, was a shrine dedicated to Maria Santissima delle Grazie—Mary Most Holy of Favors, of Grace, of Thanks, of Mercy—however one might want to translate the word *grazie*. This being Naples, Michael suspected that Mary of Favors and Mary of Mercy were the more likely translations. Then, recognizing his condescension, he amended the thought. This being the world, the earth, Mary of Favors and Mary of Mercy would be not only more likely but more appropriate.

The shrine itself was a picture of the Madonna and Child flanked by two simulated candles, with bulbs of electric flame flaring at their tips. Michael had already noticed in the small courtyard of one of the buildings a lighted shrine to Saint Francis, robed and tonsured, with a bird alighting on his hand. Michael knew that if he'd looked closer, he would have seen the stigmata dabbed in scarlet paint on the hands and on the sandaled feet.

He started back up Via Giganti, a street that could hardly be more misnamed. The Street of Giants, like many of the streets of Naples, was little more than a passageway between buildings. Its width had contributed, no doubt, to the creation of compact cars, but even they proved a tight squeeze. Twice since he'd turned off Via Anticaglia he'd had to flatten himself against a doorway to escape being skinned alive, first by a Fiat, then by a BMW. Nor was the experience particular to Via Giganti; it happened all the time. But the giants whose presence might have occasioned the naming of the street must have moved along its hundred yards or so a single boot at a time. Still, the *piperno,* the hard black Italian paving stone beneath his feet, was firm and smooth. He had yet to see in the centuries-old streets of impoverished Naples a single pothole.

One difficulty in finding the apartment was that not every building had a number in plain view. The entries to the *bassi* were marked by nothing at all, but the neighborhood was obviously on the rise: several of the *bassi* had new and freshly varnished doorways, and some of the windows in the stuccoed buildings that walled the street had the sturdy metal frames that he'd seen installed in apartments by New York City landlords eager to justify yet another raise of the rent. Perhaps Naples shared some of the insidious customs common to New York real estate.

The entry to Rosalia's building was in a small courtyard the size of a bedroom; Michael had previously mistaken it for an improvised auto repair shop. Taking up most of the space was a light-blue Fiat, the left rear tire removed and the windshield missing completely. A grease-smeared table was pushed against the steps, and on a rack to its right was a dented can of Pennzoil and a small crowbar. Above it was a niche in which stood a statue of Saint Anthony holding the Blessed Infant. There were no candles, but a small vase held two pink flowers and two blue ones, fresh as if picked only moments before.

When Michael reached the top of the five steps that led to the main entrance, he found the door locked. There was no bell that he could see. He knocked, then knocked again. No one came. Perhaps that was the reason the crowbar had been so providentially provided: It was the one means of access. Michael could think of no alternative to going back out to the street and yelling Rosalia's name.

When he passed through the courtyard gate and out onto the street, he realized why the door hadn't magically opened at his knock. Rosalia's building, like Michael's own, on the Vicolo Venezia, was equipped with an intercom, complete with buzzers. For reasons that again touched on condescension, Michael had assumed that this particular convenience had not yet reached into the depths of Spaccanapoli. The name on the bell was still Attanese, and Michael was grateful to La Calefati for mentioning the bride's name when she was making her persuasions. Otherwise he'd have to go yelling up and down the street, and who knows what kind of shouts and slops might have come down on his head. These were the midday hours of rest, and Neapolitans, like most of humanity, do not—to put it quite literally— take a disruption like this lying down.

Michael pushed the small plastic rectangle and waited to hear Rosalia's voice. He heard instead a buzzing sound at the top of the steps. He rushed to the door, shoved against it, but he was too late. The buzzing had stopped. He went down again, rang again, and rushed past the blue Fiat and up the five steps. Now, instead of the buzzer, he heard Rosalia's voice on the intercom, asking who it was.

Slowly Michael started down the stairs. His ruse worked. The buzzer sounded before he'd reached the bottom. He was back up the steps in two bounds, and the door was given a quick bash that was surely rude beyond its deserving.

The stairs and the hallway were lit by bulbs no larger than those that burned in honor of Maria Santissima delle Grazie, and Michael expected that these, showing him the way, were on a timer. There would be light enough, not to find Rosalia's apartment on the third floor, but merely to help him get his bearings so he could feel his way for at least the final flight.

The dark he could deal with, but the cooking smells that now invaded his nose and his pores almost staggered him. Surely these were the scents of heaven. Or, more likely, an earthly equivalent of angelic incense. If God could be praised and honored through his nose, then certainly a man made in his likeness could be elevated to near divinity when such pleasing odors rose to his nostrils. It wasn't that Michael could detect tomatoes or garlic or veal or artichoke or cheese or any other specific; here they were joined, the unity of all things proclaimed. Only smells like these could both stimulate and drowse, pierce and envelop, taunt and satisfy.

The hallway lights went out as Michael reached the second landing, but he made it without difficulty to the third, thanks to a small window onto an air shaft. Rosalia had opened her door to further light his way, and he was able to walk the hallway without the stumbles he'd anticipated.

"Don Michele! Zio! Buon giorno! Buon giorno, Don Michele!" Rosalia shouted the words as if Michael were on the next street instead of a few feet away. As he was planting the obligatory kisses on her cheeks, the two of them still standing in the open doorway, Michael realized that her greeting had been intended more for the neighbors than for himself, an assurance that she was being visited by a relative, a member of the family, who would in no way compromise her honor as a woman and as a wife.

Having satisfied the neighbors, Rosalia stepped back and motioned for him to enter, a slow reaching out of her hand toward the room, then its quick withdrawal back to her skirt. She, it seemed, was not quite as reassured as her neighbors that this was a permissible visit. Even when she closed the door, she winced when she heard the click and kept one hand pressed against the wood as if afraid there might yet be another sound.

Michael was in a long, narrow hallway, almost a tunnel, that led to a well-lit room, a kitchen, at the end. *"Prego,"* Rosalia said, her hands still uncertain which gesture they should make. Michael negotiated past a small table decorated with photographs in silver frames. On the wall near the kitchen door hung an accordion-style rack with a few raincoats, a hook-handled umbrella, a heavy knitted black shawl, and a blue necktie.

Michael moved into the center of the kitchen and stood next to the table, waiting for further instructions. Rosalia went past him. "Come," she said. "In here." Michael dutifully followed her into the living room. What was there was worn but comfortable: the couch, the overstuffed chairs, a rocker, even, and lamps with yellow silk shades. Against one wall was an upright piano, complete with piano bench. But on top of both piano and bench were more photographs, a veritable forest, all framed and placed with no particular attention to size. Several small ones were lost behind a large one; one of oval shape might be eclipsed by a rectangle. Precedence was apparently determined by something other than visibility. A piece of sheet music was open on the piano. Michael recognized it as an old Neapolitan song, "*Te voglio bene assàje,*" the words written in dialect, the music composed by someone whose name had been long forgotten. From the color of the yellowing pages, it seemed that no other song had been sung for quite a while.

"Please. Sit down." Rosalia indicated the easy chair. As he lowered himself into it, she went to the other side of the room and turned on the television. It was a Sony, a color set with a twenty-four-inch screen. Rosalia punched the buttons until she found—at one-thirty in the afternoon—a soccer match, probably a rerun. Smiling as though proud of the achievement, she told him, in case he might not know it, "You're comfortable now." With that, she went back into the kitchen and left him to watch the game.

Michael was dumbfounded. Was it for this she'd so tremulously asked him to come and see her? His mouth open, his body bent forward, he stared at the screen, disbelieving that this was what he was doing. From the kitchen he heard the few thuds of something being put down, then a clunk, then running water, then another clunk. Leaning forward even more, he tried to see into the kitchen, but it was impossible. He wondered if it would be impolite to get up and wander, like the new visitor he was, around the living room. Surely it was acceptable that he examine the photographs; surely he was expected to ask the history of each and every one.

But Rosalia had seemed so pleased to have found the soccer match that he stayed exactly where she'd put him. One team was Naples, the blue and white. The other team, red and black, was completely unknown to him. German, perhaps? The ball was chased and kicked, kicked and chased. The players scurried and ran, ran and scurried, changing course in mid-step as if in response to some erratic and arbitrary directions that had their source not in the ball or the rules of the game but in their instinct, a sort of animal reflex to signals put deep in the blood ages and ages before.

Michael would watch for a few minutes, then think of some pretext for going into the kitchen. As the ball arched high into the air, Rosalia appeared in the doorway. "Tell me about Rome," she said, her voice still shy, as if this were a request she really had no right to make.

"What do you want to know about Rome?"

"Has it changed?" With that, she disappeared again into the kitchen.

"Changed from what?"

Again she was in the doorway. She had a man's T-shirt in her hand and was folding it. "I was there once. To see the Pope. Some girls from school. In a bus. We had a picnic in a field. But it was after we'd seen the Pope." Again she disappeared.

"When was that?"

"Oh, long, long, long ago. I was a girl." She was back, folding another T-shirt.

"I don't think much has changed since then," Michael said. "At least not the Pope."

"He was so friendly. We were way over on the other side, and he waved to us. Way over everybody else, it was to us he waved." She laughed, then added, "Some of us almost fainted. I know I almost did. It was so exciting, and he was so happy that we'd come to see him."

Again Michael was left alone. A window was closed in the kitchen, and he assumed she'd taken in the last of the daily wash. No doubt, like the good wife, she'd done the laundry before going to work and had hung it out to dry on the rack attached to the kitchen window.

"Would you take me with you, back to Rome?" She was in the doorway, a thin cotton bathrobe in her hand. She was feeling it to make sure it was dry. With each clutch of the material, she'd bunch up her face in disgust.

"Would I what?"

"Nothing gets dry anymore." She was gone, and Michael heard the window open again, then close. He waited for her to come back. A member of the red-and-black team was on the ground and being helped up by two players in blue and white. The injured man limped slowly away from his rescuers, then began a trot back to his teammates. From the kitchen came the sound of a refrigerator door opening, of a sigh from Rosalia, of something being stirred, perhaps. Michael waited for the refrigerator door to close, but apparently it was still wide open. It made him uneasy, and he began to shift in his chair. There was the clank of metal on metal, the rim of a pot being struck by a large spoon. There was the definite sound of a plop, then silence. The refrigerator door was still open.

All the men on the field, the blue and white, the red and black, were running together, their heads aimed skyward. The ball was nowhere in sight. It was too high to be seen, and the players were looking for it, awed, expectant, as if waiting for something to descend on a cloud.

"It's ready." Rosalia crossed the room, turned up the television, and went back into the kitchen. He heard the refrigerator door close. It was only then that Michael realized that the cooking smells that had assaulted and gratified him in the hallway had come now into Rosalia's apartment. She had promised him *il pranzo,* and when he went into the kitchen, there it was. A plate of *penne* with a sharp red sauce. Even before he tasted it, he knew it was *penne all'arrabbiata,* the same pasta he'd had the evening before. Considering all the variants the Italians have for pasta, the likelihood of being served the same dish two times in a row approached odds that would perplex even a mathematical genius. Perhaps there were more *arrabbiate* in Naples than he'd suspected.

Michael noticed that only one place had been set. "Aren't you eating?"

"I have to finish the laundry." Having said that, she didn't move from where she was standing. Michael dipped into the pasta. It was less spicy than the night before. Possibly Rosalia had been reticent with the peppers, in deference to his status. In any event, Michael declared it *"squisite."*

Instead of fending off the compliment with a dismissive gesture, Rosalia said, "Yes. I'm a very good cook. My mother, she was a good cook too."

"Yes. I can tell."

Fish smells were coming from the oven, and Michael knew he was being given an exact duplicate of the meal he'd had about fifteen hours before. This time he must be more watchful for fish scales. The one from last evening had dislodged itself only that morning during a rehearsal at San Carlo.

Rosalia continued to stand there, her hands clasped in front of her, fingers locked loosely into fingers, as if she were about to sing a song by Schubert. Michael felt embarrassed. He'd made more work for someone already overburdened. She'd obviously done the laundry before going to her job, probably cleaned the house because company was coming, done the shopping during part of the hours set aside for siesta, and now was feeding him before she'd go back to work again.

Suddenly Rosalia's hands separated, and she grabbed onto the back of a chair. "You *can* take me with you to Rome, can't you?"

Michael had a mouthful and couldn't answer. He indicated this by raising his head, looking at her, and chewing as rapidly as he could. Rosalia didn't wait for him to swallow. "You're not married. You don't have a ring. I saw that right away yesterday. Whoever takes care of you, let her go. *I'll* take care of you."

She turned and looked at the unfolded laundry, then at the pots on the stove. "No, I didn't cook just to show you how good I am. I really wanted you to come over and see my— our—apartment, since you came all the way from Rome. But last night in bed, the idea came to me. You'll take me with you. I'll look after you, cook, do the laundry—all the things a man can't do."

Michael didn't tell her that at home in New York he did exactly these same things for himself and did them fairly well. All he said was, "I don't understand."

Rosalia pulled the chair back from the table and sat down. "I have to go away. I can't stay here, not in Naples. But I have nowhere to go. I have no family except my husband. And you. There's no one anywhere, except you. You're my uncle now. I am Spacagna, so it will be all right. Don Michele, please, *please* let me come with you."

Michael put down his fork. "I don't see how that's possible," he said quietly.

"Oh, don't worry. I can get a job in Rome. See? I speak Italian very well. In school I worked very hard. You won't have to support me. Just let me live with you and take care of you."

"But you're married. You can't leave your husband."

"I *have* to leave my husband. Please don't ask me why, but I have to go away. Far away. As far as Rome, even. I have to. Let me come with you. Oh, *Zio!* Please. I beg you."

Michael wasn't sure he should ask the question, but he did anyway. "But why did you marry Peppino if you have to go away?"

"I had to marry Peppino. I didn't have an uncle then. But tell me I can come with you."

Without stopping, she brought all the desperation of her request to, of all things, a plea for a bird. "And can we have a bird?" she asked. "Saturday is La Festa di San Giuseppe. The two of us, we can go together to Castel Nuovo. It's the day they sell birds there. In the moat, except it's been dry now for centuries, I guess. Birds *and* fish. Can we buy a bird and take it with us? A finch, maybe. And a cage made of wood? Not metal, but wood, because a bird is used to wood, to trees. And maybe in Rome you have a window, and the bird can live there. Or maybe there's even a balcony. Do you have a balcony? I could put the bird out on the balcony. Every morning, before I go to work. I would. I'd never forget. Oh, Uncle, please, take me with you!"

"Rosalia . . ." Michael reached across the table and took her hand in his. She quickly pulled it away, as if he'd singed her. Then, slowly, and with effort, she put the hand forward again and let it rest on his. Again he folded it in his own, and he could feel a trembling as if he held not her hand but her heart. "Rosalia—*cara*—that wouldn't be possible. I don't see how that could be possible."

"I know Peppino is your nephew and we're not really related except through him." She paused. Her next words were fierce. "Except I am your niece now. You can't just leave me here. I'm your family too. You *have* to take me with you, whether you want to or not. I am Rosalia Spacagna. You have to take care of me. You have to look after me. You have to save me. Please. You have to!"

She jumped up and started toward the window, where the laundry basket was, but turned abruptly and went to the oven. With nothing in her voice that referred to what she'd just blurted out, she said, "The fish is fresh from this morning. From the market on Via Sant'Antonio Abate. I know them there. They knew my mother."

Even though he hadn't finished the *penne,* Rosalia took his plate away and put the fish in front of him. There was some spinach as well and, a slight departure at last from the previous menu, a wedge of lemon. Rosalia resumed her Schubert position again, smiling, waiting for the praise the fish would earn her. Michael would have to say something, but it shouldn't be about the fish. He couldn't just eat and comment on the food and let that pass for conversation. Rosalia had said things that could hardly be ignored, even if she had said them to a man who didn't really exist, to Don Michele, to her beloved uncle.

But before Michael could say anything, she began to speak. "They say there aren't many fish left anymore. Soon they'll all be gone, even the anchovies. I don't believe that, but still, it's what they say. Can you imagine a sea without fish? Where would the fish go if not in the sea? The lakes, of course. The rivers, I guess. But I still can't believe there could be no fish. The men have to have jobs. How can they have jobs if there are no fish?"

She stopped and looked down at the table. "You *do* have a wife, don't you? You took off your ring because you were coming to Naples. They say a lot of men do that. I don't mind. I understand. After all, I'm a married woman. I should be able to understand these things." A twinge of a smile pushed her cheeks closer to her ears, then a calmer smile took over, one of sad understanding, and, beneath that, a look of profound acceptance, as if she were seeing not him but some sorrowful revelation to which she had become, at that moment, completely resigned.

Michael wasn't sure how much of the truth he was going to tell her, but he certainly couldn't witness so absolute a trust and continue to be a fraud himself. Sooner or later, he knew, he was going to have to say, "I am not your uncle. You are not my niece." To lead himself toward the words, he said, "No, I have no wife. And I didn't take off my ring because I was coming to Naples."

Rosalia gasped. "She died. Your wife, she's dead. I can tell by the way you said that. I'm so sorry. I truly am. Uncle, it's terrible. But you mustn't be so bitter."

"Bitter?"

"I hear bitterness in your voice. And didn't you take off the ring and throw it into the grave? A cousin of a cousin of mine did that. A cousin of Signor Scarano, the man I work for. They say he took off the ring and flung it after her just as they were closing the grave. Is that what you did?"

Michael thought he was thinking, but he wasn't. He was just waiting until he could say the word he finally said. "No."

"But you loved her very much anyway."

"Yes," he said. He was tempted to correct the gender of the pronoun but decided both he and Rosalia had had enough to deal with for one day. "I loved her very much."

"I thought maybe like him, like the man who threw the ring into the grave, you've never forgiven her for dying, for leaving you like that. I thought I heard it in your voice, that you haven't forgiven her. Have you?"

Michael answered by saying, "No, it's not that. I have no resentment about the dying. That much I know."

With her forefinger, Rosalia rubbed a spot on the tabletop as if it needed cleaning. "Then you'll probably marry again, won't you?"

"Who knows? Maybe."

"Then I can't come with you to Rome, can I? I would be in the way. Women wouldn't come to you if I was there. I understand that too. And it's all right. You came to the wedding. That's something. I . . . it's enough, really. I . . . I hope it didn't bother you too much that it was a little . . . unusual. They . . . they told me I screamed." She paused, then asked, "Did I scream? Right there? In church?"

Michael looked across the table at her. She really wasn't very beautiful. Tulle and lace had given her a borrowed beauty, and what he saw now was the common *venditrice,* the shopgirl she had always been and probably always would be. Her hair had begun to frizz from the greasy heat at the stove. Her nose was too big, her chin too small, and her skin was just a little too shiny. The eyes were round and dark, but it wasn't enough. Her whole face was too open. She had no mystery.

"Yes," Michael said. "You screamed. When Peppino fainted."

"Oh. Then. Well . . ."

There was a silence between them. Michael went back to his eating. Rosalia watched, her hands returned to the Schubert position. Michael didn't like being stared at while he was eating.

"Is it true, what Gaetano says?" he asked.

"Gaetano?" She flinched at the name. "What does Gaetano say?"

"He says Peppino . . . forgive me for saying this, but . . ."

"No, no, it's all right. I want to know what Gaetano said."

"He says—well—that Peppino raped you."

Rosalia flinched again but said nothing. Michael repented of having brought up the subject. He'd had no right; it was cruel; it was stupid. Then he heard Rosalia say, but quietly, "He—Peppino—he's my husband now."

"I shouldn't have asked what I asked. I'm sorry."

"I was all alone," she said.

"All alone?"

"I was all alone since my mother died. I have no family left. Except now I have my husband. And his family. You. But I was alone before that. I had this apartment from my mother, and I had my job from her cousin. But before I was married I had no one. No one at all."

"Then you married Peppino so you'd have a family?"

"Maybe. If I didn't marry him, I wouldn't have any family at all, would I?"

"And he didn't rape you?"

"No." She seemed to consider this a moment, then shook her head and repeated the word. "No. He didn't do that to me."

"Then what Gaetano said isn't true."

"No. I don't think so."

"You don't think so?"

"No. I don't think so." Rosalia looked at the uneaten fish and, without saying anything, took the plate and emptied its contents into the garbage pail under the sink, then put the plate under the hot water.

Michael had pushed her too far again. "I keep asking questions I shouldn't be asking. It's none of my business. I'm sorry. Please forgive me."

"But you're my uncle. You're Peppino's uncle. And . . . and Gaetano's too."

"Rosalia . . . ," he said, wondering if he was about to tell her the truth about his identity. Such faith, such trust, all unearned and undeserved . . .

But Rosalia continued talking. "It was in the living room, on the floor," she said. "I let Peppino come to see me because I was his brother's *fidanzata* and it was all right because it was the same family. He was going to become like my brother. But when I saw what Peppino was going to do, I did nothing to stop him. Except maybe scratch his face and put my thumb in his eye. But I kicked too, and I shouldn't have. I should have kept my legs stiff and straight together." She stopped as if ashamed for her mistake, then continued. "I couldn't have stopped him anyway. He loves me. He only did it because he loves me. That's what he said."

Michael listened for a trace of sarcasm in her voice, but there wasn't any.

"He cried when he was finished," she said. "It was then,

when he was sitting where you're sitting now and when I was standing over there by the window, that I told him I would marry him. It frightened him when I said that. Then I told him I couldn't marry Gaetano anymore, because I'd been with another man. It wouldn't be fair. So I told Peppino now he would have to marry me. And he did. His mother agreed with me and told him he had to. She's very thoughtful, my *suocera*."

Michael waited, then said, "But you love Gaetano?"

"Of course. But what does that have to do with it? I couldn't marry Gaetano, not after what happened, and I couldn't be all alone anymore. With no family. I had to marry someone. So I married Peppino. You were there."

"And now Gaetano says he has to kill Peppino."

Slowly Rosalia shook her head. "If I believed that, if I thought Gaetano would kill him, I would have to stop him." Before Michael could tell her that that's exactly what she should do, that Gaetano was indeed intent on murdering his brother, Rosalia continued. "I would kill Peppino myself. I have every right. After what he did to me."

"I wouldn't advise that."

Rosalia shrugged, went to the sink, and began scrubbing the inside of the pasta pot. "If you change your mind," she said, "and it's all right, then maybe I can still come to Rome. You won't love again. I can tell. So will you let me know?"

"Yes. I'll let you know."

Michael wondered if he was going to be given coffee, but Rosalia continued to scour away. He was ashamed of himself. His deception was making him irritable, impatient. He wished Gaetano would hurry up and do it, kill Peppino, and let the entire matter end there. What a foolish name it was, Peppino. Kill him and get it over with.

And what did Rosalia mean, he'd never love again? What did she know? About anything? Nothing. Nothing at all. And he wished she'd stop scrubbing. Her hair had fallen forward over her right eye, and she did nothing about it. And now she began to hum, to actually hum. And then she was singing, actually *singing,* still scouring, her hair still fallen over her right eye. As her uncle, he could tell her to stop, to be quiet, and to brush the hair out of her eyes. But he said nothing, did nothing. And Rosalia simply hummed and sang and scoured away as if it bothered her not at all that her right eye was completely blinded by her fallen hair.

7

It was a cold night for March, and when Michael came to Via Libertà after dinner, he could see on the far side of the piazza two fires lit along Via Indipendenza, where the blacks would be displaying their usual nighttime wares. There was, as well, the bonfire on the corner across the Corso and another—this one in a metal bucket—near Santa Candida. Until now, the nights, for whatever reason, had always seemed warmer than the days, almost balmy, as if the city, in the light, was cold and preoccupied, but once the dark had settled down, it would allow a more natural heat to rise up from the stones and seep out from the stuccoed walls. Michael wondered if this meant that now the days would be warmer, that Naples had at last been persuaded to subscribe to the natural order that ordained warmer days, cooler nights. More likely it meant that the morning would dawn colder than this midnight chill and that the day itself might possibly reach back to some winter memory when choosing a temperature suitable for high noon.

Michael was in no hurry, and he didn't bother to keep his head bowed toward the ground. He wasn't exactly gawking, but he was definitely interested in what might be going on around the piazza. In fact, he was hoping he'd see Piero Esposito, that the young tenor might approach him again with the smooth

"*Bello*"—a sort of "Hey, good-looking"—that managed to soothe even as it coaxed. He figured that if he walked close enough to the shadows—but not too close—he might again find himself the object of the young man's solicitation. Or at least he might spot him waiting there for a likely client. Michael hoped he'd recognize him without too much trouble; the last thing he wanted was to engage the attentions of someone who would turn out not to be Piero. What Michael wanted was to make a deal, not for Piero's professional favors but for a harmonium, the one instrument without which there could be no rehearsals of *Curlew*.

When he'd come to the hall that evening, Michael was relieved to see that the monks' robes he'd asked Crescenzo to send were there and waiting. It was his intention to have the singers rehearse in the robes to remind them that they were monks performing a play, not the operatic Neapolitans in the tradition of Bellini and Verdi that they often preferred to be. They were ascetics, and all *bel canto* ambitions were to be suppressed.

Then, too, he wanted them to see him first as a monk, one like themselves, rather than as the Madwoman. His true transformation would be from ordinary citizen to friar, and the transvestism of his role would be merely the fulfillment of a priestly duty—to perform the play in the service of God. What these graduated changes might achieve he wasn't sure. As a foreigner, he was already an outsider, and no costume could change that. Still, he thought that the respect he needed as director of the project might be better sustained, even strengthened, if he was seen first as a priest, then as a madwoman.

There had been, of course, the excitement of getting one's costume. The eagerness for transformation is universal, and a costume, like a mask, always provides an easy path to change. Velvets and brocades, plumes and fine lace, could not have prompted more preening than the simple brown woolens that robed them now. The hoods provided endless opportunities for character experiment: the sinister, the rakish, the innocent, the devout, the downright evil. The cinctures were tied in knots known only to the nautical, with one or two elaborate bows thrown in for the sake of silliness. There were complaints that sandals were not included, and when one of the baritones, greedy for the penitence that only the barefoot can experience, took off his shoes and socks, the tenors followed his example, but the basses stayed fully shod. No one, absolutely no one but Michael himself, was able to resist the temptation to repeatedly bless the person nearest at hand; there was a lot of fraternal embracing, and the mock "kiss of peace" threatened to lapse into outright orgy.

In the midst of all this, Eduardo Zongola, the musician who played the harmonium, arrived and pretended, in his usual purse-lipped way, to disapprove of the varying forms of sacrilege rampant in the room. However, when he, too, was given a priestly robe—all the musicians would be similarly clothed—his disgust disappeared and was replaced with a sacerdotal competitiveness very much at variance with monastic renunciations. He, too, took off his shoes (but left on his socks) and, like any good friar, was insistent on giving out more blessings than he received.

It was during the blessing phase of his ministry that he first began to wonder where the harmonium was. A reed instrument with a keyboard, the size and shape of a three-foot-high bookcase, it was an excellent one, electrically powered, and had been provided by the foundation at considerable expense. It would be used in actual performance, and the rehearsals were giving Signor Zongola a needed chance to acquaint himself with its idiosyncrasies and its possibilities.

Before Zongola had blessed the entire flock, it was known beyond any doubt that the harmonium was gone. Zongola was appalled. A harmonium, with its liturgical associations, was a sacred object, and the theft was well within the boundaries of sacrilege.

There was no evidence of a break-in. The lock on the door,

the locks on the windows, were examined, with no clue apparent to the naked eye. Michael announced that they would rehearse without it, that they *must* rehearse. The time was too valuable to be lost. At this point, Piero spoke up. He had a friend who owned a harmonium. He might possibly rent it to Michael for the evening, and for future rehearsals until a replacement was found.

Michael was relieved. Piero, refusing all assistance, was dispatched, and within a reasonably short time, a harmonium was delivered, carried into the room by Piero himself and a cabdriver. It was the stolen harmonium, and Zongola himself seemed about to exclaim the general truth aloud, but then, after a glance at Piero, he casually fingered a passage up, then down, and said it would do for now. Piero claimed it sounded better than the one that had been taken but that his friend couldn't possibly sell it for any amount. It was too valuable an instrument. For the time being, he would be willing to rent it out on a daily basis, but that was all. Piero, however, would intercede with his friend for an outright sale if a suitable figure was named.

Instinctively, Michael knew that confrontation and accusation would get him nowhere. Where were his indisputable proofs? And besides, there was no doubt that everyone there not only approved of the theft but felt a certain pride in the expertise with which it had been carried out.

The harmonium, now stolen property, was looked upon with heightened appreciation. Few could restrain themselves from doing a quick run up the keys to test the presumed difference between this instrument and the inferior one that had so mysteriously disappeared. The bass who sang the Abbot ran his hand along the top with fondness and affection. The Ferryman patted it on its side. A pilgrim tenor, his arm across Signor Zongola's shoulder, pointed to the harmonium, laughed, and assured the musician that the instrument had been much improved by its recent ride in a taxi.

A brotherly affection for the harmonium had sprung up, and no one, Michael excepted, abstained from the fellow-feeling. It had achieved celebrity status. And what was being celebrated was the triumph of cunning and risk, an accomplished taunt at established order, and the increase in value automatically bestowed on the illicit.

With difficulty, Michael, aided by the processional chant "*Te lucis ante terminum,*" calmed everyone down. As the rehearsal progressed, there was only an occasional disruption of discipline: Piero would be given a knowing poke in the ribs or a crooked admiring smile, or a look of mock innocence would be sent in his direction. And during an instrumental interlude when the harmonium made a solo response to the drama, the entire cast turned to Piero, their faces beaming with congratulation. The music was, after all, his achievement. Even Signor Zongola, the most prim of professionals, couldn't refrain from sending the young man a few nods of approval.

Piero himself pretended to ignore it all. Michael's only problem with him, for the moment anyway, was Piero's repeated inability to restrain the soaring voice, to cage again within the strictures of the music—the measures, the markings—a spirit acquainted with the glories of guile, daring, and, most of all, undiluted gall.

Only for a single second, also during the instrumental response, did Michael feel that the harmonium, indeed, was much improved, that it, too, had benefited from its involvement in crime and could sound forth now with a more pliant tone, a more experienced pitch. When, however, in the next exchange, between the Madwoman and the pilgrims, he heard the inspired voice of Piero raised high above all others, he returned to his first determination: It was the same harmonium, and its excursion into the unlawful had done nothing to change its old reliability, its functional sturdiness.

But then again . . .

When Michael approached Piero after rehearsal, the young

man stated very matter-of-factly that for now only rental was possible but that Michael should in the meantime give thorough and cautious thought before presenting a price for its purchase. When Michael indicated that he'd like to continue the negotiations right then and there, Piero shook his head, as if the inconvenience he was causing was a genuine sorrow to him. He told Michael he was not authorized to say anything more than what he'd already said. And with that, he finished tying his shoes— which seemed very much in need of a new pair of shoestrings.

No reference was made to the brief meeting the night before, nor was anything implied by what Michael said and did. But he couldn't help thinking that he knew where he might find the young man later on.

Michael considered crossing the Corso just before the statue to see if Piero was resting or waiting against the base. Then he realized he should be as inconspicuous as possible; Piero wouldn't come near him if he knew it was Michael. That had been obvious the evening before. And now, Piero might be even less eager to see the one person in all Naples who was prepared, as Michael was, to accuse him directly of stealing the harmonium.

Michael raised his coat collar and slumped down inside just a little. He also put his hands in the pockets, as if he might be identified by his fingernails. As he passed the shelter of the bus stop, he noticed that the fire on Piazza Principe Umberto had been rekindled and that another, farther down the Corso, was sending its orange and golden flames into the chill night air.

"Bello! Buona sera!" The intonation was familiar, but the voice was wrong. The man at his side, in a flowered brown dress that seemed like something out of a forties movie, was smiling at him, his eyes half closed, his head snaking upward as if asking Michael in a very sultry way if he liked his getup.

Michael decided to be forthright. "I'm supposed to meet Piero," he said. "Is he here?"

"How would I know? As far as I can see, there's no one

here but you. And me." He flared his eyes, coming attractions
of a performance yet to be scripted.

"*Va bene. Grazie.*" Michael nodded his head respectfully and
kept right on going.

"So handsome," the voice behind him said. "How selfish
to keep it all to yourself." Michael's ear, for better or worse, was
finely enough tuned to catch the mockery. He said nothing. "The
next time we meet, you may call me Renato. *Ciao, bello.* Don't
forget, I'm waiting for you forever—until midnight." Michael
nodded again, to indicate that he'd heard and that his rejection
intended no disrespect.

When he reached Piazza Principe Umberto, no one was
warming himself at the fire, even though a kitchen chair had
been set next to it, facing the street. Next to the bucket that held
the fire was a small pile of smashed and splintered crates and the
handle of a broom. It surprised Michael that such a treasure—a
spindle-backed kitchen chair—should be left unattended.

Piero, when Michael saw him, was looking in the window
of the shoe store across the small piazza. Above the window and
the main door was a sign in huge letters, promising PREZZI
IMBATTIBILI—unbeatable prices. This did not, Michael felt, apply
to Piero himself.

At first he wondered what effect it might have if he sat down
next to the fire. It would be both bold and nonchalant, an imi-
tation of two of Piero's primary characteristics. It would also be
stupid. What if he attracted someone other than Piero, someone
who might think that he, too, was offering *prezzi imbattibili?*

Michael went and stood next to Piero. The shoes were indeed
inexpensive, and some of them looked quite good: sturdy and
serviceable, or elegant and delicate.

"How much would it cost to buy back the harmonium?"

With no movement that might acknowledge Michael's presence, Piero said, "Please, sir, I'm looking at the shoes."

"I'm fairly sure I can get the money," Michael continued,

"but please tell your 'friend' who was kind enough to let us rent for the evening that a replacement might be found at any moment and that good as his instrument might be, it's not the only one in Naples. But I'm sure he knows that."

Piero was wearing a simple dark-blue dress, drawn in at the waist but without a belt. The neckline wasn't exactly plunging, but there was a sizable triangle of flesh visible at his chest. Considerate of the young man's professional needs, the chest had no hair.

To place his costume squarely in the early forties, or even earlier, Piero also wore a gray furpiece (silver fox?) slung across his shoulder, and Michael couldn't help thinking it would do better service worn snugly against the naked neck. Never had he seen a singer so determined to put his voice at risk. It had all the absurdity of a tubercular stubbornly standing sentry in a peat bog. Michael couldn't decide if he resented or admired Piero for the chances he was taking. Whichever, he didn't want to lose him before *Curlew River,* especially now that he held the destiny of the much-needed harmonium in his long-fingered hands.

The shoulders of the dress were padded, and Michael had to wonder again if it was tradition that made him and his colleague Renato mimic forties movie stars in their choice of finery. Had transvestites been so successful right after the war that no detail of the presentation had been altered since? Or were they trying now to revivify the excitement of what must have been a time of high prosperity? Whatever the reason, the standards seemed obviously set, and if they weren't exactly locked in amber, they were at least protected by a glow that would last as long as backlighting was available among the glooms and shadows of Naples.

"I'm not here to sell harmoniums," Piero said. With that, he turned and started toward the fire. Michael could see more clearly now why he was interested in the shoes. Those he was wearing were the same he'd worn for rehearsal, brown wing tips badly in need not only of new laces but of a pair of heels as well. With them he wore striped ankle socks, and if Michael could make out the colors in the light provided by the streetlamps, they were blue, orange, and yellow, and seemed to be falling down around his shoes. His walk made no attempt at either femininity or its parody. He moved toward the fire with no sway in the hips or shoulders. There was, in fact, a certain graceless plodding to his step, a grudging agreement to go where he was going and be quiet about it.

When Piero got to the fire, he looked down inside, then wrapped the fur around his neck. Facing the street, he raised his head and turned it away from the fire, giving the shadows the pleasure of licking the planes of his face.

Piero was a reasonably good-looking young man, but as a woman he was decidedly at a disadvantage. The long brunette wig lengthened his face so that it seemed almost to droop down toward his chin. The generous mouth became too wide, his lips vulgar in their insistence that they remain slack and passive, allowing both flesh and blood to puff them up so that they would seem at once indifferently lazy and eagerly waiting. The slanted eyes, exotic in a man, took on the narrow, slitted characteristics of a small unpleasant animal's. Michael couldn't believe that Piero wouldn't have done better to present himself as he really was, a somewhat lanky youth with floppy brown hair, long arms, and a slow smile that seemed to prefer a shy slyness to open laughter. It could be, of course, that Piero was able to present his sexual self only in this way, only at this remove from his other self, and that what he was doing now with his aloof manner was simply his insistence that he not be approached as one self when he was busy being another. He was not the singer now, or the pilgrim or the monk, and the distinction had to be respected.

Michael went to him, realizing he'd said and done the wrong thing by telling him outright that he'd buy the harmonium. He should have eased into the subject, giving each of them time to test the other's bargaining capabilities. His headlong leap into the subject was a breach of protocol, an implied dismissal of Piero's talent for negotiation. Michael decided to start all over again. "If you have a place where we might go together, maybe you'd let me come with you."

Piero squeezed his lips together, his equivalent of a furrowed brow. Michael considered mentioning the cold, that the fire would soon die down and there wasn't much more wood unless the kitchen chair was eventually intended for the flames, but he thought the outright invitation should be enough.

Piero's lips slackened again. He turned toward Michael, his face completely in shadow. "Don't you live near here yourself, Signore?"

How Piero knew this, Michael hadn't the slightest idea. Unless he'd followed him last night without being seen, a feat easily within Piero's capabilities. "Yes," Michael answered, "but I thought you might know a place more convenient."

"You have an apartment, don't you?"

"Yes, but—" Michael stopped, then realized what the "but" referred to. It wasn't what the neighbors might say, as he'd first supposed. It was that he assumed Piero would, to some degree, pillage the place. Even if he didn't return to rob it, he would no doubt make off that very night with something Michael would find difficult to replace before the original tenant returned. And yet Michael didn't want Piero to think he was embarrassed by him, because, in fact, he was. Still, if need be, he would parade him in front of his neighbors, an act of defiance that he would wish were indifference. Maybe with practice, the indifference would eventually come. He was willing to make a start.

"I understand," Piero said. Even though Michael couldn't see it, he knew the slow smile was creeping across Piero's face.

"No, you don't," Michael said. "I have an apartment, but I'm afraid that if I took you there, you'd steal something."

"I know. That's why I said I understood. After all, it's not really your apartment, and you should have some regard for other people's property. I do. In my own way. But see? I *do* understand."

"Then I'm right to be worried?"

"Maybe. First I'd have to see what's there."

"Not all that much. But enough."

"Ah."

"Maybe you could promise that you wouldn't take anything. Not only tonight, but at any other time. Could you promise that?"

"Of course." In the pause, Michael could sense the smile again, its slow spread across the face, making furrows alongside his mouth and nose. "I could promise you anything you'd like," Piero said.

"But would you keep the promise?"

"Possibly. But probably not. I might want to keep it, but then I would probably decide not to after all. I change."

"So I've noticed."

Piero leaned over to pick up the chair. The furpiece fell open at his neck, and he immediately clutched the fur together at his throat and across his chest. He reached down for the chair again, and again the fur loosened, slipping forward. Piero righted himself and, with a quick smile, now visible in the light of the fire, seemed to be apologizing for having so immodestly displayed the bare flesh of his chest. The fur was now held tightly in place, and Piero, his fingers in among the spindles, lifted the chair with one hand, braced it against his shoulder, and walked toward the darker side of the piazza.

What Michael had seen on Piero's chest, there in the firelight, was what the young man had wanted to conceal with the fur. Someone had obviously burned him in several places—at least three by Michael's count. An attempt had been made to cover the marks with makeup, but the pale pink of a healing burn still showed in the glare of the flames. Michael sensed at once the

range of indignities, the sadistic cruelties, that the young man
had to accept as part of his calling. Or was this Piero's preference?
In a thought that he didn't refuse, Michael saw him arching his
head back, his tongue hissing between his teeth with a pulled-in
breath, as the burning brand—a cigarette, a cigar, an ember—
was placed against his chest. The body itself, stretched toward
pain, the willing, even begging acceptance, the need for something extreme, the reach toward helpless giving—all this, Michael found, was not too far beyond the boundaries of his own
imagining.

"Aren't you coming?" Piero had stopped but didn't turn
around. Michael looked first one way, then the other, down the
Corso. No one was in sight, only a car far down toward the
street that led to the Porta Capuana. After gazing into the fire—
an atavistic impulse to read meanings and auguries among the
embers—he followed Piero, wondering where they were going.
He hardly relished the idea of walking the dark passageways of
Naples, even guided by an extremely knowing native armed with
a kitchen chair. Still, he followed.

Piero turned left on Via Milano, set the chair down, went
between two cars, and emerged wheeling his motorbike. He
hiked his skirt, straddled the seat, lifted the chair, and locked it
into the handlebars. Glancing back over his shoulder, he said,
"In back. Get on." The motor was started, then revved into loud
repeated whines that seemed the bike's protest at being roused
at such an hour.

"Why should I get on?"

"We're going to my place."

"To talk about the harmonium?"

Piero turned off the motor, untangled the chair from the
handlebars, and set it down on the pavement. The motorbike
was returned to its berth, and without a word, he picked up the
chair and started back toward the piazza. "You really mustn't
take up my time this way. It's almost midnight. Maybe you

should go home. The harmonium, if that's what you think you want to talk about, can wait."

Back at the Corso, he set the chair down next to the fire. With his fingers he kneaded his wig, then shook out the hair so it would fall properly to his shoulders. This seemed to rejuvenate him, as if he'd just given himself a thorough touch-up. He stood there looking straight ahead, poised and ready for whatever might happen, yet relaxed and resigned if this might prove to be the only pose required of him all night long.

"Couldn't you be dressed a little warmer?" Michael asked. Piero raised his chin a little to expose himself that much more completely to the night air. "I was only thinking about your voice," Michael said.

Still facing the Corso, Piero swallowed, his Adam's apple rising, then lowering. When it returned to its normal position, he opened his mouth and, still looking straight ahead, began, in a clear and unforced voice, a song in dialect that Michael thought he remembered from his student days. The melody was plaintive, but so simple that it seemed well beyond sorrow itself.

> *Fenesta che lucive e mò non luce,*
> *sign' è ca Nenna mia stace ammalata.*

> The window that used to shine isn't shining now,
> a sign that my Sweet is ill.

Forward the song went in an unbroken legato surge, no embellishments, no demand that the listener be moved. It was indifferent to everything but the tale it had to tell.

> *S'affacia la sorella e me lo dice:*
> *Nennella toja è morta e s'è atterrata*
> *Chiagneva sempe ca dormeva sola.*
> *Mò dorme co li muorte accompagnata!*
> *Mò dorme co li muorte accompagnata!*

Her sister came to the window and said to me:
Your little Sweet is dead and has been buried.
She always wept because she slept alone.
Now she sleeps in company with the dead!
Now she sleeps in company with the dead!

The music reached across the piazza and gently touched the windows above the *farmacia*. A shutter opened, then another, this one on the fifth floor, and then another on the third floor of the next building. Behind Michael, high up, was the creaking sound of a window being raised.

Chiagneva sempe ca dormeva sola.
Mò dorme co li muorte accompagnata!
Mò dorme co li muorte accompagnata!

Piero let the last words fall naturally into silence. There was no more to be said, nothing more to be sung.

So that he wouldn't have to look at Piero, Michael stared down into the fire. One last flare was devouring what had been the slat of a vegetable crate. The letters CAV suggested that it had contained *cavolo*—cabbage. Michael would have expected to have thoughts of Damian, but it was of Rosalia he'd been thinking. The song—its plaintive simplicity, its uncomplaining resignation—had summoned her as if it had been a chant to conjure up not the spirits of the dead but of the living. This was the tune she'd hummed and sung when she'd scrubbed the pasta pot, the long-drawn yearning of an unappeasable lament. Only now did he recognize it, the fragments she'd offered then now coming together to tell him what was in her heart, a quietly accepted prophecy of her doomed love for Gaetano and of his love for her. With its broken phrases, its lapses into wordlessness, its emergence again into song, it had seemed to Michael an offering of reassurance to the fates that she had heard their pronouncements and was preparing herself to bow down before their immutable decree.

He wished he were the uncle he was presumed to be. He'd intervene; he'd rearrange. He'd force retractions; he'd change the past, the present, and the future; he'd rescue and he'd condemn; he'd reward and he'd exact. He would bar the fates, forbid them to step beyond the line he'd draw, with an uncle's hand, at the thresholds of all who exalted in the name Spacagna.

But even as Michael was complimenting himself for the nobility of his ambitions and his resolves, his self-mockery, ever at the ready, asked for a few commonplace specifics. Exactly how would he implement these fine and daring sentiments? By what alchemy would he transform the abstract into the substantial? The emotional into the actual? The helplessness so wrathfully articulated by Fra Callisto in the confessional pressed down on him again, made all the heavier now by the vision of Rosalia summoned by Piero's song.

Three times within the week since he'd seen Rosalia, Michael had phoned Signora Spacagna and asked to see her. Three times he'd been told to call another time. When, on the third try, he'd lost what little patience he had left and blurted out, "Do you know that Gaetano talks about killing Peppino? Did you know that?" she had said, "Ah, Don Michele, you're very kind to call, but another time, perhaps, and we'll be able to talk." With that, plus a polite and unconcerned goodbye, she'd hung up.

Maybe Gaetano had been there and she couldn't speak. But all three times he'd asked to be allowed to see her, anywhere, identifying himself on two occasions as Don Michele, a person of presumed priority, but no matter what he'd called himself, he'd been promised a meeting soon—but not now. "It's so good to hear from you, Don Michele. Just to know you're still in Naples. We'll have to meet. Soon. I promise. And you're very kind to call."

After he'd hung up following the third call, he felt the urge to murder Peppino himself—gladly—not to rectify an impossible situation but to get the Signora's undivided attention. The fourth time he'd phoned—to give notice that he'd resigned his role, that he, too, had become indifferent to rape, fratricide, and Neapolitan inscrutability—no one answered.

The v and the A had been burned away from the cabbage crate, and Michael watched to see the c disappear as well. Thinking now not of the Signora but again of Rosalia, he found himself not without hope. All was not lost. Correction somehow seemed possible, rescue not far off. When he searched inside himself for the source of this improbability, he could find nothing. But then it came to him. He heard again the humming and the singing, the offered appeasement to the fates, but he heard as well the clash and clang of the pasta pot against the sink. He saw the stern pitiless arm of Rosalia as it scoured and scourged the protesting metal. This, too, was her offering. Lament she did, but in the banging and the scrapes could be heard as well the clarion signal that insurrection and refusal were distinct possibilities and that fair warning was now being given.

Repeatedly Michael told himself that there was little difference between this conjured hope and the empty puffery of his noble thoughts. They proceeded from the same despair, a necessary response to impotence, an understandable reaction to defeat. But then again he'd hear the clatter, the raw, hoarse rasp of the scouring, and the hope would rise again. And with it, below it, above it, like the intervening theme of the sonata form, were the fragments and phrases: *Mò dorme co li muorte accompagnata*—Now she sleeps in company with the dead. And the two became one: the rebellious scouring, the resigned lament. Appropriate to Naples, they were at once a cacophony and a harmony; opposites, they were a single infrangible offering from Signora Rosalia Spacagna, and the fates, the gods, and Michael himself could make of them what they would.

The cabbage crate was completely consumed, the black ash embedded with skittering sparks that spelled nothing at all. One by one the shutters closed on the far side of the piazza, and the window behind Michael was shut with a prolonged series of subdued squeals and squeaks.

After yet one moment more, Piero asked, "And is my voice still acceptable?" There was no mockery in his tone. It was a straightforward question that seemed to want a fact for an answer, not an opinion.

"That was very beautiful," Michael said.

Piero waited, then nodded. What Michael had said he acknowledged as fact. With another nod, he accepted and concurred in its accuracy. "I learned it from the man who gave me these clothes," he said. "He was my teacher. He died, and all he had came to me. To carry on his work. He was the one who taught me to sing. I know all his songs. He taught me everything I know." He paused, then added, "Which is a great deal."

Even this last sentence had no edge to it. Everything Piero had said was simple; nothing had to be emphasized, nothing had to be commented on by tone or by inflection. Like the song, it needed little beyond the telling.

Michael wanted to go home. He wanted not to have intruded into the young man's other life. He wanted not to have heard the song or seen Piero standing there, his voice rising into the surrounding night, this song of unpitying acceptance and quiet remembrance.

"Good night," he said. "I apologize if I intruded."

Before Michael had turned completely away, Piero said, "Are you a priest?"

"A what?"

"A priest. A friar. A monk."

Michael didn't know whether to be stunned or amused. But Piero seemed genuinely curious; he was making no accusation, he wasn't referring to any suspicions. He merely wanted to know.

"Of course not," Michael said. "Why do you even ask?"

Piero looked directly at him, tipped his head to the right, and lifted it a little. "You seem to be a monk."

"Why? Just because I didn't go off with you?"

"No; it has nothing to do with going with me or not going with me. You're *always* a monk, whenever I see you. At the rehearsal, the way you talk, the way you move around. You seem to have forgotten you have a body. Forgive me, but there's no tension in it. It's not expecting anything. It's not offering anything. And so you come here tonight. Not to find my body but to find your own. Unless you really are a priest."

Michael was dumbfounded. The last thing he expected to be thought was a celibate. Piero was presumptuous, to say the least, and dead wrong besides. Piero, he told himself, had said it as a goad. It was a trick of the trade, so to speak. He probably used it frequently. And with good reason. It was extremely effective. Michael felt challenged. But because he resented the challenge, the goad, the accusation, he'd be that much more adamant in his refusals.

"I am not a priest. And I came to settle the matter of the harmonium."

Piero shook his head. "You *think* you came to see me about the harmonium. But that's not really why."

"I'm afraid it is."

"No, Maestro. Forgive me, but it isn't. Think about it."

"I don't have to think about it. I know. And since we're not going to talk about the—"

"You've forgotten your body. I can help you remember what flesh and bones and blood are for."

"I've forgotten nothing. And I know only too well what flesh and bones and blood are for. Now, if you'll forgive me, I'll say good night." Michael turned toward Via Milano. "And besides," he said, "in case you haven't heard, there's an epidemic. And I don't mean cholera and I don't mean typhus."

"You're worried about the epidemic? That means you must prefer men. But don't worry. I have ways to frustrate even an epidemic. Don't forget, I'm a professional. I was trained by a master, and now I'm a master too. If you would like proof—"

"No, thank you. I'll just take your word for it."

"*My* word? But you don't take my word for anything. Admit it."

"All right, then. But in this instance I don't require any proof."

"Too bad. It would have given me so much pleasure—"

Michael laughed. "One minute my body offers nothing, the next you say it would offer pleasure."

"You've misunderstood. My pleasure wouldn't come from your body. Not exactly. My own preference is for women with ample hips. But with you, my pleasure would come from seeing you respond to yourself again. It would excite me very much to see you surrender not to me but to yourself, to watch you, be with you when it happens. And I have skills that could do it all. Truly I have." There was no boast in his voice, just a fair assurance of fact.

Michael decided he'd better stop talking and go. "Good night," he repeated. He continued toward Via Milano.

"Just a minute. One minute more."

"It's late. You said so yourself."

"I've decided to talk about the harmonium after all."

Michael stopped, sighed soundlessly, and turned around. "It's late even for that."

Piero took a few steps closer. "I understand you're singing Spoletta in *Tosca,* so you'll know what I'm talking about. Scarpia's price for the life of her lover is Tosca herself. Right?"

"Right."

"So the price for the harmonium is this. You. *You* are the price of the harmonium. Come with me, and the harmonium is paid for. That's my price. My only price."

"But that's absurd. Especially since you said you prefer—"

"I know it's absurd. Maybe that's why it appeals to me. I have no interest in priests or monks, believe me. Or in men—

except professionally. But you . . . I'd like to put myself to the test, to see what I can do. Perhaps I'll fail. Maybe you're beyond even my talents." Again he tilted his head to the right, again he lifted it. "I'm not sure."

"Don't worry. Some other arrangement can be made for a harmonium," Michael said. "But I would have thought money would be preferable."

"Money. Yes, money. I've a great fondness for it. But I have another fondness, which sometimes gets in the way. Do you think I stole the harmonium just for the money? Maybe, maybe not. Maybe it was to create mischief. And if I can create an even greater mischief by insisting on this method of purchase, I have very little resistance. Forgive me, but from now on, as far as the harmonium is concerned, money shouldn't even be mentioned. You know my price. And let's say that you have between now and the opening night of *Tosca* to make up your mind. After that, the harmonium will disappear again. But you have time to think about it. And the thoughts will be very interesting. Maybe even exciting."

As Michael watched, Piero again took the chair, retrieved the motorbike, locked the chair into the handlebars, and climbed on. The motor started, and after testing its reliability with the obligatory repeated revs, he sped off toward the Corso. He didn't wave back or even look over his shoulder. With a quick jerk of his left hand, he pulled up his skirt so it wouldn't get caught in the wheels, then used the hand to hold the fox fur tight against his chest. Across the piazza, the shutters of the fifth-floor window opened again, and someone—a man or a woman, Michael couldn't tell—leaned out to watch him go.

8

So great was the roar that Michael thought the opera house had gone up in flames and smoke. It was the rush of fire that he heard; now the beams would crack and fall, the walls crash in, and the flames, free of plaster and stone, would take their howls to the heights of heaven. The great throat of the world was letting out its final exhalation, and surely the end was at hand.

Aganice Calefati was taking a bow. The audience at San Carlo was relieving itself of its verdict for her Tosca, and all sounds to the contrary, it was not demanding blood. She had been superb. She had been perfect. Every note, every gesture, had been perfectly placed. Her ardor was the most ardent of all ardors, her jealousy the most jealous of all jealousies, her piety the most pious of all pieties, her wrath the most wrathful of all wraths. She had caressed and killed; prayed and cursed. Warm and open, cold and cunning—each emotion delivered on the promise of its direct opposite.

Michael stood just offstage, away from the folds of the great curtain, waiting to see if the stage manager would send the entire cast out for yet another call. He was eager for the evening to progress. Assunta, Signora Spacagna herself, was in the audience—the honored guest of Aganice—and their eternally

postponed meeting would take place within a reasonably short
time. He had his questions ready and his insistence, too, that she
take more seriously the crimes—the rape, the absurd wedding,
the sworn intent of one brother to murder the other—that assailed
her family. It was his hope that she'd assure him that her knowledge of the situation was complete and her control of its outcome
absolute, a hope not highly fortified by her casual response to
his previous pleas for a conversation. Perhaps she'd simply dismiss him for his insolence, reclaim his titles, and divest him of
his Roman pretensions. That would be fine with him. At least
he *thought* that would be fine with him.

Michael continued to watch, enthralled. Aganice's submission to the audience's idolatry, humble and heartfelt, had its
counterpart, he knew, in the icy dismissal she had prepared
should their verdict have gone against her. He'd seen her
rehearse—to the full—during the run-through yesterday, when,
for whatever reason, she felt the tenor singing Cavaradossi, Arnaldo Martinello, was not sufficiently appreciative of her contribution to their first-act duet.

With the *Te Deum* resounding through the empty house,
with the chorus, the Scarpia, the organ and the orchestra, rising
to their final praise of heaven's glory, Calefati had drawn the
unsuspecting Martinello off toward the lightboard. "We cannot
all be *bolognesi,* Signore. We cannot all be greatly gifted and fully
inspired. I am merely *napoletana.* And I've had to accept what
God has given me and be grateful for it. I hardly ask that you
hide your contempt for my origins or for my talents. I merely
want you to know that I am indifferent to your scorn and that
my pride is more than a match for all your *bolognese* condescen-
sions. And I ask you to consider this: Is it, perhaps, your lack
and not mine that determines your thinking? Perhaps too many
piemontese screech owls have shrieked in your ear over the years,
so now you aren't able to recognize true music ever again. Inferior
artistry has corrupted you and maybe everyone else—maybe even

the audience for tomorrow night—and you are all obviously blind and deaf to the glories that are spread out before you. But don't be afraid. None of this will affect my performance. My pity for you, for them, even, I will keep to myself; my indifference to you all will be known to no one but Aganice Calefati. You and all the world cannot corrupt me with your hisses and your boos. I hear none of it. I hear only the calling of my art; I hear only the music in my soul, placed there by the hand of God himself. And what can you—*povero bolognese*—what can you possibly do against music, against God, against the human soul?"

So exact was Calefati's timing that this final line was delivered to the ominous crashing chords that brought down the first-act curtain. Had it not been a rehearsal and the house out front empty, the applause would surely have been for Calefati's speech and not for the aria with which Scarpia and the chorus had just ended the act. Head high, she swept off to her dressing room, imperious, satisfied, and Michael realized that this, too, was a rehearsal, should she meet with calamity the following night.

The *povero bolognese* merely put his elbow on the lightboard and leaned his head against the palm of his hand. "Neapolitans eat too much fish," he said. With that, he put his fingers to his lips, made a kissing sound, and let the fingers spring forward, aimed in the direction Calefati had just gone.

Fortunately, the audience of San Carlo, inspired and incorruptible, had been able to see and hear the handiwork of God made manifest in his humble vestal Aganice. "Do they really adore me?" she whimpered when she came offstage from still another curtain call. "Tell me, do they? Do they really?" But before anyone could confirm or deny, she swept out again, and the audience did all that was humanly possible to reassure her of its adoration. Calefati knelt. If the audience had found its goddess in her, she had found in them her god, and her worship was no less abject than theirs.

With the exception of the tenor, Martinello, everyone had fared reasonably well. Boos and hisses followed his *"Recondita armonia"* in the first act, and a minor skirmish broke out between the third and first tiers when it was thought by some that he hadn't sustained his *"Vittoria! Vittoria!"* long enough in Act Two. Michael's Spoletta, however, had elicited a single *"Bravo!"* from what seemed to be the second tier on the right side of the house when he'd come out for his *very* quick curtain call. And he had no trouble accepting it as his due. Never had he been more reptilian.

The tumult for Calefati continued. Michael, still standing in the wings but no longer waiting to see if the entire cast would take another call—they wouldn't; they wouldn't dare; the night belonged to Calefati alone—was thrilled to hear the sounds. He loved applause, even when it wasn't for him. It was the sound of applause, after all, that had drawn him to singing and to opera in the first place.

Around his tenth year, he would sometimes join his father in listening to the Saturday broadcasts from the Met. But not to hear the singing or be swept away by the drama. Often, when a death scene was inordinately prolonged, he would become impatient, not for the poor heroine's death, but for the applause that would come after. The opera had to be endured so he would be eligible for the reward of hearing the ovation as the final curtain fell. Shouts of *"Bravo,"* the maddened cheering that only opera can excite, were the real music. Anarchy and disunity were at an end. All were as one, with no dissent. The tribal imperative was fulfilled at last in this frenzied accord. This was the passion he'd been waiting for. No music could match the sound of applause for abandon and for greatness. Applause validated what he'd heard; it sometimes even created the music's worth retroactively. Applause could convince him he'd been listening to something stirring and profound. Applause, if there was enough of it, would compensate for previous restlessness, and Michael would transfer the thrill of the ovation back to the performance itself and be content that he'd participated in an event the likes of which would never be heard again.

This had been his first step in the direction of opera, and it led to his second. One December Saturday when he was about eleven, there came from the radio in the living room a clamor greater than any he'd heard before. He hadn't been listening; he was in the kitchen eating an apple. He was aware that a tenor voice had been singing, but he hadn't been paying much attention. The cheers, the shouts, swelled his spirit and pricked his ears. Greatness—one of Michael's favorite words—had visited the earth, and he was eager to feel the noble awe that was its issue. He went into the living room. Since he wasn't allowed to speak to his father during the broadcasts, he'd have to wait until the end of the act to know who'd been singing. As soon as he heard Mimi's aria, he knew he was listening to *La Bohème*. The aria was beautifully, touchingly sung and was well rewarded by the revelers in the opera house.

Then came "*O soave fanciulla,*" and Michael was aware of the tenor voice itself for the first time. How simple was its sound, how pure. The music began slowly and low, ardent, intimate. Then it began to mount in long unbroken strides. The voice led the feelings upward, fearless of the sorrow already awakening within its depths. Closer and closer, it reached out now in sounds so clear and honest that Michael thought he might be hearing the truth for the first time in his life. The voice purified; it cleansed, it restored, and it would never fail him. It would be faithful. It would declare forever the presence of longing and truth, of beauty and promise, on the face of the earth.

At the end of the act, over and above the repeat of the previous tumult, Milton Cross announced who the singer was. It was Jussi Bjoerling, a tenor from Sweden, a peculiar name he'd never heard before. Listening to the applause, Michael determined that one day he, too, would be a Jussi Bjoerling, and whether the calling came from the purity of voice and honesty of singing or from the applause, he didn't bother to consider.

But there was to be only one Jussi Bjoerling; there would never be another, and if there were, it most definitely would not be Michael Ruane, a tenor from Indiana. His teacher in Rome, fifteen years before, had told him so in no uncertain terms.

A mild April day, clear after a siege of rain. Across the street, beyond Signor d'Alessio's balcony, a woman in a man's shirt, open at the neck, watering a flowerless flower box. Signor d'Alessio had just told Michael to try a little serenade the character Beppe sings in *I Pagliacci*. Beppe was a *comprimario* role, a nice little part but hardly anything a young and ambitious student like Michael could possibly be interested in. Then he thought: Someone his mentor knew had asked the old man if he had a prodigy of some kind, a tenor, who would be willing just for the experience to sing Beppe in some festival or other, and since Michael was a favored student, the opportunity was about to be offered to him. Michael doubted he'd accept; he had no intention of making his professional debut—no matter where or under what auspices—as the operatic equivalent of a bit player. He would, however, sing the piece if it would satisfy and please d'Alessio.

And so, accompanied by his teacher, he sang Beppe's little song, and quite nicely. D'Alessio kept listening even after he'd finished. He kept looking at the score in front of him, nodding his head up and down. He seemed to approve. And his approval was a rare thing. "Did you like what you just did?" he asked.

"I guess so."

"Did you enjoy it?"

"Yes. Of course."

"Did you find it rewarding?"

"Very much."

"Good." D'Alessio paused and said the word again. "Good." Then, in kindly, weary tones, he told Michael the truth.

He began by praising his Beppe, but in the end this would prove a small consolation. Michael did not have the gift to sing lead parts; the instrument itself was just not there; he did not have the top notes, and he would never have them, at least not in abundance; he might have the temperament and the stamina and a fine gift for the stage, but they wouldn't be enough.

Michael knew better than to protest, but he did make some excuses. He was aware that, for whatever reason, his high notes had deserted him, but he could train himself. They were somewhere around, and he could find them.

D'Alessio was gentle but firm. Michael must consider a career as *comprimario* if he wanted to continue in opera. A good *comprimario* was invaluable to any house interested in the integrity of its productions. *Comprimari* were actors as well as singers; they were indispensable; they gave any production the measure of its worth. It paid reasonably well; it was not without its moments of glory; it could be rewarding to any true artist—as Beppe had just proved.

Michael was enraged. He wanted to draw down thunderbolts. He wanted to cry. He wanted to humiliate his teacher. D'Alessio knew nothing: nothing about singing and less about Michael Ruane.

The woman across the way was drying her hands on her shirttail. She sniffed her fingers, then began tucking the shirt back into her skirt.

"I must tell you one thing more," d'Alessio said. "Yes, God has given you a high C, but he has put a limit on their number. You have only so many left, and you have a long life, even a long career, ahead of you. You must be warned. Six left. Maybe five. I can't be sure. But there won't be many."

What d'Alessio had said, Michael had long suspected. His natural gift was decent enough, maybe even a little better, and it had always been his hope that the schooling, the training, would take him the rest of the way. Which was why he'd studied for all he was worth, why he'd come to Rome, why he'd placed himself under the tutelage of the renowned d'Alessio. But what d'Alessio was saying was that he'd made his try—and it hadn't been enough. He'd studied, he'd worked with a diligence and a fidelity that amazed even Michael himself. And it had brought him quite a distance—but no farther. He had defined the limits of his gift, and they did not reach into the stratosphere.

But d'Alessio had said something more, whether the old man realized it or not. Michael's failure was a spiritual failure. It was not his gift, it was not his voice. It was his soul that was insufficient. The fault, he felt, was his. He had the soul of a Beppe.

But rather than nourish and expand the deficient spirit, a thought that never really entered his mind, he settled soon enough for what lay within his limitations. Which was probably why they were so limited to begin with.

The curtain calls continued, with flowers, endless flowers, raining down from above. Michael watched poor Calefati's growing delirium as the shouts and yells went on and on and on. An usher rushed past him, carrying in his arms the countless bouquets he'd scooped up from around Calefati's feet to make room for those still being showered down from the top of the house. Because Michael had been there in the wings since the pandemonium first began, he was now able to realize that the usher, ever busy, ever frantic to assure space for yet more flowers, was not taking the bouquets to the diva's dressing room but hauling them to the fifth tier so they could be thrown again and again and again in tribute to the grateful soprano, who, in humility, was holding to her breast only a single rose.

When Michael saw going past him for what he suspected was the umpteenth time a spray of gardenias and an armful of torn carnations, he decided to change from his costume and get ready for the party to be held onstage—an extraordinary, unheard-of concession—to celebrate the triumph of *una figlia di Napoli*. It was there that his scheduled confrontation with Signora Spacagna would take place.

Because the stagehands were not allowed to work past the stroke of midnight, the stage setting had to be changed before, not after, the party. They would replace the third-act set with the set for the first act—the ramparts of Castel Sant'Angelo exchanged for the church of Sant'Andrea della Valle—so that whatever calamity might befall the world between tonight and the next scheduled performance of *Tosca,* four days away, the stage of San Carlo would at least be ready to raise its curtain.

Michael took one last look at La Calefati onstage. She seemed to have fallen in a heap among the flowers, the centerpiece of a floral display, but no, she was only bowing lower than usual. Michael went to change, to prepare himself to meet his *cognata,* the unheeding Assunta.

Sant'Andrea della Valle proved to be a rather fine place for a party. Food was spread out on the scaffolding where Cavaradossi had stood to paint the Magdalen: prosciutto and chicken from Campania, fish and shrimp and squid from the Tyrrhenian Sea, olives and cheeses from the surrounding farms, and pastas of such variety that Michael felt each town in the hills around and the countryside as far as Reggio Calabria and Bari had sent its representative dish to honor this daughter of Naples, Calefati herself, on the occasion of her elevation to divinity within the sacred precincts of San Carlo.

No one had put wine in the holy-water font, but the gates of the Attavanti chapel had been opened wide to accommodate the long table stocked with every conceivable drink: wines pressed from the most delicate and the most robust grapes down to grappa, the water-clear *liquore* distilled from the trampled peelings and seeds and twigs—and, Michael sometimes thought, toenails—after everything possible had been taken from the exhausted pulp.

Wearing his tuxedo for the occasion, Michael took a sip of grappa and let it sear its way down his throat. He looked around for Assunta. She was nowhere to be seen. He realized at a glance, however, why Sant'Andrea was the best place to give a party of this kind. People tend to behave slightly better in church, and the guests crowded among the columns and arches seemed to prove it. There was less elbowing, fewer utterings of *"permesso, permesso,"* than he'd expected, and he'd been able to get the grappa more or less in turn, a first since he'd gotten off the plane.

Most of the men were wearing dark suits, with more than a few, like Michael, in black tie. The women, almost without exception, wore fur coats, most draped over the shoulders but some secured to the body by arms kept comfortably within the sleeves. One woman with polished dark hair pulled back so tightly that surely her eyes must ache was carrying a plain black woolen coat over her arm and, in spite of the lavish gown whose satin repeated the shine and sleekness of her hair, seemed with her cloth coat an affront to everyone there. At any moment she would probably be thrown into the outer darkness for want of the prescribed fur, there to wail and gnash the night away.

Far back in the corner of the stage, in the direction of the main altar, Calefati was celebrating her assumption into divinity in well-documented fashion: She was suffering the little children to come unto her. For the great event, countless nieces, nephews, and cousins had been allowed to stay up past their bedtime, and now *Zia* or *Cugina* Aganice was talking playfully to them, allowing the girls to touch the pearls threaded through her hair and the boys to make free with the censer and the candleholders that might or might not be there for the first-act procession the following Thursday.

It was Arnaldo Martinello, the disgraced Cavaradossi, who was having the best time. If Neapolitans ate too much fish, then *i bolognesi* did similar honor to prosciutto, salami, chicken, pasta, olives, cheese, bread, and red wine. He popped a zucchini flower stuffed with mozzarella and anchovy into his mouth and said to

Michael with great good cheer, "A memorable evening. Most memorable. One of the best—maybe *the* best Cavaradossi I've ever sung. And my '*Vittoria!*'—a real triumph. And what did you think of my fall during the execution? Maybe a little bit too soon, before the gunshots, but once I waited too long, and that was worse. Did you like the way I twisted first one way and then the other when the bullets hit? I got that from Pisarri at Verona, or was it Salvago at Vienna? Anyway, audiences love it. A little bit of acting once in a while won't hurt, if it doesn't damage the costume." He tossed an olive into the air, bent back his head, and caught it in his mouth.

"You're the violist," the woman carrying the plain black coat said to Michael as he was trying the olive trick himself. The olive bounced off his cheek and landed among the cheeses. "I remember you from after the Mozart, at the Contessa's." Before he could explain that he was the singer who had just given the shivers to the entire house with his definitive Spoletta, Assunta Spacagna, properly robed in the furs of some hapless animal or other, came to the scaffolding and stood next to him.

"All this food," she said. "Right in front of the Magdalen. Sacrilege. The Magdalen had just given up all this." She was right, of course. There was Cavaradossi's painting of Mary Magdalen, and there before her, instead of candles and votive offerings, was the bounty of all Italy to mock her renunciations and tempt her return to the satisfactions of, if not the bed, at least the board. At first Michael thought Assunta was trying to amuse him, but no, she was obviously disgusted by what she saw. Twice she rapped the stage floor with her cane, a just punishment for the floor's complicity in the abomination and an effective punctuation to the words she'd spoken. She then leaned her cane against the scaffolding and with great disdain heaped a plate high with tender young artichokes.

Michael watched. Her gray-streaked hair, drawn back for the wedding, had been loosened, let fall, and then drawn up so that her face seemed to be looking at him through cottage curtains. Michael suspected that she frosted her hair, that she wasn't as gray as she'd like to be, if she was gray at all.

It occurred to Michael that the Signora was eager, almost desperate, to age. She wanted to be not so much a mother as a matriarch. She seemed to have realized early on that her best time would be her later years, and after the death of her husband, she'd leapt at the chance, a fitting end to agility if ever there was one. With her cane and her hair, she would now be allowed to monarchize, to rule by edict, to be feared, and to threaten recalcitrants with that most dreaded of punishments, her displeasure. So eager was she to be venerable that she'd given at least twenty years of her life to attain her present position, to say nothing of her present posture.

The woman who had mistaken Michael for a violist, offended by Assunta's appropriation of the artichokes, moved away without waiting for his correction. He couldn't even ask her which Mozart she'd been referring to. "Did they do a Mozart earlier this year?" he asked Assunta.

"Mozart? Of course. *La Clemenza di Tito.* Mozart's greatest. Superb. Exhausting, but superb." She cut through one of the artichokes with her fork, speared a chunk, and delivered it to her mouth with a satisfaction that suggested the spearing had been the preferred part of the operation.

To continue their meeting with the obligatory small talk, Michael asked, "And what did you think of your friend Aganice?"

"Aganice Calefati is the greatest singer who has ever lived and who ever will live. I've known it all along. Now everybody knows it, and I can relax."

Michael watched her eat the artichokes. It seemed she was doing it out of annoyance, that she was cutting, spearing, and swallowing them to rid the world once and for all of their worthless presence, that she was scornful of their tenderness and impatient with their succulence. "I hope you'll be leaving Naples soon, Don Michele." Assunta was now pushing the artichokes around on the plate as if she were trying to detect something suspicious hidden underneath.

Michael assured her he was set to leave the day after the last performance of *Tosca*. *Curlew River* would have had its one showing the night before that, and his business in Naples would be at an end. He had considered staying on in Italy, but if he did, it would be to go either to Sicily or to Venice.

"Good," she said. "You mustn't stay in Naples any longer than you absolutely have to."

Michael, annoyed by so imperial a directive, decided to hint at possible rebellion. "Of course, I want to go to Vesuvio. And I haven't had time yet to visit the museums."

"I'll take you to the museums. Tomorrow. We can do them all in a day. Gaetano can take you to Vesuvio, but I should warn you: It's nothing more than a gravel pit. Two little wisps of smoke at best. If it didn't erupt once in a while, they'd tear it down and plant olives. When do you want to go, so I can tell Gaetano he won't be going to work for the day? But maybe a Sunday would be best. Sunday, then. It's all settled. I'll tell Gaetano. But be sure you're the one who pays for everything."

"I?"

"You must not forget you are the uncle. The uncle pays. Even on his name day, the uncle pays. So don't forget. Sunday, you pay."

"But Sunday won't work. There's a performance Sunday night, and I try not to do any mountain climbing just before I sing."

"Those few lines? You call that singing?" She was not being disdainful; she was merely surprised.

"I owe it to Aganice to be at my best," he said.

To this Assunta gave assent. "You'll go the Sunday after."

"Please," said Michael. "None of you must trouble yourselves. I promise I'll be out of Naples within twelve hours after the final curtain. And until then, I'll be only who you say I am."

"Good." She moved closer to him and, for the moment, gave the artichokes a much-needed rest. "The last thing that can be allowed is that any one of the children suspects you're not from Rome. They're very proud of you. And besides, I told them myself you are their uncle, and a mother never lies."

This was Michael's cue. To lead into the subject, he said, "I hope Gaetano's feeling a little more relaxed these days."

"Why shouldn't Gaetano be relaxed?"

"It seemed, at the wedding . . ."

"Oh. That. Over. Finished. And very soon it will all be forgotten."

Michael didn't find this probable. "Then Gaetano was never going to marry Rosalia himself?"

"Oh, yes. They were *fidanzati* for months. They have been insane for each other—Gaetano and Rosalia—from the day they met."

"But—"

"It was not God's will that they should marry."

"It was God's will that Rosalia should marry Peppino instead?"

"Of course it was God's will. Rosalia is all wrong for Gaetano. She's a good, innocent girl. She works hard. She will be a perfect wife and a good mother. Gaetano would weary of her in a week, and then where would she be? Her suffering would be terrible. I couldn't bear it. Her trouble is she loves Gaetano too much. She is a woman of tremendous passion. I can tell. Gaetano can tell. That's why he wanted to marry her. But he would destroy her. She's too weak, too good, too innocent, to be sacrificed to a life like that. And God has had mercy on her, and now she's set for life."

"With Peppino?"

"With Peppino."

"And Peppino is the right husband for her?"

"Why not? The important thing is that Gaetano was all wrong."

"And what if it doesn't work out?"

"It'll work out."

"How do you know?"

"I know. I'm Peppino's mother." With that, she speared an artichoke and brought it to her mouth, where it was pulled in and, Michael suspected, swallowed whole. Michael considered changing the subject, possibly even excusing himself, but he had one last thought he wasn't willing to let go of.

"On the day of the wedding, when I talked to Gaetano after he left the church, he said Peppino raped Rosalia."

"Don Michele! That's a terrible thing to say about a girl like Rosalia! She's your niece now, don't forget."

If Michael understood correctly, Assunta was saying that Rosalia had allowed herself to be raped. He decided to ask a few questions more. "Then Gaetano was lying? He made it up?"

Assunta pushed an artichoke to the far side of the plate and pulled another one toward her. "It's possible."

"Gaetano also said that you insisted, because of the rape, Rosalia must marry her rapist."

"I told you. Gaetano is all wrong for Rosalia. I did it for Rosalia's sake. And the day will come—"

As Assunta was sucking in another chunk of artichoke, Michael noticed a young man in black tie standing near the prop statue of the Virgin where Tosca in the first act places a bouquet of flowers. He was facing Michael, mouthing some word or other. The young man was Piero Esposito, hair slicked back, patent-leather shoes at a high shine. He was holding a glass of white wine. He raised the glass, mouthed the word again, then drank. The word, Michael realized, was "*bravo*." He knew now where his single call of praise had come from.

Still watching Piero, Michael asked Assunta, "And what are

you going to do when Gaetano kills Peppino for raping and marrying his *fidanzata?*"

Assunta put down her empty plate and took hold of her cane. "Don't worry. I know what I'll do when the time comes."

Michael had hoped the question would finally scare her into a less imperial approach, but apparently contingencies had been provided so that she would never have to abandon the eminence from which she viewed the common scene. "Then you think it's a possibility?" Michael asked.

"Of course it's a possibility. You know Gaetano as well as I do."

Michael didn't know Gaetano at all, but he didn't want to dispute the point. "Then what are you doing to prevent it? I mean, Peppino's your son too. And Rosalia's awfully young to be a widow."

"You make fun, *Zio*. And you shouldn't."

"I wasn't making fun, so I'll ask my question again. What are you doing to make sure Gaetano doesn't kill Peppino? And before you answer, let me add this: Uncle or no uncle, what I can do to help, I'll do. If you'll just tell me what it is."

"Get yourself some poison," Assunta said. "A little pill will do it."

"I beg your pardon . . . ?"

"Here, I'll show you." She leaned her cane against the scaffolding. With her right hand she tugged upward on the gold chain she was wearing around her neck. Michael had assumed that a pendant, a jewel, was tucked into her cleavage for safekeeping. It was not unusual. It had even become something of a fashion: The value of a piece was declared by the depth of its concealment. It was too precious for any risk to be allowed. A woman could wear a can opener on a chain, tuck it into her dress, and feel reasonably assured that she would be envied for the treasure resting secure within her bosom.

What emerged from Assunta's dress was not a star sapphire,

nor was it a can opener. The Signora had brought into the open
air a tangle of religious medals, the remains of a cloth scapular,
and a drawstring pouch too small to hold much more than a few
coins. The medals jangled and the scapular flapped against her
hand as she opened the pouch. Drawing her chin in against her
neck so she could see more easily what she was doing, she reached
into the pouch and brought out, between the thumb and first
finger of her right hand, what could have been, at first sight, a
precious jewel after all. It was as red as a ruby, smooth and shiny.

"Poison," she said. "It will kill in an instant."

"I'm not sure I understand." Michael drew in his own chin,
for a better look.

"I've had this since my sons were—what?—eleven, twelve.
Since right after their father was killed. It's always been with me.
I sleep with it around my neck. Even when I bathe, it's there. I
just wash around it. I never let it go. At the beginning it was so
they wouldn't take drugs. I showed it to them. Poison, I said.
I'll take it, I told them, the minute I even suspect you're having
anything to do with drugs. I'll take it right in front of you, and
then you'll see what drugs can do. I told them it turns into a rat
inside the stomach and that I would keep trying to vomit and
they would know I was dead when the rat leapt from my mouth
and ran across their shoes. I can tell you, *Zio,* my sons have
never touched drugs. And they never will, as long as I have this
pouch around my neck. And for the same reason, Gaetano will
never kill Peppino. On the night I told Peppino to marry Rosalia,
I showed this again to Gaetano and told him that if he even raises
his hand against his brother, the rat will be loosed inside me and
he will have to watch until I vomit it out. So far it's worked,
and I have reason to think it will go on working. If you'd like
to get one for yourself and give Gaetano fair warning, I can help
you. Would you like one? I'd give you this one, but I can't be
without it, not even for a minute. It would be too dangerous. I
may need a few days' notice, so let me know if you decide it's
something you want to do."

Assunta rubbed the pill against her fur to shine it up a bit, then carefully plopped it back into the pouch, drew the strings, and, with a jangle not unlike sleigh bells, placed the entire collection back inside her dress. She gave herself a pat on the chest, not just to make sure everything was in place, but to congratulate herself for the possession of such riches as she'd just displayed.

"It's something I'd want to think about first," Michael said.

"You wanted to know what you could do. Now you know." She took hold of his sleeve and, without really pausing between sentences, went on. "Come say hello to Peppino. He's here to take me home. Now that he's married, he has a car."

Making sure that she used her cane, Assunta strode toward the holy-water font, where Peppino was waiting. "Your uncle," she said to him, "is an opera enthusiast too. Say good night to him. It's late."

Peppino came over and took Michael into his arms and kissed both cheeks. "*Buona sera, Zio,*" he said in a near whisper.

"*Buona sera,* Peppino."

Peppino seemed to wait an extra moment before letting go of Michael, but once he'd finished with the embrace, he stepped back rather formally, as if offering Michael not only his respect but his homage. He was looking at the floor of the stage, an unruly jut of light-brown hair sticking out of the back of his head like a Spanish comb. It was only then that Michael noticed why Peppino seemed different from the way he remembered him on the day of the wedding. At first Michael assumed it was the clothes he was wearing: baggy flannel pants, a very loose-fitting suede jacket with a bulky green sweater underneath. Michael now realized that Peppino was wearing glasses. His eyes downcast, he seemed not to want Michael to see that he wore them, that he was ashamed of the need.

And then it occurred to Michael that the glasses were really a protective device provided by nature itself in the guise of deficient sight. So childlike was the face—the hazel eyes softened by a quiet confusion, the lips ignorant of their ripening fullness, the nose both fleshy and firm, and the unshaven cheeks pale and tender, unblemished even by the glandular eruptions that lay at the source of the family's present predicament—so innocent was his presentation that some disfigurement, some disruption, was required to give at least a minimal sense of normal human imperfection. The glasses, by implication, spoke of ordinary corruptibility, and it was with a prescient wisdom that the young man's eyes had been blighted, requiring now a pair of black and gleaming circles to be clamped over a beauty that bordered on the absurd and the incredible.

Michael also noticed that, as with his brother, his eyebrows, an even lighter brown than his hair, met above his nose, only here it gave the face a comfortable look, two furry little creatures touching each other, untroubled, almost cozy.

"Don't you want something to eat, something to drink, before you go?" Michael looked around the stage. Most of the guests had gone. Even La Calefati seemed to have made a quiet getaway. He could hear Martinello laughing heartily somewhere along the nave, and near a downstage column, the director, Rigutti, was talking with great earnestness to the woman with the polished hair and the cloth coat, who seemed to have found in him the violist she'd been looking for.

Michael felt as if he were offering his nephew leftovers and didn't blame Peppino when he said, "No, thank you." Then, more quietly, he added, "Rosalia's waiting." Peppino tried to smile but didn't quite make it.

"Will you tell her I send her my best?" The gentleness in Michael's voice surprised him. He really hoped his message would be faithfully delivered. He'd meant what he'd said.

"Yes. I'll be sure to. I won't forget." After swaying slightly with hesitation, Peppino again embraced Michael and gave him the two obligatory kisses. When he was near his left ear, farthest from his mother's hearing, he whispered, "Take me with you to Rome, Uncle. I beg you." When he withdrew, he looked directly into Michael's eyes, terrified.

Michael wanted to pretend he hadn't heard, but the young man's look made it impossible. How could he ignore him—especially since he'd just stunned Michael with his plea? Was there no one who didn't want to be taken to Rome?

"Peppino," Michael said, as offhandedly as possible, "I'm in Naples for a few more days. May I come to meet you at work and we can go eat together, the two of us? Is that possible?"

"I . . . I think so."

"Rosalia won't mind? I mean, if it's just the two of us?"

"I won't tell her," he said. "And I go to my mother's to eat during the day anyway."

Michael nodded, not in agreement with what he'd said but in a sort of helpless understanding, an appreciation of a man who could be so open and honest about deception.

"Not tomorrow. But the day after. All right?"

"All right."

A restaurant was agreed upon, and Assunta took hold of Peppino's arm and directed his gaze toward the statue of the Virgin in the middle of the set. "Look. The young man. He knows what it's proper to do."

The "young man" was Piero. He was lighting one of the prop votive candles at the base of the statue. After the candle was lit, he looked up at the statue and seemed to be murmuring a prayer. His look was blank; he didn't seem to be able to quite make out what he was seeing.

As he watched, Michael came to a decision, or, rather, realized he'd come to it some time before. When it had been reached he couldn't remember: possibly when he saw Piero mouth the word "*bravo*," possibly when he was having his second grappa, or when he saw again, glasses and all, the perfections of Peppino, or even now, as he looked at Piero himself, seemingly lost in prayer. Michael knew that he'd become willing to pay for the harmonium in the way Piero had prescribed.

"Come, Peppino," Assunta said. "We'll light a candle too." She led her son toward the statue. Piero crossed himself and moved away toward the wings. He seemed to know Michael had been watching him. He turned, waited, then started toward Michael.

"You're surprised to see me here," he said.

"Surprised? Only for a second or two. From now on, nothing you do will ever surprise me."

"But that would be terrible. I like to surprise."

"Then let's say I won't be surprised to be surprised."

"That's better. And for what it's worth, I thought you were very good."

"Yes, I heard. Thanks for the '*Bravo.*' I don't get that many." Piero made a slight bow. "And for what it's worth," Michael said, "I've decided to make the payment you suggested for the harmonium."

Piero glanced at him out of the side of his eyes, and the mocking, pleased smile crossed his mouth. "Now I'm the one who's surprised."

Michael shrugged. "Anything for the sake of art."

"I have my motorbike near the Galleria. You even get a free ride."

As Piero was saying this, Michael noticed what seemed to be the remains of a black eye on the ridge just above Piero's right cheek. The bruise had faded to the palest blue, but it made Michael wonder again what abuse Piero might have to accept when practicing his trade. He remembered the burn marks covered with makeup he'd seen the other night. He was tempted to say something about the bruise but was able only to look for a moment into the young man's eyes before being distracted by Assunta and Peppino. As Michael watched them solemnly light their votive candles, he said, "Yes, thank you. I accept the ride. And we'll make a fine pair, the two of us in black tie."

"This is Naples," Piero said. "It happens all the time."

Michael saw the upraised heads of Assunta Spacagna and her son, lost in supplication to the Holy Virgin, the light from the candles flickering against their throats. For a moment, he had no clear thought. Then he knew that Piero had not been burned on the chest, nor had someone blackened his eye. The blemishes were known to him from others he'd seen. They were the lesions caused by Kaposi's sarcoma. Piero had AIDS.

"It's going to be cold," Piero said. "Pull up your collar."

Michael did as he was told, without pause, without question. "How about you?" he asked.

"I never get cold."

Just before they reached *l'ingresso degli artisti,* Piero, without turning to him, said, "I'll take you to my place. All right?"

Michael gave his collar another tug. "Sure," he said. "Why not?"

9

Piero's apartment was yet another Neapolitan surprise. Apparently transvestites did rather well in Naples, better than *comprimari* in New York. The building itself was somewhat impressive, tan stucco with green shutters in good repair, and it had two palm trees in a patch of grass just outside the entry. Vinyl tiles in blue and yellow that reminded Michael of the cloister of Santa Chiara made the halls seem less dim than they really were, and the stairways were padded with a rubbery plastic so that their footsteps made no noise at all beyond an occasional squeak from Piero's patent-leather shoes.

Piero had parked and locked the motorbike under a back stairway, behind a discarded metal cabinet and an easy chair that seemed to be still in use: A copy of *Il Mattino* was stuffed between the cushion and the arm; an empty espresso cup was on the floor just to the side. Going up the stairs, Piero had put his finger to his lips, but after the second landing, he'd begun talking in a voice that must have carried at least two flights up and two flights down. He said he'd been shoved for applauding the Cavaradossi after the first act and was punched for doing it again after the third. It was Piero's theory that the tenor had to be offered up to Calefati; that her elevation to *diva*—to goddess—wouldn't be valid without human sacrifice. It happened all the time. More than once a passable soprano whose name he'd forgotten had been delivered, prostrate and uncomplaining, to a tenor so that his triumph could be all the greater.

"Baritones and mezzos they pretty much leave alone. They don't seem to need cults the way tenors and sopranos do. Their voices don't suggest the superhuman. Who can't hit an A if he has to? Bassos are everybody's grandfather; baritones and mezzos are our aunts and uncles; but sopranos and tenors, they're our first loves, and we can be very jealous."

By the fifth and final landing, he was saying, "Tonight La Calefati was made a goddess, and what better proof that we are her worshipers than to sacrifice someone to her glory? Poor Martinello. He didn't have a chance."

Michael, too, had thought Martinello did extremely well, but when he said, "I feel the same—" Piero immediately twisted around and put his finger back to his lips.

The foyer just inside the apartment door had given Michael his next astonishment. A large gilded mirror hung on one wall, in front of it a marble-topped table with a three-pronged candelabra on each side, so that there was a ready shrine to whatever image the mirror might hold. What it would have reflected at the moment, if the back of Piero's head weren't in the way, was a brightly painted marina that he recognized as Posillipo, the community at the western end of the bay, where all the natives acted suspiciously Spanish, the last vestige of the Bourbonic intrusion. It was at this mirror that Piero would make his final adjustments—hair, skirt, furpiece—before his nocturnal descent into the city below. Michael began to wonder why Piero couldn't afford a better fur. But then, perhaps ostentation was not encouraged or even permitted in his profession.

"You have many *lazzari*—many homeless people—in New York. In America. Am I right?" Piero asked.

Michael was looking around the living room, and when he heard the question he knew what he was in for: a reminder—as if one were needed—that nowhere in Naples, nowhere in Italy, nowhere in all Europe, was the poverty so clearly visible as in New York or any American city of any size. A wonderful reversal had taken place. For years Americans had been fascinated, appalled, and disgusted by the filth and the poor of Italy, of Naples in particular. Now it was America's turn, New York's turn, and Michael could hardly blame the Neapolitans for taking it with some degree of relish. What Naples had been—a city divided between the very rich and the very poor—was now New York. Of course, it wasn't that clear-cut. Naples was hardly a classless city, and New York had its clinging lower middle class, but the old visibilities had switched. If anyone in the Western world was attracted to scenes of misery, degradation, and despair, New York could provide the easy satiation that it had once been the duty of Naples to give. The subject annoyed Michael, not just because it was true, but because it was obvious. Piero and all Naples had the right to gloat, and if it was for this purpose that he'd been invited to observe such near sumptuousness, he accepted the taunt.

"And you have what are called soup kitchens, where *i lazzari* can go and they don't pay anything to eat?"

"Yes. We have those too."

"And shelters, like barracks for the army, where people go and they can sleep out of the rain and when it's cold?"

"Yes," Michael said. He had taken in the green-and-gold carpet, the plush, plumped couch, the almost elegant chairs; he was now pretending to examine the bookcases. Thank God for bookcases. How often they'd been his rescue in awkward moments like these. Michael scanned the titles, not really reading them, simply occupying himself until Piero would begin the proceedings by which Michael was to make payment for the harmonium and Michael, in turn, could ask him about the mark under his eye.

The bookcase was perfect for his purposes. He needn't look

directly at Piero, even when they did speak; he could pretend distraction when questions were asked; he could present himself as a man interested in books, obviously cultured. It would also flatter his host: His tastes were being given the notice they deserved; he was being credited with achievements not within the common scope. Best of all, a book could be spotted that would allow a question such as "You like So-and-so too?" and conversation could be started, even developed, along lines of "Have you read his Such-and-such?" More than once, in the years of his activity, Michael had headed straight for the bookcase, grateful that he'd found a way to ease himself into the situation and even more grateful for the few solitary moments, off, aloof, and alone, until it would be time for the evening's meat and potatoes.

"I know about the shelters and the kitchens," Piero was saying. "I read all about it, with pictures, in a magazine. And it's really true?"

"Yes. It's really true."

Now would come Piero's amusement that this was happening in America. Michael's only hope was that he wouldn't rub it in too deeply or with too much delight. He had no intention of defending his city or his country; no defense existed, and he felt no obligation to create one. Still less did he want to have to explain how such a phenomenon had come about. "Greed" might not exactly say it all, but it went in most instances as far as it was necessary to go, and Michael, after all, had had a busy day.

While Michael was waiting for Piero to begin his taunt, he began to see that most of the volumes were lawbooks, with a few Calvino novels thrown in and a biography here and there, one of them of John Kennedy. Piero lived with someone. A patron, a lover? A pimp? A relative? A wife? Signor Crescenzo had said it was not impossible that a transvestite prostitute of Naples was sometimes married, with a wife and children to feed. It was a profession open to anyone who got the call, to anyone willing to develop its requisite skills and tolerate its uncertainties

and its humiliations. Like any other artist. Perhaps Michael had
been brought here to be made one of the family, though he very
much doubted it.

"I'm thinking I might go live in New York," Piero said.

Michael read an entire shelf of titles, translating none of
them, squinting his eyes a little to exaggerate his interest. Words
like *legge* and *giustizia* were unavoidable; the rest he ignored.

"Do you think I should do that? Go live in New York?"

Michael thought of answering while still facing the books,
but he turned around. Now Piero was the one looking away—
out a window, and one that was shuttered, at that. He was leaning
on the wide ledge into which the window was recessed. Italian
architecture seemed always to provide comfortable and ample
space for leaning out a window, even if the view was of a street
no more than six feet wide, with a shuttered window directly
opposite that no one ever opened except to hang out the wash.
But then, what could be read from laundry more than justified
the extravagance. That very morning, to prepare himself for the
evening's performance, he'd thrown wide his shutters, opened
his window, leaned his elbows on the spacious sill, and taken it
all in.

Even his inexperienced eye could find from what was hung
out to dry more revelations than could be delivered by even the
most avid busybody. Here was the history of the entire street,
writ not only large but in bright and flying colors: an accurate
census of who lived where, the degree of wealth and poverty,
the preferences not only in clothing but in bedding. Modesties
and lures were flaunted with equal abandon, and no wife or
mother could escape the common judgment of her sewing and
mending, her ability to keep her family properly clothed and
sufficiently clean. Also, the state of her health and the degree of
her happiness were readily apparent. The condition of a husband's
underwear told much; the sight of the children's socks was, fairly
or unfairly, taken as a measure of maternal care. Scandals and

secrets, sooner or later, had to be hung out to dry; the rise and fall of neighborhood dynasties could be predicted by which flags flew. The bold emblems or the tattered banners sent out their jubilant or melancholy news, and one could tell at a glance who was favored and who was scorned by the local gods. The clothes dryer, that insidious instrument of secrecy and seclusion, had yet to come to Naples—though it was rumored to have invaded the suburbs—and one was still able to hear among the great street cries whole histories of hope and doom, flapping in the wind.

Piero pulled back a little from the shuttered window, then leaned closer again. Overcasual, he was waiting for Michael's answer—which could be framed only in the form of a question.

"Why would you want to go to New York?" he asked.

"I always wanted to go to New York. All my life," Piero said.

"Why?"

"Just to go. To say I've gone. To say I've been there."

"When will you go?"

"I don't know yet. I brought up the subject so I could think about it. Do you think I should go?" As Piero spoke, he kept moving his head from left to right as if he was tracking something through the shutters. His elbows were planted on the ledge, and he'd crossed his right ankle in front of his left. He seemed completely at ease except for the slow continuing motion of his head.

"Whatever you decide," Michael said.

Piero stopped moving his head. "If I go, I can stay with *i lazzari*. That way I won't get homesick."

Michael waited a moment, then turned away from him and said, "Piero, whose apartment are we in?"

"Nobody's. Mine. Does it matter?"

"I'm leaving."

"No, wait. I'll drive you. But first we should have a drink. How will anybody know we've been here if we don't have a drink?"

"I don't need a drink. I had enough at the party."

"A drink. The two of us. Then we'll go. I promise."

With a proprietary air centered somewhere in his lower back, Piero went to a cabinet and brought out a bottle of Courvoisier. He then tried to open the doors above to get the glasses, but they were locked. He tugged a few times, then tried turning the delicate knobs, but they refused to budge. For a moment, he seemed about to yank mercilessly at the doors; he was not about to have his determination thwarted by a couple of delicate and finely finished pieces of wood.

Just as Michael was about to tell him not to ruin the cabinet, Piero recovered his restraint. He glanced at Michael over his shoulder, an invitation to observe closely. From his pocket he brought out the metal ring that held the keys to both the downstairs door and to the apartment itself. With a bravado defined by the exaggerated assurance with which the operation was executed, Piero chose a key from among its colleagues, inserted it in the lock, and made a twisting motion. Nothing happened. He twisted in the opposite direction. The door opened. Piero took two glasses, held them to the light, checking for dust, then put them down on the small table near the couch. As he was pouring, he said, "And you haven't seen the view yet. I really brought you here so you could see the view. Come. Look." He handed Michael a glass that held what was, even for a brandy, a rather stingy portion. Piero went to the window and, facing the closed shutters, took a light sip. Michael waited for him to open the shutters, but Piero simply stood there like a child sent to stand in a corner. "Come. Look."

Michael went to the window and stood next to him. "See?" Piero stretched his head back as if trying to see the sky. Michael did the same. Now he could see the view. Through a thin slit between the slats of the shutters, he could see a few lights from Naples below them, the terra-cotta roof tiles, a broad avenue that would have to be Corso Umberto I, and the beacon light

"Don't thank me. It's you I was thinking of. You're alone in Naples. There's an epidemic. Soon you're going to get lonesome and you're going to go and do something dangerous. I can tell. But I can protect you. So you'd better come with me. Otherwise it'll become unbearable for you, how lonely you'll be. You won't have the strength to resist. And it could be bad. Very bad."

Piero, it seemed to Michael, had just given voice to his own loneliness, his own fears that he would be alone and that it would be unbearable. He had made this his way of asking Michael not to leave him.

Piero had turned toward him, the fur fallen loose from around his throat. There were the lesions on his chest, this time with no makeup to cover them. Two were still only blotches, bruises that looked as if they might even fade away, but one had begun to darken to a pink, the color of bubble gum.

"Don't worry," Michael said. "I'll be all right. I never get that lonesome. And I keep myself very busy."

Piero looked at him, and Michael felt that the young man's face might crumple into some terrible show of desperation and pleading. But it didn't. The smile curled its way along his mouth, and the eyes brightened even as they narrowed. To give an even greater emphasis to his mockery, Piero turned his head away so he could look at Michael from the corner of his eye. "And when do you expect to secure the harmonium? Remember, there's only one payment possible." He made no move away from the window, and he failed to erase from his mouth the sardonic smile and from his eyes the skeptical glance.

"Do you know you have AIDS?" Michael asked quietly.

The smile, the sideways glance, stayed fixed, unmoving. "Not yet. I expect to know in a little while. But not yet."

"Those blotches on your chest . . ."

"Yes. It does seem God has marked me for his own, doesn't it? But for now they're bruises. Later they may become something else. But not yet. And you haven't finished your brandy."

"Do you mind if I don't?"

"Not at all." Piero picked up Michael's glass and emptied it, then finished off his own.

He stopped in the foyer, not to examine himself in the expensive mirror but to consider with an appraising eye and a light touch one of the candelabra. He picked it up and checked the bottom, as if it might have a price tag. He seemed about to stuff it into the wig he held in his left hand but, after testing it for heft, set it down again on the table.

In the mirror, Michael saw himself watching Piero. His look was one of disbelief, because he'd almost said, "Go ahead. Take it." Instead he turned away from the mirror. "I'll go with you," he said. "To your place. If you want me to."

Piero nodded and quickly picked up the candelabra. He plopped it into the wig. On the way out the downstairs door, he handed the wig to Michael. "Take this. It'll be easier for me to steer."

IO

When Michael stepped inside the *basso,* the room at street level, he knew that this indeed was Piero's home and not the apartment of some unwitting benefactor whose keys and tuxedo Piero had managed to borrow. More than half the room was taken up with a huge double bed, a *matrimoniale.* It was covered with a clean blue cotton spread, and at the heavy wooden headboard were two oversized plumped-up pillows, suggesting motherly breasts more than hedonistic props. Piero had brought his motorbike in with him, much the way one might in olden days have brought in one's mule or one's horse. To complete the comparison, Piero threw a thick woolen blanket, dark green, over the motorbike, bedding it down for the night.

Against the wall was the kitchen chair Michael had seen the other night, but now it was used to hold a television set. There was another television set on the floor, and still another on one of the four cement steps that seemed to lead to nowhere except into darkness. He considered giving Piero his watch outright, but that would deprive the young man of the opportunity to exercise his skills. The undetected theft was more important to Piero than the profit his cunning might provide. Michael wagered with himself that Piero would succeed without his knowing and looked forward to winning the bet.

"You want more to drink?" Piero reached down into what would have been his cleavage and brought up the bottle of Courvoisier. What for Assunta Spacagna was a repository for medals, scapulars, and poison was, for Piero, a fair-sized compartment ready to receive whatever might strike the young man's fancy. Michael expected him next to dip in and bring out the two glasses, but apparently the magic act was over. Piero went to the shelf to the left of the door and took down two glasses, which he held up to the light, this time not searching for dust but to give Michael a chance to admire them. They were admirable indeed, delicate and clear and exquisitely wrought.

"Sit down," Piero said. "Be comfortable. I'll be right back." He handed Michael the bottle, went up the steps, and disappeared into the dark. Michael listened for the opening or closing of a door, but no sound came down, not even footfalls.

Michael had two chairs to choose from—actually three, but he didn't feel he had the right to dethrone the television set. An easy chair was angled into a corner, with a floor lamp next to it, and another kitchen chair was drawn up to a small table to the right of the street door. The easy chair had the wig on it, the candelabra poking out. The kitchen chair was empty, but on the table in front of it was a plate smeared with dried tomato sauce and a hardening chunk of bread. No fork, spoon, or knife was visible, but next to the plate was a glass that seemed coated with milk. Michael couldn't believe Piero drank milk with his meals, but there it was, the unmistakable gray like a thin syrup unevenly filming the sides of the glass. There was some left at the bottom. Michael smelled the glass. He got mostly the scent of tomato sauce. He pulled the chair away from the table, sat down, and drank what was left. He held the fluid in his mouth, testing it, tasting it, like a rare wine, then swallowed. It was milk and, possibly because of its nearness to the outside wall, deliciously cool.

"Would you rather have some milk?"

Piero was emerging from the dark. He was wearing his unpressed gray pants, a shirt open at the throat, and a rumpled red sweater. His hair he'd combed back with water, and a few drops were running down below his right ear. His feet were bare.

"No," Michael said. "No, thanks. I was just curious. You drink milk?"

"Always. They say it's bad for you, but I can't help it. I like it, so I take my chances." Piero picked up the plate and glass and headed back up the steps. Once again he passed into the dark, and once again there was no noise, as if sound itself stopped at the edge of light, unable to go farther.

Michael's feet began to feel cold, and it was then he noticed that the floor was stone, with only a small rug thrown down next to the bed. There were no windows in the room, but the top half of the door could be opened to let in what air and light could find their way down a street wide enough to accommodate no more than a wheelbarrow.

Whether it had been the narrowness of the street or whether Piero deferred to his sleeping neighbors, the last hundred feet or so of their journey had been on foot, Piero guiding the motorbike at his side, Michael still clutching the wig and the candelabra. The ride down the hill had provided Michael with the view he'd had to cut and paste at the shuttered window. Everything was in place again: the Duomo, the museums, the churches and pa-lazzi. Even the bay had receded and lay peacefully along the shore, pretending innocence, defying anyone to see it as something other than a benign and disinterested presence.

Once they were on level ground, buzzing along the streets and through the alleyways like a vengeful fly, the city seemed insubstantial again, but in a different way. These were not build-ings but the ghosts of buildings, the stuccoed walls like stained winding sheets. If Michael had any fear at all, it was that the nasal sound of the motorbike would wake not the irascible living but the bewildered dead. He very much approved that they walk, as quietly as possible, the last length of their descent deep into this graveyard of churches and palaces. It seemed a safer, more respectful way to approach Piero's door.

Michael pulled his feet back under the chair, as if that might warm them. Piero had returned and was standing unsteadily on the easy chair, trying to balance himself in the give of the cushion. Finally, he stood astride the two arms, one bare foot on each, and reached up, a lit match in his hand. Michael couldn't quite see what Piero was looking for until the match was dipped into a red glass and the flame grew. Piero had lit a votive candle in front of a picture of Pope John XXIII. A household shrine in Naples was not an oddity, any more than shrines were oddities in streets where each neighborhood seemed to have its guardian saint: Santa Maria dell'Arco, Sant'Antonio, San Francesco, the Madonna and Child, San Gennaro, Sant'Angelo, the Sacred Heart. But Michael had to wonder how many claimed Pope John as their intercessor. He considered asking Piero his reasoning but figured it was none of his business. Michael's own interpretation was that the picture had been a challenge to Piero's nimble gifts, and he couldn't have been expected to resist. Michael wondered next if Piero lit the votive each night, even when he'd brought a client home with him. A vision of the revered Pope peering past the flickering flame to see what was happening on the *matrimoniale* began to form in Michael's mind, but he dismissed it. Again it was none of his business. Still, the thought came to him that the Pope in the picture *did* peer through the flame, *did* watch, though Michael had no idea what he thought and what he did about it. Considering what the saints must have to see and hear, from the sacrifice of the innocent, through suppliants' pleas, down to the horrors of the human heart, what Piero offered must seem pretty puny potatoes. But Michael did wonder, for the first time, if the lit candle was not so much an offering as a necessary light, that for the blessed in heaven, what is human on earth is aptly seen through fire.

"You don't mind?" Piero asked, stepping back onto the unreliable cushion, then down on the cold floor.

"No. Not at all. Why would I mind?"

"Some people don't like him because of all those things he did."

"Things? What things?"

"He changed the Mass into Italian, so now we all sound like *romani* or *toscani* when we pray."

Michael could have told him that this was hardly the case, if it would have been any comfort. He'd heard them at prayer in Santa Chiara, and in no way did they sound other than Neapolitan. He doubted, however, that the assurance would be appreciated.

"And he talked to the Protestants and the Jews and to the Saracens. He listened to the Jesuits. I feel sorry for him, because some people think he was crazy. They're trying to change things back, as if he'd never existed, never been our Pope. As if he'd never loved us all the way he really did. That's why I have his picture. Maybe I'm the only one he has. Sister Procida, who told me all about him, said they had to bring in a Polish Pope to change things back again. He, she said, the Polish Pope, *he'll* never listen to the Jesuits. Poor Roncalli, she said, he'll never be a saint. Wojtyla would jump from the dome of Saint Peter's before he'd canonize him." Piero sat down in the easy chair and looked at his feet.

Michael, too, looked at Piero's feet, as if that were what they'd been talking about.

There was a light tapping at the door. Michael waited for Piero to make some move, but he had begun, now, to examine the sole of his left foot, and it seemed nothing could possibly distract him. The tapping came again, this time a little more insistent. Michael continued to look at Piero, who continued to look at the sole of his foot.

"Piero," a voice whispered through the door. "It's Gaetano.

Let me in. It's cold out, and I have to come in." There was another tapping, this one approaching an out-and-out knock.

Michael waited a moment, then reached over and touched Piero's arm. Piero looked first at Michael, then toward the door. "I'm busy, Gaetano," he said, making no attempt at a whisper. "You'll have to come tomorrow instead. But earlier."

"Tomorrow? How can I wait until tomorrow? Please, Piero, tell whoever's there to go and come back later. I won't take long. But I have to come in."

The whisper made the voice sound all the more desperate, and Michael, puzzled as he was, would gladly have yielded his place if he could have been allowed a swift, anonymous exit out another door—which, he was sure, didn't exist.

"I'm sorry, but it'll have to be tomorrow." Piero's voice was anything but dismissive. He sounded genuinely sorry.

"How can you do this to me? I'm your friend Gaetano. I've done things for you; now you must do this for me."

Piero was looking again at his foot, which he'd placed squarely on the floor in front of him. Michael was almost certain now that he, Michael, was about to be sacrificed in the name of an old friendship. Piero was thinking of opening the door, letting Gaetano in, and then allowing to happen whatever might happen. Perhaps Gaetano would see him and simply shrug. After all, Michael's wife was presumably dead; he was a widower and alone in Naples. Why shouldn't he have chanced on Piero, who also chanced to be a friend of his nephew's? But would Piero let it go at that? Would his need for mischief prompt him to say something that would force from Michael all the disclosures he'd prefer not to make in the *basso* of a transvestite prostitute?

Now Piero was rubbing his foot, deciding.

"Are you still there?" Gaetano asked. "Piero, answer me."

Piero got up and started toward the door. Michael considered grabbing him by the arm, looking up at him, imploring or possibly threatening—frightened, perhaps, and shaking his head no—anything to dissuade him from opening the door. But even with his slight knowledge of Piero, he knew that any form of interference would only excite further complications of the *commedia* already in progress. Michael sat back in his chair and, for support, grasped the edge of the table.

Piero placed his fingers on the lock to the door, ready to twist it back. Michael moved his head to one side, in the direction of his right shoulder, a show of indifference that was probably as unconvincing as it was fake.

Piero put his ear close to the door. The lock was turned back, the door was opened. Michael looked up, expecting to see Gaetano walk in. But, as was possible in the *bassi* of Naples, only the top half had been drawn into the room.

"Gaetano," Piero said quietly, "you have to forgive me. There's someone here who's important to me. You can understand, can't you?"

"But he can come back in a little while."

"I can't ask him to do that. I really can't."

"Then *I'll* ask him. Let me in. Let me talk to him. I'll explain to him. He'll understand when I tell him."

Piero hesitated. He seemed about to do it, but then said, "Gaetano, please. I would do anything for you. But not this time. Not now. Tomorrow. Make that something for you to look forward to. So will I. We both will. Let's do it that way, all right?"

There was no sound, no movement, for what seemed a full minute. Then, from where he was sitting, Michael could see the hands of Gaetano reach in, take hold of Piero's head, and pull it toward himself, out through the opening of the door. He heard what sounded like a kiss, then the grinding of shoes on the stone pavement and quick steps away from the door, down the *vicoletto*.

Piero moved away from the opening, closed it, locked it, and stood looking at it. Before Michael could do anything, Piero, still staring at the closed door, said, "Gaetano comes only to me.

He's going crazy for Rosalia, so he won't go to another woman. It would be unfaithful to Rosalia, he said. He wants to keep himself worthy. So he comes to me instead. And it works pretty well, even if sometimes he gets too excited."

He started back to his chair. As he passed Michael, he looked down at him. "And I do it all so it's safe for him. Don't worry. I'm honorable in my profession. I've always been safe, even from the beginning. That was to protect myself. Then I guess I forgot when I was with someone on my own, not for work. She was probably using drugs and she got it from a needle, but she didn't know. That happens, they tell me. But with the people who come here I'm honorable, always. To everyone. Even when they beg me not to be safe, the way Gaetano sometimes does."

Piero had sat down again and was now examining the bottom of his right foot as if looking for a splinter.

"Something wrong with your foot?" Michael asked.

Piero scratched his instep, then said, "When I first came into the profession, after my protector died and left me everything he had—the clothes, everything—and after he'd given me all that training, I was afraid. I thought I might, with those I'd be with, make a fool of myself. Except for the times my protector was training me, I'd been only with a girl or with a woman. I'd do it all wrong. I'd forget everything I'd been taught. I'd disgrace myself. So I asked Gaetano, because he was my friend, if I could practice with him, and he could tell me if it was the way it was supposed to be. At first he wasn't sure he wanted to, but then, because he's my friend, he said we should try. So we did. Some things I got wrong at first, and he let me know it wasn't working the way it was supposed to. So we'd try again and then again. And some other things too. Lots of them. All I'd learned. It took almost a whole day, but by the time we finished, I'd made Gaetano happy. Very happy. And he wasn't even tired. And since then I've been confident in what I do, no matter what, no matter who."

He began picking lightly at a spot near his heel, leaning down closer for a better look. He wiped his finger under his nose, then went back to his picking.

"I wish he could get over Rosalia, so he could stop coming back like this. He's hard to control. But I have to let him in. He's my friend. We sang for the Pope."

He bent his toes back and cracked the bones, then cracked the knuckles of each hand as if to compare the sounds and resonances. This done, he rubbed the toenail of his big toe as if its surface had some message he was trying to receive.

"Would you forgive me," Piero said, "if we just went to sleep? I'm tired. I'd ask you to go, but it's late and you shouldn't go alone and I don't want to take you. And besides, I did invite you, and I don't want to be inhospitable. But is it all right if I go to sleep? You can have the harmonium anyway. Do you forgive me?" He was cleaning between his toes with his forefinger.

"No problem," Michael said. "I'm tired too."

Piero was taking special care with each toe, examining each speck and morsel he retrieved as if it were an archaeological find, then flicking it to the floor. There was nothing for Michael to do but watch.

II

The trattoria was almost empty. On Via Mastellone, just off Piazza Dante, it wasn't far from where Peppino worked, in the piano shop, or from his mother's apartment on Via San Sebastiano. After they'd had their lunch, Peppino could either go right back to work or, more likely, go to his mother's for his siesta. Michael wished now he hadn't made the promise to Assunta that he'd continue to be the uncle for as long as he was in Naples. It would have given him a moment's ease to tell *someone* he couldn't possibly take him—or her—back with him to Rome. He could take Peppino to lunch, but that was as far as the bloodlines could be stretched. He could take Rosalia to buy a bird in a wooden cage, he could take Gaetano with him when he'd buy himself a poison pill, but none could he take to Rome.

The night before last, when he'd slept next to Piero, Michael, awake, had fought a strange battle. First he wanted to ask Rosalia if she would come with him, not to Rome, but to New York. He wanted it desperately, passionately; he wanted to find some way to be her benefactor, her protector. But it would never work, he kept telling himself. She would be lost there; she'd die of loneliness. She was in love with Gaetano. In New York she would pine away and die. Here in Naples she at least had the protection of Signora Spacagna, and that was a force he couldn't hope to equal.

The matter would be completely settled, decided, determined. No Rosalia. Then Piero would shift in his sleep, and Michael could feel his leg against his thigh or his shoulder along his arm, his hair against his ear. And he would see Peppino's frightened pleading eyes behind the dark-rimmed glasses and ache to say to him, Yes, rapist you may be, but I will rescue you. I will save you from your brother; I will help you untangle the muddle you've made of your young life.

Michael would fight an almost feverish impulse to whisk him off to New York, to free him of his brother and his wife and place him beyond the sway of the imperial Assunta. His thoughts, he would tell himself, were unreal; they would have no force when the morning came. He would be unable to believe that he had even thought them. It was a dream state; that he was wide awake counted for nothing.

Next it was Gaetano, weeping with rage, begging to be thwarted in his vengeance against his brother. Again Gaetano crammed his mouth with poisoned earth, again Michael pounded the bent back to make him spit it out. Again he heard the exhaled "Rosalia . . ." as Gaetano looked upon his *fidanzata* in her bridal radiance, and again he heard the gentle knock on Piero's door and the impassioned plea for release.

Michael was, he thought, experiencing the direct opposite of the "dark night of the soul." He felt anything but abandonment and despair; he felt crowded, importuned—by Rosalia, by Peppino, by Gaetano—and his battle was a fight against hope, against action, and against an uncle's love.

Instead of asking why he had been forsaken, Michael had to ask why he wasn't being left alone. Why these temptations to caring? What had he done that they should be visited upon him at this most vulnerable hour? He would resist; he would appeal to that most elusive commodity, common sense. He would apply his innate selfishness, and it would not desert him in his time of need.

Toward morning, halfway through his litany of reasons for doing nothing for any of them, he was startled to hear a church bell clang in the near distance, once, twice, three times, four. He stopped counting. The bell was not so much rung or sounded; it was being beaten. Someone had, it seemed, taken an iron rod and was thrashing the bell for some offense of which it was ignorant.

Piero didn't stir. Michael moved away a little and knew his nighttime battle was over. He'd been told that church bells were meant to frighten unwanted spirits, to fight off the powers of the dark, and they had indeed just now done their ancient work. The wrestling night was over and reality restored. Michael even felt stupid for having engaged himself in all that grappling. He moved back toward Piero, who, asleep, squirmed against him; then the two lay absolutely still, and Michael, too, finally slept.

The waiter was putting *l'acqua minerale* and the wine on the table when Peppino walked in. He seemed angry, resentful. Michael stood up, and Peppino made straight for his cheeks.

"*Zio! Buon giorno!*" He snapped out the words.

"*Buon giorno*, Peppino."

Peppino let go of Michael's shoulders, stepped back, and stood stiffly as if presenting himself for inspection. He wasn't wearing his glasses, and puffy mounds of flesh swelled beneath his eyes. He looked as if he'd just gotten out of bed after an overlong and murmuring sleep. At first his face seemed dirty, then Michael saw, to his surprise, that he hadn't shaved. The other evening it had seemed that he never *had* to shave; now the light-brown bristle roughened his cheeks and chin, giving the face a hint of color, even if it was more a shadow than a color itself. Peppino had aged, and very much to his advantage.

Michael gave the nod of approval he thought was expected

of him. Peppino sat down, put the morning newspaper on the table, and slid it toward Michael. It was folded open to the cultural page, and Michael recognized right away the article being offered. It was the review of *Tosca*. "Did you read *Il Mattino?*"

"Oh, yes, the opera," Michael said.

"Did you see what they said about the tenor?"

"They seemed to think he did fairly well." Which was true. The critic had ears and eyes of his own and had felt secure and beyond the influence of a San Carlo audience. He'd actually praised Martinello and given an accurate account of his achievements. It had pleased Michael. Martinello was a serious artist and deserved better than the jeers and insults the audience had seen fit to hurl his way.

Peppino leaned forward and tapped his forefinger against the newspaper. "They say as much about him as they say about Aganice. Look at his space. Now look at what they give to her. They're almost the same."

"But read what they say about Calefati. It's nothing but superlatives. They loved her. They adored her."

"It's not right. The tenor shouldn't even have been mentioned except to say he was no good. At least compared to Calefati. She's the greatest singer ever. Ask my mother."

Peppino abruptly sat back in his chair; he'd made his case, and it was irrefutable. Michael was being dared to disagree. Again it amazed him that he, as uncle, was admitted so easily and so completely into family matters. La Calefati was, because of Signora Spacagna's earlier association, definitely a family concern, her glory a family cause.

"Don't worry," he said. "Aganice Calefati is good enough to sing with the best tenors there are. She'll take care of herself. They'll never get the better of her. I can promise you that."

"Of course she deserves the best tenors. But Martinello isn't one of them. She so far outshone him he was nowhere to be seen. You know that. You were there."

Michael almost said, "And you weren't," but he kept his peace. Peppino was obviously insulted in a very personal way that Aganice Calefati, who had studied piano under his mother's tutelage, had not been made the sole object of praise. That her triumph had not included the disgrace and defeat of Martinello was intolerable to him, and Michael realized there was nothing he could do about it. Opera inspired this kind of adamantine response all the time, and all over the world, although he had to admit that Naples, San Carlo, and Peppino Spacagna had brought the practice close to an idiocy that he had previously thought was the exclusive claim of standees at the Met.

Michael wasn't willing to agree with his nephew, so he staked out a more neutral ground for the sake of peace in the family. He would purposely refrain from giving Martinello his due; he would concentrate on the many virtues, gifts, and talents of La Calefati, in the hope that the distressed Peppino would find in his words some compensation for the injustice heaped upon him by the base critic of *Il Mattino*.

When Michael, with honest ardor, was telling Peppino about Calefati's "*Vissi d'arte*," the waiter took their order. Peppino ordered *maccheroni* with tomatoes and onions for his pasta, and fish with fried potatoes, broccoli, and a mixed salad for his *secondo*. Wrath did not seem to affect his appetite. He was also quite willing to partake of the wine. Michael asked for *minestra*, then some veal and a salad, no more.

"Is it true," Peppino asked cheerfully, "that had not the hands of Jesus been nailed to the crucifix, he, too, would have applauded when '*Vissi d'arte*' was over? That's what my mother told me on the way home."

"I didn't notice," Michael said. "But your mother has a better eye than most for that kind of thing."

"And when Aganice hurled herself from Castel Sant'Angelo at the end, and when she cried out '*O Scarpia! Avanti a Dio!*' did everyone in the audience really shout, 'No, Calefati, no! Don't jump!'?"

Michael remembered hearing one lone demented voice from the top of the house express a sentiment of that kind, so he confirmed the report, and Peppino, pleased to have been correct, helped himself to more wine.

It occurred to Michael that Peppino had forgotten completely the reason for their meeting. He'd forgotten his whispered plea that he be taken to Rome. Michael was relieved that the entire meal could be given over now to a discussion of the opera and of Calefati, and if there was a lull in the conversation, Michael could always throw a bone of praise in Martinello's direction and Peppino's former energies would be restored.

Michael's soup and Peppino's pasta arrived, steaming, sending into the air scents exotic and domestic, not quite overwhelming the honest carrot-and-cooked-onion smell seeping upward from the bowl and the plate. Peppino chose to eat with a large spoon, chewing slowly, thoughtfully, warily at first. Then, assured that he had been given what he'd asked for, he began to eat more rapidly, managing to scoop up sizable mounds of pasta into his mouth before a single piece could slip back down to the pile on the plate in front of him.

Michael found himself eating slowly, carefully, even gracefully, realizing after he'd swallowed the fourth spoonful that he had instinctively taken it upon himself as uncle to set a good example, to offer rather grandly a lesson in table manners. When the fifth spoonful reached his lips, Michael purposely slurped it all in, a momentary rebellion against the complexities of the role he had so eagerly assumed.

Peppino quietly put his spoon on his plate, as if offended by such a disgusting noise. Michael almost expected a reprimand, but what Peppino said instead was, "I'm sorry about my aunt." His look was mournful, his voice solemn. Quickly his tongue licked in some sauce from the right side of his upper lip, as if he hadn't readied himself completely for his recitation. This last-minute preparation accomplished, he relaxed his face back into its former gravity, making his mouth sullen and his eyes slack.

Sorrow, for him, seemed a tranquilizer, implying that loss was, first and foremost, a relief, an easy relaxant that smoothed the brow, drooped the cheeks, and loosened the jaw.

Michael, of course, hadn't the least idea what he was talking about. After a swift glance at Peppino, he went back to eating his soup, reverting to the more majestic movements that had preceded the disruptive slurp. Maybe if he just kept on, Peppino would give further vent to his grief, enough at least to give Michael some slightest clue about the unfortunate relative Peppino had assumed they shared.

"Maybe you would rather not talk about it." Peppino leaned toward him, his forearms flanking his plate, his tie looping down perilously close to the sauce. Michael would take two more spoonfuls, then decide what to say, what to do.

"Was she very beautiful? Rosalia said she must have been."

Michael was raising yet another spoonful, but he stopped midway between the bowl and his chin. It was the mention of Rosalia that had made him pause. He remembered the lie he'd told her about a wife. He saw again Rosalia's soft horror at what he was telling her, the lies about a wife's death. With this vision of her fixed in his head, with the full sight again of her helpless hair and her inadequate chin, he said, "Yes, she was very beautiful."

"That's terrible!" Peppino said. "I mean, that she died after she was so beautiful." He lifted a spoonful of pasta, looked at it, lowered it a few inches back toward the plate, and said, "I'm sorry." His period of mourning lasted a full five seconds. He spooned in the pasta, again quickly flicking with his tongue the sides of his mouth, to retrieve on one side a chunk of *maccheroni,* on the other a smudge of sauce.

"But she left us no cousins?"

"No. No cousins."

To arrive at his acceptance of this, Peppino again regarded a spoonful of pasta, unwilling to take in both food and fact at the same time. Finally, he nodded his head and, with this self-permission, let the spoon continue its appointed course.

Michael expected to hear another expression of sorrow. Peppino, after all, was not only bereft of an aunt but left without the cousins who would have been a probable source of added familial affection. But the young man said instead, "Then you have a lot of room where you live, with no one there but you. Especially since it's too soon for you to marry again—or even to think about it."

Michael understood all too clearly what Peppino was getting at. "You want to come back to Rome with me, is that it?"

Peppino didn't seem to hear the question. He had finished the last of the *maccheroni* and was moving his spoon around on the plate, gathering together a residue of sauce he'd missed. He finally managed to align the spoon's edge with the elusive scrapings and, content with this slight success, put the spoon down without treating himself to the rewards of his exertion.

"Take Gaetano," he said.

"But the other night . . ."

"Gaetano would be better. Take him."

"What makes you think Gaetano wants to go?"

Peppino pushed himself away from the table, puzzled. "You'll tell him he has to go. He has to go with you. He would have to obey. All you have to do is tell him."

"He could say no."

"How could he say no? You're our uncle. We have to obey."

"And you? Would you obey me?"

"Of course. Why wouldn't I?"

"And if I told you to give up Rosalia?"

Peppino was stunned, amused, and perplexed, all at the same time. "Give up Rosalia? She's my wife. You saw. You were there."

"I know. But you could get a divorce."

"Uncle! A divorce? Never!"

"An annulment, then."

"That could never happen!"

"No? Rosalia can testify that you forced her." Michael paused, disapproving of the torment he was visiting on the gullible young man across the table but not yet ready to relinquish the power he'd been given, the power to command, to be unthinkingly obeyed. He pressed the issue. "You raped her. She would testify to that."

"I didn't rape her."

"You did. And I'm telling you you did."

Peppino brought his hand up toward his chin, palm downward, reflexively ready to make an insulting gesture, but he caught himself in time and rested the open hand on the table. "I was only protecting her," he said quietly.

"Protecting her? Protecting her from what?"

"I covered her with myself to protect her."

Michael was about to dismiss Peppino as a madman, to shed the whole affair as the demented actions of a lunatic, but Peppino, speaking more softly, continued. "It was to protect her from Gaetano. I thought I heard him coming up the stairs, when I was there, when I brought the flowers to Rosalia and told her how happy I was because I was going to be like her brother. I could hear Gaetano getting closer to the door. I don't think Rosalia heard him, but I did. I went to her. She was going toward the piano to get a picture of her grandfather to show me. Before she could pick up the picture, I turned her toward me. She was surprised. I thought it was because now she could hear Gaetano too. 'Quick!' I whispered to her. 'Quick! Now. Before it's too late.' I was forcing her down onto the floor. I'm not sure, but I think she was hissing something at me, but I heard it as a whisper. Then she struggled, but I thought it was to help me, that she was in a hurry and that this made her clumsy, so I did what I could to help her help me before it was too late. She was desperate for me to do what I had to do. She kept making sounds, crying, pushing, telling me something. I . . . I thought it was for me to hurry. I did my best. Gaetano was almost at the door. I hadn't yet hidden her completely. I begged her to stop helping me; I told her I knew what I had to do. I talked gently to her, promising her she would be all right. She kept on helping, flailing on the floor, even scratching at my face to get me to hurry. Any minute, any second, Gaetano would open the door. He would be there. I whispered that I was hurrying, I was hurrying. She would be safe, I told her. I heard the door opening. I screamed. But it was all right. Rosalia was safe now. I had protected her. I had saved her. There was no Gaetano at the door. I had sent him away. He had known it was useless for him to come in. He had gone away. I was safe. Rosalia was safe. There was no Gaetano."

Peppino ran his finger along the edge of his plate, collecting the sauce his spoon had failed to gather up. He leaned forward so nothing would drip onto his tie and brought the finger to his mouth and licked off what had stuck. He started to repeat the gesture, when Michael asked, "If you were protecting her from Gaetano, what would Gaetano have done that she needed protecting from?"

Peppino took his finger from the plate and wiped it on his napkin. He waited, then said, "He would not have respected her."

"And what did you do?"

"I protected her."

"How?"

"I hid her from him."

"You raped her."

When Peppino didn't answer, Michael repeated the words. "You raped her."

Peppino shifted in his chair, put an elbow on the table, and seemed about to rest his chin in his hand, but after a glance at Michael, he took his elbow from the table, put both his hands, palms down, on either side of his plate, and said, "With all due

respect, Don Michele, Rosalia is my wife, and I can't allow even
you to talk about her in this way. I can't allow such things to
be said by *anyone*." He sat rigid in his chair, his eyes cast down,
as if waiting for his uncle to reach across the table and send him
sprawling with a single blow. Michael wondered if he should do
it, if he should play his part to the extreme and let his nephew
know he could not speak to his uncle in this defiant manner.

Peppino seemed to be holding his breath, prepared for what
was certain to come. All his muscles stiffened, not in defense but
in acceptance. His surrender to the consequences of what he'd
said was complete. This, Michael realized, was the Peppino who
was waiting eternally for his brother's vengeful hand to fall.
Appalled by what he'd done, terrified, yet unable, unwilling, to
retract his actions, Peppino could do nothing but wait, knowing
full well the fate he had invited to be his own. The man was
mad, but there was a stubborn courage in him, a kind of defiant
dignity that Michael could almost admire. Peppino was not waiting for his uncle to strike him; he was waiting for his brother's
murderous thrust. He had no defense against it, nor did he ask
for any. He was prepared to wait, unrepentant, and accept it
when it came.

Then, as if conjured by Michael's thoughts, Gaetano was
standing at Peppino's side. He was smiling and cheerful. He was
wearing the grease-stained blue coveralls of his trade, but his
hands and face were scrubbed and his hair was slicked back; even
the shielding lock that always shaded his forehead had been plas-
tered down. There was no trace in his looks or manner of the
desperation and the pain he'd brought to Piero's door two nights
before.

After a bow and a greeting directed at Michael, Gaetano said
to Peppino, "Give me the keys to your car."

The waiter appeared at Michael's elbow and, with a skill so
deft and unobtrusive that it could have been executed by a ghost,
removed the soup bowl and Peppino's plate and replaced them

with the veal and the fish they'd ordered, then he disappeared.

Peppino, still stiff in his chair, looked up at his brother. "What do you want the keys for?" he asked quietly.

Gaetano pulled out a chair and sat down without drawing himself up to the table. "You must excuse the intrusion, Don Michele," he said, "but Peppino's car needs fixing. Three times it stalled when he was driving Mamma home from the opera, and she said it made terrible squeaks. She was ashamed to be seen in it, she said. I'm supposed to fix it."

"I fixed it yesterday."

"You didn't fix it yesterday. Why do you always lie?"

"I don't lie. I'll fix it this afternoon."

"You don't know how. Now give me the keys. Mamma says she won't ride in it until I fix it. She didn't say until *you* fix it. She said until *I* fix it."

Peppino, who had started boning his fish, put down the knife and fork, looked at his plate, then reached in his pocket and took out a bunch of keys tangled into a wad of lire. He flicked the keys, found the right one, and tried to get it off the ring. It wasn't going to be easy. The key ring was the exasperating kind: a compressed spiral which has to be pried apart at one tip and the key forced into and led along a course that would eventually free it. Peppino was having difficulty keeping the pried end open long enough to slip out the key. So that Gaetano wouldn't keep so close a watch, Michael said, "Gaetano, join us. Have something to eat."

"Thank you, but I can't. I'm going to eat later, at a friend's." With that, he reached over and, with Peppino's fork, lifted some of the broccoli from his plate and ate it. Peppino paused in his struggles, to watch the broccoli disappear, then resumed his labors. Gaetano picked up Peppino's knife and, with surgical ease, began boning the fish. He slit along the belly, gently eased the fish open so that it lay, two symmetrical ovals, one still possessing the head and tail, the spine connecting the two, its delicate ribs providing a ladder so that communications could proceed in ordered steps, one side perhaps traveling up, the other down.

As he lifted the skeleton cleanly from the flesh, Gaetano said, "It's a good thing I came to get the keys. He knows he's not supposed to have fish when I'm not with him. When he was five, he choked on a bone. He almost died, but Mamma prayed to San Biagio, and he told her to reach right into his mouth and down his throat, and he'd give her the bone. It was tiny, like this one"—he indicated with the tip of the knife a half-inch bone near the tail of the perfect skeleton he'd placed on the plate provided by the waiter—"but San Biagio found it and gave it to Mamma. Ever since then I'm supposed to bone his fish."

He turned to his brother and punched him lightly on the upper arm. "Why did you order fish when you didn't know I was going to be here?" The punch caused the key to jerk, and it was suddenly off the ring. Peppino put it on the table in front of his brother. Gaetano ignored it and said to Michael, "You were at the opera the other night. Why didn't you tell me you went to the opera? I'm going to take you to the opera myself. *I* will take *you*."

He reached over, snapped a bone from the spine, and carefully dropped it on the fish near the place where Peppino's fork was pulling away a mouthful of flesh. Peppino hesitated only a little, then continued eating. Michael's instinct was to snatch the bone away, but he wasn't sure how much license his status gave him when games were being played by the two brothers. Since Peppino was pretending to ignore the bone, Michael would ignore it too. It did occur to him, however, to ask San Biagio to stand by.

To demonstrate his indifference to the fishbone and his willingness to allow them their rituals without his intervention, Michael said, "Thank you, but I've seen the opera, and even though Calefati is tremendous, I don't think I'll have time to go again. But that's very kind."

"No, I don't mean that opera. And besides, Aganice is a slut and shouldn't be playing a saint like Tosca."

That Tosca had her pieties Michael knew, but somehow saintliness had never seemed central to her character. The point, however, was arguable. A concubine and a murderer she may have been, but she loved mightily, venerated the Virgin, was a genuine penitent, and, in the end, surrendered herself completely to the will of God—which, in the scale of spirituality, wasn't all that bad. What was not arguable was that Calefati was a slut. Michael knew her to be so completely devoted to her career that she'd left herself neither time nor emotion for anything so diverting. Manic she might be, egotistical and solipsistic to the point of a high and damning pride, but she had a good and generous heart that, time and time again, rescued her from herself and put her, if not into the company of saints, at least into the fallible human family where she belonged.

Michael was ready to state his defense of his colleague but reminded himself that he presumably didn't know the woman, that he had nothing to do with opera, that he was the uncle from Rome, a stranger to these parts and unacquainted with its ways.

Determined not to glance at the waiting fishbone, Michael turned casually to Gaetano. "You won't go to see her?"

Gaetano shrugged. "I might. She probably wants me to. I probably shouldn't disappoint her. But the opera I'm going to take you to will be one you've never seen before. It's being put on by an American. But don't worry. Everyone else in it is from Naples, including my friend Piero. The one where I'm having lunch. He's in it. You'll see him. I'll introduce you. It's about a madwoman, but not like Lucia or Elvira. I won't tell you any more, or maybe you won't go."

"I don't think I'll be able to anyway, so tell me. What does your friend—Piero, is it?—what does he say about it?"

"He's in the chorus, so he says what everyone in the chorus always says. He says he should be singing the lead part instead of the American."

"Oh?"

"It's the part of a madwoman, but it's sung by a man. So of course Piero should play him. Piero and I, we both sang for the Pope, that's how we know each other, but when he's not singing he's a prostitute dressed like a woman. Piero is very good at it." Michael wasn't even tempted to ask him how he knew. Gaetano went on: "He should play the part of the woman gone mad. The American will be terrible."

"Is that what Piero, what your friend, said?"

"No. Piero thinks of him as if he were a genius."

"A genius?" Michael struggled not to sound pleased, much less too eager for more. To show that he was interested in other things as well, he glanced at Peppino's plate to see how close he'd come to the fishbone. The bone was gone. Michael saw it nowhere on the plate, nowhere on the fish, nowhere on the table. He would have noticed had Peppino put it back on the plate originally intended for it. Peppino had eaten it. Michael knew he had. He would have choked and died rather than not eat it. He'd eaten it and survived. There was a forced casualness about the motions of Peppino's mouth, his jaw, his throat, a display of indifference to death, to the plots of his brother, to the trials he might have to endure before the blow came that would strike him down for good.

"He says the man is a genuine artist. And he's patient and very intelligent, and he knows all about music, and he makes it all very beautiful."

"Good," Michael said. "But can the man sing?"

Gaetano shrugged. "Well enough."

"Oh? Exactly what does your friend say about his voice, his singing?" Michael barely managed to hide his interest behind the napkin he'd raised to his lips.

While he was dabbing away, Gaetano said, "He thinks he'll improve."

"I see." Michael put the napkin down on the table, his movement slow, his placement careful.

"So you must let me take you," Gaetano was saying. "You're a stranger in Naples and my uncle. I must do something for you, or I'll be shamed. Please. I'll take you to this opera. It'll be something you'd never see otherwise. I want to give it to you. Please, let me. You must."

As if the matter were settled in his favor, Gaetano reached over and picked a fork off the next table and helped himself to some of the fish. Peppino took no notice of it. Gaetano helped himself to some more. Still, Peppino acknowledged nothing. When a third forkful was almost to his mouth, Gaetano set it back on the plate. "It needs more salt."

"It doesn't need salt." A fork held upright in one hand, a knife in the other, Peppino put his fists on the table, the cutlery now standing guard over his plate.

Gaetano picked up the salt shaker, kissed Peppino on the cheek, and began salting the fish. Peppino made no move. Gaetano paused, then salted some more. "Salt. It needs salt. It definitely needs salt. Here, let me do it."

Peppino let the knife and fork drop to the table and picked up the pepper shaker. "And you need more pepper." He began shaking pepper—fiercely—on the tablecloth in front of Gaetano.

"Salt," said Gaetano. "It needs salt."

"Pepper," said Peppino. "It needs pepper."

This, Michael realized, was an ancient rite reaching back to the mists of childhood, a competitive taunting where each rendered the food of the other inedible, consciously or not cutting off life-sustaining nourishment at its source.

Now Peppino was shaking pepper into Gaetano's hair, repeating his refrain. Now Gaetano was salting his brother's head. Even though the restaurant had almost filled, no one took any notice. Two men at the table to the right continued their silent eating; the .couples on the left went right on with an intense conversation that, if Michael understood correctly, concerned the concert the rock singer Sting would give in two weeks at the Domiziana in Cava de' Terrini. In front of them was the woman with the German shepherd. Each time the dog would so much as move its head, she'd bark, "Vasco! Vasco!" Only the dog seemed interested in what the two brothers were doing, and even he was content to be a passive observer.

It was when the dog sneezed and was reprimanded by its mistress that Michael took up his responsibilities. "*Basta!*" he whispered fiercely. "You don't waste food!" Both stopped immediately. Both quietly placed their weapons back on the table; both put their hands on their laps; and both looked down, ashamed and penitent. Michael waited for one to blame the other, for Peppino to point out that Gaetano had started it, for Gaetano to protest that he was only putting salt on the fish. But neither said a word; they simply sat and waited for their uncle to do with them what he would.

"Gaetano," he said severely, "go fix the car."

Gaetano waited, then said, "We didn't mean to disgrace you. We're sorry, profoundly sorry."

"Is that true, Peppino?"

"Yes. We're sorry. Profoundly."

"Well, it's over now," Michael said. "And besides, it was the dog I was worried about."

Peppino sneezed, then Gaetano. They both laughed, and for a moment Michael thought that surely their enmity had been brought to an end. They had reminded each other that they were brothers, that they shared a past that would always make its claims no matter what, that there was a sympathy between them that no rivalry, however primitive, could dissolve.

Gaetano stood up, still smiling. "I'll take you to the opera and introduce you to my friend. You'll be my guest." He bowed and scooped the car key into his hand. Looking down at Peppino, he said, "It makes me sad to tell you this, but the first time when you drive the car after I fix it, bring Mamma with you. Otherwise there might be a bomb hidden in it. You can't tell, can you?" He bowed once more, more stiffly this time, as befits a man who has just warned another of possible betrayal and death. As he went out, the dog sneezed again.

Peppino had put his fork to the fish and was about to continue eating. Michael reached across and touched the back of his hand. "No. I'll get you another one." He looked for the waiter.

Before the summons could be given, however, Peppino said, "Why do that? This one is fresh. There's nothing wrong with it."

He began slowly to eat the heavily salted fish, not looking at his uncle, one forkful after another, slow, uncomplaining. Only after the fourth bite did he take a drink of wine, then continued eating, still not looking up. When he'd almost finished the entire fish and had taken another drink of the wine, he said, "When I was four and Gaetano was six—it was before Papà was killed—we were coming home from school and a man was selling little model cars on Piazza Bellini. Lancias, Lamborghinis, Alfa Romeos—all the great and wonderful cars, just the way they are, only tiny. I stopped to look because they were so beautiful. I started to reach out to touch one of them, a green Maserati, and Gaetano, he so gently pulled my hand back. I shouldn't touch. We couldn't buy one. We had no money, even if Papà was still alive. I looked up at him, and he shook his head no. I put my hand by my side again. And then Gaetano reached down and he picked me up, and he began to carry me along the street in his arms, even if I was four. He carried me, just like that. And I had to wonder how did he know this—that to be carried, and by him, was what I'd really wanted? Not the cars at all. Just for him to carry me the way he was doing. I never asked him how he knew. But someday I will, before I forget."

He put his fork carefully on his plate, then his knife, crossing it over the fork. "Go with him to the opera, Uncle. Please. He'll be so disappointed if you don't."

Michael, too, put down his knife and fork. With all his heart he wanted to go with Gaetano to the opera, if for no other reason than that his nephew Peppino had asked him to.

12

The pilgrims in the boat sounded exactly the way they were supposed to sound, a derisive crowd, jeering at the Madwoman.

Show us what you can do!
Madwoman, sing!

The instrumentalists, their entrances approximately rather than specifically scored, created just the right degree of cacophony without overwhelming the pilgrims. Each singer, each musician, seemed to have found a character for himself and to have found as well his own place in the drama. Michael was amazed. Everyone knew what to do and how to do it and when to do it. He had asked more than once if they had ever worked together before. He was assured they had not; this was their first time and probably their only time. One of the baritones admitted to knowing the percussionist from a bookshop on Via San Biagio dei Librai, and a bass claimed to have taken lessons with Signor Zongola, but the Signore had no memory of him, even when he'd told him he used to bring eggplants from his grandmother's garden when he couldn't afford to pay.

At first Michael was sure it was a fluke. They got it right the first time, but they would never be able to repeat it, no matter how hard they might try. It would still have to be gone over again and again, painfully, carefully, then set. But no, the second time, the third, and from then on, they were inexplicably able to create and re-create chaos of the most exact and perfect kind. Michael was awed even as he thought: Only in Naples would he find artists so familiar with the anarchic that they could reproduce it at will and on cue.

Today's rehearsal included the principal singers wearing their costumes and masks for the first time—which meant Michael would be robed as the Madwoman. It was a central conceit of the opera that all the parts were being sung by monks, even his female role of the mother—demented by loss, crazed by anxiety, and confused by grief—who had come to the Curlew River in search of her twelve-year-old son.

Michael wondered if Piero would revert to his mocking smile to see him in woman's clothes, a switch, indicating that no one was immune to the transformation that so often brought scorn and abuse to those who had recourse to it because, like Piero, they were poor. There had been a moment the other morning, after he'd slept in the *basso,* when he expected to see the sardonic twitch curl the right end of Piero's upper lip, but it hadn't happened. Piero, awake, had slipped into his gray woolen pants and then, instead of putting on his shirt or his shoes, placed the wig on his head and proceeded in businesslike fashion to make coffee. His movements made no reference to his having long brown hair that came down to his shoulders. There was, in his actions, no sly triumph in Michael's having spent the night in the *basso.* Every move was unself-conscious and natural. The wig was taken for granted, as if it were his own hair and was always worn like this, the most ordinary thing in the world, no different from his eyes, ears, nose, and throat.

Watching him sip his coffee, make the bed, stand astride the chair to blow out the candle he'd lit in front of the nullified Pope, Michael began to wish he had, during the night, held Piero in his arms, not so much in passion but to test himself, or, rather, test his memory of Damian. In the days after their separation, nothing could summon the lost lover more quickly than for Michael to hold someone in his arms and be tender to him. The presumed means of escape, to find and hold another, had been not only denied him but by some insidious law changed into a trap. He was to find that he had no tenderness that was not a tenderness for his absent friend; he had no yearning that was not for him; he had no surrender to give, no conquest to make, that was not a surrender to Damian or a conquest that had, for its spoils, Damian's spent and satisfied body.

Damian had once thought Michael an amazement to the world, and it was to Michael that he'd offered up enough oaths and promises to support a minor god. Michael had liked being worshiped. He'd enjoyed the rites, the hymns of praise, and the prayers of supplication. He'd rejoiced in finding someone upon whom to bestow his favor, someone to make worthy, to raise up to the wobbly heights of requited love. It had pleased him to reassure, to promise, to comfort. But also he'd found that there had been aroused in him an insatiable tenderness, whose only object was Damian. It was as if even his passion itself was an eruption, a desperate attempt to escape, to find relief from the sweetness that ached and gasped in every part of his flesh.

Then, one autumn morning, Damian chose breakfast as the time when he'd give Michael the explanation he did or didn't deserve for the boot-foreshadowed change in their lives. Damian was eating Wheatena, not with milk and sugar, but simple and unadorned, which made it look like congealed sand. Michael was eating cornflakes, his chosen cereal of maturity, a replacement for the sugar-coated treats he'd clamored for as a child, a sufficient sign of responsibility and of discipline.

"You know, it's funny," Damian had said.

When he added nothing, Michael fed him the necessary "What's funny?"

"It's funny how most people, when they aren't in love anymore, they blame it on the other person."

Michael ate two spoonfuls of cornflakes before he said, "Oh?"

"Yeah," Damian said. "Most of the time, they say something like: 'I was so much in love I didn't see what you were really like.' Or: 'You've changed. You're not the person you used to be.' Stuff like that."

"And you think that's funny?"

"No, that's not the funny part. With us, the funny part is that you haven't changed. And I never saw you as anyone different from what you really are. The funny part isn't that I made a mistake about you. The funny part is that I made a mistake about me, about myself."

After another spoonful of cornflakes, Michael repeated his "Oh?"

"Yeah. *I'm* the one I didn't see for what I really am, because I was in love. I was in love so much I imagined myself to be someone completely different."

"Can't we just eat?"

"*You* weren't the one I imagined. *I* was the one I imagined. I imagined I was someone devoted and faithful. I imagined my feelings would never change, that I was a wonderful lover and I always would be. But I'm not any of that. And it doesn't have anything to do with you. I'm just not who I thought I was, the one you made me think I was, devoted, faithful. You know. And I think it's funny how so many people probably make the same mistake. They think it's the other guy, but it's not. It's themselves they got all wrong. You don't think that's funny?"

"Hilarious," Michael said. He couldn't finish his cornflakes, but Damian had no trouble spooning up the last soggy grains of Wheatena from the bottom of his bowl.

Two days before the agreed-upon breakup, Michael experienced for the first time the overwhelming terror that was to be his primary response to Damian's departure. On his way to a rehearsal of *La Bohème*—he would be playing his first Parpignol—he had stopped for a traffic light on the corner of Broadway and Seventy-third Street, in front of the Ansonia Hotel. He had no memory of what he'd been thinking—whether about Damian or about Parpignol or about what he'd have for lunch—but before the light had changed, he knew himself to be threatened, to be in some terrible danger. He moved a step back from the curb, then another, bumping into a rather large woman in a red woolen dress. He mumbled his excuses. The light changed. Everyone else crossed the street. Michael took one more step back. Something terrible was about to happen to him. This was the moment just before the blow was to be struck, his entire body alert, summoned to its full presence, not to ward off but to witness, to experience in its entirety, the devastation about to strike.

Michael moved over to the building itself, as if the great gray stones might protect him. He couldn't stay where he'd been, at the curb; that was certain. The spot had been marked for calamity. Whoever might be standing there was targeted for destruction. But the stones offered nothing. Here, too, he was susceptible to whatever it was that was about to overwhelm him. He must keep moving. He must not stop. If he did . . . If he did . . .

Numbed as if to declare himself a nonpresence, he continued down Broadway, looking neither to the left nor to the right. Twice he bumped into someone, but each time said nothing. He mustn't. He must say nothing. He must try with all his might to feel nothing, just to keep walking. It was his only hope, his only escape. He shortened his breaths, another attempt to become as absent as possible.

The traffic lights were in his favor as far as Sixty-ninth Street, and then they turned against him. To thwart their betrayal, he turned right and walked the short block to Amsterdam Avenue, then headed downtown again. Everyone he passed he envied, the chattering or the solitary people in the Butcher Block Restaurant, a sergeant leaning against the doorway of a recruiting station, even the man with the plastic coffee cup who spoke his need for spare change. They were not he; they were not Michael Ruane; they were not being forced to go through dark immutable fears that were helpless against the coming moment, one second away, less than a second away, when his mind, the gray aqueous lump of his brain, the bones of his skull, even the shreds of his hair, would explode and be flung into the surrounding air, spattering the cars like pigeon droppings, staining the sidewalk, pocking the bricks of the buildings, and fouling the leaves on the trees.

He kept walking, down past the library, down past Damrosch Park. At the Fordham tennis courts he made a left, back to Columbus Avenue. He had to go to rehearsal. He'd go, but he'd tell them he couldn't rehearse. He'd tell them he could never rehearse. That he could never sing, never act. That he was about to go insane and there was nothing he could do about it. And it would be when he'd say the word "insane" that the explosion would come. There would be a scream, and then would come the end. But first he must make sure to tell them that they mustn't send for Damian. It would do no good. He wouldn't come. Damian was leaving him. He was going the day after next, and then he'd be gone forever.

When the thought, the words, whisked through his mind —Damian was leaving—the terror lifted, like a fever broken, a delirium survived. Exhausted, relieved, almost light-headed, Michael reached the theater and went down the steps to the stage entrance. He felt giddy. He'd been given a reprieve. The decree against him had been rescinded. He was to be spared. He would not go insane. Not now anyway. As if in gratitude, he kept saying over and over and over, as if it were a chant, "Damian's leaving . . . He's leaving . . . He's leaving . . ."

His Parpignol was excellent and earned him his first mention in *The New York Times.* He sent a copy to Damian, by then living in the Village, but heard nothing in return.

Once, when Michael was waiting in line to see *Blue Velvet* at the Waverly on Sixth Avenue, Damian passed by and stopped. "You're going to see *this?*" He laughed at witnessing such an absurdity.

"It's supposed to be good."

"Of course. It's *supposed* to be good. But it isn't." He laughed again and walked on.

A third of the way through the movie, Michael became convinced that he was dying. At any moment, he would slump to the floor. There would be a disturbance. He'd have to be carried out, with everyone in his row annoyed at the disruption. To flee from death and avoid causing an inconvenience, Michael got up slowly, excused himself, and left the theater. By the time he'd walked to Bleecker Street, he began to feel that he might have eluded his death, but there was no guarantee he'd be so successful the next time.

He knew what he had to do. His only hope was to allow a fuming rage to burn and boil within him. He must permit a yearning and a sorrow to well up from somewhere inside himself and reach out to every corner of the earth, searching for Damian. He must give grief permission to take hold of him in an unrelenting grip, allow an acknowledgment of loss to exhaust his every moment, threatening at any time to bring him to his knees in futile supplication. These were the demands made by his terror. If he would agree, his sanity, his life, might be spared. Refuse, and the terror could come again at any time. Michael agreed. And the sorrow and yearning, the rage, the grief, and the loss entered in, taking full possession, locating themselves mostly in the stomach, in the throat, and in his good right hand.

When, after that, Michael and Damian would inadvertently meet—once at the Caravaggio show at the Metropolitan Museum, another time at Jan Wallman's on Forty-fourth Street, when Barbara Lea was singing Rodgers and Hart, and then again at the Strand Book Store, in the C's of the fiction section—the organs in Michael's body that housed his feelings for Damian would leap in recognition, like a child in the womb rebelling against its separation from the true object of its need. This would be followed by a threat of nausea or diarrhea or both, the clamor for release persisting until both Michael and Damian had gone at least three sentences into the banalities they would invariably exchange.

"I didn't know you liked Caravaggio."

"I'm not sure I do."

"When did you discover Barbara Lea?"

"I came to hear Wes McAfee. He's the piano player."

"You look well."

"It's the haircut."

"Good to see you."

"Yeah."

"Still cooking?"

"Still cooking. Still singing?"

"Still singing."

Numbed perhaps by the stupidities taking place, the organs would calm themselves to a mild churning, whispering to each other, exchanging comments about what was happening, complaining that they'd not been allowed to eject themselves from the confining body. In protest, they'd make a few more minor leaps, then settle for a dull turning until all was exhausted and there was no strength left beyond some slight prompting toward nausea, some feeble attack against the sphincter. And then the grief, in a great and groaning wave, would wash over him, through him, again, again, again, but be unable, for all its efforts, to drown him and give him peace.

Then, one day when Michael was rehearsing—of all things—the part of Beppe in *I Pagliacci,* the thought came to him that Damian, at his parting, had given him a valuable and lasting gift. Michael was leaning over the windowsill of the stage set while the director worked with the crowd's reaction to Il Pagliaccio's jealous rage against his wife, Columbine. He had already gone through Beppe's little serenade—youthful, ardent, as he'd sung it for d'Alessio on the fateful Roman day when the woman across the way had watered a flowerless flower box—and would sing it again once the crowd scene was taken care of. Columbine was checking the hem of her costume, Taddeo the fastness of the hump attached to his back. Michael, as Beppe, was reconstructing in his mind how he'd jump out the window later when Pagliaccio would enter—a headlong leap or one great swing, legs first. Before he could make his decision, he realized that the longing and jealousy, the loss, the grief, the rage that Damian had given him had enriched his life. Seldom did intensity leave him; not often was he without feelings alert and desperate. No fulfilled love could have given him anything to match the limitless reach of this yearning. Damian's daily presence could never have inspired moments equal in depth to this grief. For none of the old satisfactions should he sacrifice his loss or surrender his rage.

Damian, all unknowing, had bequeathed a life more full than he'd realized. Michael had been given the better part of the bargain after all, and it had a surprising worth, a remarkable durability, and an unfailing power of renewal.

Beppe sang his serenade and, when the moment came, he jumped out the window headfirst, twisting so he'd land on his side, a triumphant exit if ever there was one.

With the acceleration of the epidemic, Michael kept waiting for news that Damian was sick or that he was dead. Then he could mourn, secure in the knowledge that his loss would never be taken from him.

News, indeed, did come. Michael was in Patelson's music store, on Fifty-sixth Street, trying to find the sheet music for Mozart's Sonata in A. It would be a birthday present for a pianist friend who didn't like Mozart: Michael could be pretty sure he was getting him something he didn't already have. The sales clerk, wonderfully tenacious as was usual there, was looking in yet one more place, even though he was reasonably sure they were out of it. Michael, so he wouldn't be standing around dumbly waiting, was working his way through the Brahms file on the table near the door. His birthday friend had little fondness for Brahms as well; if the Mozart didn't work out, there was always a Brahms Intermezzo.

It was a December afternoon, a Saturday. The shop was crowded and stuffy with the smell of wet wool. The floors were slopped with partly melted slush. Michael had taken off one of his gloves, a maroon knit of synthetic fabric that looked warm but wasn't. He'd put it just to his right, on top of the Schumann, Scriabin, and Shostakovich. Someone bumped against him, then picked up the glove and tossed it over to the Handel and Haydn. Michael glanced sideways to see who was so easily familiar with his glove.

It was Curry James, who taught music theory at Columbia. Curry had introduced Damian to Michael at a gallery opening in, of all places, New Jersey. Because Michael and Curry hadn't seen each other for some time and Curry had become completely gray, Michael put a question mark after his name when he spoke it.

"Curry James?"

Curry was more confident. "Michael Ruane."

They shook hands. Michael picked up his glove and stuffed it into his jacket pocket, almost an apology for having let it obstruct the Scriabin. Each asked what the other was doing; each answered; each was pleased that the other was up to such excitements. Michael was going to Naples in March to put on *Curlew River*—in Italian—and play the Madwoman as well. He'd also be singing Spoletta in *Tosca,* at San Carlo. Curry was having a piece for clarinet, violin, and viola played in Houston in February.

The sales clerk, a baritone Michael had heard in the *Saint*

John Passion the year before, found the Mozart. It was in the complete piano sonatas, all eighteen of them, including the Fantasia in C Minor. Michael had envisioned a few pages of sheet music; he was confronted with a sizable volume that cost more than he'd planned to spend. So he'd have time to make up his mind whether to splurge or claim penury, he flipped through the pages, the better to see what he'd be getting for his money. Notes, notes, notes. Michael thought maybe the legendary fathead had been right after all when he'd said, "Too many notes, Mr. Mozart." Whoever might play these sonatas had better have a strong and sturdy left hand.

"I suppose you heard it's Damian's turn," Curry said.

Michael knew immediately what he meant. A thrill began in his groin and spread through his entire body. It weakened him, but he kept on flipping the pages of the Mozart. Köchel after Köchel after Köchel passed in front of him, like the names of towns seen from a fast train. Now the smell in the shop was of dried leather, and Michael thought he could detect a faint odor of orange peel. The thrill sent a second wave shuddering through him, this time keeping most of its force in the groin itself.

Michael told the clerk he'd take the whole volume. Because he knew Curry would give no more information until Michael had repeated the word "turn" in tribute to the original way the man had phrased his information, Michael said, "Turn?"

Curry followed Michael to the cash register, and while the Mozart was being paid for, he told him what he knew. In a voice that had settled for weariness as a substitute for sorrow, the man gave Michael what facts he had. Damian was at home, in his apartment. He was in bad shape; his mother had come from Allentown to take care of him. It didn't look good. Damian, he added as Michael accepted his change, was such a fine cook. It was all such a terrible, terrible pity.

Michael, repeating a correction he'd once received from Damian himself, said, "He wasn't a cook. He was a chef."

"Yes. A chef. Terrible pity, all of it."

For this last, Curry's weariness increased until it could almost sound like regret, but not quite.

Michael wished him well in Houston and, brushing past heavy coats and thick scarves, went outside, the Mozart held against his thigh like a fifth-grade geography book. Damian had ceased to matter. Michael's only thoughts were of himself. What was happening to Damian was incidental to what was about to happen to him. Soon he would be given a terrible sorrow and an unappeasable grief. Soon the losses of the past would wed themselves to the losses of the present, and the bond would hold forever.

Michael headed west toward Broadway, then north toward the subway station at Columbus Circle. The thrill that he'd felt shivered through him again. It was a feeling of great pleasure, as if he'd been told he'd won some award or was about to receive an enviable honor.

By the time he'd reached Fifty-seventh Street, he knew where the shudders and the thrills had come from. He had wanted Damian to die, and now he was about to be given his wish. And so complete was his satisfaction that he couldn't even be appalled by the grisly nature of his feelings. This was the final gift he'd been hoping for, and eagerly he accepted it now. In gratitude, he would lament and weep forever. Soon he would reach the other shore, a land of desolation deeded to him in perpetuity as the last will and testament of poor dead Damian.

But it didn't turn out that way. Damian, without having seen Michael, did indeed die. And now that Michael had what he'd wanted, he expected his old sorrows to be fulfilled. But a terrible trick had been played on him.

There'd been a wake for Damian at Redden's Funeral Home on Fourteenth Street, a short service before his mother would take the body back to Allentown for burial. Michael had gone to the service after having been twice refused permission to see Damian during his last days, once on the phone, the other time through the intercom of Damian's building on Waverly Place. (His mother told him that her son was resigned to his dying, that he'd let go of the world but was afraid something might happen to pull him back, an old friendship, a regret, a promise unkept. On the intercom, she'd cried and begged Michael not to call again. Michael had promised he wouldn't.)

Just before the service began, a young man, younger than twenty, came in led by a Seeing Eye dog, a blond Labrador. Two friends were with him, both his age. They went near to the coffin, the blind man stretching out his hand, touching it. So tentative, so tender was the touch that it seemed to be a form of braille, the body of the blind man gently reading the body of Damian.

During the brief eulogy, he reached down to stroke the dog settled patiently at his feet. During the prayers, he patted its flank, and once he scratched it behind the ears.

The service ended. Michael waited; he wanted to go to the coffin, to touch it himself. He looked toward the far wall. There stood the blind man, a boy almost—he was that young. His body bent forward, he was sobbing into his left hand. His two friends were quietly touching his back. The dog looked up at him, confused, then rubbed its nose against its right front paw.

Tears came to Michael's eyes and emptied out onto his cheeks, some of them falling on his sweater. He, too, began to sob. He fought the tears, but he wanted nothing more than to throw himself down on the floor and weep and weep some more.

He left the room and went outside. He sat on the third step of the stoop and put his head down on his arms, folded across his knees. And then he let the sobs, the heavings, do whatever they wanted.

But it was not for Damian or for Damian's death that he wept. He wept for the tears of the blind and for the confusion of the patient and faithful dog.

And from then on, his sorrow for Damian was taken from

192 · JOSEPH CALDWELL

him completely. His sense of loss became less than a memory; it was a vacancy, a thing that might never have existed, and Michael, in the days and nights that followed, was forced to call into question whether he had or hadn't truly loved his friend.

The answer was not in his favor. Out of his probings and his bewilderment came one irrefutable fact. He had, in the years since their separation, become obsessed with Damian. His vaunted yearning, his grief, his rage, had become an obsession, a clinging, parasitic leech that feeds on love, devouring it, leaving behind a carcass, a corpse dressed in all the trappings of love itself. It was splendidly robed in jealousy, longing, and pain, but it was a brutal yearning that made its unrelenting reach. Love's mockery, it craved possession for possession's sake, conquest for conquest's sake. His obsession was, in the end, a form of hatred disguised as love, and death was its easiest fulfillment.

The truth came to Michael not like a blow but as a slow, pervading weight, a part of his anatomy. It was in his bones, his skull, his organs, his muscles, an increase in density more than an added burden. Like yet another virus, it found lodging in his marrow and in his blood, and if it wasn't exactly fatal, its company was constant and accusing; it agitated even as it numbed.

In his prayers, in his search for sorrow and for loss, Michael, in reality, was asking for forgiveness, or even that he be allowed now, at this late hour, to love his friend at last. He was praying that his obsession be retracted and he be given in its place a fond affection, tender and mournful. Damian, whom he had refused to forgive, must now forgive *him*.

His prayer was answered, but as so often happens, the answer was no. Damian had taken with him to the grave the very loss of himself, and it was there to stay, buried, cold, and adamant. Stealthily and in justice, he had reached into Michael's heart and removed the central, sustaining emotion of his life, his sense of Damian gone. Attached, like torn nerve ends and ruptured veins, were grief and sorrow, so that they, too, were gone.

To make sure nothing remained, Damian had even closed up the hollow that had held them and had stitched it fast with needle and thread so fine that there was no scar, nothing at all to indicate that this had once been a heart full beyond bearing.

That was in New York. And now he was in Naples. And with him were the hollowed heart and the bewildered mind that were his final legacy from the man he had failed to love. And the other night he hadn't held Piero in his arms, so he had no way of knowing whether Damian would have come to him again in the dark, stone-floored *basso,* whether the closed heart would have stirred and the stitches loosened and he been given again his lost sorrow, so justly taken, so cunningly removed.

· · ·

We want to hear you singing . . .
unless you entertain us . . .
crazily singing!

The jeering Traveller and the pilgrims gyrated and made faces, one of the baritones crossing his eyes and rolling his head in a circle. The Abbot flung his arms heavenward, then brought them down to wrap around his ears, then flung the arms upward again. One bass, a fat man named Donato, leaned heavily on his left foot, raising the right one sideways in the air like a dog about to urinate, then bringing it down and lifting the left, going stiffly from side to side, while the other bass contented himself with covering his cheeks with his hands like a distraught housewife and shaking his head from side to side. Piero had found another way to mock the Madwoman. He merely raised his head high, then slowly brought his right hand to his eye and covered it with his open palm. He made no other movement, although the head seemed to be straining even higher, reaching for a greater arrogance, a more humiliating contempt.

Masked and robed as the Madwoman, Michael had stepped out of character to see how it all sounded and looked. A hip-shaking baritone was asked to look a little less as if he were in a disco. The Ferryman and the Traveller, unable to wait for the praise Michael was about to lavish on them, asked him what he thought of their contributions. They were *ottimi,* the best. They must keep it exactly that way; all of them must. Nothing must persuade them to change what they'd just done. The rehearsal went forward.

The frenzy called for at the moment the pilgrims, the Ferryman, the Abbot, and the Traveller realize that the dead boy buried on the opposite shore, where they had just landed, is the Madwoman's son was frenzy indeed. The libretto and score merely indicated the gist of what should be sung and played; musical entries overlapped, words clashed. The impression was to be one of shock, belief, and disbelief, all at the same time, and everyone did justice to the composer's and the librettist's trust.

At the harmonium, Signor Zongola, the closest the production had to a conductor, stopped the action to check on the percussionist, a wide-eyed youth who tended to be carried away with it all, and the bearded man playing double bass wanted to know if he was being heard. The percussionist was asked to hold back just a little; that might solve the problem of the double bass.

Again Michael stepped out of character to see what each was doing. The tenor was spreading the news to the baritones, who in turn let them know that

> She was his mother!
> She has only found sorrow.

while the basses asked him and each other:

> Is this a dream?
> Or is it true she was his mother?

Amid the babble and the twistings and turnings, Piero stood stock-still, gazing at the spot where, in performance, Michael as the Madwoman would be. Tears were on his cheeks and in his eyes.

"He was her child . . . ," he sang. "She has found his grave here by the river."

To distract himself, Michael concentrated on what the Abbot was doing. His eyes were raised, his palms outstretched. He had apparently decided to speak only to God, and Michael told him that this was news he might want to share with his flock. The singer liked the idea and began to move freely among the pilgrims. When the Abbot came to Piero, he saw the tears. His voice faltered. Quickly he turned to the Traveller, who was himself staring at Piero. Piero seemed to sense nothing.

One by one, the others, seeing him, stopped singing. When the last voice trailed off, he turned angrily toward the other monks. "What are you stopping for? Keep singing. Don't pay so much attention to me. I'm playing my way, and you play yours. Unless Maestro Ruane objects." He looked at Michael, defiant, daring. "Do you object?"

"You don't think the music inclines you to mix and mingle a little with the others?"

"No, I don't. It inclines me to do exactly what I'm doing."

"It's the Madwoman's part to weep," the Ferryman said. "You're trying to play his part instead of your own."

"I'm playing no one's part but mine. I am Brother Francesco, a pilgrim, and I come from the hills near Monte San Biagio, and I am in my eighth year of orders, this year of our Lord thirteen hundred forty-seven. In our monastery I am a scullion, and I am the only one from whom our mule, Tonino, will take food. In my cell, hidden under the pallet, is a shiny but worthless stone that I found one day in the butter vat. I decided then that it once belonged to my mother, who left me naked at the monastery door, and I will not part with it even if it means my eternal damnation. And now I, Brother Francesco, am here at the Curlew River and I see a madwoman and I learn the dead boy was her

child and that she has found his grave here by the river. And I
am playing my part, the part of Brother Francesco, and none
other."

"All right, then," the Abbot said. "You are Brother Francesco, and I am your abbot. You may keep the shiny stone with
my permission, until you are prepared to surrender it. But for
now, when you have come to the grave of the Madwoman's
son, you will not display your sorrow in this way. You will,
like a good friar, a faithful member of your community, share
your emotions with your brothers and not keep them to yourself,
as you've been doing. Are you prepared to obey?" With that,
the Abbot took the sleeve of his robe and wiped the tears from
Piero's cheeks. Piero looked down, nodded, then sniffed.

Michael glanced at the musicians. They were ready. He
looked at the singers. They were ready. He gave the count, then
began to sing, the musicians coming in right on time.

The frenzy began again, each repeating almost precisely what
he'd done before. Except for Piero. Piero, or perhaps it was
Brother Francesco from the hills near Monte San Biagio, spread
the news among his brethren, breathless, terrified by the words
he was singing. They seemed not to relate to the revelation of a
past misfortune but instead were a prediction of a calamity yet
to come, one that would happen at any moment. He moved
among the pilgrims, desperate that they know, that they be
warned in time. He was, Michael realized, trying to warn them
of a truth that was about to strike them down. They must prepare
themselves. At any moment they would be destroyed by the
knowledge that "he was her child." He clutched at robes, he
gestured with his thumbs and fingers joined, he moved his
opened hands away from himself, pushing back the truth of what
he was saying.

Michael thought of the shiny worthless stone hidden under
Brother Francesco's pallet. He turned to the musicians, to clear
away his confusion. It was his cue.

O Curlew River, cruel Curlew,
where all my hope is swept away.

He cried out the words and those that followed, struggling to concentrate, determined to continue the rehearsal in a thoughtful and professional way. It wouldn't be easy. He had understood Piero's tears. They were for Piero himself. He was going to die. And they were being shed as well for the scullion brother who had just seen Piero's mother come at last to his grave. When Michael came to the lines

> Did I give birth to him
> to have him stolen
> and carried far, far away,
> here to the Eastern Fens
> to end as dust . . . dust . . .
> to end as dust by the road?

he looked directly at Piero. And Piero looked directly at him, slowly shaking his head yes.

13

It was the strangest sight in all of Naples: the whole city, the bay, the stretch of land toward Sorrento, Vesuvio rising up from the surrounding plain—but no people. Not one. The defining element of the city, its frantic, determined citizens, were nowhere to be seen. The city looked like the backdrop for a giant *presepio,* a Nativity scene scaled to the God of Majesty rather than to the God who had consented not merely to have feet of clay but to be fashioned completely, tip to toe, of earthly mud. But there was no *sacro bambino,* no carpenter and his exhausted wife, no shepherds, no craftsmen and peasantry, no lords and thieves going about their workaday chores, unsuspecting that their salvation was at hand. It was a moment in creation left unrecorded, the day God made Naples but before he'd gotten around to Adam and Eve and those of their progeny who would, on some day of the Lord, people this empty scene, fulfilling the invitation to increase and multiply perhaps well beyond the original divine intent.

Michael put his hands on top of the waist-high wall, not to support or steady himself, but to touch something, to ground his awe and his unease. Behind him was the white stuccoed wall of the ancient monastery of San Martino, now a museum. Next to him was Piero, who'd insisted that they not take the bus or *funicolare* but climb the steps, La Salita di Montesanto, that began near Port'Alba, leading higher and higher, first through, then above, the gray buildings of Via Ventaglieri and Via Oliveta, past the Ospedale della Trinità, with its brick walls and tile roof, along Corso Vittorio Emanuele to the Pedamentina San Martino, where, without looking back, they passed among houses with small yards, stopped at a shrine to the Virgin long enough for Piero to cross himself and for Michael to read the inscription telling of the shrine's destruction in the war and its rebuilding by the people themselves, then through a rubble patch that seemed a perfect breeding ground for rats, up a stretch where the steps were no more than broken stones, then a final climb to where they stood now.

Michael had mentioned casually the morning after he'd spent the night with Piero that he wanted to visit San Martino, and as seemed perpetually the case in Naples, the most speculative wish immediately became a cause and a crusade for any Neapolitan within earshot. Piero would not be content until he had taken Michael to San Martino. Michael hadn't taken up Assunta's museum offer, since she'd ultimately confessed her preference to go alone. And so it finally became Piero who wanted to go to San Martino—and it was Michael who would be the half-interested companion, compelled by courtesy to accompany him there.

The climb had tired neither of them. It was as though the lure of holy ground—or what had once been holy ground—had bestowed a more limber leg, a more agile lung, a more cooperative heart. In contrast, Michael had heard that no one scales the ungraded slopes of Vesuvio—surely at times the mouth of hell—without the threat of imminent heart failure and immediate lung collapse. That the one climb was considerably shorter than the other was beside the point. The reason Jesus had so much trouble going up Calvary was that he had not yet made its heights a blessed place. For everyone since, the ascent has been easy—comparatively, of course.

There was another reason for Michael's well-being. That morning, he had gone to Sansevero to see the stage and the setting the carpenters had built. What they had effected were miracles beyond Michael's specifications. More than once he had known that at some point during his labors he would have to go to Signor Crescenzo and tell him again that all was hopeless, that the space in Sansevero was impossible. But he had been wrong. There, in the small chapel, all was perfectly arranged—the ramp, the platform, with ample room for the boat and the benches and for the pilgrims who would cross the Curlew River.

The sail was the workmen's particular pride. They showed him again and again how it could be raised and lowered without difficulty. The sculpture of the entombed and shrouded Christ —*Il Cristo Velato*—was incorporated into the set as if the entire presentation were an offering to the redemptive act. The workers were geniuses and had seemed to know, beyond Michael's ability to tell, what was needed—and there it all was. The monks would come up from below, from a circular room presided over by two grotesque skeletons with petrified veins; they would rise from this land of the dead and sing out their mystery "of God's good grace," and then they'd return to it when all was over.

Resisting an impulse to hug each workman in turn, Michael shook their hands at least three times. It pleased them, but more than that, it surprised them that this American could have had so little faith in their skills. How the audience would respond was a fear that Michael would confront at another time. Now there was only joy and possibility. He shook their hands once more and heard them mutter their amused bewilderment as he left.

Michael looked out over the expanse of orange-tiled roofs below, the domes and towers, the tops of trees, the walls and spires, so close together they concealed completely even the broadest *corso,* the most open *piazza.* In the bay, no ship moved and the water was still. Possibly the fish in the sea, too, were yet to come.

However, this was still Naples, and he and Piero were hardly alone. Off to their right, on a flat rooftop, a chubby boy kicked a soccer ball against the security fence obviously installed to prevent easy access from the nearby public steps. With each kick, a large white dog on a lower rooftop barked, only to bark again when the ball hit the fence. To their right, four people had just gotten off a bus and were heading toward a postcard stall. At the far end of the walk, a little boy of about three, squealing with triumph and delight, was moving along the top of the cement wall, his hand firmly held by a young man, white shirt open at the neck, ballooning in the wind—his father, no doubt, whose delight, if not quite so vocal, was obviously no less than the child's.

"You're not out of breath?" Michael asked. He didn't turn to Piero; he wasn't going to look for evidence. He'd take Piero's word for it, whatever the answer.

"Why would I be, when you aren't? I'm younger than you." Without letting Michael say anything, he went on. "I know. My *malattia*—my 'illness,' as you call it. But it's not *la malattia;* it's *la pestilenza.* It makes me sound so much more important, don't you think, if you say, 'You have *la pestilenza,*' instead of, 'You have *la malattia.*' I really prefer the sonority as much as the accuracy. *La pestilenza.* But no, my lungs and the rest of me aren't affected. Yet. I wanted to climb the stairs to prove it to you. And see? I did. Come, you can look at me now."

Piero was smiling, amused and pleased by his little speech, but Michael saw the slightest hint of gray in his face, surfacing from somewhere beneath the skin, but since it could be the light refracted from the cement, he decided to dismiss it. There was certainly no weariness there, only the usual wry smile indicating that Piero had just tricked someone or exercised his cunning in a particularly satisfying way.

With this, Michael knew that Piero was more ill than he'd let on, that his insistence on climbing the hill, the denial of exertion, the pleased smile, were not to be trusted. That Piero was sick Michael had known, but now he knew that he was dying, that the act itself had begun. It wasn't the gray tinge that had told him this; it was the smile. And Michael had to wonder if Piero had deliberately chosen this method to make the announcement, trusting Michael to read the auguries accurately, a method of communication peculiar to Piero and flattering to Michael.

"Do you want to catch your breath, or should we go in?" Piero asked.

"It's the view," Michael said, "not the climb, that takes your breath away."

"Good. Then we'll just look at the view. We can forget the museum. I didn't want to tell you, but there's not much there since the earthquake." He looked along the wall. The squealing boy and the beaming father were getting closer. "No, we'd better go in," Piero said. "It's what you wanted, and you should get what you want."

They both pulled respectfully away from the wall so that the boy could continue his wobbly progress along the top—as if it were the edge of the known world—assisted only by his father's steady hand. *"Coraggio!"* Piero cried as the boy passed. *"Coraggio!"*

The father, in effect, took a bow, nodding at the two of them. *"Attenzione, Guido!"* the man called in mock warning. *"Attenzione!"* Never, of course, had the boy been so safe. *"Non aver paura!"* the father called. *"Bravissimo! Bravissimo, Guido! Non fermarti! Vai! Vai, Guido, vai!"* Don't be afraid. . . . Don't stop. Go! Go, Guido, go! Each warning and each exhortation was rewarded with a squeal from Guido, and Michael had to wonder if he had ever seen two happier people—ever—on the face of the earth.

Without waiting to see Guido's triumphant achievement of the far end of the wall, they went inside the museum. Few of the rooms were open, and what they looked at—the paintings and the drawings, the artifacts and the antiques—failed to interest Michael as much as he'd expected. Only at one particular painting did they pause for more than a moment. Piero stopped first, then Michael. It was almost a primitive, an illustration more than a work of art, a scene in Piazza del Mercato, in front of the Church of the Carmine, once considered the center of Naples. Strewn everywhere in the piazza were the bodies of the dead, rigid in ghastly contortion. The few still alive, stunned, exhausted, moved among them. There was a cart heaped with corpses, but with no one, no beast, no man, to pull it. The inscription below the painting, printed on a gilded shield, told them that this was the plague of 1656, a year of the Black Death.

Piero continued to stare at the picture, then said, "How wonderful. In those days you didn't have to die alone. Everyone was doing it. The trouble now isn't that there are so many *pestilenti,* but so few. In New York, there are many, though, aren't there? Does Times Square look like this?"

"Not yet."

"If I were in New York, I could, when the moment was approaching, go to Times Square." He pointed to the figure of a woman heaped on the stones. "There, that would be me. As you can see, I would have dressed for the occasion." He laughed lightly, then went out the door into the sunshine. Michael took one more look at the painting, at the woman on the stones, at the living attending the dead. Then he followed.

Outside, everything seemed green and gold in the sunlight. Two broad terraces, cut from the steep slope of the hill, were given over to trees and walkways, to grass and the plantings that would flower when the warmer weather came. Michael and Piero went toward a parapet that, like the cement wall, looked out over the city. Above them a great stone thunderhead rose, the sheer rock wall of Castel Sant'Elmo, brooding over the monastery and—as a matter of fact—over all Naples. Like Vesuvio, its counterpart on the far side of the bay, it menaced the city

with the threat of a terrible justice and an unthinking retribution.
The great difference, however, was that Vesuvio had, in its slopes
and peaks, a certain majestic grace, and it was, as history had
proved, responsive to saintly and divine persuasions, whereas
Sant'Elmo was brutal in aspect and indifferent—or so it
seemed—to any pleadings, human, saintly, or divine.

Michael and Piero began a slow stroll down the walkway
toward the parapet.

As they walked, Michael asked Piero, "Where did you find
your character, your Brother Francesco, for the opera? Is he from
an old story?"

"Maybe. I don't know. He came from somewhere, but I'm
not really sure."

"You made him up?"

"No, I don't think so. I just looked inside myself, and there
he was, living his whole life, and I never knew he was there until
now." Piero spoke cheerfully, but it was the same cheer he'd
had in talking about the painting.

"You have a pretty vivid imagination."

"But I didn't imagine him. I didn't make him up. He was
there."

Michael shrugged.

"You don't believe me?"

"All right. I believe you."

"No, you don't. But it's true. And I'll tell you something
else and you won't believe it." They continued walking. "There
was a day," Piero said, "a long time ago, when he, Brother
Francesco, looked inside himself and found me living there, just
like he was living in me yesterday. It was a time of plague, and
he was afraid. He worried what it would be like to get *la pestilenza*. He tried to imagine it, but he didn't have to. He looked
inside himself, and I was there, wearing my wig, sitting on the
edge of my bed. He saw the lesions on my chest and the one
here beneath my eye. He knew that I had just had some milk to

drink and some bread and that beneath my pillow I keep a shiny but worthless stone that I found one day in a butter vat and had decided at once that it had belonged to my mother, who left me naked at the convent door, and I would not part with it, even if it meant my eternal damnation. And then he knew he, too, would get the plague, that his brothers in the monastery would turn him out and he would die, ravaged by the disease, alone, by the side of the road, and he would remember as almost his last thought that he had forgotten to bring the stone with him and that now it would be found by the abbot and the brothers and they would say he caught the plague because he was worldly and a man of great vanity. And he would know this to be true. And he would die with no regrets, with no repentance, and without the shiny stone."

Down on the lower terrace Michael saw a tall, thin woman in an elegant beige dress of crushed silk, looking as if she'd just come from a garden party, going from bush to tree, from tree to bush, taking a leaf from each and, after rubbing it between her thumb and fingers to test its texture, putting it in her purse. Michael watched her reach up into what looked like a ficus tree, but before she'd plucked a leaf, he looked down at the paving stones beneath his feet. Piero was wearing a new pair of shoes Michael hadn't noticed before, black. Then Michael recognized them as the patent-leather ones he'd worn with the tuxedo to the opera.

"What made you think I wouldn't believe you?" Michael asked.

"Maybe because you'd know I wasn't telling the truth, that I was making it all up after all."

Piero laughed. Michael said nothing. They were nearing the end of the walkway. Steps led down to the terrace below. There was a group of three women, a young man, and a child taking what seemed to be its first baby steps, uncelebrated by any of the adults. Two old men in shabby suits sat on a bench, both with bellies shaped like enormous eggs growing out from their coats. They weren't speaking, but one would, from time to time, nod as if the other had said something. They seemed an aged Tweedledum and Tweedledee, lost and too weary to gain again the land of irrefutable logic from which they'd strayed.

Without consultation, Michael and Piero opted for the low wall ahead. It, too, looked out over the city, the bay, and the volcano. Again there was the stillness below, a silent, empty Naples, a contradiction if there ever was one.

Piero made a broad gesture with his right arm, taking in all that lay before them. "This will I give you," he said, "if you will but bow down and worship me."

Michael wondered if the sly smile was on his face, but he preferred not to look. Perhaps when Piero mocked and smiled slyly, he spoke the truth. Perhaps when he delivered his words straightforward and unnuanced, he was lying like a rug. Michael told himself he must take this into consideration.

Piero rested his arms on the parapet. Neither of them spoke. The silent city below them seemed enough, for now anyway. A plane flew overhead, leaving behind it a vapor trail, a great white arc across the sky like a rainbow for the color-blind.

"Do you think I should go to New York to die? They have shelters there and food. Or when I slept in the street, I wouldn't be alone. Maybe I'll go to New York."

The vapor trail began to break up into small puffs of cloud, the tail of the arc disappearing altogether. "If I *do* come to New York, I'll let you come to see me. Would you like that?"

Michael wanted to change the subject, but that would have been too insulting. If Piero wanted to talk about his illness, it had to be allowed. Still, Michael wished he'd talk about something else. But when he didn't, Michael said, "I don't think going to New York would be such a good idea. You'll get better health care in Italy, in Naples. That much I know."

"Maybe. But if I do come to New York, I'll bring with me

something precious—something very precious—and I'll give it to you." He laughed, then said, "No, I don't mean *la pestilenza,* and I don't mean a shiny stone."

Michael could tell he was looking at him, but he kept his eyes on the disintegrating vapor overhead.

"I'll let you share my death with me," Piero said. "I'll let you be with me. Maybe I'll even let you take care of me. You would be able to see me weaken or maybe even go blind and mad, the way some people do. You can watch me try to catch one more breath; you can hear me cough and take away in a piece of tissue the thick green phlegm. You can clean away the diarrhea and spoon simple soup and water into my mouth. You can bear everything, even when I turn on you and denounce you, because it has pleased you to be a part of so great an act—my suffering, my dying, and my death. You can close my eyes and clean my body, and I don't doubt that you will take advantage and kiss my lips as well. And you can weep. You can mourn and grieve. You can suffer and be bereft. Who else can offer you so much as this? I can. And only I."

Michael looked directly at Piero. He was smiling. His lips, which seemed able to pout and curl at the same time, were tightly shut and thrust forward brazenly. His eyes, pulled back deeper into their sockets, both stared and danced, defiant and merry. What Michael was being offered, by proxy, was the death of Damian. Piero had ferreted out his deepest susceptibility. He had offered Michael a role he had been desperate to play.

Before Michael could say anything, Piero added, "But you must promise just one thing. At the last, you must hold not my hand but my cock. You must reach under the blanket and take it in your hand. It will probably be shriveled and cold, but you must take hold of it anyway." He brushed a hand across his forehead as if readying his thoughts for the words he was about to say. "I have always loved my cock," he said. "I am a true son of Naples. I have always thought it beautiful, just as I was taught to do. And you must promise this one thing. I don't want to die with no one holding my precious and beautiful cock."

Piero brought his hands together in front of him, then slowly spread his arms wide as if making himself completely open, completely vulnerable, completely helpless, but quietly, simply, and with dignity. His shirt was open, unbuttoned three buttons down, giving a full view of the pink splotches, the lesions on his chest. Tongue-colored, and in the shape of tongues, each seemed to have been branded into his flesh by a burning and unearthly kiss.

"I think," Michael said, "you should stay in Naples."

Piero shrugged, then stuffed his hands into his pockets and made a gesture with his elbow for Michael to follow him. They were leaving. The time had come to go.

They took the *salita* again, the wide spacing forcing them to take broad steps, careful not to land on a crumbling stone. Before they had come to the first turning, the chubby boy's soccer ball inevitably bounced past them and landed in a heap of rubble off to the side.

"*Capo! Capo!*" the boy called.

Piero waved his hand to him and went for the ball. With a kick that employed his entire body, a twist of the torso, a swing of the arms, Piero sent the ball back to the roof, but some bricks and stones beneath him gave way, and the movement ended with Piero on one knee, his hand quickly searching for somewhere to steady himself. A brick he touched tumbled away down the slope, and to prevent a more complete fall, he set the other knee on the rubble.

"*Grazie!*" the boy yelled.

Michael was at Piero's side. He helped him halfway up, and Piero sprang the rest of the way, his body shooting upward to an erect and stiffened stand. He brushed the sleeves of his shirt, even though his shirt had not been involved in the fall. Next, he took out a handkerchief and flicked it over his shoes, which, again, had suffered nothing.

"Did you hurt anything?"

"Only my dignity." With that, he gave a kick to one of the stones that had betrayed him. It went bouncing and bounding down the hill and came to rest under a scruffy bush near someone's fence.

With Piero leading the way, they half walked, half leapt down the steps. As they descended, the sounds of the city were heard again, and soon enough a street was seen between the buildings. There were people on the street, and cars. A shop-window shutter rumbled its way open. The whine of motorbikes was pitched above the sounds of the growling cars, and the long shout of a man's wail could be heard above them all, its Mediterranean origins casting it in a minor key. With each step, the city's life increased as if it had slumbered in their absence and was now awakening at their return. By the time they reached Piazza Dante, all was the same. They had never left, and Naples had never slept.

They made their way through the narrow *strade* and *vicoli,* Piero walking more swiftly than Michael. When they reached the foot of Piero's street, he stopped. Too narrow for a car, it had not escaped completely its share of modern-day intrusion. Against a wall halfway down the incline that led to the end of the street was a discarded refrigerator, its door hanging from one hinge. Garbage had been thrown the street's entire length, as if a procession had passed this way, the devout strewing neither palms nor flowers but lettuce leaves, artichokes, cabbages, and fennel, with a tomato or an orange peel tossed in by some particularly desperate pilgrim, homage, it seemed, to the god of abundance.

Overhead, tier upon tier of laundry mounted to the sky, all gray and lifeless, as if it had forgotten what sun and a fresh wind could be like. One clothesline had broken, and the family laundry had worked its way through several other lines, so that a woman's blue-checked dress and a pillowcase rested in the thin film of slime that coated the black *piperno* that paved the alleyway. Close against a wall, as if trying to scratch the fleas in the fur of its left side against the stained stucco, a rat ran about five feet, then disappeared, not into a hole but down in a stone.

Piero paused and took in a deep and satisfied breath. Gazing the length of his street, he said, but quietly, "All this will I give you if you will but bow down and worship me."

Michael did not bow down or touch the pavement with a bending knee, but after the briefest pause, he did give a slight nod of the head. That would be enough. "I'll find some way to bring you to New York. You can't be left here alone. You have to be with me."

"Maybe," said Piero. "Maybe I will. And maybe I won't. We'll see, shall we?" He wasn't smiling.

14

The last time Michael had come here to Via Giganti, the name on the downstairs intercom had been *Attanese,* but now it clearly said *Spacagna,* printed in a rather spirited calligraphy that gave some letters tails, others wings, while the *S* had been inspired by both the dollar sign and the G clef. Michael thought he saw in the lettering the fine, generous hand of Rosalia herself, which had tamed and at the same time made proud the good and biting name Spacagna.

Familiar now with the rubric for getting into the building, Michael made his way inside the door on the second try, but he found that the hallway lights that had seen him to the second floor the last time were now willing to accompany him only past the first three steps. From then on he was on his own, with aid only from what must be a skylight on the top floor, its gray light able to travel no farther than the second landing, straight ahead. He moved as quickly as the dark would allow, though he would have preferred to just stand still, to go nowhere and let nothing happen.

He had just come from a run-through of *Curlew River,* the first in Sansevero itself, on the "set." It had been not a disaster but simply a dull and empty spectacle. There was nothing there. There had never been anything there.

His well-rehearsed and gifted cast sang all the words, and the musicians sounded all the notes, and the two forces had kept themselves reasonably together. The lighting man was singularly efficient, and everything happened on cue. Nothing went wrong. Except that the opera itself was worthless; its score was boring and unmusical, its text inconsequential. Who cared about some dippy woman making life difficult for everyone? Who would believe the pilgrims' scorn and then their swift switch to compassion? Or who would even bother to make the attempt to believe? The ending was sentimental, the appearance of the spirit of the dead son a replication of Puccini's *Suor Angelica* but without Puccini's music.

The catcalls Michael had previously feared, the cries of outrage and ridicule he'd schooled himself to expect, seemed now a blessed alternative to the snores, the indifference, the casual exits that he knew were to be the final reward for all his long labors—and the end to all the hopes his old maestro had placed in him. The poor man had done what he could, even from the grave, to help his former pupil, to give him one last chance to shine beyond the shadowy confines of the *comprimario*. But now the light was about to be extinguished for good and for always, not even a quick dramatic snuff but a slow fade, and what light Michael might seek in the future could be found only and forever in the dusky illuminations allowed a Parpignol or a Remendado or, on a good night, a Goro or Basilio.

Midway during the telling of the Ferryman's tale earlier that day, he was given the knowledge that he would never sing the Simpleton in *Boris Godunov,* that the prize role of the Emperor in *Turandot* must be deleted from his expectations. Even the current acceptance of his Spoletta at San Carlo was simple Neapolitan indulgence; they didn't find him worth the strength it would take to make their rejection known. Or, more likely, the applause he'd received during his curtain calls was—and he didn't realize it until that morning—a form of mockery; some claque had been making fun of him, delighting all the more in his stupid and ignorant gratitude at their barely disguised jeers. He was a fool and a failure, grateful that he would leave Naples in less than a week. The only hope he had left was Piero's possible acceptance of his offer to come to New York. That might redeem his Neapolitan disgrace, but Piero had yet to give him an answer. Which made him feel all the more ineffectual, that much closer to nonentity.

The one effort he'd made to counter his mood had merely intensified it. He'd gone to the street market of Sant'Antonio Abate, hoping the shouts and cries would raise him from the depths into which the rehearsal had plunged him. Surely the spirit of the place would catch at him, force him to shed any feeling that wasn't celebratory.

He had headed for the market, hoping he'd repeat the experience he'd had a week before when, on a walk home from rehearsal, he'd made a wrong turn and found himself on Via Foria. A general sense of direction, not always reliable in Naples, suggested that he turn right into the next street to see if he could wind his way through the endless maze to some place near his apartment. At a *vicolo* no wider than a hallway, he made his turn. It led to a wider street, the width of an alley. No sooner had he made this second turn than he heard shouts and cries. Some great calamity had obviously happened up ahead. Michael couldn't help wondering if this is what it might sound like when an earthquake hit, the people rushing into the streets, calling out their distress, their warnings to their neighbors, their pleas to heaven and to the saints. A building had collapsed, a child run over, a shooting, perhaps.

He had no impulse to turn back. He was immediately willing to lend his voice to the general dismay—and his natural curiosity required that he find out what the disaster might be.

At the bottom of the street, he made another turn. There, laid out before him, was not the tragedy he'd come to see but a great open market, stretching as far as his eye could reach. Those were peddlers' cries he'd heard, the great shouts going up to extol their wares and excite the passersby into buying what was there for sale. Stalls of vegetables and fruit, clothing, shoes, household goods, toys and games, fish, mussels, eels, and cigarettes, more vegetables, more fruit. A boy no older than six was holding high a huge brass scale, its tray filled with lemons, the leaves and stems still there, his clamor as full-voiced as the rest. A man hawking balloons strode quickly by, an incomprehensible call coming from deep within his throat. A woman sat dead center in the street, a display of cigarettes spread out on a wooden crate: Marlboro, Chesterfield, Doral, and Winston. Her words were muttered, a low voice, an undercurrent, a bass line to the shrill cries around her.

Michael headed down the street. A sign told him he'd come upon the markets of Sant'Antonio Abate. There was *finocchio* like giant celery stalks, clumps of broccoli that seemed miniature trees, eggplants like dark and polished breasts, peppers, red, green, and yellow, the yellow the color of fire. Hats, shoes, suitcases, belts, dresses, and underclothes. No want had been ignored.

All around him now, like an anarchic chorus of jubilant madness, the cries came. He almost stumbled from the force of it. A man stood astride two tables, one filled with pants, the other with sweaters. His right arm was raised heavenward, and his cry, it seemed, was a plea for witness that these were indeed the finest pants, the least expensive sweaters, in all the Western world.

And then it came to Michael that these were neither peddlers nor vendors. They were celebrants. They were selling nothing. They had come to shout their praise, to cry out with a great voice the high worth of what they'd brought. A tiny woman with a kerchief tied under her chin defied contradiction that these were oranges like none other and pears meant only for kings.

Caps and purses were proclaimed the true glory of the earth; cabbages and artichokes the only acceptable offering to God and to the saints. There was a need for nothing in the world but this garlic, these handkerchiefs. No hymn of thanks and praise could equal what Michael was hearing now, no pagan rite could duplicate its passion and its chaos.

Near the end of the street—he'd come about a quarter of a mile—he considered buying some oranges. But it didn't seem right. These were offerings, objects of celebration, not intended for mortal consumption. Michael told himself he was being foolish. The man shouting dementedly into Michael's left ear was there to sell his oranges, and if Michael wanted to buy some, the two were well met. He stepped back to look at the display. It was bounteous indeed, three great pyramids raised to some worthy deity. The vendor's face changed from one grimace to another, the mouth now wide open, now stretched toward his jawbones; his eyes were fierce, and his right hand kept fanning the air off to his side, as if to keep the sound of his shouts from piercing his ear. Nothing could persuade Michael to interrupt him. It would be like disturbing an ecstatic in mid-vision. The man would become confused, disoriented, lost.

Michael looked and listened another moment, the great clamorous shouts of praise behind him, undiminished, unending, the man in front of him desperate that his own cry be heard above all others. Michael walked out onto Piazza San Francesco. He bought his oranges at a small shop on Via Milano, where he'd disturb no hymns, intercept no praise, and he ate them for his lunch. They'd been delicious.

But when Michael had returned to the market after the rehearsal that morning, he heard the vendors' cries not as shouts of celebration and praise but as jeers at his failure. The cries were cries of scorn that he had dared to bring to Naples something so foreign and so worthless. The fishmongers reviled him, babbling their contempt as he passed by; the cigarette woman muttered words she wouldn't dare say too loudly. The balloon man snarled his disdain, and only the woman selling broccoli and *finocchio* seemed to have any pity. Her call was a lamentation that so misguided a venture had been allowed within the city gates. When he picked up two oranges from the flawless pyramid, he was told to put them back. The vendor himself would make the choice; he knew better than Michael which oranges were best suited for his consumption. It was the vendor's profession, and Michael must not presume. Michael accepted the two oranges handed him by the man who'd fanned his ears to protect them from his own demented cries. They were decent enough oranges, but the vendor had demonstrated a truth now known throughout the city: Michael was not competent to choose an orange. He was inadequate in all things, a pretender and a failure. Far behind him, the jeers continued and were silenced only when Michael threw the oranges into a litter basket on Via Foria and strode rapidly toward Via Giganti.

Before the first landing, a stench of cat spray clogged the hallway air. It was an odor that could turn a palace into a tenement, a smell within a smell, as if the scent were repelled even by itself and had sent out a second odor in an attempt to smother the first. It was a male cat's territorial claim, and Michael, repulsed by the fouled air he had to breathe, understood its effectiveness: No one, not even another cat, would want to come anywhere near so repellent a stink.

He had come to say goodbye to Rosalia. He didn't intend to tell her the exact date of his departure; he wished only to say that he might have to leave at any moment and wouldn't want to go without having said his farewell. He must also tell her that he could not, alas, take her with him to Rome, that it was, for reasons he couldn't explain, impossible. And that he was sorry. He hoped she wouldn't ask for an address, but if she did, he'd simply tell her Signora Spacagna would know how to get in touch with him. He would let the uncle from Rome, Don Michele Spacagna, die insignificantly, a dismissed memory, a forgotten absence. In the role of uncle, as in the others, he had achieved nothing.

Gaetano would or would not murder Peppino. Rosalia would or would not eventually find some happiness in her marriage. Peppino would or would not go mad with fright. Signora Spacagna would or would not take poison. He had hoped to reconcile the brothers, to save Rosalia, to satisfy the Signora, but without wanting to, he had obeyed the commands of Don Callisto. He, the Roman, had left Naples alone. He took what comfort he could from the dreary phrase "Let Naples look after Naples." Strangers beware. Had he the energy, the spirit, he might have resented or ignored the exclusion, but he was too weighed down, too wearied with his knowledge of failure and the meaninglessness of things, to care one way or the other. He lacked even the energy for the self-pity that would have provided him with some modicum of caring, even if it was only for himself.

He would, of course, with Rosalia now, be—for the last time—the uncle from Rome. He would be all authority and affection; he would confess a sad inadequacy that he was unable to reweave an alternative pattern into the tapestry of her fate. He would give her his avuncular blessing—and promptly abandon her to her misery.

In one of the apartments on Rosalia's landing, an argument was taking place, the words in dialect, charging, retreating, then charging again into the hallway. Michael, climbing the last few steps, wasn't paying much attention, but the few words he bothered to understand seemed to indicate that the argument was over a chicken. Hearing the women's voices, he realized for the first time where *bel canto* had come from. Repeated notes in the middle register, sudden notes below the staff, a chest-voice staccato, a B flat tossed off on the way up to an E natural, then the plunge back down below middle C, a high C, a two-octave drop, then the high C again—and this was being done sometimes in duet, sometimes in solo. *Bel canto* was indeed the native utterance of Naples. To strengthen this realization, there was the added revelation that it could all be inspired by nothing more—or less— than a chicken.

Michael started toward Rosalia's door. The dim light made the entire passageway seem a sullen cloud that had solidified itself and formed walls and doorways. The cat smell was less aggressive, but there was the continuing threat that it could reassert itself at any time. He had almost raised his hand to knock when he realized that the raging duet was coming from Rosalia's apartment. One voice—the contralto—he recognized as that of Signora Spacagna. In the time that it took Michael to raise a fist, ready to knock, she demonstrated that she was quite capable of a G, and a sustained one at that. Now she retreated below the middle register, the soprano coming in a half tone higher, more intense and obviously readying herself for another quick leap into the stratosphere.

Michael could only assume that the Signora and another woman were there, assaulting the hapless Rosalia, possibly, from all Michael could make out, with competing recipes for *pollo arrosto*. He had expected her to be alone, but the presence of others might make the parting more simple. It would certainly prevent Rosalia from repeating her plea that he take her with him to Rome, and he would be spared the need for a heartfelt refusal. And his refusal would have been heartfelt. He really did want to help her, but there was nothing within the bounds of reality he could do beyond killing Peppino himself, which would create too great an inconvenience in his own life for it to be practical. And so her situation, as far as he could tell, was hopeless, and he could only pray that some contentment in the future would compensate for the agonies and idiocies of the present. With the final hope that he could keep from looking directly into her eyes, he knocked. There was an immediate silence. At least he had rescued Rosalia from the Signora and her partner, who'd been making her the forced audience for their passionate and threatening chicken duet.

Rosalia opened the door. Her face was flushed, her eyes fierce, almost imperious. The rush into his arms, the head abandoned to his shoulder, the tears of relief that he had rescued her at least from this present torment—none of this happened. Her chest heaved up and down, in and out, as if she, not he, had just climbed the stairs. She greeted him respectfully, then stepped back to let him enter the narrow hallway.

In the kitchen, seated upright a little away from the table, was the Signora, hands propped on her cane. In front of her was the plucked carcass of a chicken, its claw feet aimed at her gray-streaked hair, its limp neck a short twisting path to its still-feathered head. The soprano had obviously retreated, perhaps to the bathroom to gargle, protecting her invaluable instrument. He decided to go ahead with his farewell scene without her, whoever she might be. An interruption might be welcome somewhere along the way.

"I've come for my promised cup of coffee. Unless now is not a good time." His voice sounded suave, almost oily. That he had been a fraud from the beginning he accepted, but he had been, to the best of his ability, a sincere fraud. He must try for sincerity now. It was there someplace, and he would like to find it. Rosalia deserved no less.

"It's a very good time," the Signora said.

"No, it's not a good time." Rosalia half tossed, half brushed her hair back from her forehead, then drew her hand down, letting it pause for a moment on her breast before bringing it to rest on the table in front of her. As she delivered a recitative built around the key of G, Michael recognized the soprano he'd heard through the door. There was no one gargling in the bathroom. Rosalia was not audience but participant.

"Rosalia," the Signora said, "offer your uncle a chair."

"No, no," Michael protested, still unable to get the oil out of his voice.

"You may sit, Uncle, if you wish."

"Sit," the Signora said. "Sit. Rosalia will make us both some coffee. Isn't that true, *cara mia?*"

"I promised Don Michele coffee. I'll keep my promise." It seemed to Michael that she was struggling to find again the plaintive voice he'd heard before, that she wished to become again the young woman who'd so effortlessly made him such an impressive meal a few weeks before.

"Not if it's any trouble," Michael said. He was pleased that the oil slick coating his words had begun to disperse.

"No, it's no trouble." Rosalia smiled at him, a hesitant smile but one reminiscent of his previous visit. She even came to him and kissed his forehead, not quickly but fondly. Whatever Michael would say from here on might be a lie, but it would be sincerely said.

"Perhaps before you make the coffee you'd like to put the chicken away." The Signora pushed the bird a little toward the middle of the table, the head now twisted under the spine.

"No," Rosalia said in soft, measured tones. "I don't want to put that chicken away." Her voice didn't exactly rise but intensified itself in the direction of a *forte* as she added, "You will put the chicken away. In your own refrigerator, in your own home. Not in my refrigerator and not in my home."

"But it's for you. The boy is starving, I tell you."

"Then let him starve!" There was the crash of the coffeepot against the stove, and the cue was given for the resumption of the duet he'd heard in the outside hallway.

"You! His wife! How can you say that?" The Signora drew back, her horror possibly real.

"If I'm his wife, I'll feed him and he'll eat it. Or not eat it if he doesn't want to."

"Never has he refused chicken, in any form. This he'll eat."

Rosalia yanked open the refrigerator door and pulled out yet another plucked chicken. Holding it by the neck, she shook it in front of her. "Here's a chicken if he wants a chicken. And if he doesn't want to eat this one, then let him eat shit."

The Signora jerked herself up and sucked in air through her teeth. "Rosalia!" Even Michael sat up straighter in his chair.

Rosalia gave the chicken another merciless shake. "Here is his dinner. *I'll* fix it. *I'll* put it in front of him. He'll stare at it, just as he stares at the pasta, just as he stares at the spinach and the soup. If he chooses to feast on stares, let him."

The Signora grabbed the chicken on the table and she, in turn, gave hers a good shake, in Rosalia's direction. "Of course he won't eat that one. Look at this one. *This* is a chicken. *That* is a pigeon."

"No. *This* is a chicken. *That* is a buzzard." Rosalia slapped the bird onto the table in front of Michael. The Signora slammed her chicken down, also in front of Michael. He began to have the less than vague suspicion he was going to be asked to choose.

It would be the Judgment of Paris all over again, the contending deities forcing a mortal to make the fateful choice. No matter which chicken was chosen, the war was destined to take place, not between the Argive forces and the Trojan heroes, but between mother-in-law and daughter-in-law, *suocera* against *nuora*. All Naples could go up in flames, his decision achieving a devastation denied all these millennia to Vesuvio itself.

The inevitable happened. "Let Don Michele decide." The Signora sat back in her chair and again put both hands on the head of her cane.

"There is nothing to decide." Rosalia covered her chicken with her hand, forbidding Michael to even look at it. "But let Don Michele know this so that he'll realize I'm right in what I say."

"Know what?" Michael looked at her, her face almost softened, the old pleading almost come again into her eyes.

But before the transformation could complete itself, the Signora said, "A wife does not speak such things except to another woman. And certainly not to her respected uncle."

"I *do* respect him. But he should know the truth."

"Tell me," Michael said, hoping to head the Signora off at the pass.

"Rosalia, *cara,* you will not say these things about your husband. It will offend Don Michele."

Michael realized Peppino was the one the Signora was protecting, not himself. He turned toward her. "If I'm offended, that's my difficulty. My . . . niece has something she wants me to know." He turned to Rosalia. Her eyes were closed, her hand was still on the chicken. She could have been saying a prayer for its soul. Quickly she raised her head, tossing back her hair, revealing a look as magisterial as the one now rigid on her mother-in-law's face. Rosalia, the shopkeeper, had somehow transformed herself. Whether she had taken instruction from Signora Spacagna Michael couldn't tell, but there was in her now an indomitability, a passionate disdain, a mournful repose suggesting that she, too, had done battle with the fates, lost, and risen above her defeat. Any battle between her and Assunta would be a battle royal and a battle of equals. It was with such a look as this, Michael thought, that Maria Sofia, the last queen of Naples, had met the enemy at Gaeta. Michael doubted, however, that her emotional descendant Rosalia was about to be bested in the impending onslaught.

"Peppino is starving to death," Rosalia said. Her aria had begun, and Michael knew it was going to be magnificent. "You've seen him yourself, how skinny he is, almost nothing but bones. Yes, people joke about it, his friends, the man where he works, everyone. It's not uncommon. A newly married man exhausts himself in nights of love, without sleep. He becomes gaunt, and for a time it seems he will die for love. It pleases everyone to see Peppino like this. It amuses them and gives them a chance to make remarks. He tries to smile, to let them think they've hit upon the truth. But they haven't. Yes, his nights are sleepless, and so are mine. When we were first married, I knew my only hope was to be his wife. If I was tender to him, and he to me, maybe I would begin to forget"—she stopped and turned away, then back again—"to forget Gaetano." She had struggled to say the name as if it were ordinary, no more important, no less, than any other word in her vocabulary, but her throat constricted halfway through, there was just the hint of a choke, a glottal spasm affected by some but not by Rosalia, not now. She sniffed and lifted her chin a little higher. "No, not forget him. I'll never forget him."

"Rosalia! This is enough!" The cane hit the floor, but Rosalia ignored the sound.

"The more I was Peppino's wife, the more it would anger Gaetano. And he should be angry—and I should be the one to make him angry. He could have taken me away before my wedding. He could even have forced me to go with him when he came to the altar at Santa Chiara. He could have fought all of you, fought for me. But he didn't. He just cried and ran away."

"He would not have dared to do anything other." The Signora spoke evenly, ominously, but Rosalia paid no attention.

"My revenge," Rosalia said, her voice wonderfully dark, "was to love Peppino—not to pretend, but to actually do it. In time. In time. And I could have. The motions of love might have led me to it. I thought they might. And if one is gentle, won't one come to love what lies beneath the tender touch, the quiet kiss? And don't forget: Peppino has loved me. He said so, and I've believed him. If I lived with him, with his love, patiently, couldn't I, after a while, begin to feel some little stirrings toward a man so kind, so passionate, so gentle? I prayed to Maria Santissima delle Grazie to make it so. I prayed even that I would forget that I'd wanted to make anyone angry. There would be children. Peppino would be their father. They would show me how to love him. I would have made my life a great triumph that would have redeemed Peppino's sin. Yes, I was willing to do all that. But now just the idea disgusts me. Let him redeem his own rape. Let him die of its consequences. Let—"

"I'll listen to no more." Leaning heavily on her cane, the Signora stood up. Michael expected a bitter flash of temper, if not an outright rebuke to her daughter-in-law. But there was a new desperation in her voice. It was even possible that she was near to pleading. But Rosalia continued.

"You may listen or not listen, but here is the truth: Peppino will not eat because he's sure I'm going to poison him. Even when I exchange plates and eat what I'd set out for him, he won't eat. For a time, he would eat at his mother's, but I have forbidden him to do it, and he's obeyed. *That* he'll obey, but not my command to eat. And at night, he sleeps not at all. He lies there, certain that I'll suffocate or stab him if he so much as closes his eyes. On the first nights, I reached toward him and put my hand on his chest. He screamed, he whimpered. The neighbors, of course, gave this their own interpretation. But he has refused me as his wife, at the table *and* in the bed. Now let him die. I have no more prayers I'll pray. Let him starve, let him hang himself. Tell Gaetano there's no need to kill Peppino—unless, of course, he really wants to."

"He won't do it. I've forbidden it!" The Signora, for this, had summoned again her regal blood, and so that there could be no mistake about the authority of her statement, her royal staff, her cane, hit the floor three times.

"Then Peppino will do it himself," Rosalia said. "And I won't stop him."

"You are his wife."

"I am not his wife. He hasn't done anything to make me his wife. I'm the woman he raped, that and nothing else. And now what's he waiting for? Me to rape him back? One night I even put my mouth on him. Down there. If kissing him on the lips didn't do anything to help him—"

"This is an outrage." The Signora began with a low mutter, the first rumblings of an eruption. "How can you speak these words even to me, to say nothing of speaking them in the presence of your uncle? You are without shame, and if you aren't careful, you'll be without honor."

"I am without honor already. Peppino has dishonored me, and I, in my own turn, dishonored myself by marrying him. But since then I've found my honor again. There was honor on my lips when I kissed my husband's lips; there was honor on my lips when I took my husband in my mouth. And I'll be honored when he dies. My black clothes will tell, not what I mourn, but what I have endured. I was married to a rapist and an impotent, frightened, self-indulgent child. Let him starve. It restores my honor to see him waste away." With that, Rosalia grabbed the chicken the Signora had brought and, after struggling just a little bit with the lid of the garbage pail, threw it inside and clamped the cover down. For a moment, Michael thought she was going to sit on the top to make sure the chicken made no attempt to escape. But she came back to the table, suddenly mournful, as if not unfeeling for the chicken's fate. "*Madre mia,*" she said, "what I've said is shameful, and you must forgive me. You've made me your daughter, and I've given you my love. But everything angers me. It will pass. Be patient with me. And patient with Peppino. And I will be patient too. I promise. All will be well. Don't despise me. You don't despise me, do you?"

Signora Spacagna looked at her, then, leaving her cane propped against the kitchen table, went to the garbage pail and, with the dignity of a monarch bestowing royal favors, opened the lid, reached inside, and retrieved the discarded bird. She did not bother to replace the top but walked solidly back to her place at the table, dropped the chicken into the net bag slung from the back of her chair, took up her cane and, without looking at either Michael or Rosalia, said, "Don Michele, you will walk me as far as Santa Chiara, where I will go and pray. What I will pray for will remain known only to me and to no more than two or three saints of my own choosing. Come."

Michael dutifully got up. He looked toward Rosalia. He had

said nothing he'd come to say, but this, then, was to be their farewell. He went to her and kissed her forehead, but before he could begin his goodbye, Rosalia said, "Good Don Michele, I know you came to tell me that you would take me with you to Rome, that you would watch over me and give me refuge and protect me. But I'll protect myself, and I don't want any refuge. Not anymore. Please, forgive me for letting you go away without me. Try not to be lonely. It's from you, knowing I had you as a protector, that I found my strength." She kissed his cheeks, first one, then the other, sweetly, gently.

Michael's jaw must have dropped several inches, because Rosalia raised it for him and put it back in place, still gentle, still sweet. "Don't say anything more. Take my mother to her prayers."

Michael wanted to confess everything, but what would that accomplish except a delay in Assunta's prayers? He wanted at least to speak some exit line, perhaps even work himself into a pretty little speech, but Rosalia shook her head when, again, he'd begun to move his jaw. He offered his arm to Assunta. She looped hers through his. Rosalia went ahead of them through the hall, opened the door, and the two of them left, the naked chicken in the net bag knocking against Michael's thigh with every stately step they took.

Michael considered going into Santa Chiara with Assunta. He knew he had prayers of his own, but wasn't sure what they might be, so he released her arm, chicken and all, on the church portico. Assunta looked at him and shook her head slowly. "You are not one of my chosen saints, Signore, but I will tell you my prayer. I will pray for forgiveness. I made a terrible mistake. Who would have thought such a thing could happen, that I could be wrong?" Since she said this without irony, Michael felt no need to offer a contradiction. "It was Gaetano Rosalia should have married. You saw her just now. She is exactly the right wife for Gaetano.

She's all wrong for Peppino, and he's all wrong for her. How could I—*I*, Assunta Spacagna, a Gallifuoco—have been so mistaken? Who could possibly believe it? Well, it's done now, and there's nothing left to do but pray."

"But, Signora, if this is true—and it is, it is, I know it is— let Rosalia get the marriage annulled—"

"Don Michele, you don't know what you're suggesting."

"I do. They haven't consummated the marriage. Nothing's happened between them. Let Rosalia get free and marry Gaetano." Without hesitating, he went on. "Peppino will eventually find someone else. One hopes, of course, that his method of courtship will be a bit more orthodox than the last time."

Assunta had heard nothing of what he'd said. "No, it would be all wrong." She shook her head to dismiss the thought of anything else. "Peppino and Rosalia are married. It is God's will."

"But if Peppino really starves—or if Gaetano really kills him?"

"We must not interfere."

Michael was about to repeat the word "interfere," scaled upward to a scream and punctuated with a question mark, but the Signora went on. "Gaetano will not kill Peppino because I have threatened to take the poison here at my breast if he does. But I have promised Gaetano, in turn, not to tell this to Peppino. Gaetano must be allowed some little revenge, and Peppino's fear of him provides it. And Peppino will eat when he gets hungry enough. And that goes for his lovemaking too. Rosalia is right. We must all be patient." She moved toward the doors of the church, stopped, and, without turning back, said, "Of course, Rosalia might still poison him. I must remember that as a possibility when I say my prayers. The girl seems to be a little strongheaded lately. Well, one does what one can."

Again she started toward the doors, again she stopped, but this time she turned back. With the utmost gravity in her voice and the utmost solemnity in her gaze, she said to Michael, "I will tell you a secret I've told no one, not even God." She paused, steeled herself by surrendering most of her weight to her cane, and said, "You are sworn to secrecy. The pill is not poison. It is vitamin E."

She turned, threw open the church door, and went solemnly into the dark.

15

It seemed only right that the room should be circular and its stairway up into the chapel proper a spiral segment that could lead to either the upper or the nether regions, depending on one's present position. For the moment, Michael was very definitely in one of the lower circles, if not exactly of hell, then at least of purgatory. There seemed to be nothing here but anxious expectation, with hope present more as a component of fear than in anticipation of release. Garbed in the coarse brown robes of the monks who would present the evening's parable, the singers and musicians milled about the enclosed space, not even murmuring, but simply moving constantly, without thought or sound, each in a separate desperation, unable and unwilling to seek comfort from one another. They seemed more stunned than nervous, and looking at them now, Michael wondered if some exhortation might help, some show of encouragement, of confidence. The speech Shakespeare wrote for Henry V at the battle of Agincourt suggested itself, but Michael felt instinctively that they were all best left alone.

Michael himself tried not to feel too exhilarated, but it wasn't easy. For all his misgivings, he really did believe the evening would be a triumph. Much as he warned himself against that

most irretractable theatrical taboo—savoring success before it had
been stamped, sealed, and delivered—he was unable to feel other
than happily expectant. Even when he told himself that he was
projecting onto the entire enterprise his own personal anticipa-
tions, it did little good. Michael knew he was on the brink of
several fulfillments. Why shouldn't *Curlew River* be given, by
simple association, some share of the achievements that were
soon to be his?

For one thing, this evening he would no longer be *comprimario*. He would sing the lead role; he would be the center, the
very heart of the drama, his agony, his experience of miracle and
of grace, the first purpose of the parable. In him would meet the
human and the divine, the artist and the man. During rehearsals
he'd been too occupied with the production as a whole to give
much thought to his personal accomplishment, but now he could
revel in its reality. Soon he would take the stage and make it his
own, a moment long awaited if seldom anticipated in his *comprimario* career. Like Canio in *I Pagliacci,* who declared himself
no longer a clown, Michael could now sing out, *"Un comprimario,
non son!"* A comprimario, not I!

Then, too, his elevation above the secondary was reinforced
by the assumption that Piero would come with him to New
York. He would be given Piero's decision later that evening,
after the performance. But the answer, Michael was sure, would
be yes. His accusing failure with Damian, his inability to mourn,
would soon find correction. What Damian had taken from him,
Piero would give back. That Piero had to suffer and die to do it
was given very swift consideration, then replaced by a general
anticipation of what seemed to be rescue and redemption—not
Piero's, but his—then that, too, was quickly forgotten. This
evening and tomorrow would be a time of consummation, and
nothing must interfere.

Even more quickening to Michael's spirit was the knowledge
that he'd assumed yet another lead role, that he'd achieved a

further ascent above the *comprimario*. He had become, indeed, the uncle from Rome. He, Michael Ruane, was about to rearrange lives, correct wrongs, and help form the future. A plot—devised by Don Michele himself—already afoot—would soon pair Gaetano and Rosalia and set them firmly on the path to everlasting happiness. Michael had challenged the fates and was already well on his way to victory. He would leave Naples a hero.

His plan was simple but with enough complication to make it worthy of its Neapolitan inspiration. The next evening—or late afternoon—Rosalia and Gaetano would set sail for Palermo. Rosalia would leave a farewell note to Peppino, telling him to have the marriage annulled. Michael himself would explain everything to the Signora after the boat had safely cleared the harbor. Then, after annulment and marriage, the family could finally reunite, the consummation that justified all intrigues, betrayals, and deceptions.

To give the operation a Neapolitan cast, Michael would bankroll the escape by stealing the box office receipts from tonight's performance and handing them over to Gaetano and Rosalia to tide them over in Palermo until Gaetano got a job as a mechanic, a job absolutely assured by the supremacy of *la macchina,* the automobile, throughout unified Italy.

The prompting for the box office theft had come from Michael's recollection of a scene with Signor Crescenzo. The Signore had been apologizing for the foundation's inability to pay Michael a higher fee. Even with his San Carlo supplement, he was being pitifully underpaid.

Then Signor Crescenzo went on to tell him that it would be his responsibility to take away with him after the performance whatever money, if any, was in the till, and bring it to Signor Crescenzo's office the next morning. Michael had said he didn't want the responsibility or the risk. But the Signore insisted, telling him that no one else could be trusted. And then the moment of revelation came: Signor Crescenzo didn't exactly wink,

but he did twitch his shoulders. "Of course, there are dangers," he'd said. "But if there is any attempt at robbery, simply hand over the money. It could happen, and we'll understand. Just tell us the next morning, and we'll note it in the records of the foundation. Since the thief couldn't possibly be found"—and here the twitch ceased and Signor Crescenzo became quite serious— "there would be little need to give more than a few details. The foundation would probably not even bother to notify the police. So have no fear, Signor Ruane, you are at no risk. Simply accept the money after the performance, and we'll see you the following morning."

Michael had understood. He was supposed to keep the money and say it had been stolen. This, of course, he wouldn't dream of doing. He was from Indianapolis, not Naples. He was hardly a thief, but he was intrigued by Signor Crescenzo's invitation that he become one. And now Michael could hardly wait to appropriate the money and give Signor Crescenzo the prescribed excuse and explanation. He looked forward to saying it all with a very straight face, and he looked forward as well to the approval he was sure he'd get from the Signore for cooperating so masterfully.

The plot would unfold and spread wide its triumphant banners the next day. It would be executed in full by sundown, time for Michael to ready himself for his final performance at San Carlo and his departure for New York the next day. If Assunta Spacagna wouldn't interfere with the fates or with the will of God, Michael, the Roman, had full license to reorder, restructure, and revise anything he considered a Neapolitan misadventure. His authority had the support of historical precedent; his will had the support of Roman assurance.

From above came the sounds of scraping chairs, stern directions being given by one person to another, giggles, and the rough hum of a gathering crowd. A boy of about five, wearing short

pants and a blue V-neck sweater, appeared at the railing at the top of the stairs. He seemed to have been running, but now he'd stopped abruptly and was staring down. He was wide-eyed at what he saw, possibly chastened for disobeying a mother who'd told him to sit down and behave himself. Now he observed the scene below, this slowly shifting mass of monks seen as if at the bottom of a well, guarded by two skeletons perched high on the wall, each in its separate niche, the petrified veins threading through the bones as if the corrupting disease that had brought them to this state had survived uncorrupted itself. The boy backed away toward the door, said the one word "Mamma," then turned and quickly disappeared.

Michael looked up at the skeletons, often mentioned as one of the attractions of the chapel. How could he ever have wanted the opera, with its promise that all men, all women, shall rise again, to be done anywhere but here? This place, more than any other he could think of, could use a good stiff whiff of the resurrection.

Picro, he saw, was staring up at one of the skeletons. His mouth was opened slightly, and he seemed about to cross himself as if he were finishing a prayer. Piero's communicating with a rack of bones made Michael uneasy, although it didn't seem to bother Piero at all. He was almost rapt in his gaze, taking in a wonder that inspired a tranquil awe. Michael started toward him, but a thumping in the chapel made him look upward. Someone was running up and down the ramps, testing the strength of the platform. Children, no doubt, who had not yet been informed that there were areas of the world not open to their eager exploration. Michael even had a fearful vision that some delighted boy, at this very moment, was raising and lowering the sail, trying to see how much abuse it could take before breaking down completely.

Then the running stopped. Dario, the chapel's equivalent of a house manager, was back on the job. The sail, perhaps, might still function and the ramps and platforms not splinter and collapse before the opera's end.

Michael looked up toward the landing at the head of the stairs. He was anxious to begin the performance. Surely it must be time. Dario was to let them know with a flick of the lights. Impatiently he turned toward where he'd last seen Piero. He was still there, looking up at the petrified dead, but the look of transport Michael had seen before had been replaced by the pressed-lip smile, the cocked head, the insolent eyes. It was Piero's look of intimacy, an assurance that between them, himself and the skeletons, there was a shared wisdom, a mutual understanding. Michael continued toward him to break what he considered an unholy spell, but Dario had come to the top of the stairs and was making a "Pssst" sound. Michael looked up. Dario started to say something, then glanced behind him and decided it would be better to deliver his message at closer range. He came halfway down the stairs, and Michael himself went up to the second step from the bottom.

"I don't know what to do," Dario whispered. "They're still coming in. There are no more chairs; they're in the aisles. I don't know how you're going to get through for the opening and closing processions. I've told them they can't sit on the edge of the stage, but one woman insists. You'll have to ignore her, or maybe just give her a slight kick as you go by. It's terrible. I can't turn anyone away. They'd make a disturbance outside. Pray they stop coming. Pray, Signore, pray."

With a whimper, he hurried back up the stairs. His angry voice was heard from above, a final instruction possibly to the woman perched on the edge of the stage.

Michael didn't know what to think. He'd expected next to no one, maybe a half-dozen stragglers who had nowhere else to go, a few of his colleagues from San Carlo, and a couple of friends of the cast. Now the multitudes were arriving. The performers would be cramped as it was; now the situation could become impossible, a performance that would be all audience, a theater given over completely to its patrons. Would success create the fiasco Michael had feared? There was no escape; the answers would be given soon enough.

Michael moved slowly through the milling monks, who had begun to quiet themselves. Piero was retying the cincture of his robe, a last attempt perhaps to secure himself into his role. Michael went toward him, but the lights flickered, off, on, off, on. It was time to begin. Without direction, the cast put itself in place for the procession that would lead them upward into the chapel and onto the stage, Piero toward the front, Michael at the end. Everyone pressed, as if at a signal, the switch that lighted the tapers they carried in their hands; each assumed the reverential attitude of the monks they had become.

The singer playing the Abbot gave the sign, the Latin chant began, and the ascent was under way. There was one last thumping above, one last happy child running up and down the ramp, exploring the forbidden joys of being where he wasn't supposed to be. When the thumping stopped, the other sounds subsided as if everyone had taken his cue from the disobedient boy.

The Abbot hesitated at the door to the chapel, paused only a moment, then went on. There was a whoosh, the sound a congregation makes when it rises; there was a scraping of chairs; then silence.

Michael turned in to the chapel. People in the aisles solemnly parted to let them pass. From under his cowl Michael could see that Dario had been right. There was absolutely no room. And everyone, at the monks' entrance, had stood up as at a liturgical service. How and when they could be given the signal and the permission to sit down again, Michael had not the slightest idea.

Again and again his robes brushed against the spectators. The main aisle had been kept reasonably clear, but additional chairs had narrowed it to a very thin path indeed. So slowly did they have to move that Michael began to wonder if they could accomplish all they had to accomplish by the end of the chant: gain the stage, allow for his and the Traveller's concealed exit, and the robing of the Ferryman. He should have prepared for such an expediency, the repeat of the final verse if necessary, but it was too late now.

Thanks to the determined advance of the Abbot, the procession moved forward at close to the rehearsed pace. There was indeed a woman sitting on the edge of the platform that would do service as the ferryboat, but as the monks came nearer, she got up and slowly moved away, pressing herself into the group huddled under the statue of *La Pudicizia Velata—Veiled Modesty* —the woman apparently awed or intimidated by the inexorable approach of the robed and cowled figures chanting their evening prayer.

The monks climbed the ramp as the musicians went to the side to group themselves around the harmonium. A teenage boy and girl were surprised to have to surrender the harmonium seat. Again the monks' robes helped, and the couple moved to the wall, placing themselves under the protection of the statue of *La Sincerità.*

Michael and the man singing the Traveller managed to make their exit along with the acolytes and the boy who would later sing the spirit of the dead child. The Abbot and the pilgrims circled the Ferryman to help him into his costume and put in place the plain flesh-colored half mask that would cover only the top of the face. The opera would now begin.

Although Michael was offstage, back on the stairs leading to the room below, where he'd change himself into the Madwoman, he could hear the Abbot intone the first words:

> Good souls, I would have you know
> the Brothers have come today
> to show you a mystery:

> how in sad mischance
> a sign was given of God's grace.

Michael heard next the scraping and creaking of chairs and an accompanying sigh-like sound. The Abbot had given the audience permission to sit down. Now the Ferryman introduced himself, and the Traveller made ready for his reentry. Michael started toward the bottom of the stairs but stopped when he heard a bewildered voice call out, midway in the Ferryman's opening monologue, "When are they going to start singing?" Then came the shushes, followed by the protesting, bewildered voice again. "But this isn't singing." More shushes, then a clearer voice from the other side of the chapel: "These are monks. This is the way they sing. Listen." That seemed to shut up everyone except the indomitable baritone singing the Ferryman.

Michael felt fearless, almost defiant. As he changed into the costume of the Madwoman, he tried to prepare his spirit for whatever reaction he might get. Laughter, no doubt. Ridicule, perhaps. Open scorn was not beyond possibility, and personal physical attack could not be ruled out. He would be equal to it all.

Waiting for his first cue, Michael listened intently to whatever he might hear from the audience as well as from the other singers. As far as he could tell, no notable disturbances were taking place, beyond three sneezes followed by whispered blessings, followed by some brief shushings. Then Michael heard his cue. From now on he was the Madwoman and no one else.

Singing, Michael began the slow ascent up the curving stairs, past the watchful skeletons with the burnished bones, closer to the Curlew River, where he must act out his tale of loss and madness and bear the sufferings necessary for the eventual peace of his mind and soul.

> Let me in! Let me out!
> Tell me, tell me the way!

He was in full view, dressed in ragged skirts and shawls, strands of unkempt hair straggling to his shoulders, his face half covered by the flesh-colored mask. There was a certain amount of uneasy shuffling out front and a few whispers, but nothing really disruptive.

> I turn me, I turn me away!
> Turn me, I turn me away!

It was then that a woman's voice noted, for all to hear, "It's a man. He's dressed as a woman. A man. Like a woman."

There were a few shushes, several giggles, and a certain amount of coughing, but then another voice repeated the obvious: Michael was a man dressed like a woman. The shushes were fewer and slightly feeble, the coughs more embarrassed, until a deep voice toward the back of the chapel explained it all. "He has lost his little boy," the voice said gravely. "It has made him crazy. He thinks he is the little boy's mother instead of his father."

There was an audible "Ah" from several parts of the house, and by the time Michael had finished singing

> Dew on the grass
> sparkles like hope
> and then is gone . . .

and had prostrated himself completely, there was another "Ah."

The imaginary boat was now crossing the river, the pilgrims, the Traveller, and the Madwoman aboard. The sail had been raised, the Ferryman was plying his pole. The time had come for the Ferryman's narrative of the kidnapping, the death, and the burial of the child on the far shore. Michael, his head down as if exhausted into sleep, heard nothing stir in the entire chapel.

He made a greater effort to listen to the singer, but the story made him impatient. He was much more interested in what was happening out front. When the Ferryman sang the child's words: "'He threatened to kill me. . . . But there was no need: I know I am dying. . . .' " Michael, faithful to the script, raised his head to show that the Madwoman was beginning to understand. Staring straight into the audience, he saw Gaetano in the second row, just to the side of the statue of the veiled Christ. He was looking at Michael, probably wondering where he'd seen that face before, the one beneath the mask, above those shawls and tatters. Michael kept his gaze steady. The Ferryman quoted the child:

"Please bury me here, by the path to this chapel.
Then, if travellers from my dear country pass this
way, their shadows will fall on my grave.
And plant a yew tree in memory of me."

As the Madwoman, Michael began to ask questions. The answers were given until, little by little, she, the Madwoman, was led to the truth. Finally, the moment came, and Michael, the Madwoman, let out a great cry:

He was the child
sought by this madwoman!

Soon he must stand up and begin his lament. And when he did, Gaetano would recognize him. He was sure of it. Gaetano would stand up and call out, "Don Michele! *Zio!* Is that you?"

And Michael would have to continue, even as he'd hear Gaetano say, "But what are you doing here? Why are you dressed like that? Why have you gone crazy? When I invited you, you said you couldn't be here tonight, but you're here anyway. And you're singing about some child you lost. I don't understand. Uncle, please, explain it to me. I'm confused. I'm lost. You're the only one who can help me. Uncle, please, help me to understand."

And what would Michael do or say? He would have to continue his part. He couldn't stop. He must pay no attention to his nephew's plea. He must ignore it. He had his lamentations to make; he had his sufferings to endure. Surely they took precedence over his nephew's confusion; a performance was more important than a young man's plea for understanding.

Michael huddled even closer to himself, making himself smaller, less present. Listening to the chaos so accurately created by the performers, he knew what he would do. At Gaetano's first word, if it should come, he would slowly reach up and take the mask from his face. He would pull the tangled strands of hair from his head; he would rip away the tatters that covered him, and he would say, "Gaetano? Nephew? Help me. Help me, Gaetano. I am the one who is confused; I am the one who's lost. Why can I grieve only when I pretend I am a madwoman? I want to care. I want to grieve. But I can't, not as who I really am. I am Michael Ruane, and I am here to mourn and to lament and to receive God's grace. But first I must go mad and search in foreign places among strangers. You must help me. All of you here, good people of Naples, help me, I beg you. Tell me I am a good and decent man. Please, I beg you. Tell me that I have a right to grieve, that I have the power to love. Gaetano, my nephew, help me. Good people, I am lost. Rescue me, I beg you. Rescue me!"

His cue in the music was coming closer. Soon he must raise his head. Gaetano would see him and know him for who he was. Michael prayed for Gaetano's words, for the questions that would unmask him. Then he could make his true lament. And Gaetano would hear him, and everyone there, and they would forgive him all his transgressions.

The cue came. With a slow move, he raised his head and looked around him. He saw the pilgrims singing their disbelief, Piero, stricken, in their midst. He saw Gaetano in the darkened chapel, and he saw the slain savior, veiled, lying at his feet. His moment had arrived. He felt himself rising up not from an imaginary boat but from the earth itself. He looked straight at

Gaetano. And Gaetano looked straight at him—but said nothing.
His mouth was slightly open, but no words were there. No
questions would be asked. He was seeing no one but a madwoman, and he was waiting, open-mouthed, to hear her
lamentations.

Michael could never make his plea, not to Gaetano, not to
the good people crowded around the veiled Christ. He must
continue his part.

> O Curlew River, cruel Curlew,
> where all my hope is swept away!
> Torn from the nest, my bird,
> crying in empty air.

Out rushed the words like panicked ravens, shredding his
throat, withering his tongue.

> Chain on my soul, let me go . . .
> Chain on my soul, let me go!

As if to beg an end, Michael sank down to the ground from
which he'd risen.

> O River Curlew, O curlew, cruel bird!

With that, Michael surrendered completely to the anguished
spirit that possessed him. Freely he gave his body, his gestures,
his voice. He could do nothing other.

The opera moved inexorably to its close. The vision of the
dead child, sung by the boy soprano, appeared and moved in a
circle around his maddened mother.

> Go your way in peace, mother.
> The dead shall rise again
> and in that blessed day
> we shall meet in Heaven.

To Michael the words meant nothing. The dead child's spirit passed by and was gone.

Now there was only the triumphant *Amen* that would end the opera, and the recessional back through the chapel. Michael's task would soon be over. On cue, the monks circled around him, concealing him, unmasking him, and divesting him of his madwoman's rags. He was robed again in the monk's garb. Michael tugged the cowl low over his eyes. He did not want to be seen, not by anyone.

As the monks took up the chant and began their move down the aisle, the audience rose again, but very quietly. Some crossed themselves as the procession passed. At the back of the chapel, the boy who had come to peer at the milling monks in the well of the dead was perched on his father's shoulders, the better to see.

Michael was at the end of the procession, the last to reach the door leading to the stairway down. As he passed through, the last words of the chant faded away.

From the chapel there was nothing but silence, then the sound of about three people clapping. Violent shushings followed, then silence again, followed by the scraping of chairs on the stone floor, quiet chatter, a call across the chapel, shuffling feet.

Why was there no applause? Michael knew the answer, but still, there should have been applause. Without it, the opera was unaccomplished. Nothing had been complete, nothing finished. Applause was part of the performance itself. It was as though *Curlew River* had yet to be brought to its conclusion. Michael's task remained undone, his homage unfulfilled. Surely applause would have helped to quiet him, to give him a sense of ending. But there had been none.

He slipped off his robes, then dutifully, numbly, moved among his colleagues to thank them and wish them well. "*Bravi, tutti bravi, bravissimi,*" Michael said as he shook hands with the

disrobing monks, his voice almost a whisper, as if he were afraid
to awaken in himself a spirit of accomplishment. The performers
seemed neither pleased nor displeased by what they'd done,
merely cheerful, rather like a construction crew at quitting time.

As Michael looked around for Piero, Dario appeared with
a cigar box and thrust it into his hands. "Many people came,"
he said, then slipped quickly through the monks and up the
winding stair. Michael looked for someplace to set down the box
so he could continue his thanks and congratulations, but only
the floor presented itself, and he was a little wary of letting go
of what seemed, from the weight of the box, a rather hefty haul.

"I'm going now. I have to be by myself tonight."

It was Piero, directly in front of him. The look on his face,
completely noncommittal, told Michael nothing except that he
should not ask for reasons. But he asked anyway.

"Why?"

"I have to be alone tonight," Piero said.

"Don't go."

"I have to."

Then everyone was gone. Michael couldn't remember them
leaving except for two of the musicians, who, climbing the stairs,
had laughed at the skeletons. He hadn't even seen Piero leave.
All he knew was that he was gone.

Michael clutched the cigar box, worried now that it might
actually be stolen, frustrating his plan to steal it himself. There
was no way to carry it inconspicuously, especially since it had
become an object of his concern. He had yet to see how much
money was there, but the weight of the box and the size of the
audience told him it would certainly be enough for Gaetano and
Rosalia to get by in Palermo for a good long while. Without the
money, the entire plot would be thrown into disarray. Second
thoughts would surface, third thoughts. The plan would collapse
completely. Michael felt too incomplete himself to allow this to
happen. He'd protect the box with his life.

· · ·

Late-night strollers along Via San Biagio dei Librai, people passing quickly under the Porta Capuana or gazing into the bonfires
lit along Via Firenze—none of them seemed to show the least
interest at the sight of a robed and cowled monk walking by,
his head bowed, meditating, no doubt, on things not of this
world. Nor did they notice that he clutched to his breast, not a
breviary or the holy viaticum, but a box that looked suspiciously
as though it contained nothing but cigars.

16

Michael worried, as he made his way past the cloister's souvenir stand and the open door of an office, that he'd wrongly be identified again as the "Peppino" who had defiantly scratched his name on the forbidden wall, that he'd be denied entry to the cloister, and that the real Peppino, also innocent of the infraction, would simply sit his afternoon away in confused solitude, wondering why his uncle had told him to meet him here and then not shown up.

The young man behind the souvenir counter was reading a book, and a friar just inside the office seemed to be testing the door for a squeak, closing it partway, then quickly opening it again, trying to surprise the sound and thereby verify its pernicious existence. When Michael pushed the door leading out to the cloister, at least seven different squeals were sprung loose. Michael was tempted to pause before passing through to see if the monk would take any interest, but he decided that the less attention he drew to himself, the better.

He hadn't told Peppino where in the cloister they'd meet, but since the farther half was still closed off with chicken wire, he'd have an easier search, unless, of course, Peppino had not yet arrived. Michael considered this unlikely. Peppino was too bewildered by what he'd made of his life, too frightened, to risk provoking annoyance, especially from someone as important, as powerful, as his uncle from Rome.

This would be the last time he'd see Peppino. He wondered if he'd miss him. He'd reveled in the respect shown, he'd enjoyed his power over the two handsome young men. He had strutted his way through their lives with the haughty pleasure of the born hypocrite. Now it was coming to an end, but not quite. He was still the uncle, and he must not falter. His full authority was needed, now more than ever. He was about to tell the bewildered youth that his wife was running off with his brother, that he, Peppino, must accept this, get the marriage annulled, and eventually reconcile with his brother and the woman he had criminally raped. And he must do all this for no other reason than that it was the command of his uncle, Don Michele.

Michael's absolutism had worked with Gaetano and Rosalia. Whatever hesitations they'd offered were meant to exact further reassurances, greater permissions, and, ultimately, an uncle's blessing that would sustain them through the days and nights of their impending concubinage.

They were first shocked, then bewildered, then wary, afraid to believe in the possibility of what had been arranged; then they became skeptical: The plan would collapse somewhere along the line. Guided by their uncle's assurances, which were sometimes stern, sometimes impatient, they began to allow themselves a modicum of hope. Finally, they triumphed over marriage vows, fraternal loyalty, and simple honesty. They would obey their uncle.

What Michael had devised was this: Rosalia and Gaetano were to take the boat to Palermo. Michael himself would get the tickets, to avoid any premature sighting of the fugitives. (Gaetano had chosen Palermo over Milano. In the north, he and Rosalia would be *terroni,* a word a northern Italian would use to describe a southern Italian, a word which could be roughly—and somewhat politely—translated as "clodhopper." In Palermo, however, they themselves could pretend superiority over the *arabi* all Sicilians were presumed to be.) The money for the journey would be provided by a generous donation from the mysterious monk last seen entering Michael's apartment the night before, clutching to his breast what was, in honesty, the box office take from Sansevero. The monk, it should be noted, absolved himself of all guilt before defrocking himself and revealing to a mirror on the opposite wall the very self and person of Michael Ruane, who, earlier that night, had, to uncertain effect, presented himself in public as a madwoman.

Madwoman, monk, and uncle—each had done some service. The tenor with the spiritual insufficiencies that had placed an insurmountable barrier between him and a high C was now righting wrongs, averting catastrophes, securing happiness, and making possible the triumph of love over rapine, folly, and familial duty. As the plot took hold, first with Gaetano at the garage where he worked, then with Rosalia behind the counter of her shop, Michael could almost feel in the back of his throat a pure and trumpet-toned high C forming itself, gathering glory until it would, as the boat for Palermo cleared its moorings, ring out over the entire bay, reaching in lambent echoes to the higher slopes of Vesuvio.

At this point, Michael had cautioned himself not to get too excited; he was the even-keeled uncle going calmly about his tasks, and any thought of trumpeted high C's and lambent echoes—*especially* the lambent echoes—should be suppressed with the same cool determination he was bringing to every other aspect of his enterprise.

To Michael's surprise, Gaetano had been the one to object the most. (Rosalia, to her credit, wasted little time in doubting the excellence of the plan.)

"But I can't leave right now; I have work here, in the garage, and I haven't finished."

It turned out he'd been assigned a Lamborghini to work on,

and he'd only begun his explorations of what made it go. He didn't want to elope before he'd experienced each and every one of its sophistications. It was the chance of a lifetime, and nothing, absolutely nothing, could measure up to the thrill of taking the engine apart and putting it back together, correcting in the process the simple mechanical problem he'd diagnosed at first glance. The fulfillment of his love for Rosalia paled at the prospect.

Michael had told him, sternly, that he'd have to leave before he, his uncle, returned to Rome—and that that would be the day after tomorrow, Lamborghini or no Lamborghini.

"But what will I tell my mother?"

"Nothing. Do you hear me? Nothing. I'll tell her—when the time comes."

"I can't do it. She'll kill herself."

"She won't kill herself."

"She will. You don't know. She carries with her a pill with poison in it. She'll take it. She'll swallow it right in front of you when you tell her. It'll be terrible. I can't even think about it."

"I give you my promise. Your mother will not take poison."

"She will. If I thought she wouldn't—"

Here Gaetano stopped and seemed for a moment to review in his mind's eye a long succession of joys and experiments he had renounced under the threat of the poison pill. His mouth opened slightly, and his eyes withdrew into their sockets, narrowing a little as if to try for an even deeper retreat. Amazement and regret, sorrow and fear, passed over his face, each a different response to the separate pleasures forgone, the varying sacrifices endured, so that his mother would not, because of him, fumble with wild fingers entangled in the strings of the breast-warmed pouch, extract from it the ruby capsule, and, with a shrug, say, "I told you so," or "Now see what you've done," and pop the fatal pellet into her mouth.

"You can persuade her not to take the poison? You're that sure?"

"I promise you. Your mother will not take poison. You have your uncle's word for it."

"I have your word?"

"On the honor of our family, I tell you, she will not take poison."

After further assurances that his mother would one day actually approve his action, that by running off with his brother's wife he was making possible a family reconciliation, Gaetano agreed.

Before Michael could mention the monk's money as a subsidy for the abduction, Gaetano, his eyes fired by a vision of his own daring, very quickly outlined the plan to steal and sell Peppino's car for ready cash. When he'd made the recent repairs, he'd also made himself a set of keys. A change of license plates would be no problem. As a mechanic at the garage, he always had a ready buyer for a car. The plot, as it tumbled from his lips, seemed to excite him more than the prospect of gaining the woman he loved.

"No; I'll give you the money you'll need," Michael said, every inch the uncle.

Gaetano at first refused such generosity as if it were an insult to his manhood. He would prefer to steal his brother's car. Michael was cajoling, then insistent. Gaetano must compromise his self-esteem, abstain from the fraternal theft, and submit to his uncle's largess. Michael thought it might ease Gaetano's reluctance to accept the money if Michael assured him that it, too, had been stolen, but this would have raised complications of its own, and besides, it might cloud the image Michael had of himself. He was, after all, not the uncle from Palermo or Milano or Pisa or Naples. He was the uncle from Rome.

And so it was settled. As a concession to Gaetano's need to inconvenience Peppino beyond the loss of his wife, it was decided that his brother's car would be "borrowed" to get Rosalia and her suitcase to the dock. A friend of Gaetano's would get the car, pick up Rosalia, take her to the boat, then return the car to its usual space in Piazza Bellini, where Peppino parked it during working hours. Michael agreed to this; Gaetano agreed to everything. Michael handed him the boat tickets, complete with reservations for a private cabin, since this was, in its way, their honeymoon, and the trip would last till dawn.

Quickly Gaetano stuffed the tickets into the pocket of his coveralls. Once the hand was withdrawn, he looked directly at Michael. He pulled him into his embrace, he kissed each cheek, he held him away and seemed about to embrace him again, but he hurried instead into the dark garage and disappeared behind the Lamborghini.

Peppino was sitting on a bench at the far end of the first walkway, opposite the fountain. He was hunched forward, his hands hanging between his knees. He was staring at the water as if trying to understand the noise it was making. Because this was a cloister, there was no question of either of them calling out a greeting. Michael simply went to where Peppino was and sat down next to him.

When Peppino did nothing to acknowledge him, Michael, too, looked at the fountain, as if the explanation for Peppino's silence and immobility was in the falling water. It was an uneven flow, dropping down into the pool as if the water came in gobs instead of liquid form.

Without taking his eyes from the plopping water, Peppino sat upright. Michael wondered exactly how he should begin to tell the young man all that had been plotted against him. Perhaps some pleasantry about his mother; maybe Michael could express his admiration for some article of clothing Peppino was wearing. Michael looked first at his shoes, brown, narrow, and obviously polished with the same brush that was used for black ones. They looked bruised by the effort to improve their appearance. Michael looked next at the pants, the outsized pleatings and blousings.

The pants legs crumpled in rounded folds against the shoes as if the cloth were melting, making tubular rings around his ankles. His jacket was the same black broad-shouldered, box-shaped one he'd worn to his wedding. His shirt was white, too neutral to allow comment. All that was left was his tie. To see it, Michael would have to look more directly at him; what he'd observed so far had been within the view available to the periphery of his right eye.

Before Michael could decide whether or not to consider the tie as a conversation piece, Peppino said, "Rosalia is gone, then."

Someone had done Michael's job for him. Someone had told Peppino the whole story—or at least enough of it to justify the even-toned resignation in his voice. Michael looked at him, not at his face, but at his tie. It was navy blue, the knot pulled a little away from the throat. The top button of his shirt was open. The tie did not afford a pretext for conversation, unless Michael would confess to never having seen a knit tie in Italy before, which he was about to say when Peppino went on in the same soft voice as before. "It's probably best, the way it's turned out. For me anyway. That much I know."

Michael had not expected this part of his task to be so easy. He was about to congratulate Peppino for his maturity, along, of course, with voicing expressions of sympathy for his loss, followed by detailed reasonings why this plan was best for all concerned. First, however, he had to know who had told him what was happening. Gaetano? Rosalia? Had Gaetano told his mother by way of a farewell, and had she then passed the information on to her younger son? Had Peppino surprised Rosalia in her preparations for departure, or had Signora Spacagna asked Gaetano why he had taken the suitcase from the top of the closet and why he was taking his shirts, sweaters, and socks from the dresser drawers where she'd so faithfully tucked them? Of the several possibilities, Michael favored Rosalia having told her husband the truth, whether as taunt or as apology he had yet to determine. It seemed consistent with his idea of her: honest, straightforward, and fearless. But before Michael could ask, "How did you know?" Peppino, as if in anticipation, said, "A friend of Gaetano's told me everything."

With this, Peppino leaned forward again, putting his elbows on his knees, clasping his hands loosely together instead of letting them dangle down between his thighs. "I caught him unlocking my car. I asked him if it was his car. I didn't tell him it was mine. I wanted to trap him. I wanted to see what lies he would tell. But it was the truth he told. That he was only borrowing the car to drive a friend of his to the boat, that the car belonged to his friend's brother. I told him I knew who the car belonged to and that I thought he was stealing it. When he found out that I knew who the car belonged to, he asked me not to say anything to the owner about the car, because it would make for some difficulties. He promised the car would be returned to this exact same spot later, after he had taken the wife of his friend's brother to the boat. They were running away to Palermo, he told me. That's the truth, Uncle. They were running away together. I still didn't tell the friend who I was, that it was my car, my brother, and my wife. I just asked him when the car would be back. Not for a while, he told me. He was going now to get his friend's things at his house, while his mother was out, and take them to the boat. Then later this afternoon he would go get the wife and her things and take her to the boat before the husband came home from work. If I was to see the husband, the owner of the car, I was to tell him that his car would be returned and that he mustn't worry. But I was to say nothing about the rest of it."

Peppino paused, turned toward Michael, and said, "The friend, I'm sure he knew I was the one who owned the car. The way he kept smiling at me: He enjoyed telling me all these things. He knew what he was doing to me."

Michael quickly guessed that Gaetano's friend could be no one other than Piero. And he knew Piero had deliberately told

Peppino for the pure pleasure of it, because it would cause mischief, because it pleased him to see Peppino uncomfortable, or worse.

Still, Michael wanted some confirmation of what he already knew, but he thought his first words to Peppino—he had yet to greet him—should address the larger issue: the truth of what Peppino had been told and, more important, some elaboration of his response to it all. Had he really accepted what was happening? Had he said or done nothing after finding out what was going on in his household?

Again Peppino knew all the questions at the same moment Michael had framed them in his mind. "I told the friend I would say nothing to the car's owner except to tell him his car would come back later. He held out his hand through the car window, and we shook hands before he drove away. Then, before he pulled his arm back in, I saw him do it, with his hand, with his fingers. He made the horns, the sign of the cuckold, so I could see it. So slowly he did it, and I saw it. And then his hand was back inside the car, and he was driving away. Even from the back of his head I could see he was smiling. And now Rosalia is gone. Forever. Forever. For always."

Peppino's eyes were unblinking as he stared in the fountain across the walkway, as if he were seeing some vision of himself without his wife, ridiculed, tormented, for a time at least. Now, Michael told himself, was the time to tell Peppino what the script required: that a terrible mistake had been corrected, that his life, that the lives of all of them, had been set back on course, that he was young and his hurts would mend.

Peppino unclasped his hands and straightened himself a little, then put a hand on each knee. He looked down at the bricks that paved the walkway, the vision within the fountain no longer needed. Michael began to draw himself more erect. His spine had straightened, but he had yet to draw back his shoulders, when Peppino said, "Now Gaetano will *have* to kill me. But he'll

254 · JOSEPH CALDWELL

have to wait until I'm out of jail. But that will be only for a few
years, then maybe he can do it. He'll be in prison for the rest of
his life, of course—for killing his brother—not just a few years,
like me. After all, it's a terrible thing to kill your brother. Much
worse than what a man does to his wife when she's going to run
away with another man, especially if it's with his own brother."

Michael made no further move. His shoulders remained un-
squared, his hand half curled on the bench, his head not quite in
line with his straightened spine. For the first time since he'd come
into the cloister, he spoke to the young man at his side. "Tell
me what you're saying."

"I didn't know I was going to do it. We were in the bedroom.
Some of her clothes were on the bed. I thought I was only going
to kiss her goodbye. I'd already told her I'd come home only to
say it was all right, what she and Gaetano were doing. But then
when I was holding her, she tried to pull away. I only wanted
to hold her closer, but then I was forcing her down onto the
bed, rumpling all her clothes. She started to yell. So I used a
pillow. I didn't hurt her. I promise you I didn't. I just held the
pillow there until she stopped."

Peppino turned his head toward Michael. Slowly, Michael,
too, turned his head. Peppino's right cheek was streaked with a
jagged line of blackened blood where the flesh had been torn.
There was another mark on his neck and a deep cut near his right
eye. His look was completely blank, as if all emotion had been
eliminated, bit by bit, as he'd been speaking. Now there was
nothing left to feel, just as there was nothing left to say. But he
said it anyway. "Rosalia is gone, then, forever."

Michael felt a twitch in his right arm, then a slight lift in
both arms. He was going to shake the young man until his neck
broke. He was going to force him to say the words he'd just
said, again and again and again. But he didn't. He was already
on his feet and moving quickly toward the cloister exit. He was
going to Rosalia, not to confirm what had been told to him, but

to stop from happening what had already happened. He didn't doubt for a moment that he had the power. But he must move quickly, and he must not think. Nor must he be aware of Peppino behind him, almost catching up. Nor must he hear Peppino saying, "You don't have to go to the police. I'll go myself. I know what I have to do. I do. Honest, I do."

Even when Michael turned and glared at him, Peppino kept following, always about two paces behind. "I can do it myself. You'll see. I'll go to the police myself."

Finally, Michael stopped and jerked his body back so he could face Peppino. "I'm not going to the police. I'm going to Rosalia."

Outside the cloister, hurrying along Via San Biagio dei Librai, Michael could hear Peppino behind him. "Why don't you believe me? She's gone. I did it. Why don't you believe me?" Accusation and self-pity were in the voice, but Michael did what he could to ignore it all, to walk even faster, to lose Peppino among the cars and motorbikes and the people rushing toward him. But still he could hear the voice. "You don't believe me. But it's the truth. You'll see. I'm not lying to you. I'm telling the truth. She's gone. Forever. Gone." He even laughed a little, exasperated that he wasn't being believed.

17

When Michael turned into Via Giganti, half walking, half running, he saw a car lumbering straight toward him on the narrow roadway. Not for a moment did he consider flattening himself against the wall to let it pass. He kept right on moving, ready to break into a full run at any time. The car continued toward him. The driver more in pleading than in warning kept punching the horn. Michael went right on, past the shrined Maria Santissima delle Grazie, not defying the car, merely ignoring it. From up above, a voice called down, "*Signore! Attenzione! La macchina!*" Michael could hear a few windows being raised, and there was a lively rattle of the clothesline racks. People were no doubt leaning out to see the accident the voice had not so much tried to forestall as to prophesy. The "*Attenzione!*" was not for him but for the neighbors, a summons to leave their household chores for the moment and witness a calamity that would give interest to an otherwise uneventful day.

Four inches from Michael, the car stopped and the horn no longer sounded. As Michael, without breaking stride, squeezed between the car and the greasy stucco wall, he saw the driver looking at him, bewildered, worried that someone could, with such lack of reflection, ignore the natural law that stated quite specifically that an automobile had the God-given right-of-way.

On the other side of the car, between it and a street-level doorway, a woman had squeezed herself into the niche the doorway provided, raising up above her shoulder a plastic shopping bag so that the loaf of bread sticking out the top would not have been mashed between the car and the stucco wall at her side. Michael heard her gasp, an intake of breath that could have been an attempt to gain a further quarter of an inch between her stomach and the car or, more likely, to give utterance to her disapproval of Michael's recklessness.

Past the car, Michael ran the last few steps to Rosalia's entry. Only then did he realize it would do him no good to ring the bell. Responding to instincts of his own, he slapped his pockets, first his jacket, then his pants, not to verify the knowledge that he had no keys but to beat and punish himself for the lack. Before he reached up and pressed the entire row of buttons, certain that someone would buzz him in, he looked to his left and to his right, an expression of frustration more than a search for help. The car was gone, and a motorbike was grinding past.

It was only when its whine receded that Michael realized he was staring down the roadway at Peppino. At first it seemed that the young man was trying to claw his way up the wall. His arms were raised, reaching upward, his hands opening and closing against the dirty stucco. Then Michael noticed, just out of Peppino's reach, the small shrine. He was performing an act of desperate supplication, which now included scraping his forehead against the wall.

"Peppino! The keys!"

Peppino stopped punishing his forehead and simply pressed his left cheek into the wall, his arms still raised but no longer straining toward the Madonna, who had so steadfastly remained beyond his reach.

"Peppino! *Avanti! Presto!*"

Slowly Peppino let his arms slide down to his sides, then, after once more pressing his cheek into the stucco, he began stumbling toward Michael. As he neared him, he went to the opposite side of the road and moved only sideways, afraid to take his eyes off Michael.

"The keys! The keys!"

Peppino reached down into his pants pocket on the left, then on the right, then again on the left, still staring at Michael. With each thrust of his hand he listed slightly in the opposite direction, as if it were necessary to counter the force of his plunging hand. The movement took on the semblance of a dance being performed by a clumsy puppet, and Michael was tempted to cross over and rip into his clothes as much to interrupt the absurd dance as to find the keys for himself.

With a cry like an amazed whimper, Peppino brought the keys up out of his right pocket and held them over the roadway. Another car, speeding between them, forced him to pull the keys back before Michael could grab them, but once the car had passed, Peppino repeated his offer, even more tentative than before. Michael could see that the key ring was crowded, a great jangling bracelet fit to adorn the wrist of a gypsy. He despaired of asking Peppino to show him which key would get him into the building and which into the apartment.

"Open the door. Quick!"

Peppino warily crossed the street, not directly but in a small arc to the left. Michael, even in his desperation, couldn't help savoring the pleasures of command.

Peppino put the key into the lock. "Why don't you believe me? We should go to the police. This is for them to take care of, not us."

"Just open the door."

The click resounded through the inner hall. Peppino, instead of taking the key out of the lock, looked at it, at the ring dangling down, the other keys swaying slightly, enjoying their suspended state. Michael shoved him away from the door. Peppino gasped as if he'd been stabbed. When Michael tried to get the key from the lock, it responded not at all to his tugs and pulls. He moved it ever so slightly in each direction, then tried again. He pushed it in deeper; he pulled it toward him, trying each time to surprise it in the necessary groove that would allow its easy extraction. In frustration, he turned it completely back and forth, locking, then unlocking, the door, to no avail. Michael stepped aside. He was only too aware that his authority had been somewhat eroded. The key had shown a stubbornness that was unheard of, and it had triumphed. Michael had been made helpless, and in his helplessness he was being forced to appeal to Peppino, his presumed inferior, for rescue.

When he spoke, he expected his voice to take on an even sterner tone to compensate for his humiliation, but the words came out rather quietly and quite simply. "You do it. It doesn't work for me."

"You have to ease it out just a little bit at first, turn it slowly to the right, then pull hard." Peppino's eyes were cast down, and he spoke in a near whisper.

"No," Michael said. "You do it." Again he spoke quietly. He was approaching the moment when he would surrender his powers, and he might just as well begin now by accepting minor defeats and show himself as one subject to vicissitude and challenge, the same as any mortal.

Peppino easily slipped the key from the lock, opened the door, and stepped aside to let Michael enter first. "Do I have to come with you?" he asked.

"You have to open the door to the apartment."

"It's this key here." He singled out a key with a long, flat stem and a large bit, which looked as if it could open castle doors or unlock forbidden towers. "I should go to the police."

"There'll be plenty of time for the police."

"Will you go with me when I go?"

The last place Michael could present himself as Peppino's uncle was a police station. And yet Peppino, standing there, looking at the rusted key, seemed so needful that Michael found himself actually *wanting* to stand at the boy's side, his proclaimed protector, loyal to the last, no matter what he may have done. He wanted to show that no deed, however damnable, could dilute the blood that bound them, that no crime, however terrible, could crush an allegiance created by divine act when God himself committed this youth, this nephew, to his care and made him, Michael, irrevocably, that most awesome and benevolent of tyrants, an uncle from Rome. But this could never be. Michael was not made uncle by the grace of God. It was all an inadvertence. He had no right to the loyalties he felt any more than he had a legitimate claim to the trust and respect he had received from the two young men who had so readily bestowed on him a title descended from Spanish Bourbons, elevating him from ordinary American to Don Michele, claimant of ancient honors, object of affectionate homage. All this he must, in a few hours, forswear. The time was fast approaching when he must depose himself, surrendering his title and his honors—the sweet trust, the anguished needs, the eager confidence of two of the handsomest men in all of Naples—to whatever capricious breeze might take them up and blow them away.

Whether to force or to forestall the moment of his deposition, Michael answered Peppino's question. "Of course I'll go with you."

Once in the hallway, Michael bounded up the first eight steps two at a time, then slowed himself. There was no real need to hurry. He had come, after all, to confirm a calamity, not prevent it. His running and rushing was his denial of what had actually happened. He'd been acting as if he were needed, as if, with his frantic energy, he might stir a lifeless body. There would be the flutter of the eyelids, a slight lifting of the hand, the mouth struggling to form a word, all in response to nothing more or less than his own urgent approach.

The totality of his helplessness, of his foolishness, of his pathetic sense of being needed, came to him on the first landing. The second flight of stairs he climbed even more slowly, Peppino a few steps behind. On the fifth step he stopped. He was, in his own way, responsible for Rosalia's death. It was he and no other who'd conceived and arranged the entire scheme. He was the one who'd convinced Gaetano and Rosalia to elope. He'd financed it; he'd even bought the tickets. His meddling had killed her. The wisdom of Fra Callisto's adjuration, the priest's warning that Rome should not intervene in the affairs of Naples, struck him with full force and sickened him. Left to their own devices, Gaetano could have murdered Peppino or Peppino murdered Gaetano—or even Rosalia murder Peppino. But he had entered the fray, clothed in borrowed robes, and now Rosalia, the one innocent participant in the whole absurd *commedia,* was dead.

"Uncle, are you all right?" Peppino, too, had stopped, four steps behind, still keeping out of reach of Michael's arm. Without answering, Michael continued his climb. For the first time, he became aware that the hallway smelled neither of cats nor of cooking. It smelled as if it had been washed by a fresh rain. There was even a gentle breeze coming from somewhere above, a roof door or a window on an upper landing. Michael breathed deeper to see if he could detect the scent of scrub water, of ammonia, of some scouring agent that would dispel his near certainty that the stairway had been not so much cleaned as cleansed.

At the final flight of stairs, Michael acknowledged why he had come to Rosalia. To beg pardon, to ask forgiveness. To see with his own eyes the slumbering girl, to straighten perhaps the angled limbs, to smooth the tangled skirt and restore some modesty to the twice-defiled body.

When he got to the landing, Michael stepped aside to let Peppino go first. Here, too, was the scent of fresh rain, and the cool breeze came down from the flights above, except that now the smell of baking bread was carried along in the gentle air.

"If I open the door," Peppino said, "will you go in first?"

"You don't have to come in if you don't want to. As a matter of fact, I don't want you inside at all."

Peppino said nothing. He went to the apartment door, inserted the key in the lock, let it and the entire ring fall to the floor with a great echoing jangle, picked it all up, then unlocked the door. Instead of turning the knob or moving away to let Michael go in, he stood there a moment, his face inches from the door. He pulled back a little, placed his right hand, palm open, on the door itself, then leaned forward and let his forehead rest just to the side of the peephole.

Peppino had closed his eyes, but now he opened them, waited again, then drew his forehead and his hand away. He stepped back from the door and looked down at the floor. "I thought I was finally going to be able to make love to her," he said quietly. "That's what I thought I was going to do when I made her lie down with me."

Michael turned the knob and gave a slight push. The door stuck a little but opened when he put a little more weight on it. The entrance hall, too, smelled freshly washed. It was as if its carpet had been restored to its first elements—not the sheep's wool, but the rich coarse grass on which the sheep had fed. On the small polished table beneath the wall mirror, a paper flower, red and purple, of no known species, was sticking out of a bud vase, and Michael wondered if that was what he'd smelled instead of the carpet.

He stood a moment in the hall, then went through the kitchen into the living room, moving almost stealthily, as if he were stalking Rosalia or was worried that she might jump out at him and say "Boo!" He made no hurry as he went toward the bedroom. She would wait until he got there.

Just before he reached the doorway, he stopped. Something in the living room had changed. He looked around. The furniture was just as he remembered it; the curtains on the window were the same, even opened in the same manner as before. Perhaps it was the lack of laundry on the rack outside. Just as Michael was about to accept this as the difference he'd sensed, he saw exactly what it was that had changed. All the photographs, the whole forest of frames—oak, maple, and teak—were gone from both the top of the upright piano and from the piano bench. With one exception: a silver frame that lay facedown on the floor next to the bench. Michael picked it up.

It was a picture of Rosalia and Peppino, the groom placing the wedding ring on the finger of his bride. They were both staring down at the gold band as if they were expecting it to turn into something else once the gesture was completed. Michael considered putting the picture back on the top of the piano, or at least on the bench, then decided to lay it, facedown, exactly where he'd found it.

The floor creaked behind him. Over his shoulder he saw Peppino watching him from the kitchen. "The pictures," Peppino said. "Who took all our pictures? The pictures. They're gone."

"Not quite all." Michael jerked his head toward the silver frame on the floor, then continued toward the bedroom without stopping.

The bed was neatly made, the pillows plumped. There was no one on the bed. "Rosalia?" Michael whispered.

Behind him, Peppino, a great sob in his voice, cried out the name, rushed forward, and shoved Michael aside. In his attempt to stop himself in mid-leap toward the bed, Peppino reared back quickly, knocking Michael against the doorframe. "Rosalia?" he said. "Rosalia?" He touched the bedspread with the tips of his fingers, then turned and looked around the room. "Rosalia?" For an instant, Michael expected him to drop to his knees and look under the bed, but after another quick glance around the room, to make sure she wasn't on top of the wardrobe or hidden behind the curtains, Peppino lurched out of the room, again knocking Michael against the doorframe.

Michael could only stay where he was, staring at the empty bed, unable to move. Peppino would have to solve and explain the mystery.

"Rosalia! Rosalia!" Peppino was in the living room, in the kitchen, in the bathroom. He called the name into the closet and behind the stove. It was Rigoletto calling out to the abducted Gilda, the puzzlement growing toward terror. "Rosalia!"

Michael waited to hear the opening and closing of the refrigerator, the oven, the cupboards, each receiving in its turn the dumbfounded question formed around the word "Rosalia."

He stepped into the bedroom and went to the bed. He, too, touched the bedspread with his fingertips and stared at the two pillows, the generous, receptive breasts, propped up against the heavy wooden headboard.

"Rosalia . . ." The sound came from the kitchen, like a long sigh. Then the name was repeated, more frantically. Michael started toward the kitchen, wondering if Rosalia had been found at last, but he was met by a wide-eyed Peppino, who was struggling to speak. Each time he tried to start a word, his tongue would get in the way. It was as though he'd been dealt a blow on the head and before passing into unconsciousness, wanted to name the assailant. The one word he'd been repeating—Rosalia—seemed no longer applicable, but he was as yet unable to reclaim his general vocabulary. Now his jaw moved quickly up and down, like that of a singer trying to control a wayward note. Accepting his inability to speak, he held out toward Michael a piece of paper.

Michael took it. There was writing on it, beautifully shaped letters, wonderfully formed vowels and well-disciplined consonants, as if the writer had found in visible terms, in ordinary penmanship, an equivalent for the Italian language. Peppino had sped past him, and as Michael read, he picked up the silver-framed picture from the floor and kept kissing it with loud-suctioned smacks and guttural moans.

The note was addressed "*Peppino caro mio*" and went on to say: "It is a terrible thing for a wife to deceive her husband. It is something I would never do, no matter what. But since you are not really my husband—I am getting an annulment, which will say that the marriage never took place—I allowed myself to deceive you and pretend that I was dead. You are a terrible man, Peppino, and it would have been better, in a way, if you had killed me and gone to jail for the rest of your life, but I didn't really feel I could accommodate such a solution to your difficulties. Perhaps you can hang yourself." It was signed, each letter an extension of the cursive into the artistic, "Rosalia Attanese."

By the time Michael had finished reading the letter twice and was slowly lowering it to his side, Peppino had again let loose an anguished "Rosalia!" He then flung the wedding picture aside so that it bounced off the screen of the television set and landed on the easy chair. He rushed past Michael—again knocking him against the doorframe—and knelt at the side of the bed, sobbing into the bedspread. His arms outstretched, he clawed the covers, pulling them toward him and, at the same time, raising himself up onto the bed. The name was repeated, but now with laughter. "I didn't kill you. I didn't kill you." Laughing, sobbing, he stretched himself lengthwise on the bed and, with one fist, then the other, kept punching the two plump pillows just above his head.

Michael set the note down on the piano bench, stood the wedding picture next to it, and quietly left the apartment. In the hall outside, the breeze had died and the scents were now of cooking oil and frying fish. It was getting late. He brought his right forearm up and pressed it against his shirt. There was the sound of crinkling paper. The stolen money was safely stashed inside, just above his navel, soon to be safely delivered, and Rosalia and Gaetano safely dispatched to Palermo.

Surely it was not too soon to begin savoring some small sensation of success. Surely the gods wouldn't mind if he began, even now, enjoying this one accomplishment. *Veni, vidi, vici.* What more need be said? The words occurred to him, but he felt they were better left unsaid, at least for the moment.

18

At the opera house that evening, Michael's difficulties be gan even before the first act. Because this would be La Calefati's last *Tosca* in Naples for a while, there was a charge in the air, a feeling of history, a sensed knowledge that one of the great episodes in the long story of San Carlo would climax and conclude itself that night; the season of Aganice Calefati's triumphant *Tosca* was about to come to a close. Calefati's reception, some had said, rivaled that accorded Renata Tebaldi, also considered *una figlia di Napoli,* for her debut *Traviata* in the fifties. This, of course, was contested hotly and with all the appropriate Neapolitan gestures, intensified to the point where self-damage had been inflicted with breast beatings, hair tearings, and thumb bitings. The Calefati contingent had been making a point, therefore, of increasing and intensifying its hysteria with each performance, determined that they, if not Calefati herself, surpass the previous performance. So that the shower of roses from the galleries should be unending, a special usher had been hired to scoop them up from around La Calefati's feet as she took her bows and, as on opening night, deliver them as untrampled as possible to her enthusiasts so that the flowers could, with great shouts and calls, be showered down again onto the beaming, weeping soprano, *l'Adorata,* who, not unwittingly, had made passion possible and hysteria permissible.

From his first day in Naples, Michael had expected his own performance to be particularly inspired this night. He would not exaggerate but merely intensify all that he did; he would make that slight undetectable turn of the screw that would pitch his every note, his every movement and gesture, onto an elevated plane accessible only to the transported and the transfigured. In the first act he would come to Scarpia's side with insinuating anticipation of evils soon to be loosed into the world, the sinuous serpent, the eager viper. In Act Two, what he now referred to as his stomach aria would be delivered with a terrified fawning, a sniveling that would disgust even the most stonehearted. And in the final act, his snarling challenge to Tosca herself, his whining threat, would come perilously close to making him the true cause of the heroine's death, her loathing of him driving her to the brink—and beyond.

The uncertainties about *Curlew River* could be superseded, possibly erased, by the sure artistry he would exercise this final night. He had been faithful to his mentor and to his memory. Applause or no applause, he had fulfilled the old man's legacy. If it had all been to no effect, so be it. Perhaps his acceptance of this was the true bequest his teacher had intended, and it was not to be refused. Now he might leave Naples not without some satisfaction. He would not only have rescued two young lovers and set them safely if not too surefootedly on the path of bliss; he would have made compensation for Peppino's crimes and canceled their effects, thereby restoring the moral order, if not of the universe, at least of one small corner of Spaccanapoli.

But not everything had happened as he had hoped. When Michael first came to the opera house, the bruise and the cuts on his face were attributed to the theft of the *Curlew* receipts from the night before. Word of the thievery had spread, and everyone was shocked to realize that it had been so brutal. There was sympathy for Michael and scorn for Naples. He could have told the truth, but he was no longer sure exactly what it might be.

It had been Gaetano who'd bloodied him. When Michael had gone to the dock to hand over the money, he saw Gaetano standing at the seawall, looking out across the bay as if trying to envision the life ahead, staring past Bocca di Ponente and Diga Duca di Abruzzi, which defined the harbor, past the cliffs of Capri and the Faraglioni rocks, past even the Aeolian Islands to Sicily itself, to Palermo, where he'd live out his exile. It made Michael a little apprehensive not to see Rosalia standing at his side.

"Gaetano?"

Gaetano turned, and for just a second before the smile made his face look somewhat foolish—the stretched lips making his nose longer and, for some reason, his ears seem larger—there was an expression of quiet sorrow, as if he had been standing instead on the shores below Palermo and was gazing out past the islands and the rocks, beyond the Caprian cliffs, knowing that there, to the north, was Naples and his only home.

"*Zio!*" He spread his arms, laughed, came to Michael, put his arms around him, and kissed both cheeks. "I've been waiting."

"Where's Rosalia?"

"She's on board in our cabin, with our suitcases. She wanted to lie down and rest, and she said to say goodbye, but we'll see you again sometime before too long. She wouldn't say so, but she's a little scared, I think. I could tell by the way she didn't even want to wait to say goodbye to you. But if you want me to go get her . . ."

"No, no. But . . . but she's all right?"

"She'll be all right as soon as I'm with her." He put a hand on Michael's arm to reassure him and smiled again, the nose lengthening, the ears enlarging, even as Michael watched.

Rosalia, apparently, had said nothing of her near-fatal mishap, and it was probably just as well. Michael had a quick picture of an avenging Gaetano insisting on a quick return home to kill his brother after all. Or even now, what might he do to Michael, uncle or no uncle, for having endangered his future wife and been complicitous in her suffocation? Yes, Rosalia indeed was the right wife for Gaetano. She knew already when to keep her mouth shut.

"If she's resting, let her rest," Michael said. "Just tell her I wish her all happiness."

"She has that. Already she has that." Gaetano preened, certain that he knew exactly where the source of all that happiness lay.

Michael was relieved at Rosalia's absence. As much as he wanted to see her, to witness with his own eyes the coming, going breath, to touch with his own hands the living flesh and look one last time into the fierce and fear-filled eyes, he knew Rosalia might, by way of a farewell, charge him with at least partial responsibility for her endangerment. It could prove to be anything but a fond goodbye. He knew only too well Rosalia's splendid unwillingness to accept injury.

Michael had taken the fair-sized packet of money from inside his shirt and was holding it out to an amazed Gaetano. "Here, then. Here's the money."

"But it's too much!"

"You're going to need it."

"It's too much."

"Just take it. And put it somewhere where it won't get lost." Gaetano was right. It was, to all intents and purposes, quite a bundle.

Gaetano followed his uncle's example and unbuttoned his shirt to the fourth button. Before taking the money, he looked a moment at the medal he was wearing, the silver oval partly buried in the thick curled hair on his chest. "Here," Gaetano said, slipping the medal up over his head. "This should be Pep-

pino's now. Take it to him, please. He'll be feeling terrible with
Rosalia gone, and I'm not there either. He always wanted it. It
belonged to Papà when the wall fell. It's San Gennà, and San
Gennà will look after him. He looks after whoever wears the
medal."

Michael sensed contradictions—the protective medal, the
falling wall—but Gaetano had more to say. "It makes him
the head of the family now, while I'm away. So take it to him
as soon as you can."

Michael looked down at the medal, rubbed smooth, more
a replica of the moon than the face of a saint. It was the worn
aspect that spoke the most, the saint obliterated by the unending
faith of those who believed and trusted in him.

Michael traded the money for the medal. Swiftly Gaetano
slipped the packet into his shirt. Slowly Michael put the medal
in his pocket. The two men, their last task done, faced each other.
They had nothing more to say. Michael made a small motion
with his arms, ready to reach out, but Gaetano had already pulled
him to himself and was holding him in a tight embrace.

"Oh, Zio . . . Zio . . . !

"Addio, caro Gaetano."

Gaetano moved away, still holding on to Michael's arms.
Tears had started to come into his eyes. *"Zio . . . Zio . . ."* He
seemed about to pull Michael toward him again, but stopped.
"Zio . . ." He repeated the word, but this time with a question
mark. *"Zio . . . ?"* His jaw slowly dropped; his eyebrows knitted
themselves closer together above his nose. "You . . . you're the
Madwoman," he whispered. *"Zio.* You're the Madwoman!" He
turned his face slightly to the right, so he could look at Michael
out of the corner of his eye. When he faced him again directly,
he asked, still quietly, "Were you the Madwoman?"

"Yes."

"Aaaaah. Yes. Yes. You are," he said, the words exhaled
more than spoken. He took his hands from Michael's arms and

brought them to his own chest, crossed, one over the other. "You are a great artist," he said, awed by the sight of the man before him. "What you did, what you had the others do, it was so beautiful. You . . . you are a gift sent to Naples. A gift. Oh, Uncle, I'm so proud. That an uncle of mine—"

He stopped. He looked closely at Michael, searching his face, trying to find something that was no longer there, something that had been lost, taken away. "But you're not my uncle, then, are you? You're not Don Michele. Not my father's . . ." Again he stopped, then he uncrossed his hands and slowly lowered them to his sides. He took a step back. The searching gaze hardened, the lips tightened, the eyebrows unknit themselves. "You're not my uncle," he said. "You're not Don Michele! You're not . . . !" His fist hit Michael just below the right eye, knocking his head back so quickly that, in rebound, it sprang forward as if eager to be hit again. Gaetano obliged, this time missing the mark and glancing off Michael's left ear, creating a sound like the sea. Gaetano took another swing, slamming his fist into Michael's right cheek.

"My mother, she must have paid you. And I told you things you had no right to hear! You let me cry in front of you! And you're a stranger . . . a foreigner!" His fist started to rise again, but a hand grabbed his arm.

"Gaetano!"

It was Piero. He'd come from somewhere behind Michael. Gaetano looked at him. "And you too!" he said. "You knew it too. He's not my uncle!" He seemed about to hit Piero, but Piero paid no attention.

"Go get on the boat. Rosalia's waiting."

Gaetano lowered his head and burst into tears, but quickly he looked up again, wiping his nose with his forefinger. "And if you think I take money from strangers," he said, "you're crazy." He began to fumble with the buttons on his shirt. "We can stay here. Rosalia can go back to Peppino. And I can kill him on any day it pleases me to kill him. We take nothing from strangers. He was the crazy lady! He was the crazy lady!"

Before he'd finished with the third button, Piero put his hand on his wrist. "Do you think he deserves to get the money back?" The words were light on his tongue. The smile, the mock sincerity, was on his face, and he was looking directly into Gaetano's eyes. "He lied to you. He lied to all of you. He let you shame yourselves in front of him. Do you really think he should be given the money? You don't think you ought to keep it? Think of how he shamed you. And now you want him to have all that money?"

Gaetano looked at neither Piero nor Michael. Glancing sideways, he seemed to be looking elsewhere for enlightenment and guidance. His breathing was still heavy, but the lips had become more thoughtful than angry.

"Do you give money to people who shame you?" Piero left his lips parted after the last word, and it seemed he would leave them that way until he'd been given the answer he wanted.

The buttons were buttoned up, and Gaetano hunched, then relaxed his shoulders so the money could settle in the cavity between his ribs. "I'll take it for Rosalia," he said. "Not for me, not for myself. Only for Rosalia."

Without a farewell of any kind, he turned and started toward the ship looming alongside the terminal. Michael wanted to call him, to run after him, to turn him toward himself, to see one final time the taut hawk face, the menacing, sorrowful eyes, the twitching lips. To say some final word. But there was nothing to say. So he simply stood where he was. And watched.

Michael's difficulties intensified during Act One. Instead of being the near-gleeful accomplice, he had dumbly approached Scarpia and stared up into his surprised face, bleating his lines like a weeping sheep. Michael had no idea of what he had done until, at the intermission, Darida, the Scarpia, spoke his enthusiasm for this new insight into the situation—weak-willed Spoletta pleading near tears that Scarpia not make him an accomplice to his intrigues. That, Darida said, inflamed him further, it fed his arrogance, this piteous defiance, making him all the more determined to unleash his awful power. "And the cuts and bruises on your face," he said. "It looks like I beat you. You must keep it that way for every Spoletta. Beautiful." Darida congratulated him, praised him for being an artist, always in search of the new.

Michael nodded his thanks, more a palsied shaking of the head than a gesture of gratitude, but it seemed to satisfy Darida, and he moved on.

Piero, after Gaetano had disappeared into the *tirrenia,* had taken Michael by the arm and led him away from the seawall. They'd gone only a few steps when Piero stopped, took out an immaculate white handkerchief, and dabbed it on Michael's eye and cheek. After examining his face, he leaned toward him and said, "This is what Sister Procida used to do when I got myself beat up by the older boys." With his tongue he licked Michael's cheek clean, then the eye. Once more the face was dabbed with the handkerchief.

"Clean," Piero said, stuffing the handkerchief back into his pocket.

"Why did you let Peppino know Gaetano and Rosalia were going away together?" Michael asked.

Piero shrugged and moved his head a little from one side to the other, a small dance from the shoulders up. "I thought it would be interesting to see what might happen."

"Peppino almost killed Rosalia."

Again Piero shrugged. "Well, she *was* running off with his brother. What did you expect? But he didn't kill her. So I didn't cause so much trouble after all. Maybe some other time."

They passed through the gate and began walking along Via Nuova Marina, toward the Galleria, just beyond the Castel

Nuovo, where Peppino's car was parked. Piero looped his arm through Michael's. "I'm not coming to New York," he said.

They kept on walking. To Michael's left, the evenly spaced spearlike iron rods that fenced off the docks caught at his eye, one by one, as he passed, a kind of blinking forced on him even as he stared straight ahead. Over the *castello* the sky was a dirty gray, as if it had grown cataracts. Michael waited for Piero to say more, but after the silence had lasted for the full length of the fence, he figured he was the one expected to say something.

"What do you mean, you're not coming to New York?"

"I'm not coming to New York."

"Why?"

"I have to stay here. In Naples."

"You don't have to stay here."

"I do. I have to stay."

"Why don't you want to come to New York?"

"I *do* want to come to New York."

"Then come to New York."

"I can't."

They had entered Piazza Municipio, empty now as Naples began to feed and feast at the day's end. Piero said nothing until just before they made the turn toward the Galleria.

"Let me look at the cuts again to see if they're better." They stopped, and Piero searched Michael's face, touching a sensitive spot just below the eye. "They're not better, but be sure you wash with a lot of soap and water as soon as you can. In my condition, I really shouldn't go around slavering my tongue on people's cuts, so be sure to do it." He laughed, then leaned over and licked again at the cut on Michael's cheek, the pale lesion below his eye touching against Michael's ear. "If you get AIDS," Piero said, "tell them you got it because someone licked your wounds."

They started walking again. The Galleria was just ahead. Now Michael spoke. "After I've made the necessary arrangements in New York, I'm coming back to get you. You can't stay here all by yourself."

They had reached the steps of the Galleria on Via Verdi and stopped next to a cluster of stone columns at the entry. Piero fixed his mocking smile on his face, then let it fade. "No. I can't go with you. I'd be too far from the saints."

"The saints? What saints?"

"All the saints: the saints here in Naples. I can't be so far away from them."

"What are you talking about?"

Piero took out the handkerchief and began touching it gently to Michael's cheek, to his eye, as if soaking up tears. "The saints," he said, "they're here in Naples. Sant'Antonio, San Francesco, San Gennà, San Rocco, the Madonna, they're all here. And San Roncalli, who was the Pope, he's here where we will never forget him, no matter what they do in Rome. He and all the other saints, they're here."

"The saints are everywhere," Michael said. "You know that."

Piero pulled the handkerchief away. "No," he said quietly, "they aren't. They're here. In Naples. And I mustn't leave them. They'll want to be with me now, and I can't desert them." He put the handkerchief back in his pocket but continued to look into Michael's face. Slowly the mocking smile came back.

He looked first into Michael's eyes, then at his forehead, as if he saw there something sad and amusing. He then looked at his nose and mouth and chin, a slow traveling. When he came to the left ear, he looked again into Michael's eyes and reached up his hand. He took the lobe between his thumb and forefinger, gave a gentle tug, then let go and let his eyes look again at the forehead.

Michael stepped back, away from him, and tried to get him to look again into his eyes, but Piero was giving attention now to his neck and his other ear. He thought he might reach over and raise Piero's chin a little so he could look directly at him this final time, but instead he was slowly lowering himself to his knees, onto the sidewalk. He steadied himself by pressing his knuckles into the cement, one hand on each side of him.

With a laugh that got clutched by his throat before it could reach his mouth, he stared up at Piero. "You said if I were to bow down to you . . ." He tried the laugh again. This time it came out mostly through his nose, somewhere between a whimper and a snort. So that Piero couldn't see the terror he knew had come into his face, he bent his head forward until it touched the ground. He could hear the scrape of his hair against the sidewalk, the sound like a rough, protesting hiss.

"I beg you," Michael said, his voice low and slightly muffled. "I beg you, don't leave me. Please. Come with me. Be with me. Don't leave me all alone. I'll come to love you. I promise I will. I will, I will! I know I will. Come with me. Please." He paused, then whispered, "I beg you."

Piero had taken hold of his head and was lifting it away from the cement. He kept raising it until Michael was kneeling upright in front of him. Piero had knelt on one knee and made no move to stand. He brushed Michael's forehead and smoothed his hair. "And will you love me more than the saints?" he asked.

Michael didn't hesitate. "Yes," he said. "I would."

"I know you would. But do you need me as much as they do?"

"Yes. I do."

Piero shook his head. "The saints have asked for me by name, now, in the time of my dying, and they would be lost if I were to abandon them in their hour of need. You can understand that."

Michael took hold of Piero's shoulders. "No," he said, "I don't! I don't!" From the right side of his eye he could see that a man was standing on the top step leading down from the Galleria, just above them. Michael lowered his arms. The man seemed to hesitate, then moved to the far side of the steps, away from them, and from the sound, Michael could tell that he came down the steps, not quickly, and made the turn in the other direction, toward the Piazza Municipio.

Piero was touching Michael's bruised cheek. He leaned forward and kissed him lightly on the lips, then took him by the elbow and made him stand up. "How strange and how wonderful," he said, "that I should understand everything and you understand nothing." The mocking smile had come back. There was nothing Michael could say that would not be a curse or a wild cry, so he said nothing.

During the ride to Via Giganti, neither spoke. When Piero stopped in front of Peppino's building, he said cheerfully, "You'll come again to Naples. Check with Gaetano. He'll tell you where I am, and you can bring me some flowers. Chrysanthemums, yellow and white. Big ones, lots of them. You can put them on my grave, and for just that one little moment, that tiny little second, I'll remember you."

Michael neither looked at him nor said anything. He got out of the car and quietly, with a near-silent click, closed the door.

He was standing in the wings, stage right, watching the stagehands as they tore down the church of Sant'Andrea della Valle and put up the Palazzo Farnese. He had stationed himself among the worn ropes and rusted pulleys, which suggested that, with the proper heavings and weighings, great sails would bloom above his head, the old wooden floor beneath his feet would begin slowly to sway, and he would be moved forward, not across the Curlew River, but out to sea, toward some other land, far, far away.

Now the great room of the palazzo was being furnished: the desk, the table, chair, sofa, the candles, and the crucifix. The table was being set: the plate, the apple Scarpia would cut with the fatal knife, the wineglasses, the decanter. Soon the act would begin. Michael had wanted to ask Darida not to send him sprawling onto his stomach—he was afraid he might throw up—but Darida was already onstage, waiting for the curtain to rise.

During the act, Darida did, of course, send him sprawling, and Michael did indeed almost throw up. But as he sang out his lines, a little gargled but still in character, a thought came to him that allowed him to rise to his feet on cue.

He would steal the knife from the table. He would sidle up and sneak it into his costume. Tosca would not be able to stab Scarpia. Scarpia would live—and so would Tosca. There'd be no reason for her to fling herself from the castle ramparts at the end of Act Three. And when it would be time for Michael to lower his sword, to give the signal for Cavaradossi's execution, he would simply refuse to lower it. There would be no more deaths.

Act Two continued. Michael was standing next to the table. His hand was near the apple. The knife had to be there somewhere, but he must not look down. He moved his fingers. He touched the wine decanter, then a glass. The knife should be right there. He had to find it.

Peppino, obedient to his wife's suggestion, had hanged himself. On the shower rod in the bathroom, using the blue knit tie. Michael had come with the medal of San Gennà, to give it to Peppino and tell him he was now the head of the family.

At the street door on Via Giganti, a man was coming out with a watering can, so there'd been no need for Michael to ring the downstairs bell. When he reached the apartment itself and no one answered his knock, he found the door unlocked. He called and searched the rooms and was just about to leave the medal on the kitchen table when he saw, through the half-open door to the bathroom, the tip of Peppino's shoe moving slowly a few inches off the floor.

First Michael grabbed him around the waist and tried to

hoist him up, to relieve the strained tie. He might still be alive. But Michael knew he wasn't. He climbed inside the tub and started to unknot the noose, but he realized that when he finished, Peppino would fall in a tangled heap onto the floor or knock his head against the tub. Michael went back into the kitchen and found a butcher knife on the drainboard.

When he went back into the bathroom, Peppino was turning from side to side, as if to show first one group of spectators, then another, what it was like to be hanged. And he looked absurd. The head bent sideways, the eyes bulged and unblinking, the tongue sticking through his partly opened mouth like a thick middle lip, Peppino could merely be making a funny face to amuse and scare his uncle. At any moment, he would restore his features to their former perfection, and the two of them would laugh at how clever Peppino could be. But Michael almost heard the last strangled grunt, stopped before it could complete itself when the feet had slipped off the edge of the tub and the tongue shot forward from the closed throat and the eyes bulged in surprise that such a thing was happening.

Michael pressed his face into the young man's chest, reached up, and made the cut. At the snap that released the body, Michael moved in even closer. He dropped the knife into the tub and let his hand slide quickly down Peppino's back so he could take him onto his shoulder. But Peppino refused to bend. Instead he slid slowly downward, and all Michael could do was hold him fast, tight with both arms, so the two of them wouldn't fall. It was then that Peppino's head snapped back, the mouth fell open, the thickened tongue slipped over to the side and was left hanging there with an idiot helplessness. The bulged eyes stared at the ceiling, amazed and terrified by the blue frosted light fixture over the sink. He was wetting his pants.

Michael would have to let him go, to lower him to the floor and stretch him out there on the tiles. The police must be sent for and the Signora and Fra Callisto too. Michael reached behind

Peppino's head and brought it forward so that it rested on his shoulder, Peppino's nose and the tip of his tongue touching Michael's neck.

He would not lower him onto the bathroom floor. He would carry him into the bedroom and give him a decent place to lie down. Michael reached behind Peppino's legs and, not without effort, lifted them. His other arm he placed across Peppino's back, just below the shoulders. To test his strength, he twice slightly raised and lowered the body. He could carry it.

Going through the bathroom door, Michael took special care that not even the tuft of hair sticking up at the back of Peppino's head should brush the doorjamb. When Michael placed the body on the bed, the right leg caught under the left, and he had to put them both straight. One arm dangled, and he lifted it up onto Peppino's chest. He tried to close the eyes, but the lids couldn't cover the bulging stare. There was sweat on the forehead, and the skin was getting cold. Michael loosened the collar. There were marks on the neck, the raw welts beginning to rise.

Pressed into the flesh by the force of the hanging was a silver chain. Michael lifted it away. The medal on the end fell into his hand. It was San Giuseppe—Saint Joseph—and he was holding the Infant Child. The name Peppino—it was the diminutive, the affectionate word for Giuseppe, for Joseph. Peppino had worn the medal so he'd never be without protection and guidance. Michael slipped it back inside the shirt, careful that the chain not rub the reddening welts.

He stepped back from the bed. Phone calls had to be made. He looked down at the unmoving body. What he saw was not Peppino dead but Peppino waiting for the death that was sure to come. The staring eyes, the opened mouth, the stretched body, perfectly still—this was Peppino on his marriage bed, Rosalia at his side, when he'd meditated, alert and ready, on the terrors soon to come. It was with this rigid stillness that he'd waited, waited, for his brother's vengeful hand, for his good wife's killing kiss. But nothing yet had happened, all was still to come. And he must wait and watch and never breathe.

Here, before Michael, was the young man who seemed to have stumbled onto the wrong planet, bewildered, who'd had to resort to outrage in the hope that someone might explain to him the world into which he'd come and what was expected of him on this alien earth. And Michael had brought him to his death.

He phoned the police. He phoned Signora Spacagna, and he phoned Fra Callisto. They arrived in that order. The police asked questions, and Michael answered as best he could, including explanations for the gash on Peppino's face—the struggle with his wife her note referred to—and the cuts on Michael's: He had fallen down in his rush to get to the apartment. The police seemed more disappointed than suspicious; they apparently preferred something more imaginative, especially concerning Michael's wounds.

When the Signora saw the body, she screamed a scream that made the world stand still, then identified it with the words, spoken in low, even tones: "This is my son Giuseppe Angelino. I gave birth to him nineteen years ago, in the autumn of that year." She then turned to Michael and said in the same low voice, "You may go now, Don Michele. There is nothing more that you can do."

On his way down the stairs, he met Fra Callisto. Before the priest could say anything, Michael pointed a finger straight in the air. "Upstairs," he said, and kept right on going.

Michael never found the knife. Scarpia was stabbed: *"Questo è il bacio di Tosca!"*—Here is the kiss of Tosca!—and now, in Act Three, there would be the firing squad and Tosca's fatal leap onto the stones below. Michael would not lower the sword. There was still time to save someone. As soon as the idea came to him, he struggled to dismiss it. He was in an opera, at San

Carlo, in Naples. It was called *Tosca,* and he was playing the part of Spoletta. He had only to continue to act his role and all would be well.

But how could he continue to play his role when he was, moment by moment, becoming more and more crazed? During a hand of *scopa*—a card game particular to Naples, which he unfailingly played during intermission with Nunzio Cappozolli, the bass singing Sciarrone—he found himself, before putting down the seven of swords, staring at Cappozolli, a burly man with the generous-featured face of an exhausted fortune-teller, and whispering, half song, half speech, " 'Let me in! Let me out! Tell me the, tell me the way. . . .' "

Cappozolli kept looking at the cards in his hand. He said nothing. Michael played the seven but made no move to collect the cards he'd won.

"You don't want them?" Cappozolli asked. "Take them. They're yours."

"Yes," Michael said. "Yes, of course." With his right arm he swept the cards toward himself. Before he could count up his points, he was saying, again the half-sung whisper, " 'I turn me, I turn me away. . . .' " He jumped up from the table. " 'Love for my child confuses me. . . .' "

Cappozolli didn't take his eyes off his cards. "Are you vocalizing?" he asked.

"No, I . . . I . . ." Michael fumbled with the back of the chair, pulling it away from the table so he could sit down again. He had almost lowered himself completely, when he cried out, " 'O Curlew River, cruel Curlew, where all my hope is—' " He stopped, sat down, his spine hard against the back of the chair. He picked up his cards. He had the *putana,* the queen. He would win the game. But he wouldn't use the *putana* now. He'd wait. He'd—

Leaning forward, Michael pushed his face into the cards fanned in his hand, trying to stop the words. " 'Chain on my soul . . .' " He dropped the cards, the *putana* and the four of money drifting down to the floor. Cappozolli watched them land, face up.

"You had the *putana*," he said. "I thought so." He looked up at Michael. "Do you want to start another game? We still have time for—"

Michael must have tripped against the chair, because he heard it fall behind him as he stumbled out the dressing room door. He started down the stairs, holding fast to the rail. To keep himself from falling, he stopped and closed his eyes, but he had to open them again. He'd felt dizzy. At stage level, two of the soldiers, the firing squad for Act Three, their rifles raised to their shoulders, were testing their aim. With their sights on Michael, they followed his swift move toward the set, pretending they would fire at any moment.

Michael moved back away from them, to where there were only the thick ropes, the pulleys bolted to the floor. He grabbed hold of one of the ropes and put his forehead against it. " 'Torn from the nest . . .' " Above him he saw the great prop statue of the Archangel atop the parapet, drawing, not sheathing, his sword. Soon it would flare into flame and be raised high over Michael's head. He closed his eyes and drew the harsh rope closer to his face, scouring it into his cheek.

" 'Chain on my soul . . .' "

He had become the Madwoman again. He struggled not to whisper the words. He must breathe, only breathe, one breath in, deep, one breath out, long, one breath in . . . There should have been applause at the end. The opera wasn't over. That was why he was in danger, perpetual danger, of becoming the Madwoman, over and over again. If only the audience had applauded . . .

Michael tightened his eyes, but the dark he was seeking wasn't there. There was only light behind the closed lids, getting brighter and brighter. He was waiting for the child to pass; it was the light from his candle he saw. It was from there the brightness came. Once the child had passed, once he'd returned to the grave, all would be well. He was nearer, closer, coming from Michael's left, circling. The light was getting brighter. Michael must open his eyes. He must not see the child. It was forbidden. He must not look. But there the child was, moving slowly, circling from his left.

Michael drew his entire face even tighter together to support the shut eyes, his mouth open, his lips spread as wide as they would reach, his front teeth touching his lower lip, the cheeks straining upward. But the dark couldn't come. He must open his eyes. They had to open. Otherwise he'd see the forbidden dead.

It was too late to open them now. The spirit had rounded into view, silently, slowly. He held no candle, he sang no words. He looked at Michael, and Michael looked at him. The thickened tongue had been pulled back into the mouth, the tip still showing between the closed lips. The swollen eyes were still unblinking, but they seemed now to be asking a question or making a mournful plea. The welts had crept up the neck and were now eating at the left side of his jaw. His arms were crossed on his chest, but limply, the hands resting in the crook of each elbow, cupped open, waiting to receive something—a coin, some water, whatever might be given.

Michael waited now, alert and stiff, to hear the words the ghost had come to speak. Peppino, still slowly moving, said nothing. Michael waited. And then the lips parted, the upper lip lifting slightly away from the tongue. Now the message would come, the accusation that had forced this return from the land of the dead. The lips twitched, the tongue struggled against the teeth. Michael stopped his breath; the blood in his veins had ceased to flow. The words were beginning to form, and Michael would have to hear. But before he could speak, Peppino had completed his slow circle and was gone.

Michael raised a hand to stop him, then opened his eyes. He turned his face away from the stage, away from the looming angel, and looked only at the shredded wood of the floor at his feet. Words threatened his lips. He closed his mouth. But the words were already there.

"Peppino? Don't go! It's me. It's Don Michele. Your uncle. And . . . and I love you. Always. Peppino . . . ? Don't go . . ."

He rested his forehead against the rope. And then the sorrow he had so ruthlessly sought was given to him at last, in measures savage and convulsive. And they came to him not through the withdrawn worship of a Damian or the adamant mysteries of a Piero, but through the mediation of a rapist, a would-be murderer, and a suicide.

One by one, the stitches that had sewn up the hollow of his heart gave way. The wound that Damian had closed was opened wide, the empty heart gaped in wonder, and Peppino, with bewildered eyes and choked tongue, entered in—and with him, Damian at last, led by the blind young man, the dog unharnessed at his side; and crowding behind them, unknown but known, their faces unfamiliar but familiar, an uncounted line of the lost and the dead, come here to dwell forever in the unstitched heart that refused to close again.

This was the judgment and the reward he must accept for welcoming death and begging for grief. It was for this he had been summoned to Naples, to lure him into precincts ruled by older gods, beyond the reach of saints, and now their avenging truth had been accomplished. He would love the dead, as he had asked.

Michael let go of the rope and leaned forward just in time to keep the vomit from getting on his costume.

The third act was under way. An assistant stage manager, laughing, had cleaned up the mess, and Michael had helped. The man had seen stage fright before, but never on closing night, just before the final act. The moment was coming when Michael must lower his sword, the signal for the execution. Unable to resist the conductor's beat, he did what he was supposed to do. There were the shots, the puffs of smoke, and Cavaradossi, the passionate lover of the passionate Tosca, fell.

Offstage, waiting for his next and final entry, Michael insisted he'd cling to nothing, that he'd stand on his own two feet, unassisted. Now there was only Tosca herself he could save. But he was insane; he must do nothing. He was Spoletta, not the Madwoman. He had duties to perform, and he must be dutiful.

His sanity returned. He was all right now. He knew exactly what he must do. His cue came. Restored, secure, he rushed out to charge Tosca with the now-discovered death of Scarpia. Moving center stage, he hoarsely whispered the line *"Ah! Tosca, pagherai ben cara la sua vita!"* Ah! Tosca, you will pay dearly for his life!

Calefati made her move toward the parapet, but Michael, brandishing his sword, came quickly between her and the battlement. He jumped up onto the wall, his sword holding her off. Calefati could only stare at him, too stunned to move.

The cue he'd been waiting for came rushing toward him, the irresistible climb of the music. Michael, transposing the notes so he could end with no fewer than two high C's, sang out full voice, in tones that would have done the great, great Bjoerling proud, his revised version of Tosca's cry. *"Ah! Napoli,"* he sang. *"Avanti a Dio!"* Ah! Naples. We shall meet before God!

The last of the six high C's God had given him resounded from the foundation stones to the roof beam, out into the farthest reaches of the house, clear, impassioned, defiant. They stiffened the curtains of the royal box and tightened the plaster on the soaring walls. They froze the faces of the women in the topmost tier and set the mouths of the ushers agape.

Forward Michael flung himself and made the downward plunge. He bounced only once on the mattresses below. When he looked up, he saw hurtling toward him like an avenging demon an enraged Aganice Calefati. Her eyes blazed. Her hands clawed the air. He had less than a second to get out of the way.

FOR THE BEST IN PAPERBACKS, LOOK FOR THE

In every corner of the world, on every subject under the sun, Penguin represents quality and variety—the very best in publishing today.

For complete information about books available from Penguin—including Pelicans, Puffins, Peregrines, and Penguin Classics—and how to order them, write to us at the appropriate address below. Please note that for copyright reasons the selection of books varies from country to country.

In the United Kingdom: For a complete list of books available from Penguin in the U.K., please write to *Dept E.P., Penguin Books Ltd, Harmondsworth, Middlesex, UB7 0DA.*

In the United States: For a complete list of books available from Penguin in the U.S., please write to *Dept BA, Penguin,* Box 120, Bergenfield, New Jersey 07621-0120.

In Canada: For a complete list of books available from Penguin in Canada, please write to *Penguin Books Canada Ltd, 10 Alcorn Avenue, Suite 300, Toronto, Ontario, Canada M4V 3B2.*

In Australia: For a complete list of books available from Penguin in Australia, please write to the *Marketing Department, Penguin Books Ltd, P.O. Box 257, Ringwood, Victoria 3134.*

In New Zealand: For a complete list of books available from Penguin in New Zealand, please write to the *Marketing Department, Penguin Books (NZ) Ltd, Private Bag, Takapuna, Auckland 9.*

In India: For a complete list of books available from Penguin, please write to *Penguin Overseas Ltd, 706 Eros Apartments, 56 Nehru Place, New Delhi, 110019.*

In Holland: For a complete list of books available from Penguin in Holland, please write to *Penguin Books Nederland B.V., Postbus 195, NL-1380AD Weesp, Netherlands.*

In Germany: For a complete list of books available from Penguin, please write to *Penguin Books Ltd, Friedrichstrasse 10-12, D-6000 Frankfurt Main I, Federal Republic of Germany.*

In Spain: For a complete list of books available from Penguin in Spain, please write to *Longman, Penguin España, Calle San Nicolas 15, E-28013 Madrid, Spain.*

In Japan: For a complete list of books available from Penguin in Japan, please write to *Longman Penguin Japan Co Ltd, Yamaguchi Building, 2-12-9 Kanda Jimbocho, Chiyoda-Ku, Tokyo 101, Japan.*